The Massachusetts
Andrew Sharpshooters

The Massachusetts Andrew Sharpshooters
A Civil War History and Roster

ALDEN C. ELLIS, JR.

McFarland & Company, Inc., Publishers
Jefferson, North Carolina, and London

FRONTISPIECE: Governor John Albion Andrew,
the "War Governor" (Encyclopedia.com).

LIBRARY OF CONGRESS CATALOGUING-IN-PUBLICATION DATA

Ellis, Alden C., Jr.
The Masachusetts Andrew Sharpshooters : a Civil War
history and roster / Alden C. Ellis, Jr.
p. cm.
Includes bibliographical references and index.

ISBN 978-0-7864-6489-0
softcover : acid free paper ∞

1. United States. Army. Massachusetts Sharpshooters Company, 1st (1861–1865)
2. United States. Army. Massachusetts Sharpshooters Company, 2nd (1861–1864)
3. United States — History — Civil War, 1861–1865 — Regimental histories.
4. United States — History — Civil War, 1861–1865 — Campaigns.
5. Sharpshooting (Military science) — History —19th century.
I. Title.
E513.9.E45 2012   973.7'3 — dc23   2011050186

British Library cataloguing data are available

© 2012 Alden C. Ellis, Jr. All rights reserved

*No part of this book may be reproduced or transmitted in any form
or by any means, electronic or mechanical, including photocopying
or recording, or by any information storage and retrieval system,
without permission in writing from the publisher.*

On the cover: "The Army of the Potomac — A Sharpshooter on
Picket Duty" (*Harper's Weekly* 1862); background © 2012 Shutterstock

Manufactured in the United States of America

*McFarland & Company, Inc., Publishers
Box 611, Jefferson, North Carolina 28640
www.mcfarlandpub.com*

To the memory of all those who honorably served
in the two companies of Andrew Sharpshooters

Acknowledgments

This publication would not have been possible without the assistance of many individuals and institutions. James Fahey, the past archivist of the Military Division History and Museum of the Commonwealth of Massachusetts, provided much historic information.

The Massachusetts Historical Society of Boston was an invaluable resource, as they provided much documentation for the 1st and 2nd Companies. Libraries and historical societies across New England also contributed. The staff of the main public library in Framingham, Massachusetts, was of great assistance. The resources available at the Lynnfield Public Library were extremely valuable. The Library of Congress provided most of the illustrations.

Members of the Civil War reenacting community and living history groups have greatly assisted by sharing their knowledge. My wife, Pam, allowed me the time and freedom needed to travel for research. She gave freely of her time and talents, offering many suggestions and help in editing.

Mary Murphy, a former professor of English at Framingham State College and an officer of the Framingham Historical Society, has been very supportive of my work. Steve Pratt, of the Framingham Historical Society, gave countless hours in editing and formatting. Without his efforts, this publication would not exist. His encouragement and talents have markedly improved this book,

Many thanks have to be given to Jonathan K. Cohen. His expertise as an author and editor has contributed greatly to the accuracy of this manuscript. Through his queries, he challenged many aspects of this book until I could verify them using my previous research.

Special thanks are warranted to my son Dean, who introduced me to the living history community.

Table of Contents

Acknowledgments — vii
Preface — 1
Introduction — 3

PART I: THE FIRST COMPANY OF ANDREW SHARPSHOOTERS

1. Goodbye Lynnfield — 7
2. *Intrepid,* Eye in the Sky — 17
3. Dig or Die — 28
4. "Hell of Antietam" — 35
5. Prestige Restored — 46
6. Arduous Trek to Gettysburg — 54
7. Strange Fruit on Trees — 68
8. Death of a Dueling Sharpshooter — 82

PART II: THE SECOND COMPANY OF ANDREW SHARPSHOOTERS

9. Basil Hall's Farm for Winter Quarters — 93
10. Shell Shocked — 105
11. Horses in the Shade, Soldiers in the Sun — 114
12. The Rifle or the Cell — 124
13. Day of Thanksgiving, but No Food — 146
14. Seventy-seven Held Longstreet — 167
15. "Stuck in the Mud March" — 179
16. Breakfast with Rebels — 189

Table of Contents

First Company Biographical Roster — 211
Second Company Biographical Roster — 235
Glossary — 251
Notes — 253
Bibliography — 259
Index — 263

Preface

There have been countless books written on the Civil War. Many have described battles and profiled leaders. This book is not intended to detail of battles or depict leaders. Instead, it is the histories of two small companies of sharpshooters from Massachusetts, and their exploits during that war.

Most units had their histories written soon after the war was over, but the two companies of Andrew Sharpshooters were never written. The Sharpshooters were often used by other organizations as their special skills of long-range shooting were needed. In some cases their histories were absorbed in those organizations.

This history follows the two companies from when they left Massachusetts, through their time in the seat of war, until they returned, describing their day to day activities for that period of time. There is detailed historical and genealogical information on every man that served in the Andrew Sharpshooters.

The Sharpshooters were courageous patriots, and believed in their cause, undergoing many privations in its service. This is the story of these foot soldiers and their experiences as they lived them.

Introduction

As a Republican, Abraham Lincoln made his views on slavery well known through numerous debates. When he was elected president in November of 1860, the states of South Carolina, Florida, Mississippi, Alabama, Georgia and Louisiana in December of 1860 convened and unanimously voted to secede from the United States of America. They were followed by Texas in February of 1861.

During that same time period, the upper southern states, Arkansas, Virginia, Missouri, Tennessee and North Carolina, voted to remain in the Union and attempted to negotiate their differences. All of that would change on April 12, 1861, when General P. G. T. Beauregard shelled Fort Sumter. President Lincoln, on April 15, called for 75,000 militia soldiers for a three month term to put down the insurrection against a lawful authority. The remaining upper southern states seceded. In the North, there was a cry for revenge and a recruiting frenzy.

The Regular United States Army would have to be reorganized and a volunteer army created. There were numerous West Point graduates who had served together through the Mexican War and who remained close personal friends. They would part company as many of the Southern-born officers would resign their commissions in the United States Army and return to the South. They would become the nucleus of leadership in the Confederate States Army.

Robert Edward Lee, a West Point graduate, through President Lincoln's emissary, was offered field command of the armies of the United States. He declined and returned to his beloved Virginia. He was appointed a general by President Jefferson Davis and charged with the defense of Virginia.

Lewis Addison Armistead of West Point (dismissed from the academy after two years) had become close friends with Winfield Scott Hancock who had graduated 18th in his class. They and their families were close. It was difficult for Armistead to resign his commission to join the Confederate Army, and he vowed to Hancock he would never raise his sword against him. If that were to happen, he wanted God to strike him dead. Armistead would be mortally wounded in front of the Andrew Sharpshooters at Gettysburg as he led a charge against the middle of the line commanded by Hancock.

PART I

The First Company of Andrew Sharpshooters

According to the adjutant general's reports, 108 men enlisted into the First Company at Camp Saunders in Lynnfield. Their average age was twenty-seven-and-a-half years old. Governor Andrew referred to them as a group of men with "superior intelligence." They were to be a distinct branch of the service as long-range riflemen. Only twelve men of the 108 would return and be mustered out after a full three years' service.

Ten would be killed in action, five would die and thirteen would be discharged as a result of wounds, nine would die and thirty-nine would be discharged as a result of disease, ten would desert, and as for the other ten, they transferred to other units or their records were incomplete. An additional 106 men would join the original group of sharpshooters and share similar fates.

These men were originally recruited with the expectation of more than double the pay rate of an infantry private. They were told that their only obligation to the army would be as sharpshooters. They would not drill, stand guard, or perform other duties. They were mustered in at the regular pay rate of twelve dollars a month, and when they went to the seat of war, they performed no other duties until they were temporarily assigned to the 20th Massachusetts Volunteer Infantry. Then they were ordered to do duties which they refused under the terms of their enlistment. They were berated by General Stone and then left alone until assigned to General Lander, a friend of Captain Saunders; then all went fine for awhile.

There were doubts about how the Sharpshooters would perform in battle, as this distinct form of service was unknown and they would take orders only from General Lander. But in their first engagement at Ball's Bluff, where they retired an entire enemy regiment, they proved their value.

After General Lander's death, they would be transferred to the Peninsula and would lose their distinct status, as they were forced to submit to all sorts of duties. The promise of having their heavy rifles transported by wagons was eliminated; on long, forced marches, they carried their heavy rifles. The company's health deteriorated; the men were always at the front, in constant danger. They grew weary of sharpshooting and cold-blooded killing. At least one Sharpshooter would often purposely miss or wound a man, rather than kill him.

Eventually their heavies would be taken from them, and under the threat of artillery fire, with their escape route covered by cavalry, they would be forced to accept the Sharp's rifles. They would then be used as skirmishers. Their morale low, they began to think they had been deceived into the service of sharpshooting. When their number plummeted due to wounds and diseases, they requested to be discharged as a unit in order to reenlist into other branches of the service but were denied.

A portion of the 1st Company Andrew Sharpshooters, ca. spring 1862 (courtesy Scott D. Hann Foundation).

Their commander, Captain Saunders, would be killed purposely by one of his own men whom he had disciplined. Confused commands put them in a horrific position at the Battle of Antietam and the company was decimated. Six of the ten desertions took place at this battle. The company would be replenished with replacements of conscripts and men who had received bounties for their enlistments. Though they endured the harsh life of Civil War soldiers, they went on to distinguish themselves in their three-year service. As they had a reputation that they could be counted on in a battle, their service was in constant demand. Numerous generals gave commendations to this proud and brave lot of men for their courageous service.

The battles in which they were engaged were Ball's Bluff, Siege of Yorktown, Seven Pines, Fair Oaks, Savage Station, Glendale, Malvern Hill, Antietam, Fredericksburg, Chancellorsville, Marye's Heights, Fredericksburg, Salem Church, Banks Ford, Gettysburg, Bristoe Station, Mine Run, Robertson's Tavern, Morton's Ford, Wilderness, Laurel Hill, Spotsylvania Court House, North Anna River, Pamunkey River, Cold Harbor, Petersburg, Weldon Railroad, Deep Bottom, Fussell's Mills, Strawberry Plains, and Ream's Station.

1

Goodbye Lynnfield

In the summer of 1861, a wealthy inventor from New York City was authorized to raise special sharpshooter units. Hiram Berdan, the most proficient marksman in the country for the previous fifteen years, sent agents all over the North to recruit the best marksmen from each state to form these units. The recruits were offered special benefits, such as additional pay, the ability to bring their own rifles and be paid for them, and relief from army drill. They would be issued Sharps breech-loading rifles and not participate in line of battles or picket duty. To be accepted as a sharpshooter, the recruit had to shoot from two hundred yards at a ten-inch target and hit it ten consecutive times. The men would wear forest green uniforms with black buttons and would be known as Berdan's Sharpshooters.[1]

In June of 1861, Hiram Berdan corresponded with Governor John Andrew regarding sharpshooters from the state of Massachusetts.

Governor Andrew's first response to Colonel Berdan was on June 25, 1861. He was warm and supportive of Berdan and Secretary of War General Scott's efforts to raise companies of sharpshooters in Massachusetts. He commended Berdan for his efforts and commented on his belief that Berdan was well suited to organize sharpshooters.

On September 2, 1861, the governor sent a letter to Charles H. Dalton at the Willard Hotel in Washington. He advised Dalton that he had been authorized to raise a company of "*Sharp Shooters*" for one year or the duration of the war. He questioned Dalton on the fact that they would want to be paid an additional $25 per month. He also stated they would be supplying their own rifles and would want to be paid at least $100 apiece for them. He asked Dalton if the Government would pay for them.

The relationship between Governor Andrew and Colonel Berdan at some point grew testy. There was no correspondence confirming that, but on September 2, 1861, he sent the colonel a letter in which he stated that he could not have the Massachusetts sharpshooters. He had learned of the desire of the colonel to attach them to a New York regiment. That would bar the Massachusetts men from obtaining certain benefits for their families. The terseness is observed when the governor writes, "Besides we furnish a better class of arm(s)."

The governor then directed Horace B. Sergeant, his aide de camp, to send a letter to Colonel Berdan. In that letter he acknowledged receipt of a letter from Berdan that ordered the Massachusetts sharpshooters be attached to a U.S. regiment of sharpshooters. He stated that order "*was responded to with great alacrity.*" He referred to the Massachusetts sharpshooters intending to use different arms and maintain their independence from the New York regiment.

To make the issues perfectly clear and leave no room for doubt, Governor Andrew sent this letter to the secretary of war in Washington.

Commonwealth of Massachusetts
Executive Department
Boston September 3, 1861

To Hon. S Cameron, Secretary of War

Sir:

A company of Sharpshooters 101 men organized in Mass. leave this day for Washington, agreeably to your special request. They would have left Saturday, but the supply of telescopic rifles, though not entirely adequate, could not be made available earlier.

The company enlisted specifically and unequivocally as a <u>Massachusetts</u> Co. to be attached to some <u>Massachusetts Regiment</u>. The men are of superior intelligence, would not have enlisted in any different service, nor could they be obtained to join any regiment out of Massachusetts, partly because that would debar their families from certain advantages of State Aid. And they are this day organized and their company officers appointed solely on my promise that they shall be by you attached to some Mass. regiment for the time being subject to subsequent attachment to Gen. Wilson's regiment now rapidly forming. They wish especially to be placed in <u>Gen. Lander's</u> Brigade if possible.

Col. Wm. Raymond Lee's regiment, not yet full, will march tomorrow; and this company might conveniently be attached to his command—perhaps.

We are now forming still another company three fourths full.

John A. Andrew[2]

Colonel Hiram Berdan. Berdan, the best marksman in the country, with influence with President Lincoln, organized the National Sharpshooters, which Andrew's were to be a part of. Governor Andrew put a stop to that as Berdan attempted to assign them to a New York Regiment. It also irked the governor enough that he ordered all recruiting in the commonwealth to cease and that his office would organize all recruiting (Library of Congress).

A camp was established in Lynnfield, twelve miles from Boston, on a former racetrack near the Lynnfield Hotel. A perfect setting for a camp, the field was level, open, and surrounded by woods for training, and would accommodate troops drilling. On July 1, 1861, Colonel Lyman Dike of Stoneham arrived as the commander of Camp Schouler, named after the state's adjutant general.

This advantageous location had easy access to the Newbury Turnpike and the South Reading Railroad as well as an ample water supply from Lake Suntaug. The area used for the tents and buildings was bordered on the north by what is today the town line between Lynnfield and Peabody, and on the south by Route 128, with some spillover on the other side of the road. Individual camps within Camp Schouler had names such as the City Grays, Foster Guards, British Volunteers, Saunders Guards, and Malden Light Infantry.[3]

The First Company of Andrew Sharpshooters was raised by the Honorable W. D. Northend of Salem, in Lynnfield. The camp was named

1. Goodbye Lynnfield

Saunders, after the company commander. They mustered in and left for the seat of war September 2, 1861. They were ordered to report to headquarters in Washington and as per the special request from Governor Andrew, they were assigned to General Lander's brigade.[4]

The Sharpshooters were armed with telescopic rifles which weighed from twenty to seventy pounds. A telescope ran along the entire length of the barrel. These rifles were not furnished by the state, but by the Sharpshooters themselves who had them made to their own specifications by various gunsmiths throughout the North. It was thought there were only about three hundred of these rifles in existence in the North and very few in the South.

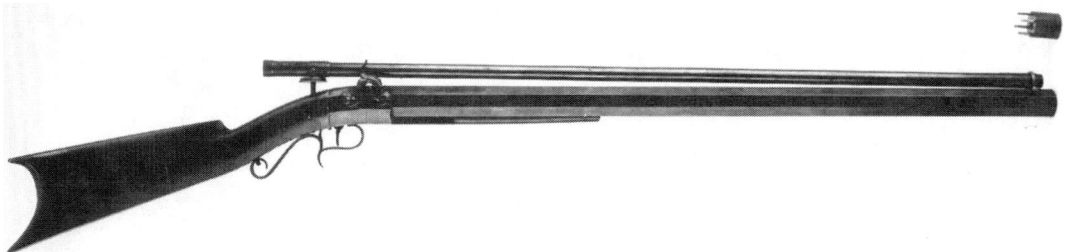

Above: A Morgan James Target Rifle, such as was used by the Sharpshooters. Both companies lost either the equipment or stamina to continue the use of these long range rifles and would be issued Sharp rifles as depicted on page 10. Both companies would strongly protest this change in their form of service. *Below:* A close view of a Morgan James Target Rifle (all photographs courtesy West Point Museum Collections, U.S. Military Academy).

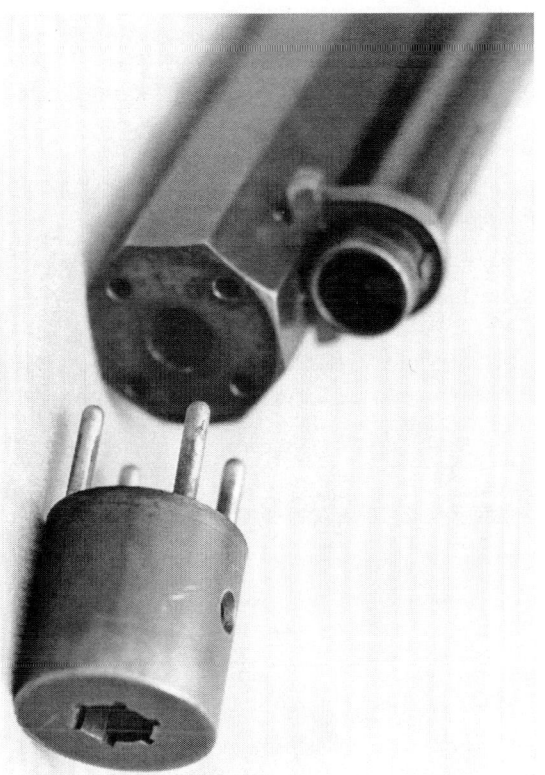

The heavily built barrel sustained a hefty load of powder and prevented large recoils from the rifles. The projectile was conical and flat at the base and was used with a grease patch. It took great skill to accurately fire these rifles. It was estimated that a projectile would fall four to five feet at three hundred yards and twenty to thirty feet at eight hundred yards; at the same time, wind would have to be factored in. Adjustments were made with a series of wedges to the rifle's telescopic scope. It would take a skilled marksman two minutes to load and fire the rifle. The shot would have to be fired from a position of rest.[5]

It is unknown whether this type of rifle had ever been used in battle. The first opportunity was presented on October 21 and 22 at Edwards Ferry. On the first day, Private Hatch shot a Rebel colonel from his horse at a distance of one-half mile and several privates at a longer distance. The second day, about forty sharpshooters lined up on a Virginia fence and opened fire as a Rebel regiment advanced on them. Sergeant Shattuck alone killed three different color-bearers. The skirmish lasted about twenty minutes, and each sharpshooter fired ten rounds. The Sharpshooters killed an estimated seventy of the Rebels who charged before they retreated for the cover of the woods.[6]

Governor Andrew, although at odds with Hiram Berdan, stuck to his convictions about the Sharpshooters' importance as he sent out the following correspondence.

Commonwealth of Massachusetts
Executive Department
Mr. A. B. Brown   Boston Sept. 10, 1861
Malden, Mass.

Dear Sir;

His Excellency Gov. Andrew desires me to say in reply to yours of this date that Massachusetts needs additional troops to fill the ranks of the fine regiments now being raised, and that companies of sharpshooters are desired for every regiment. If you can raise such a company every facility will be afforded you and His Excellency will see you at any time when not engaged.

Yours Very Truly

Thomas Drew
Assistant Military Secretary

P.S. Telescopic rifles cannot be had to any extent and company of sharpshooters will not be permitted to serve as detached companies but as the flank companies of Regiments to which they are attached.[7]

Twelve men mustered out of the 8th Regimental Massachusetts Militia Company A: John Ambrose, Luke Bicknell, John Burrows, William Forbes, Stephen Goodwin, James Hudson, Samuel Gilbreth, David Littlefield, Henry Martin, John Perley, Jason Rines, and Richard Van Moll. Massachusetts rushed to fill its quota of men. Although the 8th was a three-month

Sharp Breech Loading Rifle. Sharpshooters were forced to take these rifles and act as skirmishers. Both companies protested so strongly that they accepted these rifles only at gunpoint and the threat of execution (courtesy West Point Museum Collections, U.S. Military Academy).

INFANTRY, CAVALRY, RIFLEMEN
Artillerymen and Sharpshooters,
TAKE YOUR CHOICE WHERE TO ENLIST.

THE GLORIOUS SIXTH

Who went through Baltimore, April 19th, furnish the Nucleus of the Massachusetts 26th,

NEW ENGLAND GUARDS!

Fourth Battalion Regiment, (Col. Stevenson) the Flower of Boston's Youth.

HENRY WILSON REGIMENT!

The 22d goes next week, but a few more vacancies left. The 23d has already two-thirds the number required.

The Worcester County Regiment!

Col. Upton, a noble Representative of the Hearts of the Commonwealth.

The Massachusetts 27th, Col. W. R. LEE!

LANCERS, DRAGOONS, CAVALRY REGIMENT.

Includes the Cream of the National Lancers, the Boston Light Dragoons and other First Class Corps.

Gunners, Artillerists, Cannoneers New Battery

SHARP SHOOTERS!

IRISHMEN OF MASSACHUSETTS

RALLY FOR THE OLD WAR CRY FAUGH A BALLAUGH, let your Green Flag be turned with your Adopted Country's Starry Banner. The New Massachusetts IRISH REGIMENT, the 28th Col, THOMAS MURPHY, is now forming, join it without delay.

THE IRISH BRIGADE, GEN. SHIELDS!

This Commonwealth furnishes a Regiment for this Brigade, to be called the Massachusetts 29th.

The people of many of the towns and cities of the Commonwealth have made ample provision for those joining the ranks of the Army. If any person enlists in a Company or Regiment out of the Commonwealth they cannot share in the bounty which has been thus liberally voted.

BY ORDER OF BRIG. GEN. W. W. BULLOCK,
GENERAL RECRUITING OFFICER FOR MASSACHUSETTS VOLUNTEERS.

Recruiting Station and Barracks, 14 Pitts Street, Boston,

_____ WILL OPEN AN OFFICE IN _Boston_

AT _48 Beacon St_ FOR _Sharp Shooters_   M. H. KEENAN'S PRESS, BOSTON.

Recruiting poster for all branches of the service. This poster directs sharpshooters to report to the offices at 48 Beacon Street, Boston. This poster was probably dated sometime in late September of 1861, as the 22nd Massachusetts Volunteer Infantry were in their final stages of organization (courtesy American Antiquarian Society).

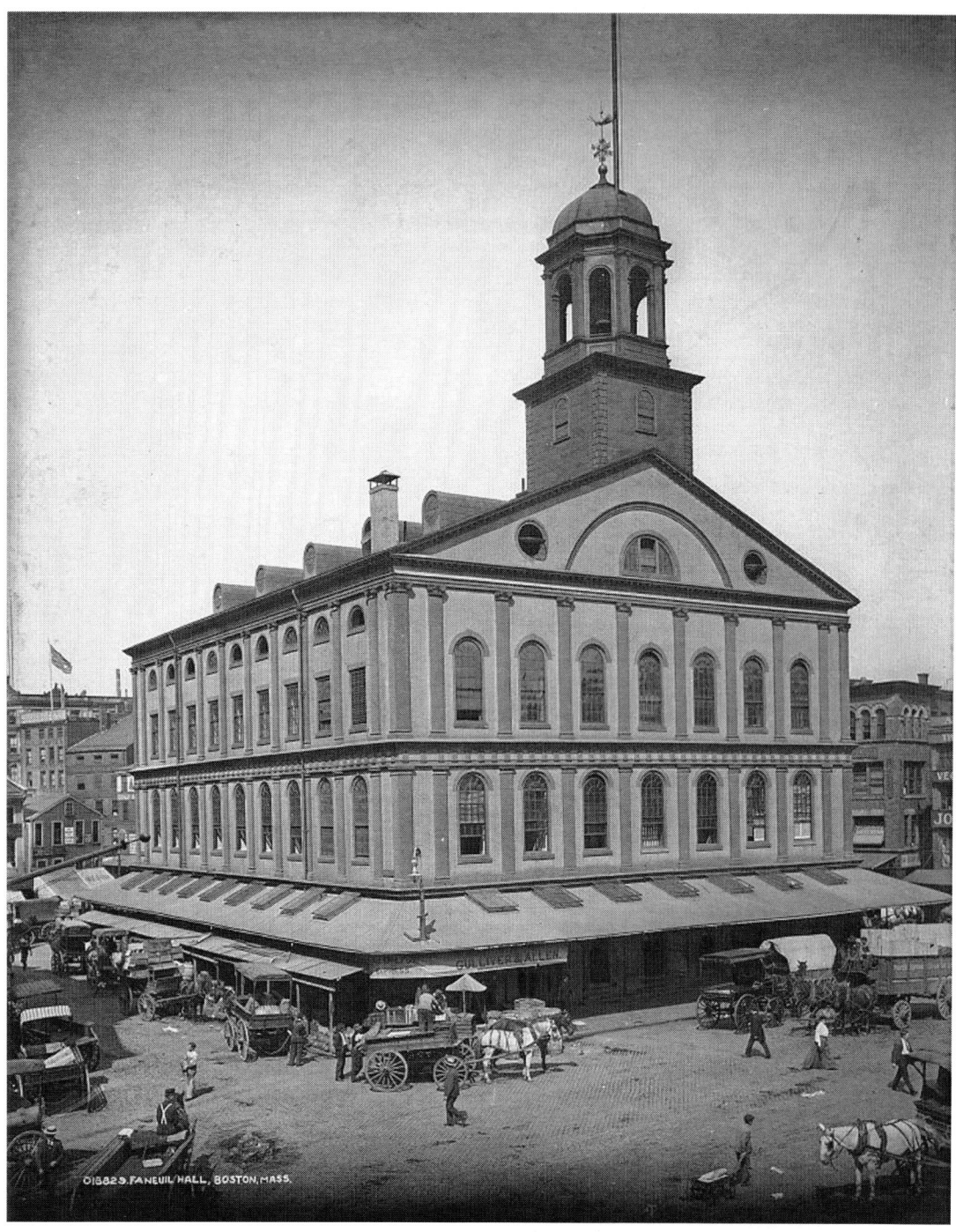

Faneuil Hall in Boston, Massachusetts, circa 1882. On April 17, 1861, the 8th Massachusetts Volunteer Infantry was organizing there. Many of the men of that 90 day regiment would return and volunteer to serve in the 1st Company of Sharpshooters. Samuel Gilbreth was denied access to the third floor where the regiment was. He was so determined to enlist that he climbed the downspout to the third floor and banged on the window to gain access. In the final days of the Sharpshooters' service, he would officer that company (Library of Congress).

unit, the recruits understood that it would be reorganized into a three-year regiment. Only later did they learn that the unit would not be reorganized. Their only alternatives were to go into other regiments that were being organized.

These men wanted to return to the war, but only if they could serve together in the same unit. Some of them turned down sergeants' positions in the 19th Massachusetts Volunteer Infantry so that they would not be dispersed into other units. It must be noted that the Adjutant General's *Massachusetts Soldiers, Sailors* did not list Samuel Gilbreth as serving in the 8th Regimental Massachusetts Militia Company A. Bicknell, on April 17, 1861, was in Faneuil Hall as the 8th Regimental Militia was organizing. There were only a few vacancies, and thousands wanted to fill them. Samuel Gilbreth tried to enter Faneuil Hall to join the company, but the guards turned him away at the door. Determined, he went to the side of the building and climbed up the drain spout until he reached Company A, on the third floor, where he was assisted through the window and was immediately voted into the company.[8]

After mustering out of the 8th Regimental Militia, these men spent a short time at their homes, visiting relatives and friends, and later met in Newburyport. From there, they went straight to Lynnfield, where they met with Captain John Saunders of Salem, who was attempting to form a company of sharpshooters that would be attached to the command of his old friend General Frederick Lander.[9]

Captain Saunders explained to the recruits that they would use large target rifles which weighed from thirty to fifty pounds each. The rifles would be loaded with a false muzzle and starter, and would have a telescope that ran the entire length of the barrel. Each rifle was to have its own set of wedges, bullet molds, charges, and powder flasks in a box made especially for it.

The company's mission would be to shoot officers and artillerists in battles or sieges. Captain Saunders stated that men in the line of battles would be free of all duties, including guard and drill. Their

Captain John Saunders (courtesy Scott D. Hann Foundation).

rifles would be stored in their boxes and carried by two wagons which the state had promised to provide them. Due to their extra-hazardous duty, they would receive twenty-five dollars a month rather than the normal twelve dollars. There would be demand for their service in many places at once, and the company would be led by four lieutenants and four sergeants. Captain Saunders said he did not care about infantry tactics or men who understood them.

He advised that the men he had already selected for his four sergeants were skilled marksmen and old friends. He had selected William Gleason, William Berry, and Charles Ingalls as his first, second, and third lieutenants, but had left the position of fourth lieutenant open and would fill it from the men who would join him.

Luke Bicknell and Henry Martin agreed that they would not attempt to obtain the position of the fourth lieutenancy and felt that John Perley, who had served in the Regular Cavalry on the frontier, would be well suited to lead the Sharpshooters. Captain Saunders tested their marksmanship and felt these men would mature into good marksmen; he invited them to join his sharpshooters and help him raise the company.[10]

They recruited with much zeal as they thought of the extra pay, freedom from normal military discipline, and the ability to always be in the forefront of the action. They soon had assembled more than two hundred men in camp for Captain Saunders to choose from. Saunders then discussed raising another company of sharpshooters that would be issued Sharps rifles. Bicknell and Martin would be their commissioned officers. Bicknell then learned from officers in the 19th Massachusetts Volunteer Infantry that they were being "humbugged" about the extra pay.[11]

Captain Saunders and Bicknell were on the next train to Boston to meet with Governor Andrews about the extra pay. Although they were not able to see the governor, the adjutant general assured them that they would get the extra pay, although there was no confirmation from Washington at that point. Captain Saunders felt reassured, but Bicknell did not, as he had enticed many men into camp under those assumptions and felt responsible to clear the air with those men.

Much to Captain Saunders's dissatisfaction, Bicknell mounted a barrel and told the men he doubted the extra pay would materialize and that they should stay in camp for the expressed satisfaction of good sharpshooting and the ability to always be out in front. Before night fell, so many men had left camp that the possibility of raising another company of sharpshooters had evaporated. Captain Saunders believed all would be corrected when they were under General Landers's leadership. Saunders was upset when the mustering officers would muster the men at only regular pay — and more so when the company would be mustered with only two lieutenants instead of the four promised. To add to his indignation, on September 2, Governor Andrew ordered the adjutant general to appoint George Gray as 2nd lieutenant. That forced Perley, Ingalls, and Berry back into the ranks, which the three accepted with good grace as they were men of pride and would not walk away just because they had lost their commissions.[12]

On August 30, Governor Andrew issued an order for the sharpshooters to proceed to Washington the following day. However, as they were waiting for additional telescopic rifles to arrive, they were not able to leave until September 3.[13] They proceeded to Washington by train. Bicknell met a Harvard College graduate and lawyer, George Whittemore, with whom Bicknell was impressed. It seemed Whittemore had poor eyesight and was unable to join the military, and had joined the Sharpshooters because the rifles' telescopes improved his vision. Bicknell told him that he had left Hardee's *Tactics*, a book of infantry tactics, at home and put Blackstone's legal treatise in his knapsack. They agreed to be tent mates when they arrived in the field.[14]

> Head Quarters Provisional Brigade
> Washington City, Sept. 7th, 1861

Special Orders No. 11

The 4th Provisional Brigade. Col. Lee Comdg. Head Quarters Camp Kalamara will consist of the following Regiments:-

> Pa. Vol.s Col. (illegible)
> Mass. Vol.s Col. Lee

Captain John Saunders, Commanding 1st Company Sharpshooters, Mass. Vol.s will be temporarily attached to the 20th Mass. Vol.s Col. Lee and report to him at his headquarters, Camp Kalamara.

> By Command of
> Brigadier General A. E. Burnside

When the Sharpshooters arrived at Washington, Captain Saunders met with Secretary of War Simon Cameron and requested the extra pay and the additional lieutenants. Although Saunders was denied, he remained hopeful as he thought Governor Andrew and General Lander's continued efforts would bring about the change.[15]

The Sharpshooters were temporarily attached to the 20th Massachusetts Volunteer Infantry and ordered to Camp Benton in Poolesville, Maryland, where they awaited General Lander's arrival. The officers of the 20th worked diligently to bring discipline and order to their regiment. They were not pleased with the Sharpshooters, who had no regular drill or duties and lacked discipline.[16]

Captain Saunders disliked drill, parades, and salutes, and refused to listen to the officers of the 20th Massachusetts. He finally relented and said that any sharpshooter who wanted to volunteer could march, drill, and stand guard with the 20th. The captain's idea of discipline was that any man who disobeyed an order or showed any sign of being a coward would be shot down. It did not take long for the Sharpshooters' special spirit to rise as the following order was issued.[17]

> Brigade Head Quarters
> Camp Benton, Sept. 29th, 1861

Capt. John Saunders
   Commanding Andrew Sharpshooters Sir;

You are requested to report in writing by what cause, and under what circumstances, alleged or otherwise your men refused to do duty when directed on service by their commanding officer, Col. W. R. Lee

> Very Respectfully
> Your obt. Lt.
> By Command George W. Butler
> Brig. Gen. Lander Aide de Camp[18]

Some of the Sharpshooters attempted to drill and stand guard with the Twentieth, but were quite awkward with their large bulky rifles and as a result just stood at parade rest during the nightly drills. One night the following order was read to all of the regiments in the division:

General Order No. 19

> Headquarters Corps of Observation
> Poolesville, Md. Sept. 30, 1861

The General Commanding has noticed, in reviewing an official correspondence, that Capt. Saunders of the "Andrew Sharpshooters" claims exemption for his company from obedience to General Orders, or any regulations concerning drill etc. on the grounds that his command came into service with the understanding that it was not to be held strictly to the rules of Camp Discipline.

This extraordinary statement, if true, exhibits a gross violation of Law and Justice, which will receive no countenance from the Commanding Officer, who cannot admit the claims of any Officer or enlisted man under his command, to especial privilege above his command.

If Capt. Saunders and his men entered the service of the Country expecting exemption from laws which apply to the other Officers and Soldiers in the Army, the sooner they waive these expectations or leave the service, the better it will be for the service and their own reputations.

The only claim to especial considerations, shall be the excellence of conduct and discipline in camp, and excellence of behavior before the enemy, two qualities of soldiers which in all of History been found to go together.

By Order of
Brig. Gen. Stone
Chas. Stewart A.A.G.[19]

That was enough for the Sharpshooters. They immediately left the field and refused to attempt to drill or perform duties or guard duty. They fell back on the original conditions of their enlistment. Colonel Lee, commander of the 20th Massachusetts, gave up, and stated that the Sharpshooters must be left alone until General Lander arrived.[20]

2

Intrepid, Eye in the Sky

On his arrival General Lander issued the following order:

> Brigade Head Quarters
> Camp Benton Oct. 3rd 1861
>
> *Special Orders No. 14*
>
> *Captain Saunders (illegible) Andrew Sharpshooters are hereby detached from the 20th Reg. Mass. Vols. And will move their camp to the ground designated by the Com. A. G. General.*
>
> *Morning reports will be made to Brigade Head Quarters of the Company Commander, and handed in by 9 o'clock A.M.*
>
> By order of
> Brig. Genl. Lander
> (Illegible signature)
> A.A.G.[1]

The Sharpshooters then set up camp by themselves on a hill in the rear of General Lander's headquarters. Perley, Martin, and Bicknell were appointed as sergeants. The Sharpshooters were issued twenty light rifles and were soon as well-drilled as any company in the army. They continued to practice with their heavy rifles, provided a guard at General Lander's headquarters, and picketed a portion of the line at night. They were transformed into the busiest, best-disciplined organization in the division and came to be known as Lander's Pets. However, other regiments retained a lingering suspicion that they might not be counted on in battle, as they yielded only to General Lander. Yet their heavy guns would be beneficial in battle, as would soon be proven at the battles of Ball's Bluff and Edwards Ferry.

The Sharpshooters' rifle telescopes revealed that the enemy across the river at Leesburg had broken camp and withdrawn from the opposite side of the river. Apparently the Confederates were moving toward Washington to attack General McClellan. A few men with Massachusetts officers crossed the river, reconnoitered toward Leesburg, and returned, reporting that the enemy's larger body had left and only a small guard remained to protect Leesburg. Although the pressure to cross the river and engage the enemy was great, only a few small boats were available.[2]

October 21, 1861, proved to be a date when both sides learned some valuable lessons about the art of war. A series of slow communications began when the general officers received communications at ten o'clock that were relevant to the situation at seven o'clock and made decisions based on that information. The general nofficers thought the enemy had abandoned

Ball's Bluff, but they had not, as they had little ability to move troops from the Maryland side of the Potomac to Harrison's Island and then on to Virginia, not to mention that they had to climb a seventy-foot hill when they arrived.[3]

The 15th Massachusetts Volunteer Infantry, the 20th Massachusetts Volunteer Infantry, and the 1st California Volunteer Infantry crossed the river to Ball's Bluff, where the enemy engaged them. Reinforcements were sent, and more men slowly crossed the river. The Federal forces were pushed back to the river and slaughtered as they tried to cross with few facilities available. About fifty men were killed in the battle, more than one hundred and fifty wounded, and many taken prisoner. In addition, about seven hundred men were missing, many of whom were either shot or drowned as they attempted to swim to Harrison's Island and the safety of the Maryland side. As a result, General Charles Stone would be jailed for almost eight months without being charged: someone had to pay for the debacle at Ball's Bluff.[4] On October 21, under General Gorman's command and as part of Stone's division, the Sharpshooters crossed the river about three miles south of Ball's Bluff at Edwards Ferry to make reconnaissance along Goose Creek. Early that afternoon, the Federal Cavalry probed deeper on the inland and made contact with the enemy. The ground in front of them was surrounded by woods on three sides, with a Virginia fence bisecting the field. Behind that fence Captain Saunders was positioned with about seventy sharpshooters.[6]

Brigadier General Frederic W. Lander was from Salem, Massachusetts. He was a graduate of Norwich Military Academy in Vermont. He was considered by some to be the best topographical engineer in the country. He was a personal friend of Captain Saunders and took the sharpshooters under his command. He favored the Sharpshooters to such an extent that they became known as "Lander's Pets" (Library of Congress).

At about three that afternoon, the enemy came out of the woods and formed in line of battle three-quarters of a mile in front of the fence. Opening fire on the enemy, Captain Saunders and his sharpshooters killed a mounted officer, three flag-bearers, and a number of other men. The enemy fell back and the Tiger Fire Zouaves of the 19th Massachusetts deployed as skirmishers. At about five o'clock, the 19th Massachusetts returned, declaring that the woods were empty and that there were a number of bodies and signs of many wounded carried off.[6]

That morning Bicknell had pleaded with Captain Saunders to be allowed to go on the expedition. As Bicknell was sergeant of the guard and Saunders dared not remove the guard from headquarters, Saunders refused to let him join the group. About midnight, General Lander returned from Washington, where he had been organizing a force that was to be sent into the Shenandoah Valley and that came to be known as the Army of

Northern Virginia. When Bicknell apprised the general of the day's events, the general was very upset and severely condemned the officers who would allow such a movement. He thought those who had crossed at Ball's Bluff would be killed or captured.

Bicknell explained to General Lander that the Sharpshooters had left in haste without knapsacks and provisions. Bicknell wanted to take their knapsacks across the river. General Lander agreed to let Bicknell cross the river and take Lander with him, telling Bicknell to advise the remaining Sharpshooters that they had no chance of returning as they would be killed or taken prisoner, and that only volunteers would be allowed to cross. Several of the Sharpshooters were willing to remain and guard the camp. Other volunteers, including Samuel Gilbreth, agreed to cross.[7]

As General Lander doubted the Sharpshooters' ability to cross the river, he arranged with artillerists to protect them. However, as General Lander had been assigned another command and General Banks had issued an order that would not allow another man to cross the river, General Lander could give orders only to the Sharpshooters. General Banks had guards placed on the river with orders to shoot any man who attempted to cross. The Sharpshooters and General Lander concluded that they were under another command and didn't have to obey General Banks.

Samuel Gilbreth pushed General Lander across the river on a borrowed skiff. Bicknell and the others loaded the knapsacks and provisions on a borrowed canal boat and pushed it across the river while General Banks' guards threatened to shoot them. They were warmly received by the troops on the other side of the river, who were pleased with the provisions and encouraged by General Lander's presence.[8]

When Bicknell and Lander's troops arrived at the plateau they found Captain Saunders and his band of Sharpshooters at the fence from which they had fought the previous day. At a fence on another side of the cornfield, the 19th Tigers were positioned, and on the other side, by the woods along Goose Creek, two pieces of artillery were located.[9]

On the afternoon of October 22, a cold rain started at about two o'clock, and Bicknell and Lander thought there would not be another battle. But having moved silently through a thick fog, the Confederates poured out of the woods at about five o'clock, totally surprising the Federal forces. Firing by ranks, a full regiment of the enemy advanced on the Sharpshooters at close range. Rain and fog had clouded the Sharpshooters' telescopic sights and made the heavy rifles useless. The Sharpshooters aimed over the top of the scopes as they fired at the advancing enemy.

As they drew the enemy into the position they had abandoned, the Sharpshooters split and moved to the right and left, and both the artillery near Goose Creek and the Union artillery from the other side of the river opened fire. Keeping up a steady fire, the Sharpshooters and the Tigers of the 19th forced the enemy to retreat. Bicknell, Martin, and Gilbreth had split to the left side with General Lander, who fell when he was shot in the calf. Although Lander gave an order to leave him there, it was disobeyed, and Martin removed the general from the field. Only General Lander had suffered a wound; the Sharpshooters had passed through a hail of bullets and not one of them had been wounded or killed. Lander praised the Sharpshooters and sent back word from the ambulance that if he had a regiment with such men he could march through Virginia. Major Howe of the 19th also had such praise for his own men.[10]

The enemy's loss was great: a prisoner said their loss at Edward's Ferry cancelled out their victory at Ball's Bluff the previous day. One of the Sharpshooters had lost his heavy rifle, which was taken to Libby Prison. Colonel Lee, who was being held there, asked about the rifle and the men who carried them, and was told that more than two hundred men had been killed by the slugs fired from that type of rifle. In their first engagement, the Sharpshooters had turned back an enemy regiment and established themselves as a fighting company.

The Sharpshooters were the last to cross the river on October 22. They returned to Camp Benton and were left alone, resting for a couple of weeks. General McClellan came to Camp Benton and escorted General Lander to Washington. Captain Saunders returned to Massachusetts for a visit and sent word to the Sharpshooters that he was authorized to raise two more Sharpshooter companies, to be equipped with Sharps rifles, and that members of the First Company would officer the new companies.[11]

When Professor Lowe came to Camp Benton with his hot air balloon, the *Intrepid,* the Sharpshooters were assigned to guard him and manage the *Intrepid.* Whenever a general wanted to ascend, the Sharpshooters would man the ropes and tackle as the balloon ascended up to six hundred feet. One day, as General Banks ascended, the ground tackle broke loose, and as the Sharpshooters held on, they were hauled high into the air. Finally, they succeeded

Professor Lowes' "*Intrepid,*" Fair Oaks, Virginia, 1862. The Sharpshooters were ordered to manage *Intrepid* in the fall of 1861. They would hold it until it rose to about 600 feet. It would be used to determine the strength and location of the enemy (Library of Congress).

in bringing the balloon down. That event became a source of amusement, and the enemy fired wildly at the balloon each time it ascended.

The chief quartermaster of the Army of the Potomac, Rufus Ingalls, arrived in camp and directed winter quarters to be constructed. The men constructed tents with wood bases, some with fireplaces. That winter, for the first time, the paymaster arrived and offered the Sharpshooters their choice of gold or greenbacks. As they thought that the war effort had stretched the government thin enough, they elected greenbacks. Uncomplaining, the Sharpshooters said nothing about their pay not being the promised twenty-five dollars.[12]

> Head Quarters Corps of Observation
> Poolesville January 1st, 1862

Special Order No. 1

In compliance with orders from Head Quarters Army of the Potomac of this date, the "Andrew Sharpshooters" are relieved from duty in this Division, and will march without delay to Frederick, Maryland, there to await orders from Brig. Genl. Lander at Hancock.

The Quartermaster of the First Brigade will furnish the necessary transportation.

A detail of forty men from the 20th Regt. Mass. Vol.s will replace that from the Sharpshooters on balloon service. The Union "Repeating Guns" now in charge of the Sharpshooters will be turned over to the 7th Michigan Vol.s.

> By order of Brig. Genl. Stone
> W. R. Nyslop
> Lt. A.A.A.G
> Head Quarters, Corps of Observation
> Poolesville January 2nd, 1862

Special Order No. 2

3. Special Order No.1 Par.11 from these Head Quarters is countermanded by Head Quarters Army of the Potomac, so far as related to the destination of the "Andrew Sharpshooters."

Instead of proceeding to Frederick, there to await orders, they will proceed direct to Hancock by Canal.

The Division Quartermaster will furnish all necessary transportation.

> By order of Brig. Genl. Stone
> C. Stewart
> A.A.G[13]

As the War Department had nixed hopes for two more companies of Sharpshooters, Captain Saunders returned to Camp Benton. On January 3, 1862, the Sharpshooters received orders to pack up and move via Hancock by canal to Cumberland, Maryland, where they would report to General Lander, who had recovered from his wound and was at his new headquarters. As their two wagons were not sufficient to carry all of their equipment and rifles over the frozen roads, they loaded their entire equipage on a canal boat, attached ropes, and began the trek to drag it fifty miles.[14]

As they started, the ice on the canal was so thin that they could pull the boat through it. As time passed, the ice got thicker and threatened to break up the boat, so they put an ice boat in the lead. The ice boat needed a detail of men, and they could not keep the icy water out of their boots. So that most of the company would be fit for duty on their arrival, they kept the same men on ice boat detail, supplying them with a keg of rum; eventually they learned that hot coffee would be better for the men.

At night, the men anchored and camped. The men in the ice boat detail were afraid to remove their boots, so the other men would elevate them, drain their boots, fill the boots with rum, and then pack the detail in bunks to make them as comfortable as possible. When they had departed for Maryland, they had thought it would take at most three or four days to reach Cumberland. But the ice cost them so much time that they ran out of rations the morning before they reached Williamsport, which they reached about midnight. In the morning they were able to obtain a small breakfast.

Shouldering their knapsacks and heavy rifles, they then marched thirty miles to Hancock without any food. They arrived late at night thoroughly exhausted, and it was too late to acquire rations. Even if they could have, they did not have the strength to prepare them. The next morning they drew rations, encamped in a barn and built fires in an adjacent open lot. That day they prepared rations for the rest of the trip, ate, washed and dried their clothes, and got some much-needed rest. They thought one good night of rest in the barn would ready them to continue, but they lost that when they were awoken and told that Cumberland was in danger of being captured.

The men felt a duty to fight by General Lander's side as he had fought by theirs at Edward's Ferry. Throwing their knapsacks and equipment on the teams, they shouldered their heavy rifles and started toward Cumberland, some forty-one miles away on a dark, cold, misty night. The roads had softened somewhat, and they sank up to their ankles in the mud with every step. They moved forward for about two miles, but about midnight their muscles gave out and they had to stop. By that time, only a few men were left. Many of the men, including Captain Saunders, were unable to keep up. They would not see Captain Saunders for a couple of days, until he arrived at Cumberland in a wagon.[15]

The remaining Sharpshooters continued on. Stopping at a small farmhouse beside the road, they begged for wood or rails to start a fire with, but the farmer pleaded poverty and old age and could not help them, but he loaned them an axe so that they could cut limbs and branches and start a fire. Returning the axe, they thought that if this was the best he had, he surely was in trouble. They stayed at that fire until morning. Giving up hope that as a company, they would reach Cumberland in time to be of use, they decided that each man would go at his own pace, and hoped a few of the heavy rifles would reach Cumberland in time to be of service.

As each man moved at his own pace, nearly every house on the roads became a free hotel. The well-rested infantry, who had followed the Sharpshooters from Hancock, nonetheless became exhausted. The Sharpshooters, far more worn, were so tired that they could neither eat nor drink coffee, and they were unable to hold water in their stomachs. The only way they were able to advance was to set their sights on an object ahead of them and attempt to reach it before stopping to rest.

At about five in the afternoon, some of the Sharpshooters reached the railroad bridge east of Cumberland, stopped, and looked down on the city. While Bicknell leaned against the bridge, a young Negro stood behind him for several minutes. Bicknell thought he was fascinated by his heavy rifle, but as he turned, the young man handed him an uncorked bottle of whiskey and told Bicknell it would be good for him. Bicknell agreed. As he returned the bottle, he thought of all the other Sharpshooters behind him who also would need it. Telling Bicknell he had plenty more, the young man urged Bicknell to drink freely. Bicknell did, and entered Cumberland feeling like a new man.[16]

The Sharpshooters who arrived that evening slept in a pit under the Railroad Round House on a foot of straw, and the engines that passed above them did not disturb their rest. The following day most of the stragglers arrived, and they all boarded a train and rode to Patterson Creek, Virginia. When they jumped off the train they sank six inches in mud. They laid down their rubber blankets to get some rest, but the mud and water seeped over the blankets and onto the Sharpshooters. In the morning, they pitched tents and forced rails and brush into the ground to create a dry floor. The sergeants chipped in money, and they bought a cone stove from an Ohio sutler. They took in as many sick men as the tent would hold.

The following week, Captain Saunders procured nine more stoves and wooden planks for floors. The Sharpshooters' camp was far less comfortable than the one they had left at Camp Benton. But they were convinced that once they had reached their beloved General Lander, there would be one great battle and the war would be over. Then they could return to Massachusetts and enjoy all the comforts of home.

In the following weeks, rain and snow fell daily. Though the Sharpshooters had no regular assigned duties, there was always something to do at headquarters, and any man who wished for exercise found something to do. Talking to some Confederate prisoners, the Sharpshooters found that the enemy suffered as much or even more than the Federals. The prisoners lacked basic necessities. They were without blankets, shoes, and other items to protect them from the elements. Bicknell intervened on their behalf, and some of their basic needs were met.

The Sharpshooters moved their camp and marched over muddy roads. Bicknell and seven others went over mountain trails with the wagon to avoid the muddy roads, cutting ruts in the road to keep the wagons from sliding over a ledge. At other places, they had to lift the wagons out of unknown depths of mud. Bicknell arrived in camp the following day and was berated by Captain Saunders for damaging the Sharpshooters' only two axes to build defenses with. Bicknell's tent mates also harassed him, saying that he should have let the wagons and heavy rifles slide off the cliff, as they were killing them on the march. But because General Lander had designated the Sharpshooters as his personal bodyguard, he said he would try to mount them on horseback.[17]

They broke camp again, boarded trains, and headed for Paw Paw Tunnel, about thirty miles from Winchester. There they labored night and day for three days rebuilding the railroad bridge, putting up telegraph poles, building stables, and erecting their own tents when they got a chance. Fever, diphtheria, and measles broke out among the depleted Sharpshooters, and half of the men were sent back to a hospital in Cumberland. On March 1, 1862, Edward Andrews of Lee, Massachusetts, was the first death in the company. He died of disease before he could be removed from camp.

Rations of quinine and whiskey were served to the Sharpshooters, and men who had promised their mothers they would not drink alcohol relented. One young man, John Brown, who had vowed to his mother that he would not drink the "accursed stuff," refused to drink and was cheered by the other Sharpshooters.

The day after the Sharpshooters arrived at Paw Paw Tunnel, they accompanied General Lander on a train to Hancock. But the troops stationed in the town were ignorant of the Sharpshooters' labor on the railroad the previous week, and despite their Federal uniforms, arrested them. Once at the troops' headquarters, General Lander was recognized as the department's commander, and the Sharpshooters were freed.

The next two weeks brought mild weather, but the company's health continued to decline. One of Bicknell's morning reports stated that only forty-three Sharpshooters were healthy enough for duty. An astonished General Lander told Bicknell to offer the entire company a disability discharge. But the men refused: they thought the advance move would precipitate one more great battle to end the war, and they wanted to be a part of it. All they requested was horses, and General Lander said he would do his best to mount the Sharpshooters.

General Lander was an engineer and one of the foremost topographers in the country. He had developed perfect maps of the area surrounding Winchester. He knew the enemy's troop strength and location, and collaborated with General McClellan on a plan to capture Winchester. Lander's plan was to strike General Lee swift and hard on his left flank and force him back on his center in front of McClellan. Then Landers and McClellan would unite, push Lee back, and take the city. McClellan continued to urge Lander to come to his headquarters and assume the position of chief of command under him.

From the morning of Friday, February 28, until the night of Saturday, March 1, Federal troops arrived by train. Marching to the woods, they encamped on the heights toward Winchester. When all the troops had arrived, they were to close in around Lee's left on Sunday, March 2, 1862.[18]

General Lander had returned to the field before he had completely recovered from the gunshot wound in his calf. He had refused any rest while the troops were arriving, and he needed rest before he could command himself, let alone the army. The surgeon administered an opiate to the general, and Bicknell was placed to guard his tent and allow no passage except for Lander's personal staff. Lander slept well into the following afternoon. When the surgeon became alarmed and went to Lander's tent, there was not much the surgeon could do, and before the night was over the Union had lost its Stonewall Jackson. The Confederates withdrew from Winchester the day Lander died.

Having been assigned as Lander's orderly, Bicknell remained alone in the death chamber throughout the night to guard Lander's body and sort his personal papers. Bicknell noted a letter from Secretary Stanton which stated that Lander was best suited to push the war in the spirit the North demanded.[19]

General Shields assumed Lander's command. Captain Saunders and twenty Sharpshooters escorted Lander's body back to Massachusetts for interment. On March 9, the remnants of the Sharpshooters loaded their equipment, horses, and wagons onto freight cars and started for Martinsburg. Their train kept getting switched off at Hancock and Cherry Run. Finally, the men, out of food for themselves and fodder for their horses, and soaked from the rain in the open cars, abandoned the train, marching twenty miles and encamping four miles west of Martinsburg on the Winchester Road.

As they traveled, the Sharpshooters subsisted on the land. Bicknell was assigned to procure forage for the horses. He rode a thoroughbred horse which the Union had never paid for. Taking several Sharpshooters and both teams, he headed two miles up the road toward Winchester and found a farm with corn and hay in its barns. The farmer was not home, as he had followed the Union Army to retrieve a horse taken from him. His wife remonstrated with the Sharpshooters as they loaded their teams with corn and hay.

Bicknell sent the Sharpshooters, with teams and provisions, back to camp. Then, in consideration of the keep of himself and his horse, he agreed to remain the night and settle with the farmer upon his return. During the night a drunken soldier from a passing regiment demanded liquor from the farmer's wife. When she refused, the soldier cocked his gun and threatened to shoot her. Bicknell interceded and got the soldier to leave, to the relief of the wife and daughter. Bicknell then spent a pleasant evening in the farmer's house, listening to "Dixie" and other popular Southern songs played on the piano.

That night the farmer returned with his horse and expressed his gratitude to Bicknell for protecting his family. He accepted Bicknell's receipt for the corn and hay the Sharpshooters took, and told Bicknell he tried not to take sides in the conflict: both sides had freely taken from him. He had greenbacks and Confederate money and asked Bicknell which had more value. Bicknell advised him to turn it into gold as soon as possible. The farmer quickly got the point, as if he were a "natural-born Yankee." The entire family invited Bicknell to return anytime he was in the area.[20]

Bicknell rode directly to General Shields's headquarters, reported his dealings with the farmer, and advised the general of the Sharpshooters' needs. Shields ordered him to ride farther ahead, take a side road, and determine whether a certain farmer had barns full of corn, hay, and oats, as had been reported to him. Bicknell was warned of guerrillas and offered a cavalry escort. But after he looked at the cavalry horses' condition, and knowing the speed of his own horse, he declined that offer.

Bicknell rode away, and as he turned off the main road loaded with Union troops, he observed on a tavern porch several young men in civilian clothes with spurs attached to their boots. He suspected they were guerrillas. As soon as Bicknell got over a hill and out of their sight, he rode his horse as fast as the wind until he approached the farm Shields had sent him to. A young Negro showed him around the barns, but as he thought Bicknell had been caught in a trap, he implored Bicknell to leave, and explained an alternate route for Bicknell to return.

Before Bicknell departed, the ladies of the mansion had closed the gates that led from the home to the highway. Bicknell's horse jumped and cleared the gates, and he sped down the road exactly the way he had approached. He saw the guerrillas just where he expected them to be, on top of a wooded hill. Whipping and spurring his horse, Bicknell rode directly toward them. Just at the edge of the woods, he turned his horse into the trees, rode at the same pace and came out on a road loaded with Union troops.

On March 18, Captain Saunders and the other Sharpshooters rejoined the company at Winchester, and General Shields started down the valley; the Sharpshooters led the way. They discovered the guerrilla General Ashby on a hill about six miles from Winchester. The Sharpshooters dropped their blankets and knapsacks. Saunders positioned the main body of Sharpshooters on a fence line just outside the village, then sent Bicknell with ten Sharpshooters around the side to sneak up on the guerrillas and shoot Ashby. But Bicknell and his squad were discovered and advanced under fire to a position near a barn where they could rest to fire their heavy rifles. They were within 160 yards of the enemy, and before they could set and fire, the guerrillas took off. Captain Saunders was enraged at the failure of his plan and approached Bicknell with a drawn pistol to shoot him. Fortunately for Bicknell, the burly Cyrus Hatch held back Captain Saunders until he cooled down.[21]

Captain Saunders attached more men to Bicknell's squad and ordered them at the double to chase down and kill Ashby, even if they had to chase him all the way to Richmond. Bicknell and his squad of fifteen or twenty men took off after Ashby. Soon they were well ahead of their expedition and found that Ashby and his men had halted. But the guerrillas saw the Sharpshooters and took off again, with the squad in pursuit.

The Sharpshooters found Ashby and his men for the third time late that afternoon. Ashby's men were heavily reinforced, dismounted, and positioned behind Virginia fences along both sides of the road to the woods. The Sharpshooters took a position behind a fence on the left side of the road, from which they exchanged fire for about a half an hour. The Confederates' weaker bullets lodged in the fence posts in front of the Sharpshooters, but the latter's bullets crashed through the Confederates' fence to deadly effect. From the porch of a house behind the Sharpshooters two men fired at them, while ladies on the porch applauded as the Sharpshooters dodged their fire. The Sharpshooters turned and fired at the two riflemen, killing them but leaving the ladies unharmed. Bicknell sent two Sharpshooters around through the woods to put a left flank fire on Ashby's men. Just then, the rest of the expedition arrived, and Ashby and his men took off, leaving their dead and wounded behind on the field.[22]

As the Confederates retreated they burned bridges to slow the expedition's advance. The squad of Sharpshooters that had just fought at the farm was ordered forward to dislodge the enemy from the opposite bank, but darkness prevented them. As they returned to the farmhouse from which the shots had been fired at them, they discovered that Captain Saunders had taken possession of the house and all that was in it, including the slaves. As the Sharpshooters returned, Saunders had the servants prepare one of the finest feasts ever created for them.

In the morning the Sharpshooters enjoyed a hearty breakfast, and Captain Saunders reissued his order to track down and kill Ashby. Bicknell selected a few men for the action and moved out. At ten that morning, the squad of Sharpshooters was concealed within enemy lines and came upon Ashby. The road to their left was filled with enemy cavalry and to the right was filled with enemy infantry. The Sharpshooters positioned themselves behind a fence on the top of a hill which overlooked Fisher's Hill. It was not long before Ashby rode partway down the hill and looked through a pair of binoculars. Although the Sharpshooters believed he was out of their range, they thought it their only and best chance to get a shot at him.

Resting their rifles on the fence, they fired in unison at Ashby. Ashby's horse fell dead under him. Before they could reload and fire again, Ashby had returned to the other side of Fisher's Hill. It was only a matter of a minute, and the cavalry was stretched across a plowed field in their rear while the infantry on their right poured a heavy fire into them. Bicknell thought they would be captured and ordered the men to surrender without resistance.

General Turner Ashby. In 1859, after John Brown's raids, Ashby volunteered and raised a cavalry unit to defend Virginia. When Virginia seceded from the Union, his unit became part of the Virginia 7th Cavalry. Ashby's brother was killed by a Union patrol in June of 1861. Ashby became enraged. He turned his command into a guerrilla unit. He followed and unmercifully murdered Union stragglers. The Union command, in an attempt to improve Union morale, ordered the Sharpshooters to track down and kill Ashby and his men (Library of Congress).

But suddenly they heard the distinct sound of their company's heavy rifles. A band of their Sharpshooters positioned at a fence behind the cavalry fired into the cavalry, forcing them to flee. Now free, Bicknell's squad retreated, although the infantry to their right continued a heavy fire into them. When they got back to camp, they learned that General Shields had become aware of their mission and had sent Martin and twenty Sharpshooters to retrieve them, advancing at the double and arriving just in time.

General Shields ordered an assault on Fisher's Hill. Under artillery cover, the Federal cavalry drove the enemy down the valley as they burned a bridge and showed a heavy force of infantry on the other side of the river. A few of the Sharpshooters returned to Fisher's Hill and dined on a delicious dinner which had been prepared for Confederate officers.

A cold rain started, and as the Sharpshooters had no blankets, they retreated to the town of Strasburg. There, Bicknell secured quarters for the night that would accommodate twenty men. In the morning, he paid the citizen fifty cents a head, and in return the men received a ham and egg breakfast. They returned and marched with the rest of the expedition, encamped, and floored their tents with lumber from a pile nearby.[23]

The following day, March 22, enemy cavalry appeared on the hills toward the south side of the town, and artillery began to shell the area. The Sharpshooters fell into a line of battle with the rest of the expedition, General Shields was wounded by a fragment from a shell, and the Federal cavalry drove the enemy away. At ten o'clock the following morning, it was thought the only Confederates near the town were Ashby's Raiders.

Several days prior, General Shields had received an order to transfer the Sharpshooters to McClellan's forces on the Peninsula, but the general attempted to get that order countermanded. He was not successful, and the Sharpshooters were given a short time to pack up and board a special train that would take them to Harpers Ferry. Accompanying the Sharpshooters to the train station, General Banks told them he would use his influence at the War Department to get them returned to his command. As the train departed, the Sharpshooters could hear the heavy artillery fire to their rear and knew that they had missed out on a great battle which took place at Winchester.[24]

3

Dig or Die

When the men arrived at Harpers Ferry, Captain Saunders wanted to keep tight control of his company. He locked them in a deserted building positioned against a cliff and placed a guard on the door. The Sharpshooters quickly arranged with the guard that if Saunders came looking for them, to the guard would fire his rifle in the air and the Sharpshooters would return. They then tore up the wooden floor boards and built a walkway to the cliff behind the house. The Sharpshooters visited the ruins of the Armory, Jefferson Rock, and the Engine House. They bought all the pies and cakes in town and managed to create a memorable day.

At about midnight, the Sharpshooters crossed the river and boarded a train bound for the Relay House. In the morning they were switched off the track at a desolate area. Henry Dike and Bicknell left the train in search of food and information. Around noon, they were sitting in the house of a settler from New England gorging on a genuine boiled dinner. As the house was close to the tracks, they heard the train begin to move, but though they ran, the train was moving too fast for them to board. The Sharpshooters onboard, particularly Captain Saunders, took great delight in their predicament.[1]

They finished their dinner, went to the encampment of a Maine regiment, and ate another dinner. They then boarded a construction train which carried them to the Relay House, where a provost guard detained them in a room at the station. But they climbed out of a rear window and went to the old campground of the 8th Regimental Militia, where they had earlier served. Dike reflected on his time there with the 6th Massachusetts Militia and described the riots to Bicknell. They examined the fortifications and ate dinner with a group of Massachusetts soldiers, then boarded an express train bound for Washington — without money, tickets, or a pass. The conductor told them they would be turned over to the provost guard when they arrived at Washington. Being the gentlemen they were, they didn't want to cause any extra work for the conductor, so as the train slowed on its approach to Washington, they jumped out of the rear of the train.

Hurrying into a camp beside the tracks, they found it to be their own Sharpshooters' encampment. But as the other Sharpshooters had had the enjoyment of setting up camp without their assistance, Bicknell's men were jeered by them. Bicknell left the camp, meeting an acquaintance with whom he went to Ford's Theater. The following day, with friends from the 10th and 15th Massachusetts militias, they toured the Smithsonian, looked at the White House and Capitol Building, and then returned to camp and found it all packed up, with no chance for supper. Bicknell returned to the Soldiers' Retreat near the depot to eat. While there, an

The *Gen. Haupt* engine in front of the roundhouse at Alexandria Station, 1863 (Library of Congress).

aide informed him that the Sharpshooters had been assigned to Sedgwick's division, and that for two hours the division had waited while they looked for the Sharpshooters' encampment.

Bicknell led the company along a sidewalk to board the ships. Captain Saunders was at his side as they passed a regiment that was liquored up. A drunken soldier jumped in front of Bicknell, cocked his rifle, and pressed his bayonet so forcefully into Bicknell that it pushed him into the man behind him. Captain Saunders acted with the speed of thought as he drew his sword and crashed it down on the drunken man's head. The drunken soldier slid to the ground without even a groan. Fortunately his rifle did not discharge, which would have alerted his comrades near them. The next morning, the newspaper identified the dead soldier and his regiment. Startled to learn that they were traveling on the same boat as that regiment, the Sharpshooters all vowed to keep silent about the affair. They avoided any contact with the remaining drunken soldiers, and it was a quiet trip, except that Oscar Clement fell overboard and was pulled into the boat through a cabin window.[2]

As they passed through the Chesapeake Bay the weather turned rough, and they had to throw their provisions overboard. The trip lasted three days and four nights. They arrived at Fortress Monroe very hungry: a difficult initiation for the twenty new recruits who had just joined them at Washington.

While the Sharpshooters unloaded their equipment, Bicknell searched for headquarters and found it five miles inland. He returned with orders for the Sharpshooters to march there; rations would be issued the following day. On April 1, the Sharpshooters settled into camp, drew rations, and performed regular duty.

On April 5, 1862, the first day of the Siege of Yorktown, the Sharpshooters arrived at a

Encampment location of the Sharpshooters at the house near Winn's Mill, Yorktown, reported to be British headquarters during the Revolutionary War (Library of Congress).

line of fortifications in Yorktown. There were no incidents, except that they were shelled as they passed Little Bethel. The Sharpshooters encamped beside a house near Winn's Mill, reputed to have been British headquarters during the Revolutionary War. It was now occupied by General Gorman, to whom the Sharpshooters had been assigned.

Lieutenant Gleason resigned his commission at Fortress Monroe. At age fifty-four, he had been worn down by the rigors of army life. William Berry was then commissioned 1st lieutenant, but for some reason it was only Saunders, Martin, or Bicknell who led the Sharpshooters under fire. Saunders and Martin moved to the right and left with squads of Sharpshooters and did great execution against the enemy artillerists in Yorktown. Bicknell took squads of anywhere from ten to fifty men and reconnoitered along the woods of the Warwick River.

Bicknell's orders were to ascertain the enemy's troop strength and kill all whom they could, whether they carried rifles or shovels. This was to prevent the enemy from strengthening their fortifications. It was very difficult to find a position of rest from which to fire their heavy guns in the swampy, overgrown woods. The Sharpshooters were issued Colt Navy Revolvers and often approached within pistol range to accomplish their mission. The Sharpshooters thought the revolvers were handy to have but an additional burden to carry.

The Sharpshooters ascertained that the woods in front of them teemed with infantry and artillery, although there were several places at which the river could be forded, and the first line of the enemy breastworks was weak. Bicknell thought it would take a force of ten thousand men to have any success against the enemy. General Gorman thought Bicknell overstated the situation. The Sharpshooters grew weary of their mission. They had come to disdain sharpshooting and its murderous work. They began to share the popular sentiment that sharpshooting was not honorable warfare.[3]

Bicknell had sent many of his best Sharpshooters to the hospital wounded while his group tried to determine enemy strength. On April 22, David Littlefield, in an attempt to get a closer view of the enemy, put himself in a dangerous position and was wounded. The following day, in an attempt to get a better view of the enemy, Captain Bartlett went to the same position, was shot in the leg and lost it. The pressure to assault the enemy grew strong.

Finally, the Union troops attempted an assault with three thousand men at Dam No. 1. The Vermont assaulting force easily overtook the first line of the enemy's breastworks, but was driven back by masses of enemy artillery which emerged from the woods ahead of them. Many of the assaulting forces were drowned as they returned across the river, as the enemy had flooded the area from a dam above the assault point. Under Martin, the Sharpshooters advanced and fired on the breastworks closest to the river. But as the enemy was reinforced, they had to retreat, and the river rose rapidly around them. Martin was wounded, and as the Sharpshooters aided him, he ordered them to leave him and seek their own safety. They disobeyed the order and returned Martin to safety, out of the range of enemy artillery.

For the following two days of the assault, the Sharpshooters rested in camp as they washed, changed clothes, and wrote letters home for the first time since they had been sent to the Peninsula. Confederate General Magruder was angry about the Sharpshooters' efficient work and refused a flag of truce unless General McClellan promised to end sharpshooting. Bicknell, with a squad of Sharpshooters, was ordered to return to the front and inflict serious damage on the enemy artillerists. The squad of Sharpshooters did just that, but was driven back by vigorous shelling. Soon a flag of truce was flown. The Vermonters who had led the assault and had been killed were allowed to be buried. It was rumored that Confederate President Jefferson Davis had met with General Magruder that day and insisted he be apprised of what had provoked the Sharpshooters.

Until the enemy evacuated Yorktown, the Sharpshooters operated only on the enemy artillery batteries. With Lieutenant Perley sick and Lieutenant Martin wounded, Bicknell acted as orderly and relieved Captain Saunders with twenty men, keeping the enemy artillery quiet at a distance of twelve hundred yards. A Union general with his staff rode up to the Sharpshooters and ridiculed them, saying that it was impossible for their fire to be effective at that distance.

Bicknell issued an order for the men to cease fire. Immediately, the enemy artillerists manned their guns and a shell burst in the woods behind the Union general, proving the point. Admitting his error, the general rode away. A colonel stationed in the woods at the rear of the Sharpshooters thought Bicknell's argument was brilliant, but requested that any future doubters be sent to him, as he did not want any more shells to rain in on his regiment.

Bicknell found his position as orderly onerous. The Sharpshooters began to think they had been deceived in accepting their commissions. Their service was continually dangerous. The promise of extra pay was long gone. And Confederate sentiment against the Sharpshooters considered them outlaws, to be hanged if captured. Added to those conditions were the difficult previous winter march and the men's health. With their morale extremely low, the men were slow to obey orders from noncommissioned officers.[4]

Although the men had very few things to laugh about, their discussion one night in camp about George Whittemore's actions at the Warwick River broke the trend. It seems the order was given to cover, and Whittemore went behind a tree about as thick as his arm and continued to fire from that position although there were considerably larger trees around him.

He had either perfect self control in a battle or no regard for his own safety. Whittemore hated cold-blooded sharpshooting, and he was known to spare many an enemy life or shoot only to wound them. When he was in an open field of battle, he stood exposed without any regard for his own life.

A man skilled as a machinist and optician was recruited as an artificer at Camp Saunders in Lynnfield. He was promised extra pay and no duty except to keep the heavy guns in order. Captain Saunders ordered Bicknell to include him in a detail to the front. The artificer refused and demanded a court-martial. Bicknell carried his request to division commander General Sedgwick, who berated him for bringing such a request while they were in the middle of a campaign. General Sedgwick ordered the man to be punished until he would do his duty.

Captain Saunders ordered the man be tied to a tree, under guard, and given only bread and water until he agreed to perform ordered duty. Bicknell pleaded with the man to no avail. Bicknell then tied the man loosely to the tree with a long open loop which the man promised to keep his hand in. A discreet guard was assigned to him. The artificer was allowed to eat and sleep at night while other Sharpshooters replaced him at the tree. But when somebody watched this happen and reported it to Captain Saunders, the captain ordered the guard also to be tied to the tree and imposed severe discipline on anyone who interfered with this punishment. A guard not in sympathy with leniency was posted. Finally, when a cold rainstorm arrived, the artificer agreed to perform duty. He was more dead than alive when he was taken down from the tree. While being supported to his tent, he vowed that Captain Saunders would die for his punishment.[5]

On May 4, the day after the Confederates abandoned Yorktown, the Sharpshooters were occupying the enemy's abandoned camps. An aide from another division rode up and told Captain Saunders that his division was to wait at Yorktown for transports to West Point. He said that his own division was to march in pursuit of the enemy, adding that he was sorry to have to leave a widow lady who lived nearby, as he had protected her house full of hams, and asked Captain Saunders to do the same.

Ordering an instant halt, Saunders hid his real intention by issuing an order that not a man was to leave the ranks. In two minutes one man stood and guarded the rifles, and not a Sharpshooter could be seen in the ranks. A feast followed: ham, eggs, biscuits, butter, chicken pie, and bushels of doughnuts. In the middle of it all stood Saunders, directing, guiding, and restraining. For that hour the Sharpshooters thought Saunders was "a very prince of a good fellow."[6]

Boarding a transport, the Sharpshooters were taken up the York River to West Point, where they disembarked at Eltham's Landing under a shower of artillery shells. Miraculously, the shells did not harm them. After a day or two at West Point, they marched seven miles up the Pamunkey River and encamped. Here the Sharpshooters were required to furnish details to provide wood and water for brigade headquarters. Bicknell reports:

> Three months before we were the proud favorites of the commander of the department; now we were ordered to perform the scullion duties for a mere brigadier, was the way the men felt about it. It was generally understood throughout the whole division that this order was intended to show the sharpshooters, once for all, that they like other soldiers must stand ready to perform any duties required of them not-withstanding their peculiar armament and promises made to them at enlistment.

Bicknell was ordered to force the men, at the muzzle of his revolver, into the wood and water details. As brave men, the troops put up all the resistance they could, but chose not to throw away their lives and reputations. A regiment which showed sympathy toward the Sharpshooters was ordered to stand at shoulder arms for two hours in the hot sun. Bicknell offered to resign his orderly position and to step back in the ranks. But the Sharpshooters would not allow it, and from that point on, no orderly in the army had an easier time with their men than Bicknell.[7]

Day-to-day subsistence had become difficult and uncomfortable for the Sharpshooters, who had not had their knapsacks since Yorktown. They had been under the impression that they were to pursue the enemy as they fled. All they were to carry was their heavy rifles and pistols, so they loaded their equipment onto teams. But they didn't pursue the enemy and camped under difficult conditions, managing the best they could in rainy days and nights, when they washed their clothing and put their uniforms on wet.

On May 31, they crossed the swollen Chickahominy River on a pontoon bridge to fight in the Battle of Fair Oaks. As the Sharpshooters approached, the farthest end of the bridge rose and floated away. They were ordered to go forward. Raising their cartridge boxes above their heads, the Sharpshooters stepped into chest-high water. Many men slipped and had to be rescued, but the division reached the other side in time to save the day.

The Sharpshooters were ordered to the rear of Kirby's Battery and were to advance with revolvers and retake the guns if they were captured. The enemy made three desperate attempts

Artillery at Fair Oaks, May 31, 1862. Gibson's Horse Battery (C. 3rd U.S. Artillery) cannons drawn by horses. The Sharpshooters were called on to protect the artillery at Fair Oaks, to ensure it was not captured by the enemy (Library of Congress).

to take the guns. Jefferson Davis was said to have led one of the charges. But it mattered little who led the charge as the enemy was met by a murderous fire from the Sharpshooters, Gorman's brigade, and Kirby's artillery. The enemy's advance had to be checked, as the swift, deep river at their rear blocked all chance of retreat.

Each time the Confederates, with their peculiar yell, approached the guns, the Sharpshooters sprang forward, revolvers cocked and muscles straining, and repulsed them. Returning to their position behind the guns, and lying on the ground trembling from the physical and mental strain, the Sharpshooters knew they had to succeed, as there was no way out.

The following day, the Sharpshooters were positioned behind a fence and could have done great execution, but the battle was fought in a swamp nearby, and they never fired a shot. The Sharpshooters watched as waves of men poured into the swamp and thought there was nothing left of the reserve unit as so many men had entered the swamp.

The Sharpshooters listened to a deafening roar of musketry for three solid hours at Fair Oaks, until all those who remained alive fought from breastworks constructed of dead bodies. Finally, an Irish brigade charged forward through the swamp, and their yells replaced the deafening sound of musketry. The Sharpshooters knew then that the battle had gone in the Federals' favor. The next day they learned that the Irishmen who fought on the enemy side had seen the green flag of the Irish Regiment and fled rather than kill their own countrymen.[8]

That night the Sharpshooters encamped in the woods from where the enemy had charged the previous day, resting among their many dead. The Sharpshooters were still without their tents and equipment, and it was rainy and cold. An exhausted Bicknell lay down between the roots of a tree in an attempt to find warmth and shelter and fell into a coma-like sleep. In the morning, he awoke to find himself on higher ground, wrapped in a blanket, dry and warm. The roots where he had lain were filled with water. Eleazer Mattoon had enlisted other Sharpshooters to help move Bicknell to higher ground and wrap him in blankets, and then walked the woods himself all night. When Bicknell asked him why, Mattoon responded that Bicknell's life was more valuable to the country than his own. From other Sharpshooters Bicknell learned that Mattoon talked about a night at Camp Benton when Bicknell had been sergeant of the guard. Mattoon was on guard duty and very sick, and Bicknell had sent Mattoon to his tent and then walked Mattoon's post.

After the battle, the Sharpshooters were in high demand and sent out many small squads to accompany reconnoitering expeditions. It appeared that the enemy had come to recognize the distinct sound of the Sharpshooters' heavy rifles. Whenever a Sharpshooter fired, from the rest or in the air, the enemy would flee.[9]

4

"Hell of Antietam"

Finally the Sharpshooters obtained their equipment and tents, and their health began to improve. When the entire company was ordered on a reconnaissance to determine whether the picket lines could advance a mile ahead, the enemy discovered the Sharpshooters as soon as they crossed the Federal picket line. The enemy pickets retired swiftly and secretly.

The Sharpshooters crossed a creek on the stringers of a bridge and entered a wheat field with a log house in the middle. Entering the house, they had a full view of the enemy fortifications and could see the spires in the city of Richmond, six miles away. They also could see that the bridge they had just crossed was held by a strong enemy picket, which had spread along the ravine to the wheat field to prevent the Sharpshooters from retreating.

The Sharpshooters quickly left the log house, running across the field and crossing the ravine ahead of the enemy pickets. Reaching the woods, they turned and fought along the ravine until they found a spot where they could ford the creek. Once across the creek, they were stuck in heavy thickets which made it difficult to retreat and fight. On their retreat they discovered a clear spring of water and were bound that the Federals would have it.

That night the Sharpshooters charged an enemy rifle pit at the head of the creek, and the Federal pickets swung into the wheat field. Before daylight the Sharpshooters were back in the wheat field and engaged in a lively battle with the enemy until ten that morning, when a Confederate waved a newspaper at the Sharpshooters. The Sharpshooters and the enemy ceased firing.

For the next two hours, a delegated Sharpshooter went forward to talk to the man who waved the newspaper. As the Sharpshooter went back and forth, swapping information with the enemy pickets, the two sides reached an agreement that if the Sharpshooters kept to the edge of the wheat field and ceased firing on them, the Rebels would hold their position and not fire on the Sharpshooters. To indicate the truce was over, either side would fire a volley overhead. Such agreements were made frequently throughout the Army of the Potomac, with officers conveniently ignorant of them.

For a couple of days after the Battle of Fair Oaks, details were sent out to the wheat field where the men basked in the sunshine. They drank water from the clear spring over which they had earlier fought to take control. Other Sharpshooters were sent to different parts of the line where their service was much livelier and more dangerous. Bridges were constructed across the creek at frequent intervals, and the Sharpshooters thought an advance on Richmond would go through that wheat field.[1]

At this time, the company had not a single healthy man. Severe winter marches, labor in western Virginia, and exposure on the Peninsula had taken their toll. Men who in better conditions would leave on disability were weeded out at Paw Paw Tunnel. The Sharpshooters who remained believed one swift attack on Richmond would end the war, and they wanted to be a part of it. They were so confident of this eventuality that when the paymaster came to pay them, they decided to wait until Richmond was captured.

At the Battle of Mechanicsville on June 26 and at Gaines' Mill on June 27, the Sharpshooters were positioned at the entrenchments in front of their camp. The first day they saw no action, so on the second day they were withdrawn to Gaines' Mill. The enemy made a feint charge which the Sharpshooters easily repulsed. Thinking all was going well, the Sharpshooters waited for orders to charge across a wheat field. But Lee had to act decisively, as Richmond was in danger. With a coordinated effort, Lee then attacked both flanks and made a frontal assault on the Federals.

Learning that the Federals were in a full retreat and that they themselves were to remain in the rear to protect it, the Sharpshooters thought McClellan had lost his mind. They wondered if the corps commanders should be responsible for disobeying McClellan's orders and holding their impenetrable position.

But the Sharpshooters retreated, their wagons loaded with sick and wounded men who died during that withdrawal, and the Sharpshooters were left to carry their heavy guns, revolvers, and knapsacks. The company was so unhealthy that it seemed the men would not

A pontoon bridge across a creek. Taylor's Bridge (a pontoon) across North Anna River, Virginia, May 1864. This is typical of a creek crossing that was too deep to be forged (Library of Congress).

survive the march. A delirious Bicknell urged the other Sharpshooters to return to the breastworks and stop the enemy's advance. At one point, he even left the ranks to return to the breastworks, but Captain Saunders restrained him and then coaxed him into cooperating.

On June 29, the Sharpshooters were at Savage Station in the reserve line. At about noon the enemy started shooting and shelling them. The Sharpshooters saw piles of equipment set on fire so that the enemy would not gain control of them. Ironically, the fires they were watching were being ignited in part by the 2nd Company of Andrew Sharpshooters. The men quickly loaded shot and shell on a train and sent it into the Chickahominy River, setting off a magnificent explosion as it careened off the tracks into the river. The battle raged until dark, when a thunderstorm stopped the action. At one point, the Sharpshooters were called out; it seemed that the Federal infantry would be driven out of the woods, at whose edge the Sharpshooters were stationed, resting their heavy rifles on stumps to support the infantry.[2]

That night the Sharpshooters were marched to White Oak Swamp. As the battle raged in the woods, they stood in the center of a field. In those dense woods, in such a closely fought battle, their heavy rifles were of no use. The following night the Sharpshooters were marched to Malvern Hill, passing by a muddy creek. The men were so thirsty that some of them fell from the ranks and filled their mouths with mud before they could get to the water.

The Sharpshooters watched General McClellan at Malvern Hill as he rode over the field and directed where each corps and artillery would be positioned. He and his horse were completely covered with mud and dust, and he showed signs of great fatigue. But he retired to the gunboats and got some much-needed sleep until the battle began.

Savage Station, Virginia, June 1862. Headquarters of General George B. McClellan on the Richmond and York River Railroad. The Sharpshooters, in reserve, were shelled by artillery there. They watched as the Union set stores of material ablaze so it wouldn't fall into enemy hands (Library of Congress).

2nd Division Surgeons. This is a later photograph taken in 1864, at Petersburg, Virginia. These are the division surgeons that were caring for the Sharpshooters in 1862, as their plights caused a reduction in their ranks (Library of Congress).

The Sharpshooters watched the entire battle at Malvern Hill. They stood at ease behind a fence near the heavy artillery, where they were positioned to protect the artillery if the Federal lines faltered. When the Federal gunboats fired their large shells with great speed and accuracy into a ravine to the left of them, the Confederates could do nothing but seek shelter. The gunboats' fire was equivalent to having an additional ten thousand soldiers on the field.[3]

The Union Army had prepared a strong defensive position at Malvern Hill, where they were protected by an elevated position 150 feet above the enemy. The Confederates, forced to attack through ravines and swampy lowland, proved to be fodder for the 100 pieces of Union artillery supported by 150 pieces in reserve on the Union flanks. The Federal gunboats opened with a two-hour barrage against the Confederates.[4]

As the Federals did not pursue the defeated Confederates at Malvern Hill, the Sharpshooters made condescending remarks to the effect that the Federals were as unfit as themselves. The Sharpshooters had started this campaign better fit for the hospital than a march. They had been without food for three days and without tents for three weeks, in many cold rains. They had been in constant battle and had marched for seven days. They were human beings and needed food, water, and rest. They arrived at Harrison's Landing and sank on the ground with one thought — sleep — as did thousands around them.

After the Sharpshooters reached Harrison's Landing, Martin, who had been wounded at the Siege of Yorktown, reported back from the hospital for duty. He relieved Bicknell of his orderly duties, and with little to do, Bicknell recovered his health and spirits. The other Sharpshooters were not so lucky. The continual deprivations, including exposure and contaminated drinking water, had taken their toll on the original men who had started from Lynnfield. As the number of able-bodied men fell, many reported to the surgeons of the 2nd Division. To add to their woes, they had lost prestige, as their heavy rifles were of little use when the Federals retreated. Clothing requisitions that went unmet left them among the most ragged companies in the army.

When asked, Bicknell drew up a petition signed by the Sharpshooters and took it to General McClellan. The petition set forth the conditions of their enlistment, outlining the company's reduction due to hardships, spelling out their heavy guns' uselessness in the past seven-day campaign, and describing the difficulty of carrying the heavy rifles on the march. McClellan read the petition with unchanging courtesy, and asked Bicknell many questions to which Bicknell would give an answer only to the commander of the army. McClellan then pleasantly asked Bicknell how he could support a petition for discharge while there was such a strong need for reinforcements.

McClellan did promise that the men would not have to carry their heavy guns again, as he would supply wagons. In a few days, the Sharpshooters learned that their heavy guns would be replaced with Sharps breech-loading rifles. But the Sharpshooters were not satisfied, as they had their minds set on a discharge. In a letter to Governor Andrew, requesting his intervention, the Sharpshooters said they would re-enlist, with some of them going with Bicknell into the cavalry and the others with Martin in the navy, as Martin had been a sailor. They wanted to continue to serve, but did not want to continue marching. Captain Saunders, who had been unaware of the petition, was not pleased. But when he found out that it had been signed by Sergeant Ingalls, whom Saunders had selected as one of the lieutenants, he calmed down.[5]

The men started from Harrison's Landing and marched to Fortress Monroe. They put Captain Saunders, Lieutenant Berry, and their heavy guns and revolvers aboard the teams. The only items they carried were their haversacks, knapsacks, and canteens. General McClellan had made good on his promise. Martin was designated acting lieutenant, and Bicknell was again orderly. As they started on the five-day march, the Sharpshooters wondered whether they would even make it five miles. Rations were not provided. They picked up green corn, unripe fruit, and any unlucky chickens or swine that crossed their path. By the time they arrived at Hampton Roads, they were well enough for a grand assault on the oyster beds.

On this march, the corps encamped for the night and the Sharpshooters were ordered to report for guard duty at General Gorman's headquarters. Bicknell put together the most ragged men he could find, some with no shoes, rimless hats, one-legged pants, and no coat; one man was without pants. When Bicknell marched them to General Gorman's tent, Gorman attempted to berate him, but broke down and laughed, ordering Bicknell to take the men away and report back with men more suitably dressed for duty as headquarters guard. Bicknell had made his point, and on the following day's march the Sharpshooters halted beside a clothing wagon, where they were told to take any items they needed without the formality of a requisition. When the Sharpshooters arrived at Alexandria, they did not see their heavy rifles or revolvers. They asked Bicknell to lead them in a refusal to accept the Sharps rifles, which they wanted Bicknell to have removed from service unless the original enlistment conditions were met. They wanted extra pay, no guard duty, and their guns to be carried on wagons while on the march. But as Lieutenant Martin was sick and Bicknell had been appointed acting lieutenant, Bicknell refused to lead the mutiny, as it would violate his duty as an officer.

Several days later, the Sharpshooters were marched into a short cross-street in front of a long, low building in Alexandria. At one end of the street stood artillery with lanyards pulled taut, while at the other end cavalry stood with drawn sabers to block any attempted escape by the Sharpshooters. This strategy forced the Sharpshooters to accept the Sharps rifles. Corporal Gilbreth, the man who had climbed the downspouts at Faneuil Hall and pushed General Lander across the river at Edward's Ferry, made a protest speech on behalf of the Sharpshooters. It would be several more days before they were allowed ammunition for their new rifles.[6]

Now armed and with ammunition, the Sharpshooters were marched by Captain Saunders toward the Second Battle of Bull Run. Their progress was slow, as there was no understanding about plans or strategy. In addition, the men lacked confidence in General John Pope, who had displayed little ability to understand tactics and correctly use the army. Although they he was unable to coordinate a supply base or retreat lines, he was a braggart. Therefore, the men did not immediately rush to his assistance.

The Sharpshooters were tired of standing at a halt in the ranks, so on their own recognizance, they moved ahead of their corps. At two o'clock, as they rested in the shade a mile ahead of their corps, they could hear the battle rage. Although they could not see the battle on the other side of the woods, they interpreted its sound as meaning that the Federals were in retreat. Suddenly a carriage dashed along the road from the front, carrying General McDowell. Recognizing Captain Saunders, he jumped out, urging Saunders to deploy his Sharpshooters to stop the Federals from fleeing the battlefield. Although Bicknell deployed the Sharpshooters and was able to detain a few men, he said it was like trying to "stop Niagara Falls with a shingle." Thus the Sharpshooters were the first to hear, firsthand, of a Union general's betrayal of his men on the battlefield.[7] When the corps arrived, the Sharpshooters fell in with them to repulse the enemy as they advanced. On September 1, the Sharpshooters went with their division to Chantilly. Lee wanted to follow up on his decisive victory over the demoralized Union Army. The Confederate general "Stonewall" Jackson led the charge as Lee wanted to find a break in the Union Army outside of Washington. That night sheets of rain poured down, and the lines went back and forth, with neither side gaining ground. At one point, with Jackson's lines in the shape of an arc, the Union cavalry mistook the Sharpshooters for the enemy and attacked them. But the Sharpshooters stayed with their division and acted as a rear guard at Fairfax. They were the last men to leave the ground. As they fell back, enemy cavalry captured some in the company's rear. They continued to march in their new role as part of the 15th Massachusetts Volunteer Infantry and finally met the enemy at South Mountain.[8] At this point, the role of the Sharpshooters had changed. They no longer had their long-range heavy rifles; rather, they had the Sharps breech-loading rifle. Instead

General Thomas "Stonewall" Jackson. The Sharpshooters, at Antietam, were far ahead of the Union lines. Lt. Bicknell lay wounded as Jackson approached him. Bicknell learned of his disdain for Union Sharpshooters. Jackson ordered his surgeon to care for Bicknell, so he could be moved to Richmond, Virginia, as a prisoner (Library of Congress).

of being used as snipers, they were being used as skirmishers, and were moving with the 15th Massachusetts Volunteer Infantry. It was evident that Captain Saunders had an extreme dislike for any type of military order or discipline. He and Lieutenant Berry resigned their commissions, were relieved of military duty, and became civilians. Neither wanted any part of infantry tactics or the new role of the Sharpshooters. But both believed a great battle was soon to occur, and they wanted to remain for that last battle. Captain Saunders and Lieutenant Berry were unfamiliar with Hardee's infantry tactics. Saunders asked Bicknell, with his superior knowledge of infantry tactics, to lead the company in the battle.[9]

At South Mountain, the Sharpshooters stood all afternoon while the battle raged on the other side of the mountain. As the Sharpshooters got closer to the battle, new lines were continually sent in. At midnight, they relieved the front line, and at daylight, they advanced to reopen the battle only to meet the Federal pickets from the other side of the mountain. The enemy had slipped away during the night. However, the company's health had improved since it had left the Peninsula.

The lighter rifles enabled the Sharpshooters to march toward Antietam at a much easier gait. Martin remained hospitalized. Lieutenant Bicknell led the Sharpshooters at twenty past seven on the morning of September 17. As part of the 15th Massachusetts Volunteer Infantry, and of Gorman's brigade, they crossed the Antietam Creek at Pry Ford. They moved about a quarter of a mile up a gentle slope and formed into a line of battle with Gorman's brigade in the lead.[9]

Moving forward to take the lead, the Sharpshooters passed through the East Woods at a quick step, under a shower of artillery shells. Then they took down a fence and passed

A print showing the Battle of South Mountain, Maryland, September 14, 1862. The Sharpshooters entered the battle at nightfall. They moved to the top of the mountain. Their plan was to engage the enemy at daylight, only to find the Rebels had fled during the night (Library of Congress).

through a cornfield strewn with bodies from General Hooker's earlier battle. There they stopped and dressed their lines. Sergeants were ordered to step two paces to the rear of their units to shoot any soldier who broke, ran, or stopped to look at or assist a wounded comrade.

At the end of the cornfield, the first fatal order was given: "right oblique." On the Sharpshooters' left flank, in the line of battle, was the 34th New York. As both sides of the road were lined with fences, the New Yorkers were unable to obey that order,. As they attempted to make a 45 degree turn to the right, they were thrown in utter confusion. They became entangled in the fences, and were further hampered by an artillery battery that dashed down the road, bouncing over the dead bodies strewn along it. The Sharpshooters had no protection on their left flank, and were among the first to enter the battle.[10] As they crossed Hagerstown Road to the right of Dunker Church and up a wooded slope, the enemy's dead were so thick on the ground it impeded their progress. They went over a fence and partway down the opposite slope, driving the enemy in front of them. A second fatal order of "dress right" was given. As they moved to their right, touching shoulder to shoulder, the smoke-filled air cleared just enough to reveal a stone wall about a hundred yards in front of them teeming with the enemy. As they dressed, the darkness and smoke thickened. Then, with a deafening roar, a large sheet

Dunkard Church, Antietam, September 17, 1862. The Sharpshooters formed on the left flank of the 15th Massachusetts Volunteer Infantry just to the right of Dunkard Church. It was a difficult maneuver, as enemy bodies lay strewn about the ground. They were further hampered by Union artillery rushing down the Hagerstown Pike, bouncing over the bodies (Library of Congress).

of flame emerged over the stone wall, revealing three lines of General Stonewall Jackson's veterans, their guns pointed at the Federal line. Three out of four of the Sharpshooters went down in that one volley. As the enemy emerged from behind a farmhouse, barns, and stacks of corn fifty yards in front of them, enemy artillery fired at them from six hundred yards to their right, trapping the Sharpshooters in the "Hell of Antietam."[11] What the Sharpshooters did not realize was that they were at the most advanced position of the Union Army and past the front of the Confederate lines, in a gap between enemy troops. There, on the left line of the 15th Massachusetts, they were totally exposed, as the 34th New York had not made it to the battlefield. Twice the Sharpshooters silenced the artillery on the hill to their right. Holding their position, they were able to advance ten yards with the 15th Massachusetts, to capture a stand of Confederate colors. They were deep enough in the enemy line to be exposed to the enemy on their front and both sides. To make matters even worse, their rear support, the 59th New York, panicked and fired through the 15th Massachusetts and Sharpshooters, increasing their losses. The New Yorkers were trying to fire at the enemy further down the slope, but the Sharpshooters had already partially descended the slope, winding up between the New Yorkers and the enemy. Bicknell instructed the New Yorkers to fire from a higher elevation, but General Sumner removed them from that position. When the Confederates were reinforced with fresh troops, they attacked the Sharpshooters on their exposed left and right flanks.

When ordered to retreat, the Sharpshooters obeyed only reluctantly, moving one hundred yards toward the North Woods, then halting, turning, and firing as the enemy advanced on them. Federal artillery near the cornfield ended the enemy's advance. The Sharpshooters and the 15th Massachusetts continued through the North Woods to the Poffenberger Farm on the Hagerstown Pike near Mansfield Avenue. There they supported artillery stationed on a hill, remaining the next day as they waited for the battle to reopen.[12]

Except for a scratch on his leg, Bicknell was unharmed by the first volley. He picked up a rifle from the ground and fired, but before he could reload, a ball crashed through his arm. As it fell useless by his side, another ball crashed through his hip. He went down on the ground beside Marcus Parmenter's body, and reached and drank from Parmenter's canteen. Then another ball crashed through the canteen and lodged in his chest.

> Thirty of the forty five sharpshooters had gone down on my left, four hundred and fifty out of the six hundred of the 15th Mass. had fallen on my right; and still the enemy poured in a steady fire upon the line of dead and wounded. They afterwards explained to me that they thought we were playing possum; and no wonder they did, for such terrible execution by a single volley was unprecedented."[13]

As the Federals retreated, the enemy charged them. Bicknell lost blood rapidly and begged for water as the enemy passed him. The first person asked Bicknell if he had had enough of the war. The second person gave no reply. The third dropped behind his comrades as they charged and held his canteen to Bicknell's lips as he drank. Bicknell continued to ask for water, and one man attempted to bayonet him, but was stopped by his general just in time.

As they advanced, the enemy were shelled with artillery from the cornfield and retreated to the fence. As the Union dead and wounded around Bicknell lay helplessly on the ground, they were exposed to the artillery fire which was intended for the enemy. Many of the wounded were killed by it. Bicknell was hit three times and thought the artillery fragments passed through his body into the ground, but he was only severely bruised.

Captain Saunders, Lieutenant Berry, John Adams, Joseph Ingalls, Marcus Parmenter, Warren Snow, Martin Strong, Richard Van Moll, and George Whittemore lay among the dead. But Captain Saunders was felled not by enemy fire, but by a shot from the artificer who

Ground walked over by the Sharpshooters as they retreated. They were ordered to the Poffenberger Farm, on what is now known as Mansfield Street. They were to protect artillery as the battle was to continue in the morning. West Woods are visible on the left (National Park Service).

had been tied to the tree at Yorktown. When the 59th New York fired through the Sharpshooters' ranks in the rear, they created a perfect cover for the artificer to make good on his promise and shoot Saunders from the rear. The artificer himself was killed instantly when Saunders fell. Although Bicknell's *Sharpshooters* does not identify this artificer by name, the only machinist who enlisted in Lynnfield and was killed at Antietam was Martin V. Strong.[14]

After the artillery barrage stopped, the enemy brought forward their ambulances and surgeons to care for the wounded. Two of the men serving in the ambulance detail were prisoners for whom Bicknell had intervened at Patterson Creek. They moved Bicknell from the field and laid him comfortably behind a stack of straw. Stonewall Jackson and his staff rode up and stopped by Bicknell. The surgeon examined Bicknell's wounds and provided him with brandy.

The staff questioned Bicknell about numerous items, including whether McClellan remained in command. Discovering that Bicknell had talked to McClellan the previous day, they tried to determine the Federals' troop strength. Bicknell responded only that there were enough to "whip" the enemy. In an attempt to catch Bicknell off guard, they informed him that although the Federals were 120,000 strong, the Confederates, with only 100,000, whipped the Union steadily. But the ruse did not work, and Bicknell drank freely of the brandy, as the surgeon urged him.

Jackson's staff tersely told Bicknell that they would see to it that he would never lead the Sharpshooters again. They would take him by ambulance to Richmond, where he would remain as a prisoner if he survived his wounds. However, when the ambulance corps' two former prisoners told General Jackson of Bicknell's kindness while they were held at Patterson Creek, Jackson's demeanor changed. Jackson told Bicknell he would provide a cavalry escort to his ambulance, which would take him to a private house where he would receive the best of care. He further told Bicknell that if he promised not to leave the city, his word would be accepted, but no exchange would be made for him. Jackson said he never wanted to see Bicknell lead the Sharpshooters again.

Jackson's forces surprised Bicknell when they said they knew of his petition to discharge the company, and the attempt to force the company to accept the Sharps rifles. As he had petitioned for discharge, they thought it was proper to retain him. Bicknell wondered whether he had a spy in his company and then remembered that they had taken a Sharpshooter prisoner at Fairfax.

The surgeon mounted his horse and ordered an ambulance to take Bicknell away. But the Federals opened artillery on the enemy, and a shell landed in front of the surgeon, causing his horse to rear and fall on him. He was killed instantly. Sharp firing broke out on the enemy line, and Jackson and his staff hastily rode away. One of the men who had moved Bicknell to the stack of straw was killed by a solid shot. The other visited Bicknell and comforted him. As Bicknell passed in and out of consciousness, the last thing he could remember was being told that the enemy was in retreat. They gave Bicknell the option to remain where he was or go with the Confederates.

The following day, the surgeon of the 20th Massachusetts Volunteer Infantry found Bicknell and retrieved him from the stack of straw. Stakes had been placed against the stack and straw pulled over Bicknell, concealing him completely. A full canteen of water, a haversack filled with provisions, and a loaded pistol were laid beside him. His gold watch and wallet, with all its money intact, had been placed under him. Bicknell observed that these courtesies differed greatly from the Confederate order to treat Sharpshooters as outlaws and hang them from the nearest tree.

David Littlefield lay beside Bicknell. Littlefield had been wounded in one leg at Yorktown and was shot through both legs on the first volley at Antietam. He told Bicknell about Saunders's death. Bicknell and Littlefield were both moved to Hoffman's barn in one ambulance and placed on straw in the barnyard. Otis K. Ladd, of the 15th Massachusetts Company I, a fellow townsman of Bicknell, was detailed as a nurse at the barn. Learning that Bicknell was there, he got both men into the barn to be treated. Each day thereafter, an hour before daylight, he went to a farm nearby and procured bread and fresh milk for them.[15]

The day after the battle, on September 19, Sergeant Henry Martin, who had been too sick to enter the battle, was commissioned 1st lieutenant and given command of the Sharpshooters. By that time only about fifteen men were available for service. Martin visited the wounded in hospitals, where he met with a recruit who had joined the company the day before the battle. The recruit complained that before the battle Bicknell had filled his cartridge box with ammunition that did not fit his rifle. Nonetheless, however, he said things worked out perfectly fine: after he fired his only two rounds of ammunition, plenty of Sharps rifles were available to be picked up off the ground. He said he would have continued had he not been shot through the lung.

5

Prestige Restored

The Battle of Antietam was the straw that broke the Sharpshooters' backs. They had been ordered to the Peninsula, out of their special service, and ordered at pistol threat to perform wood and water detail. Illness brought on by the hard marches and previous winter had shrunk their ranks. Their long-range rifles had been taken from them. They were always out in front in dangerous service conditions. They never received the additional money they were promised. Their petition to discharge their men and allow them to join the cavalry or navy had been denied.

They had just entered a battle where their commanding officer had been killed by one of their own men. Through a series of poor commands, they were advanced behind enemy lines and left completely exposed to a horrific fire. The unit to their left was lost due to confusion, and to make matters worse, their own reserve unit, on higher ground, fired through their lines. In their entire service of just over eleven months, out of 101 men, 14 men had been killed in action. Ten were killed at the Battle of Antietam. Of the nineteen men who died of wounds, ten of them were a result of Antietam. Five of the Sharpshooters deserted at Antietam.

Antietam's terrible toll represented 25 percent of the company's desertions, 52 percent of the deaths from wounds, and 72 percent of the men killed in action. But the men who deserted were not cowards. For example, Samuel Barker enlisted in a cavalry unit as Samuel Sprague. Egbert Hixon, who deserted just before the battle, enlisted as Egbert Hicks and gave his life in an Ohio regiment. Such acts of bravery probably happened in other situations but were not recorded.[1] The wounded Sharpshooters were sent to Frederick, Maryland, and were quartered in tents some distance from the town. They had the best of medical treatment but complained of the Germanic diet, which did not satisfy Americans' cravings. For more than a month they were served soup, and they did not receive knives, forks, or spoons for another month. All of them, weakened, bedridden, and in long confinement, desired delicacies. Bicknell was fortunate. He had money and purchased bread and milk from a farmer and learned to eat with just a pocket knife.

In Bicknell's tent, a man who had lost his arm at the shoulder but was healing well craved chicken. Although the man had money and could have purchased chicken from a local farmer, he felt the government was obligated to provide him with chicken. When the surgeons told him clearly that he would not be issued chicken, he rolled over and moaned — and continued to moan until his death.[2]

On September 19, the Sharpshooters advanced and found that General Lee had withdrawn

5. Prestige Restored 47

Smith's Barn in Keedysville, Maryland, September 1862, which was used as a field hospital after the Battle of Antietam. The wounded lay outside for days. Lt. Bicknell was fortunate as a fellow resident from the hill towns of the Berkshires, Massachusetts, recognized him, got treatment for him, and cared for him (Library of Congress).

his army. They tended to the wounded and buried the dead, and president Lincoln visited General McClellan at Antietam. They then crossed through Sharpsburg to the Potomac River and crossed at Harpers Ferry. On September 22, they encamped at their old site at Bolivar Heights.

All remained quiet while the Sharpshooters were at Bolivar Heights, and they spent the time performing picket guard. President Lincoln reviewed the troops with General McClellan. As they passed the Sharpshooters and the 15th Massachusetts, McClellan pointed them out to the president and explained their courage at Antietam. Their colors were furled, as they were so worn from battles that they could not stand up to the slightest breeze.[3]

On October 26, the Sharpshooters went with the 15th Massachusetts two miles up the Potomac River on picket duty. One company in the regiment was armed with sixty-nine caliber Harpers Ferry rifles, nine with fifty-eight caliber Springfield rifles, and the Sharpshooters with Sharps rifles.[4]

On October 30, they began their advance movement as part of the Second Division, Second Corps, under General Gorman's command. Moving along the Shenandoah River, they crossed on a pontoon bridge and passed the base of Loudon Heights, then encamped for the night near Hill Grove. The following day, they went up the mountain on picket duty. On Sunday, November 1, the Sharpshooters marched on, and that night the regiment encamped in a line of battle. The following day they occupied Snicker Gap. On November 4, they marched through Paris toward Ashby's Gap.

As they advanced, they pushed the enemy cavalry forward. But when they were about four miles from Ashby's Gap, the enemy took a stand. The 15th Massachusetts and the Sharpshooters led the march and were thrown out as skirmishers. They fired a few shells at the enemy and were ordered to take a hill a little to their right, which they did without much resistance. They then encamped for the night. At nine o'clock in the morning, they advanced to Ashby's Gap and expected a skirmish, but the enemy had withdrawn, leaving them in possession of the gap.

President Lincoln meeting with General McClellan and officers at Antietam, October 3, 1862. The president was irritated that General McClellan did not follow and attack the defeated General Robert E. Lee. The president went to Antietam and urged McClellan to act (Library of Congress).

The Sharpshooters and the 15th Massachusetts remained in the "dirty little village of Paris" just below Ashby's Gap until November 6. As the baggage trains passed, the Sharpshooters and the 15th Massachusetts moved to the rear and acted as the trains' rear guard. They remained a few miles from Ashby's Gap. A snowstorm on November 7 lasted the entire day. On November 8, they left "Camp Snow" and proceeded to Rectortown. After a short rest there, they marched through Salem and continued until two o'clock that morning, where they set up camp a short distance from Warrenton. The following day they marched into Warrenton and established a camp.[5]

On the morning of November 10, while the army was lined up on both sides of the Centerville Turnpike, General McClellan rode down the pike and bade farewell to his troops. General Burnside had been put in command of the Army of the Potomac, whose soldiers liked Burnside personally but doubted his ability to command as well as McClellan, at whose dismissal they felt a level of mistrust and indignation.[6]

On November 15, they continued their movement past Warrenton Junction and encamped in the woods within a half of a mile from Falmouth on the bank of the Rappahannock River. They remained there for some time. Thinking they would stay there for winter quarters, the Sharpshooters started constructing log huts. In his final letter, Samuel Haven, surgeon of the 15th Massachusetts, wrote:

Near Falmouth, Va. November 27, 1862

We are opposite Fredericksburg. Its rebel pickets and ours within talking distance. The movements of the people and soldiers in the city can be distinctly seen. We have been expecting a great fight every day, but in the meantime the rebels have erected more batteries and are largely increased in numbers, and I do not see how we can cross the river without great loss in life.... This is Thanksgiving Day and the pleasantest weather we have had for some time. It is hard work to get any eatables here, but we have been saving a turkey for this day.

General Burnside had decided to move toward Richmond through Fredericksburg, and had requested that pontoons from Aquia Creek be ready for him on his arrival at Falmouth. If his request had been obeyed, Fredericksburg and the surrounding heights might have been taken with little or no resistance. As Samuel Haven said, the Rebels reinforced and built additional batteries, and also fortified Marye's Heights, which would prove disastrous to the Federals.[7]

While these events took place, Bicknell remained in the hospital. After an abscess formed on his hip and the fractured bone was removed, he finally was able to bear the weight of his clothes and walk without assistance. He wanted to return to his home in Massachusetts to convalesce, and applied, with no success, for a furlough. At last, his commission as 2nd lieutenant reached him: he could now put on shoulder straps and pass the camp guard. He left the hospital and went to Harpers Ferry to meet General Slocum.

Working with Bicknell, General Slocum perfected a plan that would get Bicknell home over the surgeon's objections. Bicknell returned to the hospital and waited for a box from home, full of his grandmother's mincemeat pies. When they arrived, he divided them among his tent-mates. On December 8, he boarded a train for Washington. The provost guards had been warned to look out for the Sharpshooters who had deserted from Antietam. As Bicknell did not have a pass, the provost guard promptly arrested him as he left the depot. But Bicknell was honest and frank with the provost commander and was set free. Once in Washington, he went to the surgeon general and described the conditions at the Frederick Hospital, explaining that the men longed for delicacies and describing how the man who desired chicken had died. Bicknell pleaded his case for a furlough to convalesce at home, and spoke of his determination to get it, even if he had to go to Falmouth for it. But the surgeon general refused to approve the furlough and wished him luck in obtaining one. He also promised to look into the conditions Bicknell described at the hospital. The surgeon general kept that promise, as after Bicknell got home, he received a letter from a hospital tentmate which read, "We have lived tip top ever since you left. Beefsteak, butter, milk, each twice a day. I am getting as fat as a cub. For Christmas dinner, the whole camp had roast turkey, mashed potatoes, bread and butter, and ale."[8]

In Washington, Bicknell went to the War Department and attempted to get a furlough without going to Falmouth. He was advised that regulations should be followed, as they were wise and necessary. Although his case was different and the rules could be dispensed with, the War Department declined to. Having expected that decision, Bicknell headed toward Falmouth, where the provost guard told him to expect a battle as soon as he got there.

United States surgeon general Joseph Barnes. Lt. Bicknell was severely wounded at Antietam. He experienced firsthand some of the inadequate treatment the wounded had received. He met with General Barnes for two reasons. He wanted the wounded treated better, and he wanted a furlough to return to Massachusetts for his convalescence (civilwarphotos.net).

On December 9, 1862, Captain Plummer, with forty new recruits, arrived at about four o'clock at the camp near Falmouth and assumed command of the Sharpshooters.[9]

On December 10, they remained in camp. At six o'clock on the morning of December 11, they marched toward Fredericksburg as cannonading started. They had been detached from the 15th Massachusetts and ordered forward. They arrived at the riverbank at Fredericksburg at eleven that morning.

Earlier that morning, the Corps of Engineers had tried to construct a pontoon bridge across the river. But Confederate sharpshooters, protected by houses and basements on the other side of the river, kept up a steady fire, compelling the corps to stop. At one o'clock, the Sharpshooters were ordered to move forward and protect the Engineers while they attempted to lay the pontoon bridge. Deployed on the banks of the river, the Sharpshooters performed well against the Confederate sharpshooters, but they could not stop the enemy's fire.[10]

In response to a call for volunteers, five men came forward and immediately crossed the river in a small boat. They successfully cleared the houses and basements of Confederate sharpshooters, permitting the pontoon bridge to be completed. At five o'clock that afternoon, the five men crossed the bridge, and General John Gibbons lauded them for their actions. The Sharpshooters were then ordered across the bridge, where they performed picket duty and protected it. All that night, they encamped near the bridge, observing that Union artillery shells had set the town on fire in several places. The company record noted, "Tobacco plenty."

At four in the morning on December 12, they marched to the center of Fredericksburg, where they remained on picket duty. The enemy occasionally shelled the Federals who were occupying the town. At seven in the morning on December 13, the Sharpshooters marched to the front with the 15th Massachusetts and halted at the bottom of a hill within 1,600 yards of the enemy's artillery. They were in an open, exposed position, and when brisk cannonading and musketry fire ensued from their left, they were ordered to the rear.[11]

Bicknell reached Falmouth on the evening of December 12, and learned that the Sharpshooters had been engaged to protect the Corps of Engineers as they constructed a pontoon bridge and now were across the river with the 15th Massachusetts. He also learned that a new captain had been appointed to the Sharpshooters and had arrived with forty recruits. Bicknell spent the night in a crowded tent in great discomfort, as his hip remained very sensitive.

The next morning, Bicknell crossed the river and reported for duty to the officer in charge of the 15th Massachusetts. Pleased, but surprised to see him, his fellow Sharpshooters insisted that he leave for the other side of the river and take command of the encampment they had left there. They were sure there was about to be a battle and did not think Bicknell was fit to fight it. Bicknell went back across the river and sat on a porch with a full view of the city and the heights that were to be assaulted. Watching as one assault after another was repulsed and wave after wave of men in blue were brutally killed, he wondered whether the Sharpshooters lay in the lines of the living or the dead. For one, Surgeon Haven went into the battle with the 15th Massachusetts, believing that he should be with his men during a battle, and was killed in that assault.[12]

The Sharpshooters again were detached from the 15th Massachusetts and ordered to the front for special service. Deployed near the Gordon House, they remained in action all day, and performed well against the enemy artillerists and sharpshooters. Although they had expended almost all of their ammunition, they placed their fire so well that they drew the fire of only one enemy artillery piece throughout the day.

The commanding general commended the Sharpshooters for their bravery. Present at the battle were Captain Plummer. 1st Lieutenant Martin; Acting 1st Sergeant Oscar Clement; Sergeants Gilbreath and Mudgett; Corporals Upton, Packard, and Wood; and Privates Noah

Corps of Engineers building a bridge to Fredericksburg, December 11, 1862. The Corps of Engineers were continually fired upon as they attempted to build a pontoon bridge across the river to Fredericksburg. Confederate sharpshooters were entrenched in cellars of buildings. The Andrew Sharpshooters were called upon to eliminate that danger, which they did, and were commended for their bravery (Library of Congress).

Bentley, George Curtis, John Champney, Charles Gardner, Theodore Williams, Daniel Butters, Ferdinand Crossman, Robert Crane, Chilon Houghton, Lysander Martin, Frank Matt, Henry Mayers, William Roach, Henry Wheelock, Robert Wilson (slightly wounded in the hip by an artillery shell), Frederick Bestwick, Edward Hutchins, Nathaniel Penniman, Charles Harrington, Solomon Wildes, Henry Willis, Thaddeus Townsend, Horace Coburn, Alfred Batchelder, John P. Varrell, Amos Plimpton, Trask Averill, Marcus Arnold, Samuel Chase, Josiah Hunt, Edwin Hatch, Albert Young, Henry Morse, William Warner, Samuel Ainsworth, John Arnott, Lot Randall, John Smith, Charles Walcott, Nathan Ellis, and Anselm Hammond.[13]

On December 14, they were on picket duty all night. In the morning, they marched to their old encampment at the Phillips House to procure supplies and ammunition. Although shells were thrown toward them frequently, they saw no action. On December 15, all was quiet in camp until the afternoon, when Captain Plummer reported for duty to the Gordon

House with a portion of his men. With the exception of several enemy artillery shells, they saw no action that day. On December 15, the Sharpshooters evacuated Fredericksburg and marched to their old camp near Falmouth, arriving there at about three o'clock. It was a difficult march as the weather was rough and stormy.[14]

Bicknell wrote:

> After our army had recrossed the river, men from our company who went over to bury the dead told how that Confederate [g]enerals came down from the heights and talked with them of the foolish waste of life, and their astonishment to see line after line dashed so recklessly against their impregnable front, claiming to have refrained from firing on our army after the assaults, and to have allowed it to recross the river from motives of humanity and hope now the foolish attempt to crash the Confederacy would be abandoned. In this connection I may as well mention that I afterwards had it from the best possible authority that President Lincoln sent preemptory orders to Gen. Burnside to carry the heights — by assault. And that Lincoln was forced to this by public sentiment which demanded a more heroic, direct, aggressive policy at the front. The successive charges, by men who fully realized the impregnable character of the position, will never stand unquestioned amongst the most heroic acts of men.

After the battle, Bicknell finally received his leave of absence. He stopped at Washington and had more bone taken out of his hip. At first, he had enjoyed visits with friends, but he soon became sensitive to the unjust criticism of the war. In the press, the South understated her troop strength, overestimated her success in battle, and praised her generals. The Confederates attempted to secure sympathy and recognition from foreign countries. Bicknell grew weary of the rhetoric and wanted to return to his comrades, who were full of faith in themselves and their leaders.[15]

Bicknell had promised the company he would meet with Governor Andrew when he returned to Massachusetts. In the meeting, Bicknell questioned Governor Andrew about the promised extra pay. The governor quickly disposed of the question until Bicknell reminded him of the correspondence of July 25, 1861, to Charles Dalton. Governor Andrew said he had done all he could about the pay. Annoyed that Bicknell had put him on the spot, the governor requested to see his leave of absence papers. After Governor Andrew had reviewed the papers, Bicknell said he felt that the governor had done the wrong thing when he gave command of the Sharpshooters to a civilian over Lieutenant Martin. Governor Andrew justified his appointment of Captain Plummer because he had obtained forty recruits. Bicknell added that he was not in favor of the way Massachusetts filled its quotas, as she raised regiments commanded by civilians. In addition, he didn't like the payment of high bounties to recruits without consideration of their character or fitness to serve. Bicknell said the fact that civilians were sent out to command veterans was unworthy of the governor and undermined the state's claim to being the foremost in devotion to the cause of human liberty.

Governor Andrew's demeanor changed, as he sadly stated that he wished he were just a private in the front lines. As a servant of the people, he did what he felt was best to secure a victory and protect the commonwealth's interest, but some of those things were against his better judgment. Thanking Bicknell for his courage in speaking his convictions, the governor asked Bicknell how other men in the army felt about these same matters. Governor Andrew listened intently, and after that meeting, few, if any, civilians were given command over veterans.

Following his meeting, Bicknell went to Newburyport and met with Lieutenant Martin, who was home on leave. When Bicknell traveled back to the Sharpshooters, he met Captain Plummer and thought they would not get along very well. Two weeks after Bicknell returned to active duty, the division commander, General Gibbon, summoned Bicknell and questioned him on the history of the Sharpshooters. Bicknell detailed the company's actions and privations from the time it had left Lynnfield. Gibbon had received letters from Governor Andrew that covered the points of Bicknell's meeting with him, and Gibbon told Bicknell that while the Sharpshooters were under his command, the company would have no cause for complaint. When he asked Bicknell how the Sharpshooters could be used most effectively as a distinct branch of the army, Bicknell explained the special service the company could provide.[16]

The company remained in camp on December 17 and 18. At one o'clock on December 19, they were called out and ordered to protect the Corps of Engineers at Falmouth as they removed the pontoon bridges. The company returned at daylight on December 20 with no incident of interest.[17]

On December 20, as they started to build their huts for winter quarters, the weather was cold and blustery. On December 21, Captain Plummer inspected their rifles, and on December 22, he was ordered officer of the day. On December 23, they attended a brigade review ordered by General Morehead, who had succeeded General Sully. They were reviewed by General Sumner and his staff on the 24th. On Christmas Day, they had the day off and remained in camp. The following day, they were ordered to go out on picket duty with the 15th Massachusetts. They were back in camp on the 27th, and General Sedgwick was ordered to command the division. On December 28, Captain Plummer again inspected the company and their rifles.

At this time, they were in winter quarters, and boredom had set in. On January 1, their new ponchos arrived. On January 4, they were ordered to picket duty with the 15th Massachusetts. General Sedgwick conducted a brigade review on January 5, and on the 13th, General Morehead led a Battalion Drill. General Sully resumed command of the brigade on January 16, and General Burnside reviewed them on January 17. On January 26 and again on February 3, they were ordered out on picket duty.[18] On April 1, they were ordered under arms, where they remained all day but were not called out.

6

Arduous Trek to Gettysburg

Their existence in that quiet winter camp consisted of normal duties around camp, some drill, and picket duties. On April 17, the Sharpshooters were detached from the 15th Massachusetts and sent to the campground near General Gibbon's headquarters. This was thought to be the result of Bicknell's meetings with Governor Andrew and General Gibbon. The Sharpshooters made reports, drew rations, and obeyed orders only from division headquarters. Whether a colonel or brigadier general, anyone who wanted the Sharpshooters' services had to request them from headquarters. The Sharpshooters were in the same position as they had been under General Lander at Camp Benton.

General Gibbon sent to Washington and had ten of the Sharpshooters' lightest scoped rifles sent to his headquarters, carrying them on his own team so that they would be available when needed. Headquarters ordered Bicknell to train and drill the new recruits, who were trained as skirmishers with the Sharps rifles and in target practice with the long-range rifles. As skirmishers, the recruits were able to advance and retreat and to conceal themselves so well that they disappeared completely in the terrain. Because of Bicknell's experience and Captain Plummer's lack of it, headquarters chose Bicknell to train the recruits and ignored the captain. As a result, Lieutenant Bicknell and the captain didn't have the normal interactions of a lieutenant and a captain.[1]

The company remained in that camp until the 3rd of May at noon, when they were ordered to report to the Lacy House for duty. At eight-thirty, they were ordered to cross the Rappahannock River, move to the front, and act as skirmishers. Although they moved ahead three miles, they did not come in contact with the enemy. They re-crossed the Rappahannock and encamped by the Lacy House.

At the Battle of Chancellorsville, the Sharpshooters joined the assault that captured Marye's Heights in Fredericksburg. Bicknell's diary records the following:

> Lacy House, May 5th, 8 P.M. It rains torrents. At midnight of the 2nd, we left camp and marched to the Lacy House. At day break of the 3rd our division laid pontoon bridges and crossed without the expected resistance, the 6th Corps, across below the city, having cleared the enemy from the opposite bank for us. At 1 P.M. our division charged Marye's Heights in the front, the 6th Corps charging them from the left at the same time. The heights were carried after a sharp struggle.
>
> As the enemy fled in the direction of Chancellorsville, a battery with infantry supports halted and began to shell our lines, reforming on the heights. I deployed the sharpshooters and routed and chased the battery and supports about three miles back to

Lacy House in Falmouth, Virginia. This photograph was taken by Timothy O'Sullivan in December of 1863. The Sharpshooters were at first ordered to bivouac in the Lacy House on May 3, 1863. They would soon be ordered to encamp outside on the grounds of that house. It appears there were complaints by the Sanitary Commission as the Sharpshooters stripped fine imported wood from the walls and burned it in the fireplaces for heat (Library of Congress).

the woods: the battery halting and shelling us several times during its retreat. We did considerable execution without losing a man ourselves. At dark our division fell back to the city and the sharpshooters were ordered back to the Lacy House.

On the morning of the 4th the enemy reoccupied Marye's Heights without opposition and their sharpshooters soon began to annoy our division in the city. I was ordered to cross the river with the company and report to Colonel Hall in the Cemetery back of the city. The colonel ordered me to occupy some buildings across the street south of the cemetery, so that his men would not be annoyed by the return fire we should draw. When I reached the street I found that it was continuously swept by fire which made the surface fairly boil and [made] the air as blue as twilight. Nine out of ten would have fallen in crossing the street; so I commenced drilling holes through the brick wall of the cemetery. Firing from the top of the wall was out of the question until we had the enemy quieted down, for a ramrod held above the wall was hit again and again, and a hat pushed up was riddled in a moment.

Before we had perforated the wall, an aid[e] brought me a peremptory order to cross the street. I declined to obey unless he would lead the way. As this looked like instant death he concluded to go back and report. Before he had returned we had perforated the wall and reduced their fire on the cemetery to an occasional shot. We could not however from our position stop the fire which rendered the street impassable, so the aid[e] said [to] stay where we were.

We held the enemy as we had them till dark, excepting that when they left their trenches during the afternoon to assist in the attack of the 6th Corps in their rear, they suffered fearfully from our fire delivered rapidly from the top of the wall; their dead were literally piled in heaps. At dark we retired to the Lacy House, having suffered no loss.

Early in the morning our division evacuated the city and took up the bridges, the enemy then taking quiet possession of the opposite shore. It had rained hard for the last five hours. The floor of the room in which I am writing is covered to the depth of an inch with blood and water; the room having been used for amputating. May 6th, 9 A.M. I have just learned from President Lincoln's private secretary, who is down here, that we had been badly defeated at Chancellorsville. The whole army has recrossed the Rappahannock.[2]

The storm continued while the Sharpshooters were at the Lacy House. Bicknell found an officer from a Massachusetts regiment lying on a floor in an upstairs room. He had lost so much blood that a fire was needed to keep him alive. As no wood was to be found, Bicknell began tearing rich foreign wood from the house to start a fire. In another amputation room, the other Sharpshooters started a fire in the same manner to warm themselves. Mrs. Harris of Pennsylvania and her Sanitary Commission were headquartered at the Lacy house, and she was horrified at the destruction of the mansion. The longer she lectured the Sharpshooters, they more they liked her, but they continued their fires nonetheless. Soon after that encounter, the Sharpshooters were ordered out of the house to tents at the rear of the house — by Mrs. Harris's request, they assumed. Bicknell was ordered to see that the Sanitary Commission ladies were not disturbed.

At the Lacy House, Bicknell saw a woman wearing major's straps and Turkish men's pants. Talking to her, he learned she was Dr. Mary Walker, a pleasant woman and very courageous. She had gone to the river and beyond to attend to the wounded, but was turned back as she did not have a pass. As she found in civilian life, women doctors were not readily accepted. Ironically, she received the Medal of Honor for her gallantry while attending the wounded soldiers on the battlefield. The Rebels had captured her while she was attending to wounded Confederates and held her prisoner for four months. Around the Lacy House she attempted to interact with the officers, and all went well. However, one day, Mrs. Harris went to Bicknell as the officer in charge of the Lacy House and said, "Young man, you are in charge of the Lacy House. Either I leave this house and the army within twenty four hours, or this Dr. Mary Walker does." Bicknell took the information to General Hooker, who had quite a laugh and said he could not spare either Mrs. Harris or the Pennsylvania troops who would escort her home. General Hooker ordered his adjutant to have Major Walker report to Washington on the next train.

Dr. Mary Walker. This illustration almost appears to be a woodcut. It is not known when it was created. Walker was a contract surgeon for an Ohio regiment and was assigned to the Lacy House. In spite of the fact she was a Medal of Honor recipient, she clashed with Mrs. Harris of the Pennsylvania Sanitary Commission, and Walker was removed from the Lacy House and assigned to Washington, D.C. (etc.usf.edu/clipart).

The company remained in that camp until May 15, when they were moved to their old campground at brigade headquarters. All was quiet in that camp until June 9, 1863. At noon, Captain Plummer crossed the Rappahannock with ten men and protected the picket duty from enemy sharpshooters. At midnight the captain and five men returned to camp; five remained in the breastworks. On June 10, Lieutenant Bicknell was ordered to take sixteen men on duty at the south bank of the Rappahannock, the area known as Deep Run. There they met with the five men who were left at the breastworks and continued the operation. Captain Plummer had badly sprained his knee or ankle, which proved to be a permanent injury. He had not silenced the enemy, who were well concealed by a fringe of timber on their side of the ravine, and the Confederate sharpshooters' volleys of fire on the 6th Division were worse than before.[3]

On June 11, Lieutenant Bicknell accomplished no more than Captain Plummer had done the previous day. Bicknell determined that unless the enemy sharpshooters were driven from the ravine, the Andrew Sharpshooters would have little success. Bicknell saw that the Andrew Sharpshooters had finally met their match as far as drill, discipline, and skill were concerned, and were outnumbered five to one. That night, when the enemy sharpshooters withdrew and posted pickets about twenty yards from their ravine, Bicknell saw an opportunity and obtained a detail from the 6th Division. They constructed three rifle pits on the enemy's side of the ravine, quietly filling sandbags with loose dirt from the ravine so as not to alert the enemy to their movements.

With steady and persistent effort, they completed the three rifle pits by morning. The twenty-one Sharpshooters manned them, masking themselves with twigs and branches. As soon as it was light enough to fire with effect, the Andrew Sharpshooters opened fire and drove back the pickets from their posts in front of them and from a clump of trees on their left. Then, using one of their long-range rifles, they shot a mounted officer.

Suddenly their Rebel peers appeared in a long skirmish line about two hundred strong. Advancing through a wheat field in front of them, the Rebels tried to drive the Sharpshooters from their rifle pits. The Rebels were unsuccessful in the front, but managed to gain a clump of trees on their left and silenced the left rifle pit. Lieutenant Bicknell was in the left pit and jumped out and rolled to the bottom of the ravine to get clear. He was badly scratched and ruined his uniform. Losing no time, he posted two men from the center pit to position themselves where they could see the clump of trees and fire on the enemy. That allowed the left pit, silenced and full of Andrew Sharpshooters, to be activated again.

As soon as that task was accomplished, Bicknell ordered Lysander Martin and Ferdinand Crossman back to the center pit from where he had taken them. Bicknell was concerned about their exposed position, but when they pleaded with Bicknell to stay in that position a little while longer, he acquiesced and went to the center and right pits.

Returning to where he had left the two men, Bicknell found Crossman wounded. Crossman had been firing through a hole in the tree, and a Rebel sharpshooter had fired into the hole. The bullet passed along the barrel of Crossman's rifle, split open his finger, and passed through his hat as he took aim. Bicknell then ordered Martin to the center pit, but Martin begged Bicknell to allow him one more shot, as they thought the shot that wounded Crossman was just a lucky one. Against his better judgment, Bicknell granted Martin's request. Martin went up the bank, fired a shot, and then tumbled down the bank, mortally wounded.

Bicknell called for assistance from the center pit, and as they carried Martin down the ravine, he looked up and said, "Never mind, Lieutenant. I have wiped out a score of them today." As the news of Martin's fatal wound spread, the Andrew Sharpshooters recklessly exposed themselves, blazing away at the enemy and inflicting as much damage as possible because Martin was a favorite of the Andrew men.

At this time, David Temple, who served as the brigade butcher, appeared on the scene. Bicknell didn't understand how Temple had appeared at Deep Run that day: hatless, coatless, and bare-armed, with a rifle in his hand. Asking for the location where Martin had been shot, he went up the bank with a full box of cartridges, barely stepped behind a tree to load, and then exposed himself to the enemy as he stood there and fired. After using the whole box of cartridges, he came down from the bank and said he had doubled Martin's score. Those who knew how good a marksman Temple was did not doubt his claim.

Private Roland E. Bowen from Millbury, Massachusetts, and serving in the 15th Massachusetts Volunteer Infantry Company B. sent this letter to his friend Guild from the Lacy House on June 11, 1863;

> Friend Guild,
>
> David Temple a member of the Andrew Sharp Shooters and more commonly known as "Old Dave" is called the best shot in the company. [He] is a reckless old Cuss and cares nothing for anybody. He has been detailed in the Commissary Department for sometime past. Yesterday he volunteered to go over as he says "And kill a few God damned Johnnys in revenge for the death of Capt. Saunders at Antietam." So down he goes with two more men gets the most advanced position he can find and proceeds to give them Hell. He bangs away all day. Both men that go with him get badly wounded. He r[e]turns at night unhurt himself and glorifying over the fact he has caused 20 of the damned Skunks of Hell to have a reckoning with their Eternal Creator. It is my opinion he can beat Theede Barton in the way of Profanity.[4]

Shortly thereafter, the Rebels sent over a truce flag and proposed the mutual withdrawal of sharpshooters. General Howe agreed, and at eleven that morning ordered the Andrew Sharpshooters to abandon the rifle pits but stay in a state of readiness should he need them again.[5]

At noon the following day, Captain Plummer relieved Lieutenant Bicknell, who returned to the Sharpshooters' encampment at the end of the pontoon bridge in the rear of Howe's Division. Bicknell was pleased to have the opportunity to get some rest, as he had not slept in three nights. Before he was wounded at Antietam, he could sleep in the middle of a battle as well as in a peaceful place. Afterwards, however, he required a long period of rest between excitement and fatigue. He observed that he was unable to dodge bullets as before, as his muscles would not respond as quickly as they were ordered to. Both of these effects would prove to be lifelong.

As they began a march at eleven that night, the Sharpshooters were unable to get the rest they needed. A series of marches led them to the Battle of Gettysburg. As they did not know where their own corps was, they marched with the 6th Corps until June 17. Although Captain Plummer rode on the march, Lieutenant Bicknell was determined to march with his men. His hip and back pained him terribly day and night. The bullet that had smashed his hip also had clipped his backbone as it exited his body. When he stopped to rest he found some relief, but the pain was so severe that he then stiffened. When he was back in motion the pain eased a little bit, but then would return. That cycle continued on the long march from Fredericksburg, Virginia, to Gettysburg, Pennsylvania.

While they were with the 6th Corps, they ran out of rations. Lieutenant Bicknell approached General Sedgwick and asked for food for the Sharpshooters, but the general gruffly told him he had all he could do to feed his own men, and that Bicknell should have obtained food for his men from his own corps. When the 6th halted, Bicknell learned his own corps was not far ahead. Unable to find Captain Plummer, he led the Sharpshooters toward his own corps, thinking that they would raid a farm while they looked for their corps. Before they were out of sight of Sedgwick's quarters, Sergeant Gilbreth led the men on a raid of a sutler's wagon. Overturning the wagon, they loaded their haversacks.

They marched forward as aides rode all over the area. Thinking something was up, Bicknell ordered his men to bring their cartridge boxes to their fronts. An aide galloped ahead of the Sharpshooters and stopped ahead of them with six other men — and enough soft bread to feed a regiment. When the Sharpshooters approached them, the aide urged them to fill their haversacks and take all the bread they wanted. The aide told Bicknell the lack of food for the Sharpshooters was inexplicable and regrettable. General Sedgwick was a soldier and a gentleman, but could not control his instinctive aversion to sharpshooters or sharpshooting. Perhaps he had a premonition, as an enemy sharpshooter struck him in the head and killed him as he was setting up artillery in front of Spotsylvania.

The Sharpshooters found their corps at Wolf Run Shoals and marched with it through Fairfax to Centerville. At midday on June 20, they marched to Thoroughfare Gap, arriving there at midnight. General Owen was across the creek and thought that enemy cavalry on the road beside the stream would launch a charge. He ordered the Sharpshooters forward to stop the enemy. Lieutenant Bicknell ordered the men to drop their knapsacks and go forward. Although they moved forward a mile, expecting a running fight back through the woods and streams, they did not come in contact with the enemy. A cold rain started, and Bicknell sent all of the men back for their knapsacks and something to eat. Keeping four men with him, he remained there. In the afternoon, Union cavalry scouts reported that the enemy had advanced. Bicknell, with his four men, moved forward, but still made no contact with the enemy.

The Sharpshooters marched with the division on the morning of June 25. From the other side of the creek, the enemy shelled them as long as they were in sight. The enemy had attacked the rear guard, and the Sharpshooters were sent to the rear of the rear guard, where they were engaged with the enemy for the entire day. Captain Plummer was unable to obtain a horse, so he limped along at the head of his company. Seeing the captain struggling with his injured leg, the men took it easy and walked at route step. They did not march, and stayed just ahead of the Union cavalry to keep out of their dust.

At about five o'clock in the afternoon, the Sharpshooters were stretched over a quarter of a mile, each man walking at his own pace. Captain Plummer was at the front and Lieutenant Bicknell was at the rear of the group due to the pain in his hip and back. Dashing up to Bicknell, cavalrymen told him the enemy had come from a side road and cut their unit in two and now were close behind them. Bicknell ordered his group of men into the brush of a covered ditch to assail the enemy cavalry. As he looked forward, the cavalrymen gave the same information to Captain Plummer, who ordered his men to rejoin the division at the double. Captain Plummer's men ran off. Bicknell told each man to select an enemy cavalryman, shoot him, and take his horse. They waited awhile for the enemy cavalry, but then feared the enemy would flank them from the woods behind them. They could easily be separated from the division, and there would be no way for them to retreat, so Bicknell ordered his men forward to rejoin the division.

Bicknell and his squad arrived at the rearguard camp after dark. The captain and his squad were nowhere to be found. Bicknell sent word to headquarters that they were absent without leave, as he was too tired to go to headquarters and explain what had happened. The next day they marched in the middle of the regiment, and Bicknell thought he should go to headquarters and explain what had happened the previous night. Bicknell's contraband, with all of his blankets and rations, was lost with the captain. But some of his closest friends were with him and shared what they had, so he suffered little inconvenience.[6]

On June 26, they marched with their division and crossed the Potomac at Edwards Ferry, camped on the Maryland side. In the distance they could see the chimneys at their old camp, Camp Benton. The captain and his squad rejoined them at Frederick, Maryland, as they had taken a detour through Washington.

On the 27th, they left camp and marched through Poolesville to Frederick, where they encamped for the night. Bicknell's uniform had been severely damaged at Deep Run, and he suffered as he marched in winter clothing on hot days. So he went into the town of Frederick, and with his last cent purchased a lightweight outfit. When he remembered that he did not have shoulder straps suitable for the lightweight jacket, the dealer attached gilt braid on each shoulder, telling Bicknell that he had done so many times for other officers. Bicknell's only objection was that it made him appear to be a staff officer in search of a horse.

When Bicknell returned to the division, he learned that the Sharpshooters had left on a forced march to Uniontown. He left his contraband to follow with his blankets and rations as best he could. Pushing on, he met up with the Sharpshooters in the afternoon. That night, at the end of their thirty-two and thirty-six mile march, the Sharpshooters sank to the ground utterly exhausted.

They marched until June 30 and were mustered for pay by Captain Wood. On July 1, they marched at seven o'clock in the morning, traveling through Taneytown and arriving within two and a half miles of Gettysburg, where they encamped for the night. At this point, the data are contradictory. The Company Record states that they started to march to Gettysburg at four o'clock in the morning on July 2, but Bicknell's "Sharpshooters" states that he led the company of Sharpshooters to Gettysburg all day on July 1, arriving at nine o'clock that night and encamping in a peach orchard in front of Round Top. At daylight, Bicknell and his men joined the division, which had encamped south of the cemetery on the east side of the Taneytown Road. It is highly probable that the Sharpshooters did continue to Gettysburg that day and the division had encamped two and a half miles from Gettysburg, and marched at four in the morning. It is also very probable that Bicknell took a squad of volunteer Sharpshooters forward, while Captain Plummer and others remained with the division.

Bicknell mentions a long march in which many strong men lagged behind. He also mentions having thrown away his scabbard, pistol, canteen, and haversack along with photographs, letters from home, and anything else that weighed an ounce. He carried only his naked sword. As the men encamped at the peach orchard, pain, excitement, and lack of blankets made sleep almost impossible for the Sharpshooters. Bicknell was grateful to reach the scene of battle. It was his desire to lead the Sharpshooters into one more great battle and then resign his commission.

When they rejoined their division that morning, they were posted behind a stone wall by the Taneytown Road to silence Rebel sharpshooters. The company was heavily engaged in severe fighting all day long, and suffered no casualties that day. Several squads of Sharpshooters were detached and sent to different parts of the line of battle.

Bicknell found his contraband, which had arrived with his wagon during the night. As he had not eaten in twenty-four hours, he consumed a hasty breakfast. He then met with General Gibbon, who commanded the division that day. Bicknell described his physical condition and requested that his Sharpshooters select a location in which they could do severe damage to the enemy. General Gibbon sent an aide with him, and Bicknell selected a position on the field. General Gibbon ordered the aide not to leave that location except at Bicknell's discretion or the general's orders.[7]

Bicknell had selected a position behind a low stone wall on the slope of Cemetery Ridge, to the left of Ziegler's Grove and the cemetery. The Emmitsburg Road ran along the foot of the slope. Behind the Sharpshooters, an apple orchard extended over the ridge toward the Taneytown Road. Bicknell believed that this spot on the field must either be held by the Sharpshooters or taken by the enemy — to win or lose the battle. He further assumed that the ridge behind the Sharpshooters would draw enemy artillery fire which would go over their heads, and that they would be safe behind the wall. Bicknell's description implies that the group of Sharpshooters was about 1,400 feet southwesterly of Meade's headquarters. The elevation to their right was about 460 feet, and that to their left was about 440 feet, putting them in a twenty-foot sheltered area.[8]

The enemy was positioned across the Emmittsburg Road with infantry and artillery. The 2nd Corps was positioned on top of the ridge and moved forward. Five of the Sharpshooters went with their skirmishers and took possession of a brick barn across Emmittsburg Road. They fired so effectively on the enemy's artillery that the Rebels turned their artillery on the brick barn. The artillery soon gained proper range to attack the barn, and completely leveled it. In the middle of the afternoon, Sickles's 3rd Corps, on the Sharpshooters' left flank, advanced until they had gained control of Seminary Ridge, where they rested. At about four thirty in the afternoon of July 2, the Rebels started an all-out attack, which lasted until about seven thirty that evening. Forming a large semicircle around the Union forces, the Rebels attempted to completely encircle them.

At about six thirty, the 2nd Corps sent forward reinforced skirmishers past the Sharpshooters and left them to just observe the action. They noted that Sickles was pushed back so swiftly from Seminary Ridge that the Sharpshooters thought the Little Round Top was lost, but it was quickly reinforced by the 5th Corps. The Rebels were pushed back to Seminary Ridge, where the battle ended for the day. The ground between the Little Round Top and Seminary Ridge was left strewn with dead and wounded.

General George G. Meade's Headquarters on Cemetery Ridge, Gettysburg, Pennsylvania. This photograph was taken by Alexander Gardner in July of 1863. The Sharpshooters initially encamped in front of these headquarters (Library of Congress).

On the morning of July 3, Captain Plummer appeared in an ambulance and assumed command of the company. Lieutenant Bicknell advised him of General Gibbon's orders regarding leaving that position. Shortly thereafter, General Alexander Hays, of the 1st Corps, arrived and requested the Sharpshooters' help. General Hays wanted the Sharpshooters to enter Ziegler's Grove to silence the fire from enemy rifle pits that had been firing on his men. Captain Plummer ordered Lieutenant Bicknell to take twenty men and go with the general. Bicknell reminded Plummer of Gibbon's orders, but Plummer told Bicknell to select his men and go. Bicknell selected Sergeant Gilbreth and his other favorites and went with Hays.[9]

The Union troops had been driven out of Ziegler's Grove. Bicknell and his band of Sharpshooters entered a ravine at the rear of the grove and fought their way into the grove, tree by tree and rock by rock. They looked down into the enemy rifle pits in front of them and to the town of Gettysburg behind those pits. They occupied a knoll to the right of the grove, and the ridge to its left. Bicknell believed the Sharpshooters could hold that position as well as an infantry brigade. He felt all they could accomplish was to hold the position and keep the enemy rifle pits silent, as they were again opposite the position of the counterparts they had met at Deep Run.

The Sharpshooters were exhausted from their efforts. Looking out and seeing a heavy line of dead Union troops in front of them, they knew the grove had been given up only with a gallant resistance. The Sharpshooters continued to fire relentlessly into the enemy pits, which suffered severe casualties. Noticing that one of his men, Sanford Fuller, was in a position that exposed his ankle, Bicknell advised him to seek better cover. Fuller resented the order and did not immediately respond; he was shot through his ankle, and later died from that wound.[10]

The cannonading that preceded the Confederates' great charge opened up, and the Union returned the same fire. Two Union artillery pieces just behind the grove exploded in quick succession, and the cannonading was so continuous that the ground trembled and men staggered as they walked. Other Union troops sought shelter in the grove. As they entered they threw themselves face-first onto the ground, covering their ears and trying to shut out the horror of the sights and sounds. The grove soon was filled with men.

A general rode into the grove and halted at the foot of the ridge; his orderly was struck and killed by an artillery piece. Bicknell's "Sharpshooters" states that he did not know the general. Johnson and Buel's *Battles and Leaders of the Civil War* identifies the general as Alexander Hays, the commander of the 3rd Division 11th Corps. Bicknell removed the orderly from his horse amid a barrage of artillery. Removing the orderly's revolver, he buckled it to himself and tied the horse to a tree. Observing how fatigued Bicknell was, Hays offered him a canteen full of whiskey. Bicknell drank half its contents.[11]

Bicknell went to the top of the ridge and studied the battlefield, then returned to the grove and described it to General Hays. Hays proposed that Bicknell clear the grove of all of the men except the Sharpshooters. Bicknell sent all of the men out of the grove. Each man whose unit was close by was sent back to it. All the others were sent to the top of the ridge, where General Hays formed them into line and put them through the manual of arms to steady their nerves.

Bicknell returned to the top of the ridge and viewed the mass of Confederates which steadily came forward. By the direction in which they moved, Bicknell thought they would strike the 3rd Corps further south on the Taneytown Road. He returned to the grove and yelled, "Sharpshooters, rally on the left!" He moved the Sharpshooters to the top of the knoll between the grove and Taneytown Road, from which vantage point they intended to pick off Confederate officers. The Confederate ranks showed confusion when their officers went down.

Bicknell ordered the Sharpshooters not to fire until he gave the command, which would be to point his sword at a Confederate officer. Then, they fired together at that officer.

The Sharpshooters watched, as under the cover of smoke, the Confederates changed their direction and concentrated on the middle of the 2nd Corps, which was closer to the Sharpshooters' position. The Confederates charged quickly, steadily, and unchecked by the Union artillery's cannonading. The 2nd Corps's advance lines crumbled. Bicknell stepped in front of his men and observed that the Sharpshooters' lips were compressed to whiteness and all of their features set like granite. He had seen that look before in the Sharpshooters, and knew that they would fall on the battlefield and not be driven off. The Sharpshooters believed the Confederates were close enough in front of the 2nd Corps to receive fire, and wondered why the 2nd had not fired.

Suddenly, the Sharpshooters heard a loud crash and saw a wall of flame erupt from the 2nd Corps line. The Confederates reeled back, regrouped, and moved back again toward the 2nd Corps, not so much an orderly military maneuver as a confused rush. The rear lines tried to pass the front lines, as they were anxious to make contact with the Union forces. All the time, they drifted toward the knoll occupied by the Sharpshooters.

As a mounted Confederate officer came within the Sharpshooters' range, Bicknell pointed his sword at him and nodded. The Sharpshooters fired, and the officer fell. The Sharpshooters wanted to open fire on the Confederates, as the enemy's closeness warranted rapid fire, but Bicknell held them in check as he selected Confederate officers as they tried to bring order to the confused Confederates. The Sharpshooters continued to display discipline and concentrated on high-level Confederate officers. The Company Record notes that they "did great execution against the enemy." The order then was given to fire at will. As the enemy rear regiments pressed forward, each Sharpshooter selected his own target, and the Confederates became fodder for the Sharpshooters' rifles. This came to be known as Pickett's Charge. Pickett made a slight left oblique and pettigrew came straight forward, both into the 2nd Corps, penetrating the Union lines. They attempted to widen their attack and gain the important position of Ziegler's Grove.

General Hays appeared and gave the order, "Left wheel, charge bayonets and give them hell." Bicknell took command of the small band of men Hays had assembled and, with the Sharpshooters, moved down the lane from Ziegler's Grove to the Emmitsburg Road, toward

Pickett's Charge from a position on the enemy line looking toward Union lines, on July 3, 1863. Ziegler's Grove is shown on the left, a clump of trees on the right. The Sharpshooters were at that grove. They would left flank Pickett's Charge (Library of Congress).

Bryan House, Gettysburg, Pennsylvania. This photo was taken in July 1863. As the Sharpshooters did severe damage to the Confederates during Pickett's Charge, they themselves were attacked from the rear. Woodruff's Artillery stationed on Cemetery Ridge saw the danger the Sharpshooters were in. Woodruff ordered two cannons in position at the Bryan House. Those cannons churned out grape and canister shot into the enemy. That saved the Sharpshooters from demise, and they pursued the enemy (Library of Congress).

the Bryan House. There they found the last Confederate charging division crossing Emmitsburg Road. Bicknell ordered, and his men fired into the Confederates' flank. It was a devastating fire into the enemy. Bicknell was soon aided by the 8th Ohio Regiment, which had been on the Emmitsburg Road, just north of Ziegler's Grove.

The Sharpshooters forced the Confederates to the fence on the other side of Emmitsburg Road, where they massed together and returned. Muzzle to muzzle with the Confederates, the Sharpshooters fired. Bicknell looked behind him toward the apple orchard and realized the Union no longer held the slope alone: blue and gray mingled together in hand-to-hand combat.

The Confederates moved north on the Emmitsburg Road. Bicknell's men were being attacked on the flank and the rear, so he ordered them to fall back. As they did, they loaded and fired. At that time, Woodruff's artillery battery viewed the danger the Sharpshooters were in. Woodruff wheeled two cannons into position at the head of the lane near the Bryan House. His battery opened on the Confederates on the Emmitsburg Road with grape and canister shot. The Confederates retreated behind the fence, regrouped, and came forward again, standing on the dead bodies of their comrades only to be repulsed again by the artillery. So ended the charge of the Confederates.

Bicknell wrote in his "Sharpshooters":

> Anything but words of praise for the coolness, and steadiness, with which the charging lines advanced; and the bravery and desperation with which they clung to our lines, so long, seem strangely unjust to one who looked upon the scene. They were repelled only by the coolness, the steadiness, the desperation, equal to their own with which they were met.

Woodruff pursued the retreating Confederates, firing grape and canister shots into their ranks. Many of the Confederates took shelter behind a fence across the Emmitsburg Road. With five Sharpshooters, Bicknell worked his way behind the Confederates and captured 130 prisoners, along with their colonel, without a struggle.

As they attempted to capture more prisoners, the band of Sharpshooters moved along the same fence until they were well in front of the 2nd Corps. Those Confederates fought back. Bicknell found himself in hand-to-hand combat as he disarmed a Confederate with his sword as the Confederate attempted to shoot him at point-blank range. Alfred Batchelor was wounded in the shoulder and died from his wound within a week. The Confederates sent forward a skirmish line to cover their retreat. The Sharpshooters loaded and fired with great speed and fatal effect but were driven back as they were outnumbered.[12]

As the Confederates concentrated their fire on Bicknell, the Sharpshooters scattered and ran. Bicknell threw his arms up and fell to the ground as if he had been shot dead, at a great distance from the Union lines. As he had used up all of the strength from the whiskey Hays had given him, he lay there and rested. After he rested enough, he arose and ran, zigzagging, for the Union lines. The 2nd Division rose to their feet and cheered him, while the enemy fired wildly at him.

Returning to Ziegler's Grove, Bicknell found the Sharpshooters assembled by Samuel Gilbreth. They were astonished to see him as his ruse had also deceived his own men. The Sharpshooters had only six rounds of ammunition among them and they could not obtain more, so Bicknell led them back to the Taneytown Road. In case they were to march that night, Bicknell took the horse that he had tied to a tree in the grove.

They had not eaten since morning, and they lit a fire and cooked coffee in front of General Meade's headquarters. However, as Bicknell's contraband had found the Sharpshooters, they soon had some nourishment. The contraband had its own story of the day: Bicknell explained that he had been huddled under a tree at the bottom of a pile of contraband, and a cannon shot hit the pile of men, going clear through the man at the top.

An aide rode up and asked why the Sharpshooters had left the grove. Taking Bicknell's horse, the aide rode off, but soon returned, saying that General Meade had ordered an advance on Seminary Ridge and that Bicknell was to lead the Sharpshooters on the right side of the skirmish line. General Meade ordered the Sharpshooters back to Ziegler's Grove, where he said they would be furnished with ammunition. They returned, and soon after, a cavalry squad arrived and supplied them with ten rounds of ammunition each.

While Bicknell waited in the grove, he sent for an officer in the 2nd Corps for whom he had a high regard. He explained to the officer that while the Sharpshooters were out capturing prisoners, he had made some observations of the battlefield. Among them, a large buildup of Confederates was in a position to repel any advance by the Union forces. Bicknell said they would be entering a "hornet's nest" and would throw away the victory they had fought so hard for. The officer insisted that Bicknell should have a personal interview with General Meade.

The general and his staff listened intently as Bicknell explained that he had seen a regular-officered organization move down from the ridge and was prepared to thwart any assault by the Union forces. A colonel at the meeting disagreed, and suggested he should take his own men and lead the assault if Bicknell did not want to. But General Meade rebuked the colonel, saying that Bicknell had showed courage in coming forth with information rather than blindly obeying the order.[13]

General Meade ordered Bicknell to take the Sharpshooters and advance as skirmishers. If it appeared that the Confederates were ready to receive an assault the main line would not be ordered forward, and the Sharpshooters were to remain as a picket line that night. The general requested that the Sharpshooters deploy and take out Confederates in rifle pits who had been harassing the 2nd Corps before they returned. Bicknell explained that the Confederates were not a few men who were stuck behind the fence as they retreated, but a full officered regiment.

To strengthen the skirmishing force, General Meade assigned additional men from the 15th Massachusetts and two hundred men from a Pennsylvania regiment to Bicknell and the Sharpshooters. The force they faced was the "shattered remnant of Wright's Georgia Brigade": the same men who had driven the Sharpshooters from the field as they had attempted to capture prisoners after the assault of Pickett's charge.

At five o'clock, Bicknell moved the men out of the grove and to the foot of the slope. An aide approached him and said that General Meade desired to avoid another major engagement. With only ten cartridges apiece, it seemed doubtful that much of an engagement could be made. Bicknell and the Sharpshooters waited until the movement started and the skirmishers were thrown out along the entire front of the 2nd Corps. They then advanced to the Emmitsburg Road. Two men from the Pennsylvania Regiment had been shot from the rifle pits, and the rest were nervous as they made easy targets.

Bicknell had them lie on the road, which had a slight slope that afforded protection, and ordered them to shoot at the rifle pits across the road. He sent the remaining men down the lane to crawl along the fence and flank fire into the pits. Bicknell saw no reason to charge the pits, as they were well fortified with rear artillery support. Bicknell and fourteen Sharpshooters crossed the lane to the left, deployed, and connected with the 15th Massachusetts Skirmishers, who were in front of the 2nd Corps.

Surveying the scene, Bicknell and the Sharpshooters found what they had expected. The enemy had concentrated their forces in the center, upon which they had expected a charge. Bicknell talked with an officer from the 15th Massachusetts and ordered a halt to their movement. The enemy brigade in front of them fired wildly, filling the air over their heads with bullets.

Under the protection of the 15th Massachusetts, Bicknell and the Sharpshooters ran to a fence close to their front, selected enemy officers as targets, and fired a volley into them, riling them up even more. Bicknell ordered the men to conserve their ammunition, as he expected to hold that position through the night. Looking to his rear, he observed that his line had disappeared and assumed that the enemy's wild, high fire must have fallen on them. As they ran out of ammunition, some of the Sharpshooters crept back to the grove.

Bicknell was left alone. He crept to the rifle pits to observe how much damage the regiment had done. His approach drew a hot and personal fire, and he retreated. He believed he would lose many men if he tried to withdraw the regiment in the daylight, so he let them lie there until dark, when he thought their own officers would withdraw them.

On his return, Bicknell found a dying Confederate general beside a log house. The Confederate offered Bicknell his gold watch if he would take him into the Union lines, but Bicknell said his duty as an officer would not allow him to accept it. The Confederate told him he was personally acquainted with General Hancock and other men fighting for the Union. Speaking to officers of the 2nd Corps, Bicknell identified the Confederate as General Lewis Armistead, who soon was brought into the Union lines. Samuel Gilbreth had brought in a young Confederate officer who had gone down in the last desperate charge. The Sharpshooters made him as comfortable as they could. Staring death in the face, the young officer said that he was sorry he had taken up arms against his country and requested that the Stars and Stripes be placed by his side. As he drew his last breath, the Sharpshooters met his request.

At about nine o'clock, Bicknell was summoned to meet with General Hays. The general thanked the Sharpshooters for the services they had rendered that day, and said that General Meade had ordered him to thank Bicknell for the way he had followed Meade's instructions. When General Hays reminded Bicknell that it was time to bring in the men who were left in the depression in the road, Bicknell remembered that only the Sharpshooters had the privilege of leaving their positions after dark. Bicknell walked down the slope among the dead and wounded. The moans of the dying filled the nighttime air. When he returned, he learned that the Sharpshooters were down by the Taneytown Road. Bicknell retrieved George Roundy's body and returned to the Sharpshooters.

George Roundy had been a friend of Bicknell. When the Sharpshooters had had wagons, he had been a teamster for them, and he performed the same duty for the brigade. When his shoes had worn out, Roundy had marched to Gettysburg with bleeding feet wrapped in rags. Bicknell had stationed Roundy on the knoll between Ziegler's Grove and the lane, which Bicknell thought was a safe position, and asked the men to look out for Roundy's safety. From that position, Roundy saw the Sharpshooters as they were flanked on the Emmitsburg Road. He called on the remaining Sharpshooters to follow him and help the company. He made it to the top of a crest, where he was seen to fall.[14]

Little is known about what the remaining Sharpshooters did on that day. The Company Record states that the company was divided into four squads, and was stationed at different positions on the field. In a letter in the Bachelder Papers dated March 20, 1885, Captain Plummer stated:

> "On the morning of the 3rd, at the personal request of General Hays I detailed Lt. BICKNELL, with a few men, to take a position in General Hays' Division, to silence, if possible, a battery of the enemy's. Lt. B remained in this position the whole day, doing most excellent service, and taking a large number of prisoners. For his valuable service, he was personally complimented by General Hays. Shortly after I had detailed Lt. B I was ordered to take a position opposite the town of Gettysburg, where the Co. did very effective service against the enemy sharpshooters stationed in the front and the houses near, from which they killed and wounded many of our men. It was here that Sergeant Edward HUTCHINS of my Co. was mortally wounded. He was one of the coolest and bravest men I ever knew and a splendid rifle shot. He was the clerk of the Co. and was respected and beloved by all. I believe there never lived a better type of the citizen soldier than Sergeant H...."[15]

On July 4, the enemy abandoned the rifle pits near Ziegler's Grove, and the Sharpshooters returned to their first position at the stone wall. As Bicknell sat on an ammunition box with several officers reclining around him, two Confederates advanced toward him. One raised his rifle and fired through the branches of an apple tree behind Bicknell, a second shot went into the body of the tree, and a third clipped the hair over his ear as smoothly as a razor. Bicknell had not fired at a man since Antietam. He accepted the challenge. Picking up a Sharps rifle, he aimed high on a pine tree on a ridge behind the Confederate. He fired, and the Confederate dropped. Bicknell later said that the Confederate was a better marksman, as he fired from his shoulder on the run, while Bicknell fired from a position of rest, on a fence. Observing the damage to the trees all around, Bicknell wondered how anybody could have survived the battle.[16]

7

Strange Fruit on Trees

On the morning of July 5, the Sharpshooters buried Roundy's body in Ziegler's Grove and marked the spot where he rested. With the excitement of the battle over, Bicknell's body ached so much he could barely move, and he had to ride in an ambulance. He greatly detested this, as he felt a man leading soldiers should march with them, and the ambulance should be made available to the sick and wounded. He said that it was time for him to resign his commission.[1]

At eleven thirty, the Sharpshooters left Gettysburg and marched out on the same roads they had marched in on. They marched about six and a half miles and camped at a place called Two Taverns, where they remained camped through July 6. At eight o'clock on the morning of the 7th, they left camp and marched toward Taneytown.

They marched until one thirty and stopped and set up camp. Sergeant Clement went to the 1st Brigade, 2nd Division of the 2nd Corps and drew fifteen pairs of shoes for the Sharpshooters. Lieutenant Bicknell issued strict orders for no one to leave the camp without his permission. Sentries were placed by the brigade to prevent straggling. The Sharpshooters had marched six and a half miles that day. That night, Henry Willis and Nathaniel Penniman were reported absent without leave.[2]

On the morning of July 8, they left camp at five o'clock. Penniman returned to the Sharpshooters. Willis was still missing. They marched in a heavy rain until three thirty that afternoon. They had marched twenty-one miles toward Frederick, Maryland. The Sharpshooters were in good condition, but Bicknell continued to ride in an ambulance.

The Sharpshooters broke camp on July 9 and marched until they reached the eastern side of South Mountain, where they camped for an hour. At five o'clock they broke camp and marched over the mountain, where they camped in a pleasant valley on its western side. They had marched twenty-one miles that day.

On July 10, they broke camp at five o'clock in the morning. As Lieutenant Bicknell remained confined to the ambulance, Sergeant Clement commanded the Sharpshooters. They marched for three miles and halted. Ahead of them they could hear the sound of a heavy battle. They continued their march to the old Antietam Battlefield and camped. They had marched about eight miles. On the morning of the 11th, they marched two miles toward Hagerstown and camped for the night.[3]

On July 12, the Sharpshooters moved about one mile into a field. Forming a line of battle, they moved in a northeasterly direction, advanced one mile, and halted. They then advanced one mile in the same direction from which they heard shots fired by their skirmishers.

An ambulance train July 1863. Bicknell felt the effects of his wounds after three days of battle. He detested riding. He believed if a man was not fit to march with his men, then he wasn't fit to lead them. He was ordered to ride in an ambulance train as depicted (Library of Congress).

They had moved three miles that day and remained in that camp on July 13, when Sergeant Clements received a commission as 1st lieutenant from Governor Andrews. But Clements refused to accept that commission, as long it would put him in command over 2nd Lieutenant Bicknell. The only way he would accept the commission was if the captain were to resign and Bicknell were commissioned captain. Then he would command the Sharpshooters until Bicknell rested in the hospital. Later, after Bicknell resigned his commission, Clements would muster in as 1st lieutenant.[4]

At six o'clock in the morning of July 14, the Sharpshooters were ordered to the front. The 2nd Division of the 2nd Corps and the Sharpshooters with the 3rd Brigade moved forward as part of a reconnaissance. The Sharpshooters went ahead of the picket lines and found that the enemy had retreated. The brigade moved forward to within one and a half miles of Williamsport, where they formed a line of battle, changed direction, and marched in columns along the Potomac River, two miles to the right of Williamsport. The Sharpshooters were engaged with the cavalry and another regiment. Bicknell once again commanded the Sharpshooters under fire at Falling Waters.[5]

Bicknell recorded the following regarding this action:

> We had them penned up on top of a wooded hill, and were expecting their surrender. A line came out of the woods and grounded arms. One of our regiments advanced in their front. When they were within short range, the enemy bent forward and picked up their guns, and delivered a volley into their faces. Before Kilpatrick could restrain his men the limbs of an apple orchard, near by, bore much unnatural fruit."[6]

After that action, they continued to march about ten miles, and camped at about nine thirty that night.

On July 15, they left camp at seven in the morning and marched toward Harpers Ferry for twenty miles. Then they camped within two miles of Harpers Ferry. On the 16th, they marched about five miles, passing Harpers Ferry on their left, and camped at Sandy Hook, Maryland. Lieutenant Bicknell and Captain Plummer arrived in camp that day. The Sharpshooters remained camped there through the 17th. In terrible pain and thinking he would never be able to lead the Sharpshooters, Bicknell tendered his resignation that day.

On July 18, Bicknell was summoned to corps headquarters. He reported to a large number of general officers, who requested that he withdraw his resignation, complimenting him on his service and their need for his special knowledge of sharpshooting. They wanted him to rest in a hospital and would contact Governor Andrew to rectify what they considered a mistake in Clement's being commissioned a 1st lieutenant. Moved by their compliments, Bicknell said he would leave the decision to the corps surgeon. He disrobed for examination, and wrote in his "Sharpshooters," "As soon as I disrobed the surgeon exclaimed that the youngest soldier in the service would die, gray headed, before I should be fit to march again, so he made out my discharge."[7]

At eight o'clock that morning, the 2nd Corps broke camp and marched to Harpers Ferry, across the Potomac River. While he waited for the train to take him to Washington, Bicknell sat on the balcony of a house in Harpers Ferry. As the 2nd Corps marched past him, the Sharpshooters gave him many friendly salutes and the honor of present arms.

The Sharpshooters then marched across the Shenandoah River for twelve miles and camped. Captain Plummer, too ill, did not march with them, but was sent to a hospital in Frederick City. The Company Record on that day stated, "Williams missing."[8]

On July 19, the Sharpshooters marched six miles and camped. On the 20th, they were notified that the enemy had taken Theodore Williams prisoner. The Sharpshooters left camp at six o'clock that morning, marched through Snickers Gap, and continued for twelve miles, then camped. They remained there until July 22, when they marched eight miles to Paris and encamped again.

Bicknell's "Sharpshooters" records that the Sharpshooters were not in the habit of keeping up correspondence with one another while in the service. If one of his comrades who stood by his side at Antietam had not had time dragging on his hands, Bicknell thought he never would have received the following letter, which confirmed the Company Record regarding Williams.

Headquarters College Green Barracks
Annapolis, Md. Oct. 8th, 1863

My Friend Bicknell,

Doubtless you are aware that I am not where I ought to be which is wholly the fault of a squad of the 7th Va. Cavalry (Ashby's old regt.) they gobbled me up, between the Ferry and Snickers Gap; on the same day I bid you good cheer, en-route for the North. While with the fighting men of rebeldom I was treated quite well; but I cannot begin to describe the sufferings of Union prisoners at Richmond. You, nor anyone else who has been a captive in the hands of those men at the front can conceive the difference which exists, between them and the cursed rebels—the Home Guards—who having no courage to go into action must vent their spleen upon the unarmed Yankees whom they have charge over. For most of three months I was on Bell Island, Richmond, most of the time there was about 4000 there. Each morning the dead had to be carried out before breakfast, for fear a few of the living might get an extra mouthful. I saw men murdered, without any excuse or provocation whatever. Men starved to death for want of food, others killed themselves, eating bones, which they ground up between stones, they found the bones in a solid mass within the men who ate them; preventing any passage; since we have reached this camp our Surgeons have cut out many of these formations.

Our daily rations on the Island was 5 ounces of bread and 1 ounce of fresh meat, for breakfast, 5 ounces of bread and one ounce of beans or rice, for supper. We never had more, but sometimes less than the above.

I stood it full as well as any of the men tho' I weigh less than 100 lbs. At the present time, I am doing very well here, am acting as a Sergeant, have charge of [a number of] Barracks at this camp, under Major Chamberlin 1st Mass Cavalry. I have 150 men to draw and issue rations to, have everything I wish myself, suppose I shall remain here until I am exchanged.

Major Hooper was taken prisoner at the same time, and near the same place that I was, believe he is in Richmond yet. I hope this may find you gay and festive; and produce a speedy answer.

Your Friend

———[9]

On the morning of July 23, the Sharpshooters left camp at five o'clock, marching about ten miles to Front Royal and halting. They then marched another four miles and met with the 3rd Brigade, and went out on picket duty about two miles from Manassas Gap. At ten o'clock that night, they moved another mile and a half and remained for the night. They had marched about eighteen miles that day.

At five in the morning on July 24, they marched five miles and rejoined their division, camping high on a hill about a mile and a half from the eastern entrance to Manassas Gap. At two o'clock in the afternoon, they broke camp and marched with the whole army, returning the way they had previously traveled. They camped for the night about five miles from Manassas Gap. They had marched twelve miles that day.

At five o'clock on the morning of the 25th, they marched through the western entrance of the Gap, turned right toward Warrenton Junction, and marched twenty miles, whereupon they camped at White Plains. On July 26, they broke camp at four thirty in the morning, marching through Warrenton Junction, going on for twenty-two miles, and camping. On the 29th, they received official notice that Sanford Fuller had died of his wound.

The Sharpshooters remained in this camp until six in the evening of July 30, when they marched seven miles and camped four miles from Warren Junction. On the morning of August 1, they left camp at nine o'clock, marching toward Falmouth for about six miles and camping in Morrisville, where they remained until the 3rd. At three o'clock that afternoon, they marched a mile and camped. On August 4 the Sharpshooters left camp at noon, marched about two miles, and encamped with the rest of the 2nd Corps.

On August 5, the Sharpshooters remained in camp near division headquarters. They were informed that in future all company letters would be delivered to the headquarters of the 3rd Brigade, 2nd Division, 2nd Corps. On August 6, payrolls were signed and the Sharpshooters were paid. They remained in that camp, and on August 11, 1st Lieutenant Oscar Clement was placed under arrest. The Company Record states that the charges against him were unknown. The Sharpshooters then were temporarily assigned to the 20th Massachusetts Volunteer Infantry and put under the command of the 20th's Lieutenant McKay, as their own company had not a single officer to lead them.[10]

The Sharpshooters remained in camp with the 20th Massachusetts. On August 14, John Smith, who had enlisted under Captain Plummer in November of 1862 but deserted in January of 1863 near Falmouth, was discovered among the substitutes to fill the rolls of the 19th Massachusetts Volunteer Infantry. Made aware of this, Lieutenant McKay had Smith arrested and sent to the provost marshal of the 2nd Corps. The Sharpshooters remained in that camp until August 17, when they marched a mile east and set up a new camp.[11]

On August 19, 1863, the General Order Book indicates the charge against Lieutenant Clement as follows:

Special Order No. 137   Headquarters 3rd Brigade 2nd Division 2nd Corps
11th August 1863

1st Lieutenant Oscar H Clement of Andrew Sharpshooters Mass. Vol.s is hereby placed under arrest and confined to the limits of Brigade Camp.

1st Co. of Andrew Sharpshooters Vol.s is temporarily assigned to the 20th Mass. Vol.s and will report to the commanding officer of the Regiment.

By Order of Col Smith
Sgt W.R.Driver
Adj (illegible)

General Order No. 121

Headquarters 2nd Division 2nd Corp
August 19th 1863

Before a General Court Martial convened by General Order No. 118 of August 16th 1863 from these HQ 2nd Corp was assigned and tried.

1st Lt. Oscar H. Clements 1st Company Andrew Sharpshooters Mass. Vol's on the following
Charge: Conduct prejudicial to good order and military discipline.
Plea: Not guilty
Finding: Guilty
Sentence: To forfeit one half of one months pay and to be reprimanded in General Orders.
II. The proceedings, findings and sentence are approved.

Private Brown should have appealed to his Company Commander if he thought he had been illegally punished. The advice Lt. Clements gave him, shows a culpable ignorance of the Acts of Congress which have been published to this Army, and Lt. Clements is advised that unless he shows a true military spirit and informs himself of his duties, he will place himself in a position, where he will be protected from such appeal by the respect that such as comes with command.

By Commander Brig. Gen. Webb
Commander of Division
From (illegible signature)
A.A.A.G.

Headquarters 3rd Brigade, 2nd Division, 2nd Corp. August 19, 1863.
Official   from R. Driver
A.A.A.G.

Special Order No. 138

Headquarters 2nd Division, 3rd Brigade

August 22, 1863
V. 1st Lt. O. H. Clement having been arraigned and tried before a General Court Martial and the proceedings there having been published in General Orders Headquarters 2nd Corps will return to duty

By Order of Col. Baxter Commander of Brigade
From R. Driver
A.A.A.G.

On August 18 Brigade Commander General Webb inspected them. On the 22nd, Lieutenant Clement was returned to duty. As they remained in camp on the 27th the returns of deserters, absents, and sick were sent to the headquarters of the 2nd Corps. On August 28, John Smith was shot by order of general court-martial.

> Headquarters 2nd Div. 2nd Corps
> August 27th, 1863

General Orders No. 133
Privates William H. Hill of Co. K 20th Mass. Vols. and John Smith of 1st Co. Andrew Sharpshooters Mass. Vol.s found guilty of desertion and sentenced to be shot, by General Court Martial, condemned in proceedings of General Orders No. 118 of Aug. 16, 1863 from these Headquarters and the sentence having been approved by the Major General Commanding, and ordered to be executed by General Order No. 86 of August 24th, 63 from Head Quarters Army of the Potomac. The sentence will be carried into effect tomorrow at 3 pm on the grounds near the road in front of Division Head Quarters leading to Bealton.

Brigade Commanders will form their commands promptly at half past two and march to the grounds assigned them, which will be pointed out by a Div. Staff Officer.

They will also see that each Regt. of their commands are furnished with a copy of the order promulgating the sentences and the order for execution of the prisoners.

The band of the 2nd Division will report to the Adjutant Gen. of Division promptly at 2:30 pm tomorrow.

> By Command
> Brig. Gen. Webb Comdr. Div.
> Signed J. P. Wood
> A.A.A.G.[12]

The Sharpshooters remained in that camp until they were awoken at two fifteen on the morning of August 31. At three fifty that morning, they packed up and marched ten miles, halted and were mustered for pay for the months of July and August. At about four that afternoon, they marched another six miles and encamped.[13]

September 1, 1863, in the morning edition of the *Boston Journal*:

Two Massachusetts Soldiers Shot for Desertion. Last Friday, 29 August ult: Wm. H. Hill of Co. K, 20th Massachusetts Regiment, and John Smith of the first company of Andrew (Mass.) Sharpshooters, were shot near the headquarters of the Second Army Corps in Virginia for desertion. Eugene Sullivan of Co. F, 20th Massachusetts Regiment, was also sentenced to be shot at the same time, but was reprieved. His crime was also desertion, but his extreme youth, some palliating circumstances in his case, and the intercession of the officers of his regiment, induced Gen. Meade to suspend the execution of his sentence until the President's will should be known regarding it. The correspondent of the New York Herald gives the following account of the histories of the condemned, and of the execution of Hill and Smith:

Sketch of Wm. F. Hill's Case.

Wm. Hill was nineteen years of age, and he was born in North Brookfield, Mass.; was a laborer before he enlisted, has an aged father, two brothers and three sisters. He was unmarried. He enlisted on the 14th day of July, 1862 in the 20th Massachusetts Regiment. He said that a man got him drunk and had him sworn in before he knew what he was about. Up to the battle of Antietam he followed his regiment without arms. The reason he gives was that the regiment was short of guns and could not get any. After the battle of Antietam his regiment went to Bolivar Heights. Here they encamped about two months. When leaving there the regiment went up the valley towards Fredericksburg. "When twelve miles from Bolivar," he continued, "Lieut. Ropes, of my company, gave me permission to fall out of the ranks and get along the best way I could, as my feet were sore and my head ached. On going to a citizen's house, I saw a number of our soldiers. They advised and persuaded me to desert, and gave me information on how to cross the river, and the direction to take when I was on the other side. On account of my father, who is seventy-five years of age." He continued, "as well as a sister, who is thirty-five, and are not able to take care of themselves, I deserted, and reached my home at North Brookfield a few days after. Here I remained until the middle of June, when I was arrested by a policeman by the name of Charles Ruggles of Worcester. He had an order from the Provost Marshal for my arrest. I was taken under guard from there to Washington, and from Washington I was taken to Harper's Ferry, where our Corps then was, and given in charge to the Provost Marshal of the second division."

The Case of Smith, Alias Waters.

John Smith, according to the account of himself, was a native of Philadelphia, was a tailor by trade, and resided in Boston, Mass., when the war broke out. He was 37 years of age last February. Smith was a married man, but had no children. His father and five brothers are living, some of the latter being in the service. He enlisted in Captain Plummer's company of Andrew Sharpshooters about the 1st of December, 1862. He said he was in the battle of Fredericksburg, "and did my duty, as the officers will say at any time." About the middle of January, 1863, he deserted his company, which was then at Falmouth, attached to the 15th Massachusetts. He said that large numbers were deserting about that time, and when he left his company he did not think of the consequences. The morning he deserted he fell into the company of some men who had liquor. He drank to excess, and while intoxicated said that he should like to get home, when his new friends answered that that was easy enough, for all that he got to do was to start now he had the chance. He said the men were unknown to him, and even if he knew them he would not expose them. When he reached home he did not feel satisfied, and felt that he ought to get back to the army again, and had made up his mind to re-enter the service by joining Col. Frankle's artillery regiment, as he had a particular friend there. This friend advised him not to enlist at that time, as he was going to have a furlough, and that when it expired it would be time enough.

About this time Mr. William Ayers, a carpenter, residing in Waltham, Massachusetts, was drafted. He met Smith, and proposed to pay him the sum of three hundred dollars as a substitute, preferring to do this to going to the substitute office. Smith said after some persuasion he took the money and agreed to go as a substitute, though he did not want to go as such. He gave the name as Thomas Waters. He said that his intentions were good at the time; but they (the officers) do not look at it in that way. He at once applied to Col. Frankle to be mustered into his regiment, and the Colonel gave him a note to the Provost Marshal General, making that request, which Captain Herrick, Provost Marshal of the 6th Massachusetts District, dating from Lawrence, August 3, endorsed. Stating that Waters (or Smith) appeared worthy and deserving and he conducted himself well since his enlistment. These letters were sent to Gen. Devens at Long Island, who declined interfering in the matter, as he had no authority to transfer any to the Army of the Potomac. Accordingly on the 8th of August, Smith and about one hundred others started for the Army of the Potomac, with orders to report to the Nineteenth Massachusetts Regiment; but to his surprise he found himself face to face with his old comrades, the company of Andrew Sharpshooters having during his absence been transferred from the Fifteenth to the Nineteenth Massachusetts. He was immediately recognized and arrested, the lieutenant of the Sharpshooters saying he had no doubt all would be right, but that he wanted him back to his old company.

Smith said that when he deserted he went to Boston to his friends, and remained there up to the time of his coming away as a substitute, that no one interfered with him, and that no one said a word to him about his desertion, and that he had no fear of being arrested as a deserter. Officers of Smith's regiment say that he had deserted several times. He had $300 when arrested, which he wished back to Mr. Ayers, whose substitute Smith had engaged himself to be, but the government took possession of the amount.

Both men petitioned for an extension of the time for the execution of the sentence, but without success. Hill's officers refused to intercede in his behalf, for reasons not favorable to his character.

Sketch of Sullivan's Case.

Eugene Sullivan, the writer describes, is a youth, between seventeen and eighteen years of age. He was born in Boston, Mass., and was an errand boy at the time of the breaking out of the rebellion, though occasionally assisted his father, who was a tailor by trade. Both father and son enlisted in the same company, fought at Antietam and at both battles of Fredericksburg. I asked him where his father was. "He was killed by my side at the second Fredericksburg fight," was the modest answer. This is true. Up to the time of his father's death he acted bravely, fighting by his side in these battles, but after his father fell the lad appeared to be afraid of death. Just before the battle of Gettysburg he fell out of the ranks to get some water, and did not return for three days. "But I returned of my own account," he said. This had been a terrible lesson to him, he says, and that if he ever gets out of it he will remember it as long as he lives. I said "You are charged with insubordinate conduct also." "Yes" he said, "It was this; I refused to obey the order of the corporal to go into the woods after poles. This was the cause of my death sentence, for when I returned to my company I only received a slight punishment; but after disobeying orders the old charge of desertion was brought up with it. I tell you," He continued, "that sentence made me shiver and feel bad. Do you think I will get clear?" I told him that I had no doubt he would, "but how did you feel when the reprieve came!" I asked him. "That I can't tell you," he answered; "it seemed as if a great weight of misery lifted itself from me, and that I was in a new world."

The Execution.

The execution took place last Friday in front of the Division headquarters, at three o'clock in the afternoon. The preparations were of the usual character. The condemned men were taken from the prison, an old barn — the Second Army Corps having been previously disposed so as to form three sides of a square — and marched to the open side of the square, where their graves were already dug, and near which their coffins were placed. A Sergeant and sixteen men of the Andrew Sharpshooters, commanded by Lieut. Black, formed the firing party. The men walked to the place of execution with slow and steady step. The Reverend Mr. Collins of the 72nd Pennsylvania volunteers attended the condemned in their hour of extremity. The religious services being over and the last farewells expressed, the men were blindfolded and knelt before their coffins, when Lieut. Black shook them by hand and hastily turned a few paces to the left, at the same time giving the command "Ready, aim" and then instantly, before the word "fire" could be given, the rifles had belched forth their contents in one report, and the same instant the two unfortunate men fell forward, Smith on the left and Hill on the right. The former lay motionless on his back, at full length, with his arms partly folded over his breast; the mouth opened and shut a few times, a heave and a sigh followed, and he was dead. Between the time Lieut. Black shook him by the hand and the firing of the volley he raised both his arms to Heaven and casting up his face, exclaimed twice, "Oh God have mercy upon us!" Hill said nothing.

For a few seconds after the volley, Hill remained perfectly still, and, it being supposed that both were dead, the military were about moving off, when he commenced to writhe, and, this continued for over a minute, one of the reserve sharpshooters was ordered up. He presented his piece and shot him through the head, the ball passing through, and causing the brain to ooze out on the grass. He still continued writhing, when the other order was ordered to fire. He did so, and another ball passed through his head, and, strange as it may seem, it was a full two minutes before his life was extinct.[14]

On September 1 and 2, the Sharpshooters remained in camp and were inspected three times. On the 3rd, they left camp at five o'clock in the morning and marched three miles. Lieutenant Clements was put in charge of a picket duty. The remainder of the Sharpshooters marched with the 20th Massachusetts Volunteer Infantry as part of the 3rd Brigade to a camp near Morrisville, a distance of sixteen miles. They remained at this camp through September 11, where they were inspected and performed company and battalion drill.

On September 12, they broke camp at ten o'clock in the morning, packed everything, and marched to within one mile of the Rappahannock Station. At eleven o'clock that morning, Major Abbott placed Lieutenant Clement under arrest for drunkenness on that march. The day was laborious, and the troops endured much fatigue; many fell out of the ranks over the nine-mile march.

On September 13, at seven o'clock in the morning, the Sharpshooters crossed the Rappahannock River about one mile below the railroad bridge and marched in a direct line toward Culpepper Courthouse. As they skirmished in their front they heard the cavalry, and the firing became brisk at times. The enemy retreated as the Sharpshooters and infantry approached. The Sharpshooters continued their march and at about noon reached Brandy Station, which showed evidence that a great struggle had occurred there. A number of wounded cavalrymen were lodged in houses. They stayed there for a half hour and continued their march until they were within a mile and a half from Culpepper Courthouse. There they camped after the twelve-mile march.

They remained in camp on September 14, but heard heavy firing toward their south and southwest. On the 15th, they also remained in camp as the 1st Division of the 2nd Corps marched toward the Rapidan River. They broke camp at seven o'clock in the morning of

The Union Army crossing the Rappahannock River. This photograph was taken by Timothy O'Sullivan on May 4, 1862. It depicts a crossing of artillery over the Rappahannock River (Library of Congress).

September 16 and marched through Culpepper, camping two miles south of it. They had marched three and a half miles. At six in the morning of the 17th, they broke camp and marched toward the Rapidan River. They heard the sounds of battle in the distance, and could see a number of dead horses, which had been killed in the previous day's skirmish. They marched eight more miles, camped, and sent out pickets.[15]

The camps now held a large number of conscripts and new recruits. The men were loud and boisterous, and order and discipline in the camps broke down. In response, the following order was issued.

H.Q. 3rd Brig. 2nd Div. 2nd Corp
Near Gerrmannaville Ford Oct. 2, 1863

General Order No. 14

The vice of gambling having immersed amongst enlisted men within the Corps of this Brigade to an alarming extent is hereby forbidden, commanding officers of regiments are directed to use every effort towards stopping such a practice. Enlisted men of this command discovered at gambling, will be tried for disobedience of orders and will be punished with the utmost severity.

A few professional sharpers, can after play win the earnings of many, which are so much needed by their families; this entailing misery, want and wretchedness on the innocent.

No poor man can afford to risk one dollar for the chance of making another, it is hoped by forbidding the practice of gambling it will at once cease and if it does not the most stringent measures will be resorted to, to put and end to gambling. Here after all lights in the tents of enlisted men must be extinguished at Taps, all noises in the Company Streets must cease at this time. The officers of the day in each regiment will see to the enforcement of this order. Offenders must be promptly and severely punished.

By order of
Col. Mallon Comdr. Of Brig.
(illegible signature)
A.A.A.G.[16]

They remained in this camp until October 5, performing picket duty daily. By now, the Sharpshooters had lost their officers. Captain Plummer had received a disability discharge on September 27, and Lieutenant Clement was court-martialed and cashiered out of the Sharpshooters' service. About eleven o'clock on the night of October 5, the Sharpshooters and Company F of the 20th Massachusetts Volunteer Infantry were a little boisterous, and Lieutenant McKay ordered them to change their ways. Soon after he walked past the Company F camp, a shot rang out and he fell dead. Although all arms were inspected immediately, the murderer was never identified.[17]

On October 6, the men broke camp at six o'clock in the morning. They marched through Culpepper and camped about two miles east of it. At the Rapidan River, the 6th Corps relieved the 2nd Corps. They remained in that camp until October 9 and performed picket duty each day. They were happy to receive fresh meat as part of their rations.

On the morning of October 10, they left camp suddenly at eleven o'clock, marching back through Culpepper and moving a mile and a half to the west of it. Halting and forming a line of battle, they remained in that position until three o'clock the next morning. With the corps, they then marched in a northeasterly direction, stopping only occasionally for a short rest. They arrived at Brandy Station about noon, then continued their march across the Rappahannock River and camped. Having marched for eighteen hours after being in a line of battle until three in the morning, they then learned that no rations were to be had.

The Sharpshooters were up at dawn on October 11, and left camp hastily about one o'clock that afternoon. They marched by way of Bealeton to the Rappahannock, then advanced four miles toward Brandy Station, where they heard heavy firing as the cavalry was in a battle ahead of them. They were formed in a brigade line of battle and advanced another four miles. They had moved eight miles that day and remained without rations.

At one o'clock on the morning of October 13, they marched back across the railroad toward Bealeton. They marched three miles and halted, forming a line of battle and waiting for four hours as the cavalry scouted the terrain in front of them. They made an about-face and marched for about a mile, then marched in a northeasterly direction until six thirty in the evening. They had marched eighteen miles, bringing that movement to a total of about thirty-five miles, without rations.

At six o'clock in the morning on October 14, the Sharpshooters heard heavy firing on their left as the enemy attempted to capture the Union wagon trains. The firing came from the advanced 3rd Division, which made contact with the enemy first. The Sharpshooters marched about one and a half miles and halted at Catlett Station at ten o'clock that morning. At one o'clock, they were ordered on the double toward Bristoe Station, which they did in short intervals of marching. Shortly after they reached Bristoe Station, their flankers were attacked; those not driven in were captured.

The Sharpshooters, attached to the 20th Massachusetts Volunteer Infantry, were ordered to face the enemy and were placed behind a railroad embankment, along where the road ran. The Sharpshooters held their fire as the enemy approached, but were given the order to fire when the enemy got within one hundred yards. Supported by Ricketts and another artillery battery, the Sharpshooters and the 20th Massachusetts dealt an enormous blow to the enemy, who withdrew, leaving many of their dead and wounded strewn in front of them.[18]

As the enemy retreated, Major Abbott, the commander of the 20th Massachusetts, sent Sergeant Hammond and three other Sharpshooters to the right front to determine the enemy's position. Sergeant Gilbreth was ordered to move forward as a skirmisher with all of the Sharpshooters, who numbered about eight at that time. They advanced directly toward the enemy's artillery batteries.

What happened next is best described by Richard F. Miller:

> The rebel infantry continued its retreat right through Major McIntosh's battery, no doubt sidestepping its forty-four "disabled" horses and three dead and thirty-nine wounded artillerists. McIntosh tried to rally the infantry to support his pieces but in vain. With no animals to haul off his guns and no infantry to protect them he faced every artillerist's nightmare — losing guns to the enemy....
> According to Henry Abbott that credit was due to twenty-four-year-old Corporal George Curtis, a West Chelmsford shoemaker turned sniper who belonged to the First Andrew Sharpshooters. Lieutenant Colonel Wass had thrown out skirmishers to pursue the retreating rebels, and Curtis and his squad were the Twentieth Massachusetts's contribution to that detail. Seeing that McIntosh's guns were only defended by skirmishers, Corporal Curtis perpetrated a time-honored battlefield fraud. "He frightened the skirmishers back by ... pretending he was leading a heavy body of men to attack, and giving commands in a loud voice as if to [suggest] that a regiment [was] close behind." The rebels fled and Curtis triumphantly (if foolishly — the nearby ruins and woods teemed with rebel sharpshooters) mounted one of the guns and waved his hat.[19]

Major Abbott reported:

> The First Company of Andrew Sharpshooters, attached to this regiment, thrown out as skirmishers immediately after the enemy retired, gradually advancing at first, finally at the run, captured two pieces of a battery which the enemy had placed in front of our line, but which had been deserted except by a few skirmishers. The first man at the guns was Corpl. George Curtis, of the same company, to whom belongs the credit of

originating and effecting the capture of these two guns, the first which were taken from this battery.[20]

At about nine o'clock that night, Sergeant Hammond's picket guard returned, as did Sergeant Gilbreth's skirmishers. The 2nd Corps then moved off the right flank and marched to within two and a half miles of Churchville, where they encamped. The Company Record noted that Cyrus Hatch had been wounded in the face and was immediately placed in the ambulance train, and that their day and night march had totaled thirty-two miles.

They marched at daybreak on the morning of October 15 for about one and a half miles southeast of Bristoe Station, then halted to rest. They could hear the enemy shelling the forward pickets. About nine o'clock that morning, they marched northeast for another mile and a half and occupied trenches with the 3rd Brigade. They could still hear firing in the distance, and supposed it came from Union forces engaged with the enemy at the railway. Rations of fresh meat and hardtack were delivered to the men, as they had marched about three miles that day.

The Sharpshooters remained in this camp through October 18, still assigned to the 20th Massachusetts Volunteer Infantry. Sutlers came into camp; the men drilled and were inspected daily. They were issued three days' rations, giving them a total of nine days' worth of rations. They supposed they would soon march again, as whenever they were about to march the commissary would issue more rations than they could carry. On October 19, they were awoken at daybreak and ordered to pack up everything. At eight o'clock, they marched three miles past Manassas Station, halted, and encamped. They had marched twelve miles that day. On the morning of the 20th, they broke camp at six o'clock and marched southwest for twenty-two miles, where they encamped within one mile of Little Auburn.

The Sharpshooters remained in that camp until October 23, performing picket duty daily. On the morning of the 24th, they packed up and marched until three o'clock that afternoon, and then encamped within two miles of Warrenton. They had gone nine miles. The Sharpshooters remained in that camp until November 6, 1863. The entire time they performed daily picket duty, and on all but five days, they performed regimental and division drill. They were mustered and paid on October 31.

At seven thirty on the morning of November 7, the Sharpshooters marched seven miles to Warren Junction, seven miles to Bealeton, and seven miles to Morrisville. Then they went another five miles, to within a mile of Kelly's Ford, where they halted for the night. They had marched twenty-six miles carrying seven days' rations. It was a hot and dusty march.

They left camp at six thirty in the morning of November 8. They marched toward Kelly's Ford and crossed the Rappahannock on a pontoon bridge, where they formed a brigade line of battle. Moving forward a mile and a half, they came upon a Rebel camp that had just been vacated. They found fresh beef in the huts and many tools strewn around the camp, and they captured six prisoners. They remained there for some time, and then moved toward Brandy Station, where the 3rd Division was engaged with the enemy. They marched until four o'clock that afternoon and camped for the night. While there, General Meade and his staff passed through their camp. They had marched eight miles, and their position was four miles southwest of Kelly's Ford. They had heard heavy firing all day.

They remained in that camp until November 10, when they left at eight in the morning, marched three miles, and camped in the woods. They remained camped in the woods until November 23, performing picket duty each day up to the 19th. They also took part in division drill and inspections. On November 24, they were awoken at four o'clock in the morning, had breakfast, then marched about two miles and were ordered to return to camp. They remained until the 26th, when they left camp at six o'clock in the morning. They marched toward the Rapidan River and halted one mile from Germanna Ford. From noon until four o'clock, they waited for pontoons to be set. They then crossed the river, marched two miles south, and encamped along the Orange Plank Road. Sergeant Curtis and three Sharpshooters were sent out on picket duty.[21]

At seven o'clock in the morning of November 27, they broke camp and marched about three miles southwest. There they heard firing ahead of them as the front columns met the enemy about one mile from Robertson's Tavern. They were halted and loaded arms, and the entire 2nd Division ran on the double toward the sound of battle. The Sharpshooters were ordered to support an artillery battery engaged with the enemy, who were being driven into the woods by the skirmishers of 15th Massachusetts Volunteer Infantry and the 8th Ohio Volunteer Infantry. On the left of the road beyond Robertson's Tavern, the 1st Division was heavily engaged with the enemy, and succeeded in driving the enemy back. The Sharpshooters with the 20th Massachusetts were moved forward and sent out on picket duty to relieve those men who had been skirmishing. They had moved twelve miles that day.

On November 28, the Sharpshooters were up at dawn, and half of the regiment was deployed as skirmishers. The Sharpshooters were sent ahead on picket duty, and were heavily engaged throughout the day. They captured three rebels, and two of their own men, Corporal Joseph Wood and Private George Bancroft, were wounded. They were under hot fire until dark, when Sergeant Curtis rejoined the Sharpshooters with his two men. At this time Private James Shepard was reported missing, presumed to have been either killed or taken prisoner. He had last been seen fighting with guerrillas near Ely Ford. The Sharpshooters marched back about one mile and encamped.[22]

They broke camp at eight o'clock on the morning of November 29 and marched back to Robertson's Tavern, where the 2nd Corps changed position with the 5th Corps. From there they marched to the intersection of the Orange Plank Road and White Hall Church, where a Federal cavalry post was located. Because enemy cavalry were believed to be in the woods formerly occupied by the 5th Corps, the Sharpshooters and 20th Massachusetts were sent forward on reconnaissance. They found the enemy about four miles into the woods. The 20th Massachusetts were sent forward as skirmishers, while the Sharpshooters remained in a line of battle and drove the enemy farther into the woods. The enemy opened fire with shell, and as the Sharpshooters did not have artillery in position, they formed a skirmish line and remained there until eight o'clock that night, when they were relieved by the 59th New York Regiment. They then marched about a half a mile and encamped beside brigade headquarters. They had marched about twelve miles that day.

As the Sharpshooters were awoken at two in the morning of November 30, they learned that General Lee had selected his field of battle and entrenched his men behind Mine Run. With a swamp and river about one hundred feet below him, he was well fortified. The Union generals decided to attempt to go around his right side and flank Lee's army. The 20th Massachusetts and Sharpshooters were part of that movement.

At three in the morning, they marched across the Orange Plank Road about a mile and a half and formed a brigade line of battle along the entire front of the 2nd Corps, part of the 3rd Corps on their right, and part of the 6th Corps on their left. General Warren was to fire a shot that would signal a charge of 28,000 men against the Rebels at Mine Run. General Warren had stated that every Rebel in those works should and must be taken. They were to charge without knapsacks. As the cold was intense and no fires were allowed, the men suffered greatly. The Sharpshooters' nerves were in ruins at the thought of leading an assault against such an impregnable position; it seemed that many would fall that day.

That shot never came; there was to be no movement that day. At daylight, it was observed that the Rebels had greatly increased in number and also had increased their fortifications. Had the Union advanced, it would probably have sacrificed a great many men. Instead, they marched back one mile and encamped for the night. They had marched three miles that day.

On December 1, 1863, the Sharpshooters spent all day in a line of battle. They threw up breastworks in front of them, and by eight o'clock that night, they had packed everything and begun their retreat. As usual, the 2nd Corps and the Sharpshooters formed the rear guard. At midnight, they had only moved three miles, as they stopped frequently to allow the wagon trains and artillery to pass them. They moved along the Orange Plank Road until daylight, the woods filled with stragglers worn out with fatigue. Continuing on, they halted two miles north of Ely Ford, crossing the river after the 3rd and 6th Corps. They then formed a line of march and headed toward Brandy Station, which they reached at nine o'clock at night on the 2nd. It had been the most difficult march they had endured. They had marched thirty-five miles in twenty-five hours, and were completely worn out. They dropped their knapsacks, made coffee, and tried to rest.

The Sharpshooters remained in that camp until nine o'clock on the morning of December 5, when they marched three miles and camped at Stevensburg. They left that camp at nine in the morning of the 7th, marching two miles to Lookout Mountain. There they encamped and were assigned picket duty. On December 8, they were mustered and paid for the months of September through December, and their clothing accounts were settled. As usual, when they received pay, the sutlers arrived. The men were ordered on picket duty until December 15, when Sergeant Curtis received a ten-day furlough. They remained in camp and did not appear to have any duty assigned to them.[23]

In late 1863, the government realized that for more than half of all volunteer units that enlisted in 1861, their three-year service term would expire later in 1864, creating a great shortage of troops. The War Department and state governments devised General Order No. 191, which would make reenlistment payments of $402.00 by the Federal Government, $60.00 by local towns, and $325.00 by the state. The volunteers also would receive a thirty-day furlough and free transportation to their homes.[24]

On December 21, a list was made of the entire group of veteran Sharpshooters who would reenlist. Only three came forward: William Packard, Jason Rines, and Alonzo Bartlett. Bartlett must have changed his mind, as he mustered out at the end of his enlistment, on September 2, 1864.[25]

As they remained in camp on December 23, a list was made of all the old and new men of the Sharpshooters. The same privileges would be extended to the men who had enlisted in 1862. The original veterans' time would expire in September 1864. On the 24th, Lieutenant Gilbreth, a sergeant, and three Sharpshooters were ordered to three days of picket duty near Kelly's Ford.

The Sharpshooters remained in camp on Christmas Day. Only a portion of the new men who had signed their reenlistment papers were allowed to go on furlough. The 20th Massachusetts supplied the Sharpshooters plum pudding, a ration of whiskey, and roasted turkey. On December 26, Sergeant Curtis returned to the Sharpshooters. All was quiet as the men remained in camp on the 27th. On the 28th, Nathan Ellis, Frank Matt, Henry Morse, William Packard, and Jason Rines were discharged retroactive to December 19. The following day they all reenlisted as Veteran Volunteers under the provisions of the War Department's General Order No. 191. As they remained in camp through the end of December, nearly all the men were engaged in picket or fatigue duty.[26]

8

Death of a Dueling Sharpshooter

For the month of January 1864, the Sharpshooters remained in camp. Each day no fewer than four men were on fatigue duty. On January 5, Packard, Rines, and Morse left for home on a thirty-five day furlough. Lieutenant Gilbreth took a fifteen-day furlough, and a sergeant and two Sharpshooters were assigned picket duty. On Sunday, January 11, Major Abbott inspected them. Starting on the 20th, they performed battalion drill for ten days in a row. On that day, Sergeant Nathan Ellis also was commissioned as 1st lieutenant and transferred to the 20th Massachusetts.[1]

All remained the same in camp until reveille sounded at three o'clock in the morning on January 6. The men packed up, leaving their tents and sick in care of the camp guard. At seven o'clock that morning, they marched to the Rapidan River, arriving at Morton's Ford at about eleven o'clock that morning. They halted, and the 2nd Division formed a brigade line of battle. The 3rd Division waded across the ford and took shelter in a ravine, then sent skirmishers forward. Without much effect, the enemy fired their cannons at them with shot and shell. General Hays advanced his line of skirmishers and received fire from a Rebel battalion, driving the Union men back to the ravine. They remained there until about nine that night, when the 2nd Division, with the Sharpshooters in the lead, crossed a hastily-made wooden bridge and relieved them. The 2nd formed a line of battle and remained in that position until the 3rd Division had crossed the river. Then they buried the dead and removed the wounded from the field. The Sharpshooters crossed the river without casualty and remained in a line of battle all night and through the next day. At seven o'clock on the night of January 7, they marched by way of Stevensburg and returned to their camp about ten o'clock on that night.

The Sharpshooters remained in that camp until May 3, 1864, performing the usual winter quarter duties. They were inspected constantly. Some men went on and returned from furloughs. The Sharpshooters were in good health and spirits as they marched at nine o'clock the night of May 3. The Sharpshooters remained with the 20th Massachusetts, and the two units took their place in the 2nd Corps.

They crossed the Rapidan River at Ely's Ford at daylight on the morning of May 4. Their march continued until two o'clock that afternoon, when they arrived at Chancellorsville, and encamped near the old battlefields. The weather had been very warm and the roads dusty on that eighteen-mile march. On the morning of May 5, the Sharpshooters packed up at three o'clock, and at five o'clock they marched four miles to Block House and formed a line of battle. Lying on their arms all night, they heard heavy firing on their front and right.

At four thirty on the morning of May 6, the Sharpshooters were ordered out on a skirmish line. Heavy firing attacked their front and left, then changed to their right and rear. At four o'clock that afternoon, they were ordered to the Plank Road, where they formed a line of battle and expected to be attacked. On the 7th, at four o'clock in the afternoon, they were ordered to move to the right. Doing so, they lay on their arms, as they expected to be moved again.

At five o'clock in the morning of May 8, they were ordered to move four miles to the left, near Todd's Tavern. They remained there until two o'clock in the afternoon, when they marched to the left and supported the 5th and 6th Corps. They lay on their arms all night. At six o'clock in the morning of the 9th, the Sharpshooters moved right about a mile and built breastworks. At nine o'clock that morning, they advanced all the way to the Po River, arriving there at six o'clock. That night, Sergeant Curtis and six Sharpshooters were ordered to protect the crossings at two fords. Before the Sharpshooters were sent out on picket duty that night, General Gibbon highly complimented Sergeant Curtis, Alonzo Bartlett, Samuel Chase, Cyrus Hatch, Charles Harrington, Nathaniel Penniman, and Albert Young for the manner in which they protected the fords that day.[2]

At daylight on the morning of May 10, as they remained on picket duty, they were ordered to advance as skirmishers. The Sharpshooters were engaged heavily until about eleven that morning, when the enemy flanked them and forced them to retire across the river. They moved about a mile to the left and rejoined the brigade, where they lay in line in front of the skirmishers that night.

At daylight on May 11, the enemy sent out skirmishers, but met heavy resistance from the Sharpshooters, and was forced to take shelter behind its breastworks. During the skirmish, Sergeant Packard was slightly wounded in the face. The Sharpshooters began digging rifle pits with their hands, bayonets, and old knapsacks. General Webb visited them and ordered them to provide two men for pioneer duty. At about midnight the Sharpshooters moved out and marched to the left about five miles.

On the morning of May 12, the Sharpshooters formed a line of battle with the 20th Massachusetts, to fight in a battle that would be known as the Bloody Angle. Just before daylight, in a heavy fog and rain, they charged the enemy's works and captured twenty pieces of artillery and about five thousand prisoners, including one major and two brigadier generals. The enemy repeatedly attempted to retake its works, but each time was repulsed and suffered heavy casualties. The armies fought furiously throughout the day and into the night. Often they were only a few yards apart as they clubbed and bayoneted each other. The Sharpshooters were so close to the enemy that four of them were taken prisoners: Sergeant Anselm Hammond, Corporal Austin Upton, and Privates Ferdinand Crossman and Henry Morse.[3]

In the pre-dawn hours of May 13, the enemy withdrew. Ordered out to perform sharpshooting, the Sharpshooters did very good service that day — not without loss, as Amos Plimpton was severely wounded in his right leg. As the men walked onto the battlefield, they could not believe the horrific sight. The *Historical Times Illustrated Encyclopedia of the Civil War* recounts, "In a square mile of terrain, 12,000 men lay as casualties. One particularly sanguinary area became known as the 'Bloody Angle.' A Federal soldier described the ordeal as *the most terrible day I have ever lived.*"[4]

On May 14, the Sharpshooters were ordered to the field to protect men as they withdrew two guns and eight limbers that lay between the armies' lines. At three o'clock in the morning of May 15, the Sharpshooters moved about two miles to the left as the brigades closed en masse. They rested until about six o'clock that evening, then moved another mile and encamped.

The Sharpshooters remained in camp until six o'clock in the evening of May 16, at which time the brigade and one battery escorted the ambulances loaded with wounded to the hospital. On the 17th, at eleven thirty at night, they moved to the right and occupied the old enemies' works that were taken on May 12.

Thirteen hundred yards behind those works, over uneven ground, General Lee had constructed a highly defensible new set of works at the base of Mule Shoe. At three thirty in the morning of May 18, the Sharpshooters and the 20th Massachusetts led the charge on General Lee's new position. They hotly contested them, raking them with artillery shot and canister as well as infantry fire, and repulsed them. The Sharpshooters fought not only the enemy, but also the stench from the decomposed bodies which had been partially buried or remained exposed on the battlefield since the battle of the 12th. Driven back to the first line, the Sharpshooters paid a price in that battle, as Sergeant George Curtis was mortally wounded and Privates Nathaniel Penniman and Thomas Smith were seriously wounded. The Sharpshooters then were ordered out on the skirmish line.[5]

At five o'clock in the evening of May 19, the Sharpshooters were ready to march. At seven o'clock that night, they marched about a mile to the right and then returned and encamped for the night. At three thirty on the morning of May 20, the Sharpshooters were awakened and ordered to prepare for a march. At eleven forty-five that night, they marched down the Bowling Green Road, arriving at Bowling Green at ten in the morning of the 21st, and at Milford Station at three o'clock that afternoon. They built breastworks and camped for the night two miles south of the station. At two o'clock on the afternoon of May 22, they crossed the Mattaponi River and encamped. Sergeant Packard and three Sharpshooters were sent out on a picket line.

At five o'clock in the morning of May 23, reveille was sounded, and at seven o'clock, the Sharpshooters marched toward Ox Ford. They crossed the Richmond and Potomac Railroad at four thirty that afternoon, threw up breastworks, and camped for the night. It had been a difficult march: the heat had been intense, and they had had to walk through thick clouds of dust raised by thousands of men marching in front of them.

At ten thirty in the morning of May 24, they moved across the North Anna River and were sent out on a skirmish line. General Lee's army was heavily entrenched on the south side of the river across from Ox Ford. The Company Log reported heavy firing, and that the Sharpshooters did good execution. That night they were sent out again on picket duty. They remained in a line of battle until ten o'clock at night on May 26, when they moved to the river crossing. Although there was more distance between the Sharpshooters and the enemy, Lee's artillery had good coordinates and managed to drop shells among the Union forces. On May 27, they marched to the left along the Pamunkey River toward Hanovertown and camped within five miles of the river.

The Sharpshooters crossed the Pamunkey River at noon and marched up the Peninsula two miles, where they halted and constructed breastworks. Not too far in front of them, the cavalry was engaged with the enemy. On May 29, the Sharpshooters marched about a mile to the left, halted, and formed into a new line of battle. Then they were ordered to march through the night. At four thirty on the morning of the 30th, they had advanced about three miles, and at eleven o'clock that morning they were sent out as skirmishers. In their intense engagement with the enemy, Privates George Allen and Benjamin McLaughlin were mortally wounded, and Private Albert Young was slightly wounded. On May 31, the company was sent out to do sharpshooting all day.[6]

At about nine on the morning of June 1, the Sharpshooters charged the enemy lines with a skirmish line. They were successful and drove the enemy back to their main entrenchment. At five that afternoon, the brigade charged those entrenchments and was repulsed, leaving the Sharpshooters in the front as skirmishers.

2nd Corps crossing the North Anna River, Virginia, May 23, 1864. That is the bridge the Sharpshooters crossed at 10:30 A.M. on the 23rd. Timothy O'Sullivan, traveling with the 2nd Corps, captured that picture (Library of Congress).

At daylight on June 2, the Sharpshooters followed the army to the left, arriving at Cold Harbor about four o'clock in the afternoon. The brigade closed en masse and camped for the night. At ten o'clock in the morning of the 3rd, the Sharpshooters were sent out to support the 10th Massachusetts Battery. They stayed on the line and did sharpshooting throughout that day and June 4 and 5. There was an enemy artillery unit with three pieces directly in front of them. The artillerists dared not load their cannons, as every time they exposed themselves to operate their equipment they were shot down by the Andrew Sharpshooters.

On June 6, they were out sharpshooting again and were reported to have done excellent execution against the enemy works, at one point as close as fifty yards. On June 7, their sharpshooting involved them in a particularly vicious battle. Although pickets often agreed not to fire on each other without warning, such courtesy did not prevail here. Anyone exposed was shot.

Finally, a truce flag flew on June 8. As the men went out to collect the wounded and inter the dead, the battlefield lay strewn with decomposed bodies which left a putrid stench. The armies met between the lines, conversed, and swapped newspapers. Under a general agreement, the men reverted to the old rules and refrained from firing on each other until the other side was warned.

At nine o'clock in the morning of June 9, the Rebels yelled across the line that the firing would start. The Sharpshooters remained on the line and did sharpshooting through the morning of the 11th. There was some sort of informal truce, as the Sharpshooters exchanged papers with the Rebels that morning before ten o'clock, when the firing resumed.

The Sharpshooters were relieved at one o'clock in the afternoon of June 12, when they went back about a half of a mile and camped for a much-needed rest. At eight o'clock in the evening of June 13, the Sharpshooters marched toward the Chickahominy River. They marched through the night for about fifty miles, crossed at Long Bridge at two in the afternoon of the 14th, and arrived near Charles City Courthouse just about midnight.

On June 15, they marched to the James River and arrived at Akins's Landing at about five thirty in the afternoon, when they were ferried across and landed at Windmill Point. They then marched two miles and formed a line of battle. At noon on the 16th, they marched along the River Road, then turned left and headed toward Petersburg, where they arrived at eleven thirty that night. They formed a line of battle in the enemy's old works and relieved the 18th Corps. The Sharpshooters were assigned picket duty, and at four o'clock in the morning of June 17, they were sent out as skirmishers. They quietly dug rifle pits, in some cases as close to twenty yards from the enemy works.

At five o'clock in the morning on June 18, the Sharpshooters and the 20th Massachusetts led the division in a charge on the enemy works, only to find them empty. At seven twenty that morning, the Sharpshooters and the 20th Massachusetts advanced a quarter of a mile through some woods and entered an open field with a sunken road in front of the line of enemy works. They moved forward, and when they were within one hundred yards of the works, the enemy opened fire on them. Immediately they constructed breastworks, hunkered down, and held their position in the sunken road. The battle was short, but they faced horrific fire from the enemy.[7]

The Company Record states that Lieutenant Gilbreth was killed by a ball in the face. In *Harvard's Civil War: A History of the Twentieth Massachusetts Volunteer Infantry,* Richard Miller sheds more light on his death:

> [A] man of extraordinary coolness and daring. There was no reason to question either judgment, but on the afternoon of 18 [June] the lanky sharpshooter's virtues had become something else. Firing had tapered off along the Twentieth Massachusetts's front as men warily eyed the opposing earthworks. Suddenly a Confederate [s]harpshooter, his mind warped no less than a few of his blue counterparts, leaped onto his parapet and challenged any Federal sharpshooter to a duel. Lieutenant Gilbreth decided to oblige. Probably at some arranged signal, both men fired; when the smoke cleared, the rebel was down. Now Gilbreth offered a challenge and several rebels accepted; Gilbreth dropped them all. Meanwhile, frantic comrades tried to persuade the lieutenant to stop his craziness. But no! He would not listen, became very excited as his success multiplied.... Finally darkness ended the contests—but not the craziness. The lieutenant was so exhilarated that he claimed with much bluster a charmed life.... The lieutenant announced that he would renew the contest in the morning.... The charm gave out the next morning. As promised, Gilbreth mounted the works, issued his challenge, and was met by an obliging duelist from the rebel line. Just as the two men raised their muskets the contest was ended when a third rebel sent a bullet zinging through Gilbreth's mouth and into his spine. Paralyzed from the neck down, he was taken to [Doctor] Perry, who pronounced the wound mortal. Lieutenant Gilbreth's last words: "I hit him anyway, Doctor."[8]

On June 19, the Sharpshooters were assigned sharpshooting in the front. On the 20th, they marched to the left and were relieved by the 6th Corps. They then moved off the front line at eleven that morning and encamped. On June 21, the Sharpshooters were sent back to the front.

General Grant asked his staff if the Union army was fit to assault and capture Petersburg. All reports said that the men were worn down from their previous battles and the extremely difficult march to Petersburg. The march had been especially grueling due to its speed and to the extremely hot weather, in which the men had marched entirely without water. Rather than assaulting the city, Grant decided to besiege it.

On June 22, General Lee had sent a regiment around the Union earthworks. The 20th Massachusetts met and stopped them. Part of the Sharpshooters' regiment was detailed with the 20th Massachusetts, and the remainder was with brigade headquarters, assigned provost guard duty. In the confusion caused by the enemy's flanking them, some Union men tried to run off, and it was the Sharpshooter provost guards' responsibility to stop them.

On June 23, the Sharpshooters remained part of the Siege of Petersburg. They moved several times to different locations, and were on picket and skirmish duty, manning or building trenches until June 26, when they marched at five in the afternoon toward the Point of Rocks on the Appomattox River, where they arrived around midnight. They crossed the river, arriving at the James River near Deep Bottom. At five thirty on the morning of June 27, they crossed to the north bank and formed a line of battle. A lieutenant took six of the Sharpshooters out on a skirmish line.

On June 28, they moved to the right and formed in a line of battle. They could hear a heavy cavalry fight going on in front of them, so they built and occupied trenches. Later in the afternoon, they moved to the left and camped for the night. At eight fifteen in the morning, they retraced their same route and returned to their old works, continuing the Siege of Petersburg. It appears that General Grant feigned a movement toward Richmond in an effort to force General Lee to remove some of his troops from Petersburg to protect Richmond. The Company Record states that they were in camp at Petersburg until August 9, which is when the Company Record ended. It is unclear what the company did from that point on, though they remained assigned to the 20th Massachusetts. The fact that Private Daniel Eaton was wounded on August 25, 1864, at Ream's Station, confirms that they marched on August 12 with the 20th Massachusetts.[9]

At noon that day, the Sharpshooters marched to City Point with the 20th Massachusetts. On August 13, they boarded steamers which were to move five miles downriver to give General Lee the impression that they were going to reinforce Washington. They then reversed direction and headed to Deep Bottom. For some time, the weather was extremely hot and without rain, covering everything with a fine dust and making the march difficult. Some of the men dropped and died from heat exposure and sunstroke.

They arrived at Deep Bottom at two thirty in the morning of August 14. The commander of the 2nd Corps realized that Deep Bottom would not be deep enough to accommodate the steamers, so he sent a work crew to construct temporary wharves. When the first steamer attempted to dock, the ebbing tide made it clear that the wharves were too few and too short. The steamers docked parallel to each other, and men leaped from one boat to another, a feat made difficult by multiple decks loaded with men and gangplanks that were only large enough for two files of men at a time. It took five hours to disembark, and the Sharpshooters did not clear the steamers until dawn.

They lined up in formation with their division, rapidly advancing in columns to the right of Mott to the Jennings's House, west of Bailey's Creek and north of the Darbytown Road. The men were dehydrated from their voyage, and the extreme heat caused many to fall to the side of the road. A surgeon from another regiment found one unidentified man of the 20th Massachusetts; his body was rigid and convulsing and his mouth closed so tightly that the surgeon had to pry it open to give him water.[10]

The Sharpshooters and the 20th Massachusetts were under the command of General William Barlow and Colonel George Macy. Barlow suffered from acute diarrhea and was also grieving, as he had interred his wife two weeks earlier. Barlow did not lead his troops in his usual aggressive manner, at a swift pace. He proceeded cautiously while he maintained connection with Mott. Barlow advanced west on Darbytown Road in a line of battle. His skirmishers came in contact with dismounted enemy cavalry armed with repeating rifles. Barlow ordered his first troops to go forward and a New York artillery unit to shell the enemy. The New York Artillery unit "did not do credit to itself," and his first line of troops veered sharply to the left, avoided the enemy, and met with the Union skirmish line on their left. He then

Landing at Deep Bottom, Virginia. In August of 1864, General Grant feigned a movement toward Richmond. He attempted to have General Lee remove some of his troops from the siege at Petersburg to defend Richmond. At the same time Grant ordered transport to move some of his troops, which included the Sharpshooters, in an attempt to have General Lee think his troops were moving out to defend Washington, D.C., but they went to Deep Bottom. As the Sharpshooters arrived, possibly on board the transport *Linda,* of Philadelphia, they could not debark. As seen the water was too shallow to land. Crews were called out and temporary wharves were constructed (Library of Congress).

sent in an Irish Brigade that "behaved disgracefully," veered sharply to the right, avoided the enemy, and took shelter in the woods.[11]

At this point, the enemy was well-reinforced and shelled Barlow's open position from Fussell's Farm. Barlow sent out another brigade to concentrate on Fussell's Farm but was also disappointed in their efforts. He then called up Macy's brigade, which included the 20th Massachusetts and the Sharpshooters. They advanced to a crest behind Fussell's Mill, went prone on the ground, and waited while an assault plan was being formulated.

Macy formulated a plan, and the 20th Massachusetts and the Sharpshooters went forward. Advancing over the crest, they found two ravines, one with two ditches about thirty feet apart and the other an ascending bank of about forty-five degrees. Thirty to sixty yards beyond the steep incline were the enemy breastworks. Bailey's Creek separated the ravines from the enemy breastworks. On their right, the creek had been dammed to form a mill pond. The ravines, matted heavily with blackberry bushes and dense brush, were almost impossible for men to pass through. The Sharpshooters could see the enemy being more strongly reinforced by the minute.

The order to charge was given. Over the crest and into the ravine, the Sharpshooters and 20th Massachusetts charged. As they moved down into the ravine, they were exposed to a steady enemy fire, and most of the losses occurred at that time. In an attempt to inspire his men, Macy led the charge on horseback, and his horse was soon shot out from under him. Returning with a second horse, he suffered the same result, only this time the horse fell on him and caused severe internal bleeding. The Sharpshooters and 20th Massachusetts advanced to the second ravine, and a few men moved forward at the mill pond flank. Seasoned veterans, those men could see the enemy's impregnable position, and thought it wise to stop their futile advance.[12]

The Sharpshooters and the 20th Massachusetts were in an unmanageable position, unable to either advance or retreat. They remained in the second ravine until dark and then made a hasty retreat. For the remainder of the Deep Bottom campaign, the Sharpshooters and 20th Massachusetts acted as picket guards. On August 20, in a heavy rainstorm, the men marched back to their camp at Petersburg by way of Point of Rocks, where they arrived at six thirty in the morning of the 21st. The condition of the roads in the heavy rain made the march difficult, and their uniforms were soaked.

South of Petersburg, at Weldon Station, General Lee had a food and munitions support line which General Grant wanted to close. On August 18th, he ordered the 5th Corps there with the intent of disrupting Lee's line of supplies. Grant ordered the destruction of rails and bridges as far south as he could protect his working parties.

On August 23, the Sharpshooters and 20th Massachusetts, not yet rested from their last campaign, were ordered to Weldon Station. They marched at five o'clock that evening, and arrived at Ream's Station on the morning of August 24. They were ordered to destroy the railroad up to eight miles south of Ream's Station to Rowanty Creek. The 20th Massachusetts and the Sharpshooters were ordered on picket duty to protect the workforce that destroyed the railroad and bridges. The Federal entrenchments were poor and noncontiguous due to the railroad's elevation and various locations of woods, out of which the enemy could quietly advance. These conditions made the workforce and the pickets vulnerable. General Hancock was aware of the poor fortifications, but with reports of no major enemy activity, he continued destroying the rails. Amid reports of some minor skirmishing with dismounted Rebel cavalry, the work continued.

The Union cavalry returned and advised General Hancock that a large enemy force was on the move toward the work party. Having been relieved as pickets, the Sharpshooters and the 20th Massachusetts moved behind the breastworks. General Lee had thought about abandoning Weldon Station and fortifying other railroads west of it, farther out of the Federals' reach, but General Sheridan already had destroyed most of them. Lee had no choice but to take back Weldon for no other purpose than to obtain food for his besieged men.

On August 25, the Sharpshooters and 20th Massachusetts were placed in a reserve position toward the center of the noncontiguous Federal lines, on the eastern side of the railroad cut, twenty yards to the rear of the Consolidated Brigade. From this position, they were protected from enemy fire and could easily support any part of the line that needed help. The ground rose at the rail bed and protected them from enemy fire, but it also obstructed their view of the battle. They nervously waited in a cornfield as they heard the battle roar.

At five o'clock that afternoon, the enemy attacked the Federals' front and left side, raking them with rifle and artillery fire. For fifteen minutes, the enemy opened with such a barrage of artillery that Federals jumped out of their entrenchments, as they preferred rifle fire over artillery fire. After the barrage, the enemy infantry attacked. The Federal line held their fire until the enemy was close enough that they could do serious damage to them. The Rebels retreated, and it seemed the Federals' line held.

But the Rebels attacked again, and the Federal lines retreated. The Sharpshooters could hear the roar of the battle as an officer climbed to the top of the railroad cut to view the action. To his amazement, he saw Federal troops cut and run and saw the Federals to his left drop their rifles and flee. The enemy poured through the open gaps in the line and advanced on the Federals' center, right, and left lines as they broke and ran.[13]

The Sharpshooters and the 20th Massachusetts soon found themselves exposed on both sides of the cornfield and in their rear. Most of the men held their position and fought as others broke and ran. They managed to fire two volleys and did considerable damage to the enemy. But they soon found themselves completely surrounded, and further resistance was futile. They had no other option than to surrender.

Among the Sharpshooters who were taken prisoner were Isaac Mudgett, William Packard, Joseph Smart, and Charles Stone. Wounded were Daniel Eaton and Charles Harrington. This would prove to be a sad day for the Sharpshooters and the 20th Massachusetts. Adding to the unfortunate circumstances, the Sharpshooters were only a week away from their expiration of service. Two months later, Joseph Smart died of disease as a prisoner at Salisbury, North Carolina.[14]

This was the last action the Sharpshooters would see as an organization. There is no record of their return to Massachusetts, except for the mustering out of Sharpshooters on dates ranging from September 3 to 15, 1864. The remaining Sharpshooters who had enlisted later than those at Lynnfield, and those who had reenlisted, eventually would be assigned to the 19th Massachusetts Volunteer Infantry, Company K. Thus came the end of the 1st Company of Andrew Sharpshooters as a military organization.

PART II

The Second Company of Andrew Sharpshooters

One hundred forty-seven men were assigned to the Second Company. Their service was somewhat different than that of the First Company. Assigned to only one regiment for their entire length of service, they were a part of a special regiment which included infantry, artillery, and sharpshooters, the only such regiment to leave from Massachusetts. When they lost the equipment to maintain their long-range rifles and were forced to accept Sharp's breech-loading rifles, they refused to take the new rifles and were called "mutinous traitors." Their own commander threatened to have them shot to death or sent to a federal prison. The infantry trained them on battle tactics, and their entire form of service changed. Primarily used very effectively as skirmishers, they did an enormous amount of pioneer work.

Like many Civil War soldiers, their three years of service were very difficult. They marched over a thousand miles through snow, rain, mud, and dust, often without rest, food, or water. Complaining among themselves about their type of service, they believed they were not used as they were told they would be. They believed their recruitment promises were broken and felt deceived by the government. This honorable and proud group of men was prompt to obey all orders without complaint to their superiors, but they did complain about their superiors among themselves.

As skirmishers they spent horrific nights under deadly artillery and infantry fire. In positions so overpowered that the men could not be relieved, they tried to bury themselves in the ground. At times they were in such fear that they aged overnight, and thought they would not survive until morning. When they passed through the Shenandoah Valley, the sights reminded them of good old New England, and they longed for home. Yet they honorably did their service and led the way when it came to strict military discipline. Their camps and equipment were always in good shape. A mature group of men, they took care of themselves as best they could with the materials available to them.

They fought battles at Gaines' Mill, Yorktown, Mechanicsville, Malvern Hill, Fredericksburg, Chancellorsville, Gettysburg, Bristoe Station, Rappahannock Station, Mine Run, Cold Harbor, Laurel Hill, Spotsylvania, Totopotomoy, Bethesda Church, Siege of Petersburg, and numerous skirmishes as vedettes as well as in support of other units.

In the early part of the war, ignorance of sanitation methods took a toll on the 147 men, as twelve men died of disease and sixty-four were given disability discharges. Thirty-one men were wounded in action, of whom two died of their wounds. Nine men were killed in action. Four men were taken as prisoners of war, and two men deserted.

Though they honored and served Massachusetts well, they paid a heavy price. Their commanders respected them, and when fearless skirmishers were needed or reconnoiters were required to get good information, they frequently called on the men to provide these services, for which they earned their honorable and courageous reputations.

The 2nd Company Sharpshooters was organized at Camp Saunders, Lynnfield, Massachusetts, in September 1861. A number of these men were left over from the organization of the 1st Company. The 2nd Company was raised to full strength during the month of September, was commanded by Captain Lewis E. Wentworth, and left Lynnfield to enter the war on October 8, 1861.

They were attached to the 22nd Massachusetts Volunteer Infantry, commanded by Colonel Henry Wilson. Structured differently, the 22nd Regiment would include an infantry regiment, an artillery battery, and a company of sharpshooters. It was created on September 28, 1861, by Special Order No. 483 from the office of the adjutant general of the Commonwealth of Massachusetts.

9

Basil Hall's Farm for Winter Quarters

On October 8, 1861, the Second Company of Andrew Sharpshooters broke camp at four o'clock in the morning in a drizzling rain, after seeing to it that all their equipment was packed for transportation. That included about twenty-five telescopic rifles; the remainder were heavy, open-sighted rifles. The infantry was armed with Enfield rifles. Boarding train cars in Lynnfield, they arrived in Boston without incident or delay. They went into formation at Haymarket Square and, under a heavy rain, marched through the streets of Boston to the Common. There they partook of a collation provided by the citizens of Boston. The Hon. Robert C. Winthrop made a lengthy speech, and a stand of colors was presented. Colonel Wilson responded with a speech, none of which could be heard by the Sharpshooters, who were too far away.[1]

They marched in review and then marched to the Worcester Depot, where they were loaded on a special train, which began moving amid thousands of cheering friends and relatives. At every station along the route people were cheering the soldiers. On one car a steam calliope was installed, and those nearing the train at stations were treated to patriotic music by the strange machine. At Natick, the home of Colonel Wilson, a large assemblage of people was on hand and the regiment was saluted by artillery. They arrived in Worcester at seven o'clock in the evening and stopped for an hour but did not leave the train.

The train arrived in Springfield at ten at night, and remained there about one hour. While there, the fire department entered the cars and provided the soldiers with pails of hot coffee and baskets of food. Ex-lieutenant governor Trask introduced Colonel Wilson to Mayor Bemis, who persuaded the colonel to exit the train and give a speech. Although he did not want to speak, his speech was received with great enthusiasm. The train left Springfield, and the men got as comfortable as they could to sleep. At about three in the morning, the train stopped in New Haven, where the crowds provided the men with coffee and crackers. The men remained there for about forty-five minutes.[2]

At six o'clock in the morning on October 9, they arrived in Bridgeport. The citizens had assembled at nine o'clock the previous evening to greet the men, as that was the time they were to arrive. The citizens had all gone home, and someone, disgusted, had spiked the cannons that were to salute the soldiers. At this short stop, some of the men got off the train to stretch, including a Sharpshooter who was slow to return to the train. Captain Wentworth got off to hurry the man and both were left behind, so they took a regular train and rejoined the unit in New York. Just before they arrived, a soldier riding on top of the train struck his head on a bridge, but fortunately was not seriously injured.

At ten in the morning, they arrived in New York, exited the train, fell in line, and were marched to the railroad company's milk depot, where they were each provided with soup and a New Testament. As no spoons were provided, the soup was not as warmly received as one might expect. The officers, including 2nd Lieutenant Evans, went to the Fifth Avenue House and partook of a fine breakfast provided by Colonel Frank Howe of Massachusetts. Reverend Henry Bellows, of the Sanitary Commission, gave a speech to the officers, and Colonel Wilson replied in kind. Their remarks were followed by those of a number of other people, and the officers returned to the station where the men were. The regiment fell in and marched to Madison Square, where the Hon. James T. Bradley, on behalf of the ladies of New York, presented the regiment with a flag. Colonel Wilson accepted the flag on behalf of his men, replying patriotically and expressing appreciation.

Then, escorted by the Sons of Massachusetts, they were marched down Broadway to the Park Barracks amid the cheers of people who lined the sidewalks and filled windows. Sharpshooters were the subject of enthusiastic remarks, were applauded, and were cheered. Once assured the men would be comfortable and provided for, the officers returned to the Fifth Avenue Hotel for supper.

It was nearly dark when the order came to sling knapsacks and fall in. They marched to the wharf and embarked on the steamer *Battery* and got under way for Amboy at about nine o'clock at night. While under way, two men of the regiment, George Furness and Edward F. Davidson of the 22nd Massachusetts, fell overboard. Although the steamer stopped and lowered boats in an attempt to rescue the men, the attempt was unsuccessful. It was thought that the men in heavy uniforms and equipment sank immediately. While disembarking at Perth Amboy, Alden Burrill of the Sharpshooters fell overboard, and was rescued only with some difficulty.[3]

They boarded the cars of the Camden and Amboy Railroad, got as comfortable as possible, and fell asleep, arriving at Camden in the early morning on October 10. They took ferries across the Delaware River and disembarked in Philadelphia at five thirty in the morning. They were welcomed with a hearty, warm breakfast at the Baptist Bethel Church, on Church Street near the Soldiers' Relief Society. They greatly enjoyed the meal and gave a rousing three cheers to the society. They marched through Fourth, Chestnut, and Broad Streets, ending at the Baltimore and Wilmington Railroad Depot, where they boarded the train and traveled about thirty miles. When it started to rain, the men became uncomfortable.

Arriving at Perryville, Maryland, they boarded ferries and crossed the Susquehanna River to Havre de Grace, Maryland, where they boarded trains to Baltimore. Several delays prevented them from arriving in Baltimore until midnight. They marched across the city, which they found very quiet and peaceful, to the Baltimore and Ohio Railroad Station. A number of the men had served in the 6th Massachusetts Volunteer Infantry (90 days) and had been attacked during the Baltimore Riots while passing through that city. The sharp contrast was not lost on them. At the station, the Relief Society provided them with hot coffee and bread.

They boarded the cars, and were pleased with the expectation that they would be in Washington before morning. But the train sat for five hours before it moved. On the morning of October 11, they found themselves stopped just nine miles outside of Baltimore at the Relay House, waiting for regular trains to pass them. The hungry men complained bitterly; breakfast time had come and passed, and their haversacks were empty. At about eight thirty, the train started again, going but a few miles before it stopped again. This happened several more times, wearing the patience of the men and Colonel Wilson, who informed the conductor that if the train stopped again before reaching Washington, his men would take over and run the train, at bayonet point if necessary. There were no more stops, and the train arrived at Washington at two in the afternoon on Friday, October 11.[4]

It did not take long to disembark from the train, as the men were hungry and uncomfortable from being on the train so long. They fell in and marched to the Soldiers' Rest, but there was no rest. Then they marched to the Soldiers' Retreat and were provided with their first government-supplied meal. After eating and resting they were ordered to fall in and march around the Capitol, down Pennsylvania Avenue to Willard's Hotel, and back to the Retreat. While marching they saw President Lincoln; they saluted him, and he courteously acknowledged the salute. As they ate supper and prepared to situate themselves for the night, the order to fall in was given. They were marched to Woodward's Hall on Pennsylvania Avenue and quartered there, sleeping on hard, wooden floors.

Saturday the 12th found the men quite rested and in good spirits. Details of men unloading equipment more or less filled their day. On October 13, they arose quite early, cleaned up, and awaited orders to march to breakfast. They found out that they would not receive rations until noon, so they went to where they had left the wagons, made coffee, and had some hard bread. They later marched to the Retreat, but received no rations and returned to their barracks.

2nd Lieutenant Alvan Augustus Evans (U.S. Army Military Institute).

At two in the afternoon, the order was given to sling knapsacks and prepare for a march. By way of Long Bridge they crossed the Potomac River past Arlington Estate. They continued on to Ball's Cross-road, by the Chain Bridge Road, for a mile. They then turned to the left toward Falls Church. Inexperienced soldiers found the first long march a trial. Several from the regiment and one Sharpshooter straggled and were picked up by ambulances. During the march they passed many encampments and thought there were enough troops to besiege and conquer the entire Southern Confederacy.

The march brought the regiment to Hall's Hill — a farm so called because it was owned by Basil Hall. Arriving there at eleven at night, the regiment sent out pickets. After dinner was served, just enough tents were pitched to accommodate everyone.[5]

On the morning of October 14, they got up and looked around to see what sort of place they were in. Expecting to be there for some time, they pitched the rest of the tents and cleared the area. By nightfall they had quite a respectable looking encampment. October 14, 15, and 16 were spent bringing their camp up to strict military regulations. They cleaned their guns, cut patches, molded balls, and got their equipment ready for battle. They also cleared a larger area of the camp. On the 15th, Captain Wentworth left for Washington in the early morning and didn't return until late that night. On October 17, they started company drill.

Long Bridge as seen from Washington, D.C. in May of 1865 (Library of Congress).

On the 18th, there was company drill, and in the evening, a regimental dress parade. During this parade the men saw for the first time the "aerial branch of the service," as they observed a hot air balloon ascending from Alexandria, which was in view for about an hour. On Saturday, October 19, it rained heavily, and there was no duty, with the exception of picket duty.

During October, the Army of the Potomac was organized. The Regiment was assigned to General Fitz John Porter's Division. Their brigade was commanded by General J. H. Martindale. On Sunday the 20th, General Martindale was curious to see his new Massachusetts Regiment, the only one of its kind. The men were ordered to pack their knapsacks and fall in for the general's review. He was observed to be a splendid horseman and made quite an impression on the troops. He was well pleased with the troops' appearance and the camp's condition and expressed himself accordingly. After the inspection, he went with the Sharpshooters to their camp and inspected them. He seemed to like their peculiar rifles. In the afternoon the Reverend John Pierpont, the regimental chaplain, conducted divine services, which were attended by many. On October 21, Captain Wentworth started for Washington immediately after breakfast. The Sharpshooters took their rifles and went out for target practice, but found no suitable place to fire their rifles, and returned to camp. There was nothing to do until dress parade.

There was excitement around camp on October 22. Orders were given to cook and pack three days' rations and be prepared to march at five minutes' notice. The soldiers waited patiently until noon, but nothing happened. News began to circulate about the battle at Ball's Bluff. They heard that the Union Army suffered a defeat and that the 15th Massachusetts Volunteer Infantry was badly cut up. They heard that the colonel of the 13th Massachusetts

Volunteer Infantry was taken prisoner, and that Colonel Baker, of a California regiment, had been killed. Although there was no way to verify this information, this information, combined with rumors of orders to march, stirred up the camp. But no orders to march came, and the company retired. On October 23 there were just camp duties, and no news regarding Ball's Bluff. On the 24th all was quiet. Captain Wentworth spent the day in Washington and returned confirming the news of Ball's Bluff.

On October 25, the first cold weather arrived. The officers ordered the men to build furnaces in their tents, and sent men out to gather bricks from the destroyed dwellings that formerly belonged to secessionists. They used Virginia's natural red clay for mortar. They spent October 26 practicing firing their rifles.

The 27th was spent on inspections, divine services, and dress parade. During the dress parade Colonel Wilson resigned from the regiment to assume his senatorial duties. Governor Andrew commissioned Captain Jesse A. Cove, of the Tenth United States Infantry, to the rank of colonel, and he himself assumed command of the regiment. Nothing of importance occurred on October 28.[6]

On October 29, all of the Sharpshooters were ordered to do picket duty. This was the first time the entire company was deployed since encamping at Hall's Hill. They took two days' rations and marched over to the New York 25th Regiment, where they were inspected. From there they marched to their picket post, which was about two miles, northeast of Hall's Church, on the Luvinsville Road and Leesburg Turnpike. Two squads were detached and the rest held in reserve. On October 30, an officer of the 22nd Massachusetts requested that the Sharpshooters be allowed to do their duty as pickets without the aid of infantry, so the infantry was removed. There was no indication that the Rebels were anywhere near their posts. The men were relieved at noon on October 31, marched back to camp, ate some lunch, and went to the woods to discharge their rifles. A short time later it was heard that while one member of the 22nd Infantry was discharging his rifle, a soldier from Cass's Regiment, the 9th Massachusetts, was shot.

From November 1st through the 3rd, it was camp life as usual. The weather was cold and rainy, and at one point a high wind threatened to take down the tents. The Sharpshooters did not lose any, but others were not as fortunate. On the even-

Major W. S. Tilton. The date of this photograph is quoted as being between 1860 and 1870; however, it was probably taken early in the war. He was later promoted to colonel and in 1864 was promoted to brigadier general (Library of Congress).

ing of November 3, the Sharpshooters were told to report for picket duty at seven thirty in the morning.

The Sharpshooters reported for duty as ordered, and marched to the same posts they had held earlier. On November 5, their 1st lieutenant and one of the Sharpshooters were out on a scouting expedition and reported seeing Rebel pickets within two miles. Strict orders were given for the night. Officers and men rode through the area, and led the Sharpshooter to believe there was going to be a battle before the day was over, but nothing happened. All was quiet until they were relieved on November 6 at eleven thirty in the morning. The only thing that bothered them was the rain. After they marched back to camp, they felt as though they were getting home from a disagreeable visit.

In an attempt to break the monotony of camp life, Major Tilton presented the regiment with a football and had checkerboards placed in all of the tents. After dress parade, when the weather was pleasant, there was always a lively football game. That had a positive effect on the men's health and spirits. After retreat was sounded, candles were lit in the tents and the men played checkers or cards. With the aid of the regimental band, there was singing and music, all of which were good for the men's spirits.

All was quiet on November 7 and 8; Captain Wentworth went to Washington again, but came back without any news. On November 9, the Sharpshooters went out for company drill. When they returned, they were ordered to pack their knapsacks, as there was to be a review of General Porter's division. At twelve fifteen in the afternoon they fell in and marched to the parade ground of the 25th New York. They had just gotten to their position in the brigade when it began to rain heavily. General McClellan was received with all the honors of war: salutes from the batteries, music from the bands, and cheers from the men. The Sharpshooters marched in review; after passing they were dismissed at once. They returned to camp thoroughly soaked and cleaned the rust from their rifles.

On November 10 and 11, they performed the usual duties with the addition that they built tent furnaces, probably in the officers' quarters. On the 12th, Captain Wentworth was appointed officer of the day. Being the only line officer to have a regard for camp neatness, he formed fatigue parties and had the camp thoroughly cleaned. By that evening the camp was in better shape than it ever had been. All was quiet on November 13, when the soldiers performed usual duties. On the 14th the Sharpshooters were ordered to fatigue duty. They fell in with axes, picks, and shovels and marched to the field of labor, on which they worked all day. The 15th was again quiet. On November 16, while they were in ranks, it was so windy that they could not hear orders and thought it difficult to execute those orders that were not heard. On November 17, their duties were to prepare for an inspection by Colonel Ingraham, of General Porter's staff. In the afternoon they witnessed a very solemn scene. A funeral procession from the 2nd Maine passed through their camp to bury one of their comrades, and the band played the dirge. It was rather solemn to those unaccustomed to such a scene. November 18 and 19 were filled with usual camp duties. They had company drills, but no dress parade. The coldest weather yet was upon them—so cold that the water had frozen in the casks—and they executed the usual drills at double-quick time, with no objections, as it helped them keep warm.

November 20 was a day thousands long remembered as one of the most eventful days in their lives. As Nathan Haynes's journal records:

> Never before in this country has there been assembled together such an immense body of armed men as were reviewed today on the sacred soil of Virginia. Our company with the 22nd Regiment left the encampment at an early hour arrived on the review ground about ten o'clock A.M. Gen. McClellan and Staff accompanied by the President,

Artist rendering of Lincoln and staff reviewing troops at Munson Hill through Bailey's Cross, Virginia, on November 20, 1861. With President Lincoln was Simon Cameron, secretary of war, and William Seward, secretary of state, along with many general officers. The Sharpshooters arrived at ten o'clock that morning. They were awestruck at the large body of armed men stated to number some 100,000. Such a force had never been seen (Library of Congress).

> Secretaries Cameron and Seward on horseback did not arrive till half past twelve o'clock followed by several regiments of cavalry, together with a mounted brass band. The immense throng cheered as he passed along. The location of the review ground was between Munson's Hill and Bailey's Cross Road in the large open fields. The divisions reviewed were those of Gens. McCall, McDowell, Heintzelman, Fitz John Porter, Franklin, Blenker and Smith comprising nine regiments of infantry twenty batteries of artillery numbering one hundred pieces and nine regiments of cavalry forming an aggregate of about 70,000 troops: Our boys arrived in camp about dark tired and hungry. The large balloon Intrepid passed directly through our camp about five o'clock on its way to a distant hill to ascend to reconnoiter the enemy lines. There was considerable excitement in camp today caused by the report that a large body of cavalry was advancing on our pickets. The Officer of the Day armed every man in camp, cook and sick men: did not see any Rebels at a late hour at night.

It should be noted that the 22nd Regimental History states the body of men to be 100,000 in number.[7]

Governor Andrew proclaimed this day, November 21, a day of public thanksgiving and praise. Colonel Gove ordered all duties except necessary guard to be dispensed with. The men amused themselves by sparring, playing ball and other games not spoken of. It was reported that the Sharpshooters were as quiet and orderly as on a Sunday. The day closed, as was the custom in Massachusetts, with a thanksgiving ball" which was held on the parade ground, with music provided by the Regimental Band.

The 22nd Massachusetts and a squad of Sharpshooters were ordered on picket duty. The camp was as quiet as if Thanksgiving had never occurred. On the 23rd, they received information that they were to be paid. The usual duties, with the exception of guard, would be dispensed with. At noon the Sergeant Major brought in the payrolls, ordering them to be signed, and the company to be held in readiness for payment. The Sharpshooters waited patiently until night, but the orders never came.

On Sunday, November 24, it was ordered that the usual Sunday inspection would be held on company streets and performed by their respective commanders, to facilitate payment of the rest of the companies. As the prospects of speedy payment grew brighter, the men's spirits followed suit. Once they had been paid, they were happy, and immediately tried to devise ways to get the money home to friends or family, rather than spend it on useless items being sold by the sutlers and peddlers. The air was cold and raw, and it began to snow that night.

When the men turned out the morning of November 25, they expected to see the ground deeply covered with snow, but it was barely covered. It was a busy time in camp, as the men secured their money in packages to send to Washington with the captain. When the business was completed, the captain left for Washington at nine in the morning. Except for officers and sergeants, the Sharpshooters were paid $17.76, which represented one month and eleven days' service. As a group, the Sharpshooters sent home the sum of $1,650.74. One must remember that these were not men who collected bounties; they had no other means. The care for their families is commendable.[8]

At about this time Reverend Pierpont resigned his position as chaplain, as he was unable to endure the rigors of camp life. The Reverend Joseph C. Cromack, a Methodist clergyman from Malden, replaced him. There were a large number of professing Christians in the regiment, and the new chaplain sought them out. He held prayer meetings in his tent, reorganized the regimental church, and created articles of association and a summary of faith. Three of the Sharpshooters, George Burdett, John J. S. Williams, and Sylvanus Bartlett, were part of the committee to organize the church. Young or new Christians could join the church subject to probation terms. The services were quite impressive, resembling those of churches back home. But they were to be short-lived, as less than five months hence the active campaign started, at which time Reverend Cromack resigned his commission and returned to the North. It would be nearly two years before the regiment would get another chaplain.[9]

Surgeon Simmons of the 22nd Massachusetts Volunteer Infantry. This photograph was said to be taken between 1860 and 1870 (Library of Congress).

The quietness of the camp on November 26 was disturbed in the afternoon by a report that parties of cavalry scouts had skirmished with the Rebels, and were soundly defeated. The Sharpshooters who were out target practicing were hurried back to camp. They were ordered to be ready to march with a five-minute warning. At nine o'clock they were ordered to turn in.

November 27 revealed that the excitement of the day before was that a body of cavalry, out scouting, mistook a portion of Blenker's division for Rebels. Unaware of their mistake, they returned to camp circulating a report that had no foundation or cause for alarm. The camp was as quiet as if nothing had happened the previous day. The entire company of Sharpshooters was ordered to report for picket duty at seven thirty in the morning. They were not looking forward to that duty, as it started to rain and the morning was very cold and raw. While out on picket duty, as they were not allowed fires under any circumstances, they were chilled to the bone. They also heard something New Englanders were not used to at that time of the year: thunder. They were relieved on the 29th at eleven in the morning and returned to camp at one in the afternoon. The rest of the day, they cleaned guns and clothes, and drew from the quartermaster hats, shoes, and socks.

December 1 was spent preparing for monthly inspection. The colonel spent little time with the Sharpshooters, as they were always ready for any emergency. In the afternoon about forty Sharpshooters attended a funeral for a member of Company B of the regiment. The rest of the day was spent with the assistant surgeon, providing descriptive rolls of their height and other descriptions of themselves. On December 2, the men were ordered to be ready to march at midnight with two days' rations.[10]

The march started, and at a short distance from camp they overtook the 2nd Maine, which was attached to the expedition. As the men thought they were going after Rebel cavalry, they were excited about the prospect of engaging the enemy. The march was somewhat difficult. The roads were in a condition that prevented an orderly march. It was so cold that the water in the moving canteens froze. One of the Sharpshooters fell down and broke his rifle. He was left at one of the picket posts and ordered to return to camp the next day. Once outside of the picket lines they were ordered to march in silence. They marched until daylight, then took a favorable position for an ambush and waited while the cavalry passed, as they attempted to draw the enemy into a trap. The cavalry returned two and a half hours later without success. In the absence of fires, the men tried all means to stay warm. Happy to get the order to march, they marched twelve miles back to camp without a halt. They were somewhat tired, so they boiled a dish of tea and turned in.[11]

The morning of December 4, the men turned out in good condition. Some of them complained of the ill effects of the wild goose expedition. The colonel cancelled all regular duties so the men could rest, but Captain Wentworth got none as the colonel ordered him to take a company from the regiment and drill them as skirmishers. On the 5th, Captain Wentworth again was named officer of the day. The next two days were spent performing usual camp duties and target practicing. Another man from the regiment died of disease, and there was a funeral for him. On the morning of December 7, a thick fog settled in, blocking the sun and making the air very damp and unhealthy. As the men returned from target practice, they heard that another man from the regiment was dead. Apparently, when a member of Company I was cleaning his gun, he put on a cap and fired it to clear the nipple. Unfortunately, it was loaded, and a shot was fired into the tent of William Heath of Dedham while he was standing in it. The ball went through his body, and he lived only a short time afterwards. On December 11, by General Order No. 40, a board of officers, presided over by Major Tilton, recommended that Corporal Lewis Stevens, of Company I, face a court-martial for violating Army Regulation No. 106, the general rule that a rifle's muzzle was to be held at eye level. They wanted Stevens prosecuted for his actions in Private Heath's death.[12]

On Sunday, December 8, the usual drills were moved up an hour earlier so that the men could attend church services. Not many attended. On the 9th, Corporal Thomas was removing the false muzzle from his rifle when it accidentally discharged, sending the ball through his right thumb. The surgeon thought that if the thumb was treated properly, he would not lose it. December 10 and 11 were spent primarily in target practice. The Sharpshooters' shooting skills continued to improve. On the 12th, Captain Wentworth went to Washington and picked up some packages at the Express Office that family and friends had sent to the Sharpshooters. With the captain gone, little drilling was done.

Union soldiers building winter quarters, on the James River, Virginia, near Fort Brady (Library of Congress).

On the evening of December 13, a man came into camp claiming to be a Federal soldier who was captured at the Battle of Bull Run. He claimed he was taken to Richmond as a prisoner, his wounded leg was amputated, and then he was exchanged as a prisoner. He talked at length about how the Rebels were treating prisoners, but the Sharpshooters doubted some of his stories. Since he said he was a member of the 2nd Maine Company C, he was assisted over to the 2nd Maine, but none of the officers or men recognized him. The last they heard of him, he was in custody at brigade headquarters.

On December 14, squads went out to target practice, but were ordered back to camp at the double. When they arrived the major ordered the captain and twenty men on a scouting expedition. Soon after they started, another corporal came in with his thumb blown off. The regimental surgeons were not around, so he went to the brigade surgeon to have it dressed. At about five in the evening the scouting party returned, having accomplished nothing but a long march.

On December 15, the Sharpshooters' rifles were closely inspected, and it was determined that twenty-four of them were out of order. The armorer immediately began work on them. On the 16th, they target-practiced again, only to be ordered back for another scouting mission. They returned after dark with one contraband (escaped slave) as a prisoner; he was quartered in the guardhouse. The next day there was more target practice.

On December 18, Colonel Gove made his intentions known. He ordered all the tents to be raised two or three feet above ground to make the men as comfortable as possible. He believed they would spend their winter quarters at Hall's Hill, so the Sharpshooters began to cut logs, using Virginia mortar to set them in place and build a solid foundation for their canvas roofs. The Sharpshooters also were ordered to build a cookhouse. Every day they heard rumors of a forward movement or a return home, but none were reliable, and all the department heads kept that information to themselves. On December 19, they continued to raise their tents. Captain Wentworth went to Washington with the intention of procuring Sharps rifles for the Sharpshooters. But he returned at six thirty in the evening without accomplishing his goal. They had a dress parade, and at that time eleven men from the regiment received court-martial sentences for drunkenness and disobedience of orders. Three of the men were non-commissioned officers and were reduced to the ranks.

On December 20, Captain Wentworth again was named officer of the day. He started in earnest to get more tents raised. But the tents required more work than they thought, and although they started three of them, only two were completed. As a result some of the men were quartered with others. At eleven at night, a hospital attendant awoke the Sharpshooters and informed them that company member Henry Williams had died after a ten-day illness with typhoid fever.[13]

The next day they resumed working on the tents but were ordered to fall in for a review. At noon, they fell in and marched to the parade ground of the 25th New York. The troops of General Porter's division were formed into brigades, and were reviewed by General McClellan and staff along with Generals McDowell, Heintzelman, Blenker, Burns, King, and Williams, as well as Secretary Cameron General Wilson, and Commodore Wilkes. The division's brigadiers, Butterfield, Martindale and Merrell; the Prince de Foinville; the Duc de Chartres; the Comte de Paris, and a large number of civilians also watched. They marched in review at quick time, and again at the double quick. The brigades were formed in battle order and the Sharpshooters were deployed as skirmishers. They then rallied on the reserve and were sent back to camp.

Sunday, December 22, started with a weekly inspection, and they listened to 101 articles of war which were read to them. They then proceeded to desecrate the Sabbath by working on the tents. During the day, the men got together and agreed unanimously to contribute money to send Henry Williams' body home to Lynn. The morning of December 23, Captain Wentworth and Private John L. G. Williams (Henry's brother) took the body to Washington, and arranged to ship his body to Lynn. Christmas Eve was spent working on the tents. The ground had frozen, making the work slower and more difficult. A friend of Captain Wentworth from Salem visited the camp. When the captain's friend returned, many men from Salem loaded him with items to give to friends and relatives.

On December 25, Christmas Day, the colonel suspended all duties. There was considerable noise coming from neighboring regiments. During the day the men heard that two members of the 18th Massachusetts were shot during a brawl that occurred in the Garibaldi Regiment. In the 22nd Regiment there was little or no excitement except for a pretense of a dress parade that the Sharpshooters did not take part in. Instead they spent Christmas Day in raising their tents. On the 26th, Captain Wentworth was detailed for regimental court-martials. He turned his tent into a court. There were more cases than could be tried, so court was dismissed at three in the afternoon. The Sharpshooters continued zealously working on their tents, not wanting to be outdone by anybody. As the weather had turned terribly cold, it was also important to get them done as soon as possible. About three thirty in the afternoon, they observed a fire in the direction of Washington. They would have to wait another day to find out its cause. Corporal Thomas found that his thumb had grown worse instead of better. It was amputated that afternoon.[14]

Courts-martial began again on December 27, in the captain's tent. The men learned that the fire's source was seven stables on E Street in Washington. Each contained two hundred horses that belonged to the State of Massachusetts. A teamster's careless handling of a lantern set them ablaze, and only eleven of the horses were saved. The loss was estimated to be $100,000. In the evening an order came for forty Sharpshooters, two corporals, one sergeant and a lieutenant from this company to go on picket duty. While forming this group, many of the men suddenly got sick. The rest of the year was spent with the captain on court-martial duty. The men continued to gather materials to improve the cookhouse, and there were inspections and guard duty.

10

Shell Shocked

January 1, 1862, began a new year, and all remained the same. From the neighboring regiments, sounds announcing a holiday indicated that they had a pleasant time. The 22nd Regiment had been relieved of duties for the day, and mostly worked on their quarters. The Sharpshooters continued to gather materials and worked on the new cookhouse. Some of the Sharpshooters complained about letters they did not receive. It was learned that a large number of them were in an office in Washington, so Captain Wentworth sent for them. When they arrived there were nearly two hundred of them, some dated as back as far as November 2, 1861. It appeared that someone unnamed had ordered them held for some unknown reason. The entire situation remained a mystery.[1]

On January 2, there was little drill as the officers prepared company muster rolls to send to the paymaster. Captain Wentworth ordered the Sharpshooters to do pioneer duty. With the aid of picks, axes, shovels, and fire, heaps of brush, logs and stumps disappeared, leaving a clear view of the 23rd Maine Regiment, camped next to them. On the 3rd, they finished the grounds they had worked on the day before, and the cookhouse as well. It was quite a respectable kitchen and very comfortable. Soon a rumor ran through camp that they were to leave Hall's Hill; it caused quite a sensation. On January 4, the only duty required of the Sharpshooters was to gather wood to keep the fires going. The captain had gone to Washington in the morning. Missing the team that returned to the camp, he walked the entire distance back. The Sharpshooters all received new light blue pants. Additions to the previous day's rumors lent them more credibility.

From January 5th to the 8th, it continued cold and threatened more snow, making inspections very uncomfortable, with strong winds from the northeast. The Sharpshooters' hands were cold as they carried the cold steel of their rifles. When they turned out the morning of January 9, the ground was frozen, as it had rained all night. The rain froze as soon as it hit the ground. Later it melted, leaving an inch of mud to walk around in. Lieutenant Stiles left for his home in Salem, Massachusetts, on an eight-day furlough. There was no duty this day except dress parade. When the Sharpshooters turned out, instead of taking part in the parade, they were ordered to form a square around some prisoners. The prisoners listened to the charges against them, and then the Sharpshooters returned to their quarters. The next couple of days it continued to rain, eliminating all the frost from the ground and making it very difficult to move around. Captain Wentworth became extremely sick and remained in his quarters. The evening of January 11, the men heard rapid and heavy firing down the river. The remainder of the month was spent in camp doing duties such as gathering and splitting

Wooden cookhouse, There were many carpenters in the Second Company of Sharpshooters. Their skills were often called on. This would be a typical cookhouse built by the Sharpshooters as they prepared for winter quarters (Library of Congress).

wood for the cookhouse, drill, and dress parades. Captain Wentworth began to feel better. On January 29, the men learned the sad news of Edward Burrill's death, caused by typhoid fever. After breakfast the company met together and unanimously agreed to raise the money to send his body home.

During the first part of February, the sun came out, and the Sharpshooters referred to signs from the Old Farmer's Almanac as indicating that they would be in for a spell of good weather. February 3 hit them with a New England snowstorm. On the 5th, they went out for drill; the company was divided into squads and had a "sham fight." Nature provided the arms, and the ammunition was snowballs. In the drawn battle, neither side was willing to retreat, as that was a maneuver they had not learned. On February 8, they were left in peace and quiet and were not assigned duty. About twenty of the company went out for target practice and heard some favorable news: Fort Henry, on the Tennessee River, had been captured and prisoners taken. They also heard of Federal forces' successful scouting expedition in the vicinity of Fairfax Courthouse.

On Sunday, February 9, the first order of the day was inspection. The men were ordered to wear gloves and leggings, and the captain told them they looked as good as he had ever seen them. The men questioned whether the country needed men of fine appearance or moral courage in the time of battle. That day, the camp learned that a Burnside expedition had attacked Rebel forces at Roanoke Island and that the battle continued to rage.

On February 10, fourteen Sharpshooters were ordered to do fatigue duty. For a reason that apparently remained to be learned, they assisted on road repairs from Munson's Field to

Washington. The remainder of the company was either chopping wood or target shooting. At retreat the men learned that one of the Sharpshooters was missing and had not been seen since morning. Vague rumors about his absence circulated, but the men heard nothing definite and felt that in time they would learn more than they wished to know. On the 12th, the good news of Burnside's expedition was confirmed, and the men were elated. With the Rebels' defeat, the men's thoughts were of a short campaign, and they talked about hopes of being home in early spring. A sergeant and file of men were sent to Alexandria, Virginia, to search for the missing man. Nothing was learned, and he was thought to be a deserter. This day the men heard that smallpox had broken out, but there was only one case in the regiment. The fatigue detail continued to repair the road.[2]

On February 14, the company was disturbed by orders that nearly the entire company was to go out on picket duty. A detachment of one sergeant and ten men left camp on a scouting expedition. The remainder—two lieutenants, two sergeants, three corporals, and forty men—left an hour later for picket duty. Barely enough men were left in camp to do the necessary work. The scouts returned to camp at dark; they had been about five miles beyond Vienna. Their object was to capture a party of Rebel horsemen and some infantry which had been encamped there, but the Rebels had left the area. February 15 brought a three-inch snowstorm. Company streets were cleared in the evening as it turned bitterly cold. The Sharpshooters' thoughts were of the men out on picket duty in the extreme weather. Corporal Burdett returned from Washington with news that Fort Donelson had been taken and fifteen thousand prisoners captured, including Rebel Generals Pillow and Floyd. On Sunday, February 16, the pickets returned from duty at about noon, having suffered severely in the cold. The only duty this day was the usual Sunday inspection, which took very little time.

On Monday, it continued to rain and freeze, making it slippery and difficult to move around. The order was given to fall into formation without arms. The men marched to the encampment of the 18th Massachusetts Volunteer Infantry, where General Martindale confirmed the news of Fort Donelson. The men responded with three rousing cheers, and all afternoon cheers could be heard from surrounding camps. Over the next few days, it continued to rain. Warmer weather created so much mud that it was impossible to do much of anything. The men heard news of Savannah's capture and Fort Pulaski's fall. In camp, a story circulated that three hundred Rebel cavalry rode in and surrendered themselves.

February 22, Washington's Birthday, was intended to be a day of great celebration. Several regiments around Washington were to parade, and artillery salutes were to be fired by the batteries attached to them. But a death in the president's family dampened spirits, and out of respect for the commander in chief, the celebration was truncated. The Sharpshooters marched over to the 18th Massachusetts and listened to General Washington's final address, then to band music. They returned to their camp for the evening. February 23 found no improvement in the weather. All inspections and duties were cancelled, as nobody could move around in the mud.

The morning of the 24th the sun appeared for a short time; then the skies grew black and the wind and rain started. The weather worsened violently, becoming a perfect tornado that swept nearly everything before it. Barely ten tents were left standing in the regiment. The Sharpshooters' tents resisted the tornado's force and remained standing. But, except for them, all other regiments in the near area suffered the same fate. On February 25, the weather cleared, and the men of the regiment were employed repairing the damage from the tornado.[3]

The Sharpshooters spent the morning of the 26th gathering and cutting wood for the cookhouse. That afternoon, several squads went in various directions for target practice, but at four o'clock rain put an end to that. That evening the long-expected order was given to prepare two days' rations and be ready to march at a moment's notice. February 27 was spent making out rolls for the paymaster and waiting for the order to march, which did not come. The following day was consumed mostly by the paymaster, as he paid the troops. Hearing nothing more of the order to march, the men began to think it was a false alarm. So ended the month of February 1862.

The first eight days in March were quiet ones. The Sharpshooters claimed that the weather in this country was as treacherous as the inhabitants. They spent their time gathering and cutting wood for the cookhouse, and received gratifying news that Federal forces had taken Columbus, Kentucky. As every Rebel stronghold had been taken, they believed the war was nearer to an end. Target practice saw some confusion. The Sharpshooters had their sights set at two hundred yards, but the targets were set at a quarter of a mile, and very few were hit. The men then were to practice at a distance of a half-mile. Again, through confused orders, the same result ensued.

On March 9, a sergeant and ten men were assigned to a scouting expedition with General Morrell. After the usual Sunday inspection an order came for the Sharpshooters to provide a corporal and ten men to go on picket duty. Once it was decided who would go, the order was countermanded. Another order, to cook three days' rations and be prepared for the entire company to march at daybreak, caused excitement and confusion in camp.

The men turned out at four in the morning on March 10, and the march started at seven thirty in a heavy rain. All of the Sharpshooters were anxious to go and did not want to be left behind. But the rain, wagons, and thousands of men walking through the mud made the march very difficult. Some of the men were not able to keep up, and after several miles fell out and returned to their camp. So much mud clung to their shoes that they could scarcely lift their feet. They toiled on until noon, when they halted on a low piece of marshy ground. The colonel had the Sharpshooters lean their rifles on a fence, as the ground was not suitable for stacking arms. After stopping for an hour and eating hard bread and salt pork, the men resumed the march, which was more tedious than that of the morning. To lighten their load, many of the men in the regiment began throwing away their knapsacks, coats, and blankets. The Sharpshooters refused to part with anything, no matter how insignificant. As the wagons and artillery pieces cut up the roads more and more, it became increasingly difficult to march in order. At about three in the afternoon, the weather cleared and was hailed with delight by the wet and weary soldiers.

At four thirty in the afternoon, they entered the town of Fairfax, passed through it, and then halted about a quarter of a mile south of it at an old Rebel encampment. They were amazed at how fortified the area was, with earthworks in the camp and on top of surrounding elevations. As they were to march again in the morning, they began preparations for a night's rest. The last straggler came into the Sharpshooters' camp at eight in the evening, and others from the regiment were still coming in at midnight.[4]

On March 11, they turned out for reveille, stiff in the joints and complaining of soreness in their shoulders from the weight of their knapsacks. They were somewhat pleased that sleeping on the damp ground did not have the adverse effects they had expected. When it was light enough, some soldiers went into Fairfax, and broke into and destroyed personal property. They were stopped by a provost guard detailed there to keep things within the bounds of decency. None of the Sharpshooters were reported to have been involved in the unlawful action. Soldiers seemed to have a propensity for destroying all kinds of property on the march, which only the strictest of measures could prevent. For example, two buildings close to the Sharpshooters' camp were demolished and their wood used for cooking.

General McClellan passed their camp at eight o'clock in the morning, as he went toward

Centreville. It was later reported that the Rebels had evacuated Centreville and Manassas, which meant that the forward march would be stopped for a day or two. The Sharpshooters rested that day and prepared for the night. Wagons were sent out to obtain hay for the men to sleep on.

On March 12, the weather remained favorable for an outdoor encampment. There was no indication of a forward movement. Some of the officers had traveled to Manassas and returned with sad accounts of how the Rebels had destroyed everything. The Rebels had burned all they could not carry, leaving blackened ruins, and they had blown up a bridge on their retreat. About dusk, the regiment fell in, receiving General McClellan with deafening cheers. He passed the Sharpshooters first and they returned to camp, where they stayed for the next couple of days, as McClellan's plans had been altered by the Rebels' retreat. The men were anxious to go to Manassas to see the Rebels' late stronghold. Captain Wentworth returned to Hall's Hill to arrange for the removal of the Sharpshooters' equipment. Not much had been done. It was reported that a sutler's wagon was tipped over and robbed of barrels of ginger-cakes. The sutlers took such advantage of the soldiers that the soldiers felt justified in robbing them every chance they could get. At six in the evening, the order was given to cook rations and be prepared to march in the morning. The Sharpshooters gathered fence rails and waited for the rations. As of nine at night, when they retired, the rations had not come.[5]

On Saturday, March 15, they turned out at five in the morning, drank a dish of coffee, and fell into the line of march, which started at seven thirty that morning. As they marched back through the town of Fairfax toward Alexandria, the men were happy to be on the move again, and were in good spirits when it started to rain again. The long, fatiguing march was made more difficult by the added extra weight of the water held by their soaked wool uniforms. They marched for twelve miles and halted at Cloud's Mill, where they ate hard bread and drank coffee. Soon after they resumed their march, they came upon a river and crossed it on logs, which took considerable time, leaving those in the rear to stand in the pouring rain.

Marching to within three miles of Alexandria, they halted for the night. While the officers were provided quarters, the men remained standing in the pouring rain. They were finally told to find quarters wherever they could. Along with a few infantrymen, they crowded into a hospital tent not large enough for half of their company. As nothing better was to be had, the jam-packed group of men steamed like a boiler in their wet wool uniforms. They were so tired that they spread their blankets in the mud and rested.

They turned out on the morning of March 16, a discouraged group of men who found themselves in such close and filthy quarters. There was nothing to eat, nor was there any wood to cook with or fire to dry their clothes or warm their numbed bodies. Their rifles were covered with rust, and they decided to clean them before doing anything else. As the day passed, they were the most uncomfortable group of men anyplace. In the afternoon, they were issued poncho blankets. Rather than stay in the crowded tent, as they had the previous night, some of the men pitched their new ponchos on top of a high knoll. They preferred to risk the rain rather than being crushed.

As they were cold, the men who camped on the knoll rose early. Obtaining some wood, they built a fire that kept them from freezing. They longed to see the sun rise. But unfortunately, when it did, a cold wind came with it. Going over to their company quarters to get coffee, they found a number of company members sick and quartered in barns. The day was spent cleaning rifles and drying blankets and overcoats. The men tried to get as comfortable as possible and attempted to make themselves look respectable. They pitched their ponchos so that all of the company could be together except the sick ones, who were quartered in the barns. At dark, an order was issued to draw and cook six days' rations. The men believed that a long march would take place and were anxious to move. They turned out from their ponchos early on the morning of March 18, expecting an order to march, but it never came. It was a pleasant day, and the men were in much better condition. Only one man, Corporal Archer, went to the hospital. Another man, who had been left at Hall's Hill, rejoined the company.

The morning of March 19, they arose early, as they were very uncomfortable in the cold. They felt the ponchos would be good for the rain, but they did nothing for the cold. Considerable excitement in the camp was caused by the Irishmen celebrating St. Patrick's Day. The only duty done that day was an attempt to preserve the quiet. At three in the afternoon, the order was given to pack up and be ready to march. At four o'clock, they started marching toward Alexandria. It was a pleasant march of three miles, with much to observe along the way. The scenery kept their minds off of the weight they carried. They arrived in Alexandria about five that evening. The Sharpshooters took up quarters in the upper story of a building that was used as a post office and customs house. Making themselves as comfortable as possible, they appreciated the luxury of being in a building. On the 20th, they awoke from their hard beds and realized that they had found dry quarters, as it had rained all night. There were no indications that they were going to move soon, and no duties, so the men walked around the area sightseeing.[6]

On March 21, their hopes of staying in Alexandria ended, as they were ordered to pack up and be in the line of march by nine in the morning. They were ready at the appointed time, but did not start the march until noon. They marched up the river toward Washington, to wharfs where they would embark on the *Daniel Webster* to go to a location unknown to them. It was slow boarding, and they did not finish boarding until after dark. They made their way below deck, where there was good ventilation. The steamer left the dock and anchored while the rest of the division loaded. In the morning they went above deck and watched the other ships loading. They also observed that it was raining; with no protection, the men on deck were having a hard time of it. The river was crowded with a fleet of about twenty-five boats of all types. Around noon, all the troops were loaded and they got under way, moving very slowly down the river. Using opera and field glasses they saw several deserted Rebel batteries on the high banks. The fleet stayed close together and was escorted by the Potomac flotilla of gunboats. They anchored at about ten at night and waited for daylight.[7]

They got under way about four in the morning on March 23, and were in the Chesapeake Bay by sunrise. As they passed Capes Charles and Henry, Fortress Monroe came into full view. Men from several companies were detailed to remove equipment from storage areas, which indicated that they would be landing. Everybody tried to pack up their gear at once, creating so much confusion that all efforts were retarded. The Sharpshooters tried to lie down and sleep, but there was so much noise from the confusion on deck they could not sleep. Once it was known that they were not to disembark until morning, all quieted down and they slept.

On the morning of March 24, they were ordered to go ashore. The Sharpshooters were the first to disembark and had a long wait for the others. They wanted to walk around the fort but were ordered to stay together. They waited on the sidewalk until noon, and then they got into the line of march. They marched about three miles and came to the ruins of Hampton, which had been burned by the Rebels in August of 1861. They went a mile beyond and encamped in a large field, where they pitched their ponchos and gathered fence rails to cook rations, which did not arrive until a late hour.

The morning of March 25, they turned out for reveille, prepared coffee, and waited for orders. Nearly half of the Sharpshooters were ordered to go out as an advance guard. They packed their knapsacks and reported for that duty; then the order was countermanded. They returned to the rear of the regiment, and the march started. They marched rapidly for about three hours, halted, then encamped. No Rebels appeared to be in the area.

10. Shell Shocked

On March 26, the Sharpshooters were ordered to prepare twenty-four hours' worth of rations, in light marching order. They went on a reconnoitering expedition. Getting started about eleven in the morning, they marched slowly and cautiously for seven or eight miles until they came in view of Big Bethel. Two Sharpshooters went ahead on a scouting mission, saw two Rebel cavalry men, and fired at them. They then were ordered back to camp, where they arrived at about six in the evening. The next several days at the camp near Newmarket were spent in both regimental and brigade drilling. One night it rained heavily, flooding the camp. The men built fires and stood in front of them to dry. While their fronts dried, their backs were getting wet, and as they turned, their backs would dry and their fronts would get wet.

The governor of Massachusetts had appointed April 3 as a day of fasting and prayer. None of the Massachusetts regiments were required to do any drilling or duties. The officers and enlisted men played ball against each other. The ball playing stopped when the order came to be ready to march in the morning. The rest of the day was spent in cooking rations and preparing for the march.

On April 4, they turned out at four o'clock in the morning, distributed clothing to those in need, packed three days' rations, and were in the line of march at six forty five. General Wyman took notice of each and every Sharpshooter, and they gave him a hearty three cheers as he left and returned to Massachusetts. The march began at seven-thirty; it was a comfortable march, and they stopped at the battlefield of Big Bethel, where they prepared hard biscuits and salt pork. They stayed for an hour and rested. When they started out, they set ablaze the Rebel barracks and stables. As they marched through the abandoned Rebel fort, they noted how extensive and strong their earthworks were. About three in the afternoon, they came upon an artillery piece of the 5th Massachusetts Battery which had a broken carriage and the gun dismounted. They later learned it had been broken while the 5th Massachusetts had been shelling the Rebels' earthworks. At about five in the afternoon, they passed the shelled-out earthworks, marched a half mile beyond them, and encamped in an open field. The men were too worn down to look around; they just pitched their tents and lay down.[8]

On the morning of April 5, the march started at an early hour. The traveling was more difficult as the roads were muddy and cut up by wagons. The Rebels had felled trees on the roads to block their movements as they retreated. At nine thirty, a heavy rain came down, making the march even more difficult. At noon, artillery was heard in the distance and they were hurried forward, regardless of the water and mud. They came upon the Rebels in force about two miles from Yorktown. Taking off their knapsacks, they marched out to reconnoiter and found themselves face to face with a Rebel breastwork that immediately began shelling them. They retreated out of range and waited for one of their batteries to come forward, which it did and then began shelling the Rebel position. The Sharpshooters then took a position of safety in the nearby woods and listened to the whirring sound of shells until four o'clock.

At that time, Company B and ten Sharpshooters were ordered out in the front; the Rebels wasted no time and showered them with grapeshot. Seven men of Company B were wounded. They retreated to the woods more to the left and prepared to spend the night under arms. A squad of men was allowed to return for blankets and knapsacks while the rest remained. It proved a difficult task to find their way through the water and brambles, but they succeeded. A watch was set up to alert the men if something were to occur, and the men rolled themselves in blankets for the night.[9]

On April 6, they got up at daylight, rolled their blankets, and waited for orders. The Rebels fired a couple of their guns to let them know they had not evacuated during the night. The Union heavy guns answered, and a strong picket force was sent out. At seven in the morn-

II. The Second Company of Andrew Sharpshooters

Commonwealth of  Massachusetts.

BY HIS EXCELLENCY
JOHN A. ANDREW
GOVERNOR.

A PROCLAMATION
FOR A DAY OF HUMILIATION, FASTING AND PRAYER.

The time is at hand when the people of Massachusetts are wont to unite in their annual public and penitential offering to Almighty God, of Prayer and Humiliation.

I do, therefore, with the advice and consent of the Council, appoint THURSDAY, the third day of April next, to be observed throughout this Commonwealth, as a day of public HUMILIATION, FASTING, AND PRAYER.

From every altar may the flame of pure devotion arise to Heaven, and the sweet incense of contrition, penitence and humility, ascend on high; so that worthily lamenting our sins we may humbly hope forgiveness of the same through the Infinite and Divine mercy and favor manifested in the life and doctrines of the blessed Saviour of mankind.

May our self-examination be sincere and faithful, searching out all the hidden causes, in our selfishness, prejudices or ignorances, of every public disorder and evil, as well as every private disobedience and wrong.

May the trying experiences through which this people are borne lead them to a manlier, as well as more Christian, faith in the providence of God, and the power of His Truth. May they learn the wisdom of humble and constant obedience to duty, to reverence the rights and to value the happiness and to serve the welfare of all that great family of immortal men, to whom the Gospel is sent and to whom the inspiration of the Almighty has given understanding.

In tender sympathy with the bereaved, the suffering and the broken-hearted, with "all those who are in any way afflicted or distressed in mind, body or estate," let us pray for their consolation and deliverance; while we also pledge ourselves in solemn vows to God, to our Country, and to Mankind, to stand always for the defence and maintenance of Truth, Justice and Righteousness in all the trials of life and in the work of duty.

And may the Divine Mercy be meted to us all, according to our several necessities; granting a happy issue to our country out of all the trials which beset the nation; restoring peace and good will between all her people, delivering the oppressed, rebuilding the waste places, reviving the energies and hopes of busy enterprise, blessing us on the land and on the sea, in all the ways and arts of useful industry, and in all efforts to cultivate the intellect and to expand the heart. And while the voice of commanding duty shall continue to summon our sons and brothers to the fields of war, may Almighty God shield them from the arrows of the foe; cover their heads in the day of battle; shelter, strengthen, and encourage them; and give to them constant deliverance and victory.

Given at the Council Chamber, in Boston, this eleventh day of March, in the year of our Lord one thousand eight hundred and sixty-two, and of the Independence of the United States of America the eighty-sixth.

JOHN A. ANDREW.

BY HIS EXCELLENCY THE GOVERNOR:
OLIVER WARNER, Secretary.
GOD SAVE THE COMMONWEALTH OF MASSACHUSETTS.

Governor Andrew's Proclamation of Humiliation, Fasting and Prayer on April 3, 1862. All Massachusetts soldiers, no matter where they were, were not to be assigned any duty (Library of Congress).

ing, they were ordered farther into the woods and allowed fires to cook coffee, which not many of the Sharpshooters had. At eleven o'clock, they were ordered back to where they had left their knapsacks the previous day. The men prepared to pass the night there when they were ordered to go on picket duty at dark. The idea of spending another night in the woods, some going with no food in their haversacks, was not pleasant. At eight at night, they took their position near a fence in a peach orchard about six hundred yards from the Rebel line. Three companies attacked them during the night, but they held their position. They remained flat on the ground all night. One of the Sharpshooters fired at a man coming into their line but did not hit him. He was taken into camp, where he gave valuable information about the Rebels' location and strength.

The morning of April 7 had not improved their position. They still had nothing to eat, and if a man attempted to rise from the ground, he was shot at from Rebel rifle pits. To make matters worse, it started raining at eleven in the morning and continued all day, soaking the men thoroughly. It was a long day for them, and they were not relieved until the safety of dark. They returned to camp with stiff joints, cold and hungry after being out there for thirty hours. Hot coffee was waiting for them, along with a half an inch of mud on the ground. They chose to sit by the fire rather than to lie down in the mud. The rain continued on the 8th; the men were nearly worn out with exposure and exhaustion, and some of them had not slept for three nights. The batteries were busy getting their guns in position. It was not known to the men when they would attack.

The rain continued on April 9 with colder weather. The conditions of the past five days had taken such a toll on the men that thirty of them attended surgeon's call. Scarcely a man in the company was free from some ill effect caused by lying on the damp ground. They spent a miserable day standing around large campfires, able to dry only one side of themselves at a time. They turned in early, but without many comforts, as their blankets were thoroughly soaked. At eleven that night, they were ordered to fall into the ranks. Telling them that the Rebels were slowly approaching, the lieutenant colonel ordered them to extinguish all fires. They equipped themselves, formed into ranks, and marched out looking for the Rebels. Chilled through to the bones, the men were amazed that such a large body of men could move through the darkness so quietly. All orders were given in subdued tones. Then they were ordered to return to camp. It appeared that a Massachusetts regiment, led by Barnes, had gone out to relieve the picket; unable to find the men, they returned and reported them captured. Colonel Barnes of the 18th Massachusetts Infantry was an object of many smothered curses.

On April 10, they were ordered to pack up and prepare to move to another camp location, which they did cheerfully. Breaking camp about noon, they marched about two miles toward the York River and camped on some dry ground at Wormsley Creek. On the 11th, the sun came out, creating a more beneficial effect than all of the surgeons in the army. Ten of the Sharpshooters were assigned to picket duty. The pioneers of the regiment built bridges across the creek, so that Porter's Division could get to the banks of the York River. William Allen and Isaac Cowdrey were taken to the hospital that afternoon. A dense smoke could be seen in the direction of Yorktown. The Sharpshooters were unable to determine the source of the fire, as they did not know the Rebels' position.

April 12 was another good day. The guns were quiet, and no picket firing had been heard. The Sharpshooters who had been left in the hospital at Hampton returned to the company. Vigorous efforts were made to get the heavy guns in position, and the pioneers were laboring on the bridge. All was quiet on the 13th; nothing was done except necessary picket and fatigue duty. Heavy firing was heard in the direction of Fortress Monroe; they thought the *Virginia* (*Merrimac*) was battling, but no news was heard.[10]

11

Horses in the Shade, Soldiers in the Sun

Early on April 14, the Sharpshooters were turned out for picket duty. They arrived at eight in the morning. Ten of them were sent to outposts, and the remainder stayed a short distance to the rear, in the woods, as reserves. Nothing happened during that day. There were no reports of any pickets being shot at on either side, although some shots were exchanged. They rolled into their blankets to spend the night, ready at a moment's notice to fall into line. About midnight a squad of infantrymen with three Sharpshooters went out to reconnoiter, but returned without any information. The 15th was a quiet day; they were relieved of picket duty and returned to camp. They were surprised that the two armies were so close together, yet had exchanged so few shots.[1]

April 16 was hot and sultry, with very little air stirring. The cannonading was very heavy on both sides. At night a shell landed near the Sharpshooters' campground, burying itself ten inches into the ground. Soon after it landed, the men were called into formation and were not dismissed until eleven at night, not knowing the cause of alarm. On April 17, many of the men from the regiment were taken out for fatigue duty and worked on the bridges. They were again called out at night and dismissed. On the 18th, they remained on fatigue duty. As artillery was fired toward them, they worked just as calmly as if the cannons had been forty miles away. They also learned the cause of the alarm from the previous evening. It was said that Rebels had attempted to capture a piece of artillery which was being guarded by the pickets. Although the Rebels had been repulsed with a severe loss, they had succeeded in taking the piece some distance.[2]

At about one in the afternoon on April 19, a large detail for fatigue duty took nearly all the men in the regiment. The Sharpshooters were dismissed and ordered back to their quarters, as there were not enough tools to go around. They were told to stand in readiness to relieve those who used the tools, but that call never came. Captain Wentworth, who was too sick to perform his duties, was taken to see Dr. Marshall E. Simmons. Lieutenant Stiles took command of the company. The Sharpshooters were woken by an orderly sergeant in the early morning of the 20th. A detail of men was taken. They thought they would be on guard duty but ended up doing fatigue duty and built foundations for the siege guns to be set up around Yorktown. Isaac Cowdrey, a popular member of their company, had died of disease at about nine that morning, and it was not possible to send his body home. They built him a coffin, finishing it at dusk. They did not like the idea of interring him in enemy territory so far from home, friends, and family. They also realized that that could be the fate of many more of their com-

The Sharpshooters built foundations for siege guns at Yorktown, on April 20, 1862. They were growing weary of fatigue duty; they wanted to sharp shoot, as that was what they were recruited to do (Library of Congress).

pany members, as sickness was so widespread. The fatigue detail returned while the funeral procession was just finished. They regretted not having been able to pay their respects.

On April 21, there was no drilling in camp. At dark, they were to provide a fatigue party to work on the trenches, but it rained so hard that the detail was cancelled. At about six o'clock on the evening of the 22nd, the camp was alarmed by seventeen artillery shots fired in quick succession from the Rebel batteries. They later learned that those shots were fired at the reserve pickets, but no one was injured. Captain Wentworth became quite feeble and was taken to the hospital. On the 23rd, it was well set in their minds that drill and fatigue duties were commonplace, as just about all of the Sharpshooters had been assigned to fatigue duty.

At four thirty in the morning on April 24, they were called out and told to prepare breakfast and be in line of march at five thirty with equipment and a full canteen of water. Seeing surgeons and ambulances within the formation, they thought something serious was about to happen. Nonetheless, they marched off in good spirits, and it proved to be only a reconnoitering mission. Ten of the Sharpshooters were sent forward and the rest held in reserve. They returned to camp about noon, and were ordered to be ready to go out on picket duty early in the morning.[3]

On the morning of April 25, they turned out at three. Each man had prepared coffee and was in the line of march at four thirty. They crossed the creek on the newly built bridge and went a short distance. The outposts were manned, and all but six of the Sharpshooters were held in reserve in the woods. Those six were stationed in an old house along the banks of the York River, and they passed the cold and rainy day comfortably indoors. At dark, they rolled themselves into blankets, thinking they were fortunate to have comfortable quarters while their comrades were out in the woods with only a few boughs for shelter. They were relieved early on the 26th and returned to camp. The men wore their ponchos all day to protect them from the storm's severity. A story circulated in camp that during the night the 1st and 11th Massachusetts regiments had stormed a Rebel earthwork, driven out its men, spiked their gun, and destroyed their works.

On the afternoon of April 27, half of the company was ordered out for fatigue duty, and the other half was ordered to relieve them at five in the morning. Although the Rebels fired a lot of shells, there were no reports of anyone injured. The men were called out early on the morning of April 28 and marched to the entrenchment for fatigue duty. Instead of being ordered to perform labor, the Sharpshooters' rights were finally respected. They were stationed in rifle pits to protect the fatigue party. Although a number of shells were fired near them, nobody was injured. For the first time they felt they were finally being used as a company of their description should have been.

The morning of April 29 was quiet. After lunch, the Rebels shelled the fatigue party that was building breastworks in front of their camp and continued to fire at intervals all afternoon. They did not succeed in driving the fatigue party out, but many of the shell fragments fell within the camp. There were no reports of anybody being wounded. They heard rumors that New Orleans was in the hands of Federal forces and hoped it was true. Late in the evening, a detail for the fatigue party, consisting of a lieutenant, sergeant, corporal, and five Sharpshooters, was ordered out.

At five o'clock on the morning of April 30, a fatigue party was called out. The Union forces opened fire with heavy guns for two hours, astonishing the Rebels, as nearly every shell fell within their works. They occasionally responded but did no damage. The Sharpshooters were mustered for pay at one in the afternoon, but the rain was so heavy that pay was put off until evening. During the night, both sides continued cannonading until early in the morning, when there was a heavy rain, and the shelling stopped for awhile. It continued later in the day. It rained heavily during the day, making it very difficult for the fatigue party. One of the Sharpshooters received a disability discharge and was to go home the next day; all the men in the company wished they could go with him.

The morning of May 2, the men were ordered out at four and detailed to fatigue duty. Through some bad management, they were marched to General Porter's headquarters without having had breakfast. At headquarters, the Sharpshooters were ordered to take shovels and go into the trenches with the infantry. Although they felt that was not what they had enlisted for, they knew they had to obey orders from superior officers. So they took the shovels and went with the infantry to the riverbank, where they dug entrenchments and were exposed to a Rebel battery directly across the river from them. They also were in a crossfire from the gunboats. Each man was required to dig a space six feet square and four feet deep. They had just gotten started when the shelling began. Many shells exploded within three hundred feet, and three shells within twenty feet, but fortunately those did not explode. They would not be driven out. Completing their task at one in the morning, they hugged the ground in the trenches they had dug, waiting to be relieved while the shells flew over their heads.[4]

On the morning of May 3, they did their usual drill. The Rebels continued to throw

Four men in front of the Augustine Moore House, at Yorktown. These could have been the Sharpshooters under Lt. Stiles that searched the city for intelligence of Rebel movements. As they entered the Moore House Lt. Stiles found a dead Rebel officer and maps of costal surveys of the Northern seaboard states. On May 4, 1862, Stiles thought he found evidence of a possible Northern campaign by the Confederates (Library of Congress).

their shells carelessly. That night, they threw them into the Sharpshooters' camp. At seven in the evening, one exploded directly overhead; a large piece went through the surgeon's tent, creating quite a commotion among the staff. All lights and fires were ordered to be extinguished, but that had little effect, as the shelling continued until midnight. The Sharpshooters were ordered to be ready for picket duty the next morning.

At five o'clock in the morning of May 4, they started out for picket duty. As they got into position, they were informed that the enemy had evacuated Yorktown during the night. Colonel Gove was notified, and deployed two companies into the enemy works to determine whether they had been evacuated. Colonel Gove and Lieutenant Stiles, of the Sharpshooters, went over the ramparts together, going over the parapet. At six thirty in the morning, they planted the regimental colors on the parapet amid the regiment's deafening cheers. The remainder of the regiment was formed and marched toward Yorktown. About halfway there, an "infernal machine" exploded, wounding five men from Company G. It was learned that the Rebels had buried shells underground designed to explode when any weight was placed on them. They marched into the town carefully, avoiding any place where the ground was freshly disturbed.[5]

Lieutenant Stiles, in command of the Sharpshooters, was ordered to deploy his company and enter the town. After they did, the Sharpshooters were ordered to rest in place. Several of the companies from the regiment roamed the town and looked for trophies. It was learned that the entire town had been set with land torpedoes. Guards were stationed to keep the men from roving in the town. They heard rumors that the entire town had been undermined and could blow up at any time. The cavalry rode through town in pursuit of the enemy as they fled. A horse stepped on a torpedo; two horses were killed and their riders injured. When a Telegraph Corps member placed a pole in the ground in front of the Sharpshooters, it exploded as it made contact with the ground torpedo, injuring him so badly that the Sharpshooters thought he would die.[6]

In a tent, Lieutenant Stiles found the body of a dead Rebel officer. On his table was a copy of the Confederate Army Regulations, which was a curiosity for Union soldiers. At the Moore House, which had been used as a hospital, Stiles found a full collection of maps and coastal survey charts of the Northern seaboard states, evidence that the Rebel officers had studied the possibility of a Northern campaign. Lieutenant Stiles wrote:

> One thing occurred which made its mark on my person and on my memory for life. In a square near the center of town stood two stone buildings, a two-and-a-half and a one-and-a-half story. The smaller one had an outside flight of stairs leading to the upper story, and the lower floor was filled with shells and all sorts of ordnance, apparently arranged so that a careless or incautious movement would explode them and blow up the town. I had been in the building early in my explorations, and, getting out again in safety, I posted a guard to keep everybody away. By some means, however, a civilian eluded the sentry, and was going up the outside stairs as I was crossing the square. I ordered him down. He came down at once, and advanced toward me, and within four feet of where I stood, he stepped on a buried torpedo. He was blown to pieces, a hole made in the ground larger than a barrel, and I was knocked over backward. The only injury I received was a small splinter of copper from the cap of the torpedo, which entered the knuckle of the forefinger of my right hand. [It] remained there two years, and I finally lost the use of my finger. The torpedo-cap, after its upward flight, descended near some of my company, and they gave it to me, and I still preserve it as a relic. The unfortunate victim of the torpedo was a telegraph repairman from Ohio, who was entering the building to detach the torpedo wires. His remains were gathered up in a box by the men of our regiment, and received a decent burial."[7]

The Sharpshooters remained in town until two thirty and were ordered back to camp by Lieutenant Colonel William Tilton. They made their way very carefully through the fields, and returned to camp about four o'clock. They were ordered to cook three days' rations and be ready to march at a moment's notice. Hearing a rumor that Richmond and Norfolk had been captured, they hoped it was true. Captain Wentworth returned from the hospital; the men did not think he looked any better.

In a heavy rain on the morning of May 5, they turned out, expecting the order to break camp and march at any moment. They had listened to the din of battle all day and were impatient to strike a blow in revenge for the torpedoes left in their path. They wanted to end the rebellion here, rather than chasing the Rebels any further. Night came but the order to march did not, so they turned in, more to get out of the rain than for want of sleep. Just as they fell asleep, the order to fall into formation came, which they did immediately. They did not know how far they were to go but packed one day's rations in their haversacks, filled their canteens, and left everything else in camp. They marched toward Yorktown, arrived near the works, halted, and waited for orders. Having marched in rain ever since they had arrived in that part of the country, they thought the general was determined to drown his brigade. They remained standing, and no orders came. They were glad to lie down in the mud and get a few hours' sleep, and they slept as soundly as if they were home in their beds covered with eiderdown. They did not wake up until the morning of May 6.

It was learned that General Rains had set torpedoes under the ground. He had originated land mines, as he ordered Columbaid artillery shells buried 8 to 10 inches. The shells would explode when moved or were stepped on. Officers on both sides of the conflict were angered, as they thought buried mines were an unethical form of warfare.

That day they awoke to a bright and sunshiny day, which they welcomed. They stayed on the ground until nine in the morning when they were ordered to return to their camp to pack their gear and to prepare to march to another camp. They saw Captain Wentworth in camp as he attended to his baggage. He told the men he was sorry to be separated from them. At one, they marched to where they had been in the morning, halted, and set up camp. Instead of pitching their ponchos, they went into the Rebel fort and took some Confederate tents. It was difficult to find good ones. When the enemy had fled, they had destroyed as much as possible. Nonetheless, they found the Confederate tents better than not having any protection from the elements. They pitched the tents, made themselves as comfortable as possible, and turned in early, attempting to make up for the sleep they had lost the previous night.

On the morning of May 7, the men thought they would be there for a day or two, and set up all the comforts they could. Just as they completed those chores, they were ordered to fall into marching formation. They remained there, resting on their arms for the entire day. Concluding that they would be there for the night, they pitched their tents. They just had lain down when the bugle sounded for them to fall into the ranks again. They marched through Yorktown to the wharf, expecting to embark immediately, but they remained on the wharf all night. In the morning, as soon as it was light enough, the men scattered in all directions and looked for something to eat other than hard bread and salt beef. During the morning, a boat came in to take the sick to another location, and Captain Wentworth went on it. At noon they began to embark, and at three o'clock the *Elm City* departed for West Point, twenty miles up the river. That trip took about three hours. Landing on the south bank of the York River, near the mouth of the Pamunkey River, they went ashore on pontoon boats, as there was no wharf. They moved a short distance from the river and encamped in a cornfield.[8]

When they awoke on the morning of May 9, they learned that a battle had taken place where they had been camped on the 7th. The Confederates had attacked General Franklin's division as it landed there, but ten thousand Union troops had pushed back forty thousand Rebels. They did not know the losses on the Union side, but they saw a number of graves, one with nineteen bodies. Some of the bodies remained unburied, and their throats had been slashed from ear to ear, though the soldiers didn't know whether this happened before or after their deaths. It was a savage act from an enemy who claimed to be chivalrous. At noon, they were ordered to fall into ranks. They marched about half a mile and set up camp. They had to make room for other troops that had landed and gone on ahead of them. Because of that troop movement, it was evident to the Sharpshooters that they were in the reserve division. There was little commotion in camp other than the usual, as they prepared their accommodations. The lack of rest for several nights affected the officers and men, who turned in early for needed sleep.

May 10, 1862, was spent digging wells. The men found water at about six feet deep, and thought it was the best they had had since they left Massachusetts. There was a brigade drill and usual inspection, at which time they were ordered to prepare three days' rations and be ready to march on a moment's notice. The men complained of the extreme heat, to which they were not conditioned. The 11th was a more comfortable day. They were marched about a mile away to collect firewood, and had no duty until the dress parade and inspection in the evening. Lieutenant Stiles and a couple of the men went to the river and boarded a sutler's schooner. When they returned to camp they heard rumors that Federal forces had taken Norfolk and the Confederates had blown up the long-dreaded *Merrimac* so that it would not fall into Union hands. At night the rumor was confirmed, and there was much excitement in

The White House landing on the Pamunkey River, Virginia, circa 1864, from the Brady Collection (Library of Congress).

camp as the men cheered loudly. No orders were issued on May 12 other than to be ready to march early on the 13th.

They were awakened at three in the morning and ordered to pack up and prepare breakfast. They broke camp at five thirty and marched about a half of a mile, then halted until ten o'clock. Then, for two hours they proceeded at a slow pace, which felt more like a forced march. All of the troops who marched ahead of them made the march hot and dusty. Under those conditions they marched a total of fifteen miles, arrived at Cumberland, and encamped. They were told a scouting party had captured a Rebel brigade during the day. They were too tired to look around, so they prepared coffee and slept on the ground without pitching their ponchos.

They awoke stiff and sore on the morning of May 14. Thinking it was going to rain, they pitched their ponchos but did not complete the task before the rain started. They did not have much to do that day. Early in the evening, they were ordered to fall in with arms and equipment at the double quick. They observed that the ambulances were harnessed hastily and thought for sure they were going to skirmish that night. It was only when the formation was completed that they were told they were there for a review by Secretary of State Seward. They were not happy about being called out in the rain for such a reason. The Sharpshooters and their rifles got wet, and they had no time to clean them as it was dark when they returned to camp. Twenty-six prisoners came into camp and were placed in the guardhouse a short distance from them. Receiving orders to be ready to march at one in the morning, they turned in.[9]

They were called out at three in the morning on May 15. They packed up everything and fell into formation at four o'clock. They were ordered to unsling their knapsacks and fall in at parade rest, where they remained, in the pouring rain, until three in the afternoon. Then, thoroughly soaked, they marched three miles in mud one foot deep to an area called the White House. They camped in a grove near Dr. John Mayo's house, pitching their tents as soon as they could to get out of the rain. They were disgusted with a soldier's life. Every time they marched, they lost two to five men, and their ranks were rapidly diminishing. On the 16th, around noon, they fell into marching formation. The weather was clearing, and they marched three miles, in six to ten inches of mud, to the White House landing. When they arrived they could see thousands of troops who had arrived and encamped before them. They were told their wagons would not arrive that night, so they made coffee and prepared to turn in.[10]

May 17 was a quiet day for them; their only duty was to gather wood and water for the cookhouse. On the 18th, they grumbled about being called out for two inspections, for which they saw no purpose. They believed the inspections were only for the gratification of the commanding officers and probably did not realize that the army's organization had changed. They were detached from the 3rd Corps and attached to Porter's 5th Provisional Corps, and General Morell became the division's commander. That night they were issued new ponchos made out of cloth, which they thought would be cooler than the ones made of rubber. On May 19 they turned out, made breakfast, and marched two miles to Tunstall's Station, encamping above the York and Richmond Railroad, in a mud hole as usual. They pitched their new ponchos and found them to be much more accommodating.

They turned out early on the morning of May 20th. They had company drills and inspections, but were not happy about being called out for a dress parade as well. In the evening, they were ordered to prepare and pack three days' rations in their haversacks and be ready to march at three in the morning. They were tired of hearing stories about Richmond and wanted to get there and see the place themselves. They were led to believe there would be no fighting until they got there.

They were called up at five in the morning on May 21. They prepared rations and packed their knapsacks and were ordered to leave three men there: Corporal Grover and Privates Dearborn and Morris were assigned to remain as camp guards. Their march started at seven o'clock, just as the rain started. They got thoroughly wet, but the weather cleared about nine o'clock. They thought they were in a pleasant part of the country. The lands were cultivated and the houses much denser. It appeared they had gotten into the vicinity of civilization. The weather was comfortable, and the roads were in good condition. Many new scenes attracted their attention. They did not realize they were tired until the five-mile march to Lipscomb's Farm march was almost completed. It was a field of sandy soil, without a tree to protect them from the sun's rays. Seventeen yards in front of them was a grove of pines, sufficient in size to encamp the entire division. But they were ordered not to enter it, as this area was reserved for the officers' horses. They realized it was their lot to be privates in the army and that those horses were more important than they were. They quickly set up their tents to get out of the hot sun. They were about fifteen miles from Richmond.

At five in the morning on May 22, they were called up and resumed their march. The twelve-mile march to a mile beyond Cold Harbor was long and difficult. While they encamped at Barker's Mills, word circulated camp that Beauregard had been defeated at Corinth. The men got up early on the 23rd and went out foraging, as the quartermaster did not have provisions except for hard bread. They found strawberries, sweet potatoes, and green peas; these foods were all common to the area and ripe. They returned to camp with quite a load, so much so that they looked like a cooking company rather than Sharpshooters. Everyone had kettles, so they could cook their vegetables. Learning that the news of Beauregard's defeat was not true, they were disappointed. The 24th was a quiet day with normal drill. The quartermaster had only hard bread and no vegetables or meat of any kind. Many of the men took a swim and bathed in the millpond. May 25 was a quiet day, with neither drills nor signs of a forward movement. They were finally given a little bit of salt pork, which proved difficult to cook.

Before sunrise on May 26, they were turned out, and ordered to prepare breakfast, dry out their ponchos, pack their knapsacks, and be in marching formation at seven o'clock. They marched about three miles to Gaines' Mills and encamped there. Orders were given to be ready to leave camp at four in the morning, in light marching order, but they were given no hint of where they would be going. They were within five miles of Richmond, and several skirmishes had taken place in that vicinity over the past week; the Union had been victorious in those actions.[11]

They were turned out early in the morning of May 27. They made coffee and were ordered to fall into marching formation. Hastily disposing of their coffee, they fell into the ranks, then began the march in a pelting rain. As usual, the men were tired and in bad condition. They had to ford every stream they came across, and were thoroughly soaked from head to foot.

Arriving in the vicinity of Hanover Courthouse, they found the Rebels in force, and skirmishes immediately started on the right. They were deployed to the left, marched around a small field, entered a wooded area, and halted. Through an opening of the woods they could see the enemy fall into a battle line. The 5th U.S. Battery opened fire on them with such accuracy that a caisson, four horses, and some men were killed. The Rebels retired to the woods to the left and rear of the Sharpshooters. A small picket was sent out to observe their movements. It was feared the Rebels had flanked them and could attack them from their rear and side. Colonel Gove thought they were in an unsafe position, so he called in the pickets, and, as ordered by General Martindale, marched through the woods to the railroad tracks. On the slow, three-mile march to the railroad station, they removed rails and cut telegraph wires. Later, they learned from Rebel prisoners that as they were to turn onto the railroad tracks, a Carolina regiment was to ambush them from the top of an embankment directly across from them. But the Rebel commander thought the regiment was a brigade and ordered the Carolinians not to shoot.

When they arrived at the station, the Sharpshooters were ordered to destroy an overhead water tank. While doing so they heard shots from their rear, but kept up the destruction until it was completed. Colonel Gove's fear was realized, as their regiment was attacked from the rear. The Sharpshooters went to the battle as fast as their weary limbs permitted them. They arrived at the battle about seven in the evening, soon after the firing had gradually slowed down; it ended after dark. The enemy had been driven from the field, and the Sharpshooters camped on the battlefield, among the dead and wounded Rebels. It was a deeply moving experience as they viewed the carnage around them. They were proud that their little company had battled bravely and had not flinched.

The Sharpshooters also repulsed the initial attack. Some of them, burdened with their heavy rifles, could not keep up with the march and had fallen behind. When the Rebels attacked the rear of the regiments, those who had fallen behind formed a very respectable skirmish line, and held the Rebels until the rear guard, the 44th New York Regiment, could reinforce them. One of the Sharpshooters who could not keep up was Nathan B. M. Ingalls. While lying prone he raised his head to make an observation and saw a Rebel doing the same. Drawing a bead on the foe, he remarked, "I guess I'll take you into camp." The Rebel saw that Ingalls had the drop on him and surrendered.

Charles Lewis, of the Sharpshooters, drove a four-horse ambulance near the Hanover Courthouse. He was assaulted by the Rebels, but escaped capture as he carried a wounded officer back to camp. When he stopped at the plantation of G. W. Jones, near the battlefield, Mrs. Jones said the Rebels had told her the Yankees were coming and would take all of her corn. She complained that one of her young male slaves had run off to the Union army and begged Lewis to return her slave. A short time after, when the contraband refused to do some work around the camp, Lewis threatened to return the ex-slave to his master. "You don't know whar I belongs," said the ex-slave. "Yes I do," replied Lewis. "You are George Washington Jones's boy, of Hanover Courthouse, and you go back unless you behave yourself." The boy admitted his identity and promised to be faithful if he could remain.[12]

On May 28, they were ordered to collect and bury the dead. Parties were detailed for that purpose, while others surveyed the field to determine the loss of Union forces. They did not attempt to come up with a number but stated that losses were heavy on both sides. Many prisoners were taken, mostly from North Carolina regiments. The Carolinians said that they had gotten tired of the service and were glad to be out of it.

After the dead had been buried, the Sharpshooters were ordered out on a reconnoitering mission. They went in the direction of the enemy's retreat. As they moved forward, they came across knapsacks, haversacks, canteens, blankets, guns, cooking utensils, camp equipage, and everything else carried by an army. They thought the Rebels must have been completely routed to leave all of that material strewn on the road. As their object was to ascertain where the enemy was located, they left all that material there for others to collect. They marched about four miles, came upon the Rebels' rear guard, and were ordered back to camp once the Rebels' location was known. As they returned, one of the Sharpshooters picked up a Rebel tent for shelter that night. His officer ordered him to put it down, which he did. Two members of the regimental band picked it up, and when they unfurled it in camp they found the regimental colors of McCowan Guard. They camped in the same place they had been the night before, and several regiments advanced past them. Although they were ordered to be ready to march on a moment's notice, they did not move.

On May 30, they were allowed to sleep in as long as they wanted. When they turned out they all complained of soreness and stiffness. In three days they had marched fifty miles and fought a battle. A large number of them had gone to the surgeon's call, but none were seriously ill. In the early evening a heavy thunderstorm started, the likes of which the Sharpshooters had never seen. Lightning flashed all around them, striking in a regiment camped next to them; this killed a sergeant major and seriously injured five other men. Saturday, May 31, they were not ordered to march, although they expected to, as heavy firing and smoke were heard and seen in the direction of Fair Oaks. They had hoped the next day, Sunday, would be a day of rest, as it was needed. Their numbers had diminished: many were in the hospital, and several of the Sharpshooters lay in their quarters unfit for duty.[13]

12

The Rifle or the Cell

The Sharpshooters were called out at seven thirty in the morning on June 1. They marched at daylight without knowing where they were going. Marching about a mile to Dr. Gaines's house, which was being used as a hospital, they halted in a meadow. In front of them, troops moved across a bridge where Rebels were observed at a distance across the creek. Two batteries were there to protect the marching movement. It appeared to the Sharpshooters that they were there to support those batteries. They remained there until the middle of the afternoon, when they returned to camp. After dark they were ordered to be ready to march in the morning.

While at this camp, Sergeant Sturtevant had gotten apples and proposed to make a batch of pies. Lieutenant Stiles obtained the flour, Sturtevant had a Dutch oven, and it was agreed that the pies would be divided among the Sharpshooters. Four pies were cooked and set on a cracker box to cool. Nearby, a tent's crew observed that process and waited until Sturtevant was called away, then stole and consumed the pies in an instant. The cry went out, "Where's my pies?" Having consumed the hot pies in extremely hot weather, the thieves got little satisfaction. The youngest of the pie-eaters was nominated to return the pie tins, which he did, unobserved. That further angered Lieutenant Stiles and Sturtevant. The company was called out and every man questioned, to no avail. Although Lieutenant Stiles said it would go hard for the thieves, they were never caught.[1]

On June 2, the men turned out at sunrise, expecting to march after breakfast. They prepared and filled their haversacks, but no orders were issued. The hot air balloon *Intrepid* confirmed Corinth's evacuation by Beauregard's forces. Reconnoitering continued through the day, but they learned nothing of those missions' results. Sickness continued in large numbers among the regiment and Sharpshooters. They heard that two men in the regiment had died of disease but could not learn their identities.

On the morning of June 3, the Sharpshooters turned out tired and sore. As no orders were given, they thought they would remain in camp for several days and get needed rest. Receiving an order to fall in, they quickly obeyed, stood in the ranks for awhile, and then were ordered back to quarters. Within fifteen minutes the order was given to fall in. They were marched to guard a bridge that crossed the Chickahominy River. The regiment was too large for that duty, so they returned to camp and the Sharpshooters remained on guard duty. They set up their posts just as it began to rain. On the morning of the 4th, it continued to rain. They thought they would remain on guard duty and would be relieved after dark. About ten in the morning, they started a fire to make coffee and attempted to dry their clothes. Soon after they started their fire, General Martindale rode by and told them they could return to camp. Returning there, they heard of a large battle fought on May 31, with immense losses on both sides, but all of the particulars were unknown.

On June 5, the Sharpshooters were not called out. At about nine in the morning, they heard a rapid artillery discharge for a two-hour period. They prepared for and expected to be called in a line of march to support the battery at any time. They soon learned that Union skirmishers had found a masked battery of the enemy, and that the Union artillery unmasked it. There was no duty that day except for dress parade. Three company members, Faulkner, Reed, and Pinkham, were sent to the division hospital. The 6th was a very quiet day in camp, which they thought remarkable, as the armies were so close together. There was no drill that day. The Sharpshooters looked for a speedy end to the war, without much exertion from their reserve corps.

On June 7, they were ordered to prepare for fatigue duty. Waiting patiently until noon, they fell in and marched four miles to the site of their duty. Once there, they realized they were only a mile from their camp. It appeared to them that army officers intended to march them the farthest possible way to get to a certain point. They dug a trench along the side of the road that led to the bridge that spanned the Chickahominy River. After about two and a half hours of labor, it rained heavily. They sought shelter until five o'clock, when they were ordered back to camp. Once they were back, the Rebels fired some artillery, which was returned by twenty-pound rifled Enfields. The cannonading lasted until ten at night. Although all kinds of rumors about the action circulated, none could be confirmed. On the 8th, all was quiet in camp. It was a cooler day, and the men's clothes were wet from the previous day, making them quite uncomfortable.

On June 9, they received word that James Reed, who had gone to the divisional hospital in New Bridge on the 6th, had died of rheumatic fever there at about three o'clock in the morning. The Sharpshooters made a crude box and intended to fall out in full ranks to follow his remains to his grave, but were ordered to fall into the ranks to receive a distinguished foreigner. They marched to an open field on the right of the road from Gaines' Mills to Mechanicsville, where General Prim of Spain, General McClellan, General Porter, and a host of officers of lesser rank reviewed them. They were dismissed and returned to camp, and learned Reed's body had been buried. They were upset that their small company had not been excused and allowed to pay tribute to their fallen comrade. They were not called out again during the day.

On the morning of June 10, Nathan Haynes awoke cold and uncomfortable to rainwater leaking on his face through his tent. The men expected to be called to fatigue duty some distance from camp, but were not disturbed. At the end of the day the artillery opened up to let the Rebels know they remained in position. The 11th also proved quiet.

On June 12, they were ordered to pack their gear and report for fatigue duty. Thinking they were going to work on the railroad, they marched about two miles to a swamp and were informed they were to build corduroy across it. They pitched their tents on the side of a hill, as they thought they would be there for several days. Arming themselves with axes, they made a large dent in a young grove of pines. They worked right along, and night came upon them before they knew it.

On June 13, the din of artillery on their left awaked them and heavy cannonading followed for an hour, then subsided. At five in the morning, they were armed with axes and returned to where they were the previous night. As it was very hot, they worked until noon and quit for the day, then went up to the camp, had vegetable soup, and rested from their labors. At two o'clock, they were ordered to pack up and fall in. They were taken by surprise, as they thought they would be there a few days to finish the corduroy road. They packed up and began the march. They wondered where they were to go, but if they asked they would not be told. They marched to their old camp at Gaines' Farm, where they were ordered to unsling their knapsacks and be prepared for a light march. They fell into the ranks, awaited orders, and observed other regiments return from expeditions. The order was given to break ranks and encamp. This entire arrangement seemed foolish to the Sharpshooters. Although they presumed something was contemplated, they had no idea what. The order then was given to prepare to march at two o'clock in the morning. (The sudden move was due to a raid on White House.)

They awoke on the morning of June 14 and assumed that the previous night's order was countermanded, as they were not called out until sunrise. The early march had been a response to a rumor that fifty of their wagons had been attacked by guerrillas. But all was quiet that day, and the men chose not to stroll around camp but instead stay in their tents which kept them out of the hot sun.

On June 15 the Sharpshooters thought something strange had happened. Colonel Gove decided to have guard duties performed by companies rather than by detail. He had a large steel triangle made, on which the guard duty was posted, in order to eliminate bugle calls, which could have given their position and troop strength to the enemy. The Sharpshooters were assigned to guard the camp, which was something they had not done since being in the service. They shouldered their rifles and relieved Company G. The heat was so intense that it overcame one of the Sharpshooters while he was on post. At about three o'clock, a thundershower accompanied by high winds cooled them down.

The regiment was called out for picket duty at six thirty in the morning on June 16. The Sharpshooters had not been relieved from guard duty, so they stayed in camp. They wondered why they were not relieved and ordered to go with the regiment, as they had never escaped such duty before. Early in the morning of the 17th, they heard firing in the direction of the James River, which lasted about two hours. They thought it was from Federal gunboats. After being relieved from guard duty, they had nothing to do. The regiment returned from picket duty about nine o'clock in the morning.

They were called out at midnight to fall in light at marching order. They marched but did not know where they were going or in which direction. They marched without halting until they saw the gray streaks of dawn, then halted. They were allowed to rest until daylight of the 18th. They resumed their two-mile march through Mechanicsville and came to a halt; they remained there until noon. As the buildings testified, Mechanicsville had been the scene of a battle. The men were there long enough to catch a glimpse of the ill-fated citizens. They were within five miles of Richmond and could see spires in the Rebel capital. They were ordered to march back to their camp at Gaines' Farm, where they arrived exhausted just after dark. The Sharpshooters could not understand why they were ordered out there and back but were willing to remain in ignorance. (The intention was to relieve General Taylor's brigade, the 1st New Jersey, but for some reason that order was changed.) They awoke on June 19 tired and sore; Nathan Haynes was so exhausted he could barely lift his head and thought he should go to the hospital.[2]

On June 20, they were ordered to pack everything and break camp. They left Gaines' Farm and marched about a mile to Dr. Curtis's farm on the Mechanicsville Road. There they pitched their tents on the site of an old encampment, sheltered on three sides by woods. They spent the next several days laying out company streets, each forty feet wide. They planted shade trees around their tents and dug wells outside of the lines but in view of the camp guard. When they arrived there it was sandy and barren, but after their work it resembled a garden.

Savage Station Field Hospital, June 27, 1862. Many of the wounded from the Mechanicsville battle of June 26, 1862, were taken to that field hospital (Library of Congress).

Having taken so much care to set it up, the Sharpshooters thought it would be a permanent camp. Providing constant maintenance kept it clean and neat. They thought it was the best and healthiest camp they had been in since leaving Hall's Hill. They learned that they had left their camp at Gaines' Farm at the right time. A deserter had given the Rebels their old camp's location, and the Rebels had shelled it, along with Dr. Gaines' house and outbuildings, which the Rebels knew were being used as hospitals. The Sharpshooters thought it was a reprehensible act.

Orders to fall in and a light marching order were given at two in the morning on June 24. The men stayed under arms until daylight and then were ordered out on picket duty. After they marched a short distance, the order was countermanded and they returned to camp, after which small details were sent out to guard telegraph wires.

On June 25, they were awakened by cannonading, which continued into the night. They learned that General Hooker had engaged the enemy and driven them half a mile. He would have gone farther, but he was ordered to stop. The artillery on the Union side of the creek was engaged and shelled the Rebels into the evening. The men were not given any duty and spent the day nursing the company back to health.

The Sharpshooters were detailed on camp guard on June 26. The morning was quiet. At around noon the bugle sounded for the regiment to fall in. The men of the regiment were ordered to arm themselves with eighty cartridges apiece. Rifle firing was heard in the direction of Mechanicsville. Contrary to what was expected and usual, the Sharpshooters were ordered to stay behind, break camp, load the wagons, and bring them to McClellan's headquarters on the other side of the Chickahominy River. There was not enough time for the entire equipage to be taken.

They decided to leave a small squad to guard the property that remained until a commanding officer sent a team back so it could be loaded. They thought that would be about midnight. The battle in front of them raged furiously until ten o'clock that night. There was no sleep for the Sharpshooters who were left to guard the camp. They waited for the wagons while fires burned on all sides of them. Hearing the teams rumbling hastily toward the rear, they knew a retreat was taking place. They were in an alarmed state, as no one returned to camp and told them which way the tide of battle had gone.[3]

As dawn appeared on June 27, the regiment returned. They hastily slung their knapsacks over their backs and immediately left camp. Colonel Gove came over and told the Sharpshooters to leave camp unless they wanted to be taken as prisoners. The Sharpshooters collected all of the equipment left behind and burned it to keep the enemy from taking it. They marched to find the rest of the Sharpshooters, and as they left the camp they were shelled, as they had inadvertently walked onto the battlefield. They did not find the rest of the Sharpshooters until four o'clock in the afternoon. They had wandered through the great battle of Gaines Mill, in which the 22nd Regiment had suffered great losses. They remained at headquarters with the wagons of equipment until dark, then were ordered to move to Savage Station. They arrived there late at night, tired and sleepy. They were anxious to hear which way the battle had gone and their regiment's fate, but no one could tell them. They spread their blankets where they could among the wagons and lay down to pass the rest of the night.[4]

Gunboats shelling the enemy at the Battle of Malvern Hill, sketched from McClellan's headquarters, July 1, 1862 (Library of Congress).

On the morning of June 28, the Sharpshooters at Savage Station thought their regiment was in the area. Going out to look for them, Lieutenant Stiles found they were badly decimated. Colonel Gove had been killed, Major Tilton was wounded and taken prisoner, the surgeons were missing, a hospital steward was seriously wounded, and Adjunct Sherwin was wounded. The senior captain, Captain Sampson, from Company A, was commanding the regiment, which had marched to Savage Station, where Captain Sampson was taken sick and turned the regiment over to Captain Wardwell of Company B. The regiment stayed a short time, marched through White Oaks Swamp, and camped just beyond it. The Sharpshooters left Savage Station about two o'clock in the afternoon, marching until night, when they rejoined their regiment.[5]

Attempting to determine the regiment's strength, the Sharpshooters counted the stacked rifles. They counted 259 from the 750 men who went into action on June 27. They thought their information was not accurate, as an allowance had to be made for stragglers. After they gathered their information, they had some coffee and spread their blankets in the mud for some rest. About midnight they were aroused by a stampede in the regiment as they heard the yell, "They are among us! They are among us!" The Sharpshooters did not panic. Not one of them attempted to run. Instead, they followed Lieutenant Stiles' order to roll their blankets and be ready to march. All was quiet in a short time. Using their knapsacks for a pillow, they lay back in the mud for the rest of the night. Later they learned that a runaway mule team had created the excitement.[6]

On Sunday, June 29, they turned out from the damp ground and made their coffee. Seeing no sign of a movement, they went out and gathered rails for firewood to cook meat. They were ordered to fall in. They were deprived of their meat, but would not be deprived of their fire. They stacked up all the rails and set them on fire. The rails had a lot of pitch in them and sent up a column of black smoke that could be seen for miles. Still in retreat, they marched at ten in the morning, proceeded about two miles, and halted. They were on grounds where Union troops had skirmished with about two hundred Rebel cavalry two hours before. The small squad of troops was victorious: they had killed several Rebels, wounded about forty, and taken fifty prisoners. The Sharpshooters remained there until sundown, and were ordered to fall in. They marched about a mile, turned into a field near Charles City Crossroads, and encamped for the night. They were disturbed several times that night as they thought guerrillas were in their camp, but that proved to be wrong.

They were called out at three in the morning on June 30. They marched a short distance, came to a halt, and stayed there for a considerable time, supposing that the enemy was all around them. Reconnoitering parties were sent out every few miles, and they thought that was why they had stopped. At sunrise, they marched through White Oak Swamp and halted in a grove on a rise of ground just beyond the swamp. The men boiled coffee, but with only coffee and hard bread for nourishment, they began to feel the effects of their hard march. They were given only enough time to drink their coffee and then form into a line of march.

They marched to Malvern Hill, in sight of the James River, where they saw Federal gunboats and thought their trials were over. With all the support around them, they did not believe they would be assailed. They marched into a small ravine and halted; they were not able to rest as they were ordered to the crest of the hill. They took a battle position in a cornfield and faced the rear. It appeared that the regiment was covering the entire army's retreat. They remained there in the scorching sun for two hours, then marched through the ravine to a rise of ground and halted.[7]

As they began to set up camp, they were ordered to fall in. They thought they were to go to a better encampment area. Arriving at the top of Malvern Hill, they discovered all of General McClellan's army before them in a field. They contemplated the vast number of

The bow of a Confederate gunboat captured July 4, 1862, by the U.S.S. *Maratanza*. It was towed down the James River by the Union Navy. It was anchored across the river from the Sharpshooters' camp. They did not get a chance to view it (Library of Congress).

troops in front of them. As far as the eye could see, brigades and divisions marched in. They wondered where there was an army large enough to compete with them, yet they had been compelled to retreat for the last three days. The congregated men on top of the hill were ordered into the ranks and marched to the front for picket duty. They were stationed three to five men on a post and remained until midnight, when they were relieved. They marched a short distance, slept on their arms, and got some rest.

The morning of July 1, the Sharpshooters remained watchful. About nine in the morning, the Rebels shelled them, and the Union artillery replied with the assistance of Federal gunboats. At about eleven o'clock, they were ordered to form a battle line. They unslung their knapsacks, which held molds, patch cutters, and other things peculiar to their long-range rifles, and fell into line. Moving out to support an artillery battery, they lay flat on the ground for five hours and listened to the most fearful cannonading they had ever experienced, or ever wanted to. Several men of the regiment were slightly wounded by shell fragments as they lay on the ground. They found it a nerve-wracking experience and a trying position to be in, exposed to fire but unable to return it. The cannonading was so horrific it aged them as they lay there, and they dared not move.

The Sharpshooters were surprised when they were ordered to form a battle line. They thought they were not in a place for any type of formation, but they resolved to do their best. Twice they were almost flanked but repulsed the enemy. The battle lasted until eight o'clock that night, when the Rebels retreated at the double quick. The Sharpshooters rested on the ground, and at midnight marched in retreat for the rest of the night. They arrived at Harrison's Landing at six in the morning.[8]

On July 2, they awoke to heavy rains. Troops continued to come into camp all day and trampled over the ground, soon working it to a consistency of soft mud a foot deep. Fortunately for the Sharpshooters, they halted in a wheat field. Collecting the wheat, they laid it on the ground to keep them out of the mud. That was the only protection they had as they had lost their knapsacks, blankets, ponchos, and tents on the battlefield on July 1. (The regiment had lost theirs at the battle of Gaine's Hill.) The men had nothing but what was on their backs. Stragglers came in until dark, and the Sharpshooters assessed their losses. Privates James Graham and John Q. A. Sturtevant were wounded, and Private Sewell D. Richardson was wounded and had been taken prisoner. It continued to rain. The men were in deplorable condition, worn out and hungry. They lay down on their piles of straw and attempted to get some sleep.[9]

They awoke the morning of July 3, and it continued to rain. It was not long before the Rebels shelled them. The troops were ordered into a battle line. While they took their position, several shots whistled past them. They had not heard of anybody being injured. The Sharpshooters' position was in a deep ravine, and they could not hear or see what was going on in front of them. While they were in the ravine a company member who had been sent home sick appeared, and all the men were surprised to see him. They gleaned all of the home news they could from him, and then he left and reported to the hospital. Remaining in the ravine until past noon, they marched to a small piece of woods and encamped. Then they learned what had happened in the morning. Federal forces had gotten behind the Rebel battery that had shelled them in the morning, capturing the entire battery and taking a large number of prisoners. It was near dark when they arrived at the wood lot, and they sought what protection they could find and prepared to pass the night.

On July 4, they remained in the enemy's vicinity, but celebrated the day with spirit. Several batteries and the gunboats on the river fired the national salute, and a number of bands played national airs. The men enjoyed themselves as well as they could under the circumstances. Making their camp as comfortable as possible, the Sharpshooters passed the day and provided their officers with a list of items they needed for comfort.

The morning of July 5, they experienced the South's extreme heat and felt that Northerners would be rendered useless if the heat continued. The sick were returned to camp, except for Richardson, who had been missing since the battle of July 1. They learned that Graham had boarded a boat bound for a Northern hospital. The remainder were wounded only slightly, and would soon be fit for duty. They heard heavy firing in the morning down the river, and in the afternoon they learned that a Rebel field battery had gotten below Federal lines and cannonaded transports as they traveled on the river. The Federal gunboats soon quieted them. Later they learned that a Rebel gunboat had been captured and towed down the river, and had landed across from the Sharpshooters' encampment, but they did not get a chance to see it.[10]

A thorough inspection of the regiment took place on July 6. The Sharpshooters had been rendered unfit for duty. They had lost the equipment for their rifles at the battle of Malvern Hill, and there was no way to replace it. On July 7 they received the news that they were relieved from active duty, and they were upset. As an unfit unit, they received only hard bread and smoked meat. Other regiments received all that Army regulations would allow. Although unfit for duty, they provided fatigue squads. They felt their officers should have stood up for them, but that did not happen, so the Sharpshooters made the best of it.[11]

The morning of July 8 passed very quietly. In the afternoon, they heard reports of artillery fire. They were informed that those shots were without cartridges, and they wondered who the salute was fired for. They found out when they were ordered to fall in to be reviewed by President Lincoln. It was dark when the president passed the Sharpshooters, and they returned to camp disappointed. On their arrival, they heard the rumor that Federal forces had captured Vicksburg. The 9th was very warm, and they did fatigue duty around the camp. There was no duty on the 10th. On the 11th, some of the Sharpshooters performed camp guard with Company C. Since the late battles some of the companies were greatly reduced in numbers, and a detachment of Sharpshooters was required to join them so that there would be enough men to guard the camp. A new doctor appeared from Boston and attended to the regiment's sick. He appeared to be quite young, and the men thought him to be inexperienced. In the afternoon of the 12th they did company drill for an hour. Nothing else had been done that day. At night a squad of Sharpshooters went on camp guard with Company B. On the 13th, they had a regimental inspection and did nothing else for the day. At night, the remainder of the Sharpshooters went on camp guard.

On July 14, the Sharpshooters were thrown into a high state of excitement. They learned that by order of Colonel Barnes, Lieutenant Stiles had sent a requisition for Sharps breech-loading rifles. The men protested loudly against taking them. All day they talked about how much they hated the Sharps rifles, and the conversations extended late into the night. They had carried their old rifles so long they had become attached to them. To part with them would be the same as parting with a tried and valued friend. They resolved to use all means and power to prevent such a disaster falling upon them. Colonel Barnes thought the new rifles would be better for the Sharpshooters. They would be lighter rifles, better for the men's health, and they could march, drill, and carry them into battle more easily than their heavies. A ready supply of ammunition also would be on hand. The Sharpshooters had made their own balls from molds, as the caliber of their telescopic rifles was different from the standard army issue.

On July 15, the regiment was mustered for pay. They had not been paid since February 23, and they needed pocket change to provide themselves with a few articles the government did not supply. Colonel Griswold returned to the regiment and took command; he had been sick since the regiment was in Yorktown. Colonel Gove's death had enabled him to succeed to the colonelcy.

From July 16 to the 20th, camp was very quiet. The men did normal company drills, fatigue duty around camp, and some camp guard duty. They turned out on the 21st, and nothing occurred to break the previous two weeks' monotony. In the evening, they were issued new, small tents. They thought these would be preferable to the scanty protection they had, but when they saw one pitched and were told how many men it would accommodate, they resolved to sleep one more night in their old ones. It was rumored that they were to move early in the morning.

On July 22, they were called out and expected an early order to pack up, but the order never came. They spent the morning in the shade. At noon, they were ordered to pitch their new tents. Most of the men preferred their old tents, and it seemed unlikely that they would be crowded into the new tents that night. There were no new cases of sickness, but the sick men had not improved very fast. They finally admitted to themselves that as a company they were worn out. Several of the men went to be examined to determine whether they were fit for service, but did not hear the results. At dark, they were ordered to be ready to move in the morning.

They were awakened at five in the morning on July 23 and were ordered to pack their equipment. They had ample time to get their breakfast, collect all their baggage, and take it some distance to the teams before they fell into line. After getting into formation, they remained at rest for a long time in the hot sun before the order to march came. They marched about a mile toward the river and halted in an open field, where they were ordered to encamp. The Sharpshooters saw no advantage, as they would have to travel half a mile for wood and water. They thought that with some labor they could make the camp neat and clean, which they felt would be to their benefit. After they removed their equipment, some of them returned to the old camp to get things that were left behind. Those who remained pitched the tents. They got settled and turned in for the night.

On July 24, they turned out under a sky threatening rain, but it cleared around nine in the morning, and they were scorched by the sun. They sought the shelter of their tents, and all was quiet until they were ordered to fall in at five o'clock. They marched about a mile and were reviewed by Generals Morrell and Howell. They marched in review and returned to camp, and were not pleased to learn they would do the same thing the next day.

They formed a line of march at seven in the morning on July 25. They marched to the parade ground, which was about a mile from their camp, and when they arrived they found it nearly full of troops that had preceded them. General Porter's entire command was formed by brigades. It was a splendid sight, so large that the Sharpshooters could not see all of the troops. The artillery batteries were formed in the rear, except one, which was in the front to fire a salute when the generals arrived. They remained at rest for an hour, and the guns in front were fired when the generals appeared. The review was very brief, as Generals McClellan and Porter, with their staff, rode along the front line. When the men returned to camp, some excitement surrounded the case of a sergeant who had had a severe headache and thought the sun would be bad for his condition, so he had not attended the review, but remained in camp. He was arrested, and his punishment was to stand in the hot sun all day. Although the surgeon did not excuse him from duty, the Sharpshooters thought the punishment was given in a spirit of revenge. They thought it was cruel, and that caused considerable excitement. July 26 and 27 were quiet days, filled with normal camp duties, and the company was inspected. Their most important duty was to try to keep cool, as the days were very hot.

The morning of July 28, the paymaster appeared and paid the Sharpshooters two months' pay. Although they were owed four, they were happy to have some money. The greenbacks circulated quite freely. The Sharpshooters were in fine spirits as they filled their stomachs with delicacies that could only be found at the sutler's wagon. But their spirits were soon dampened when they learned that the dreaded Sharps rifles had arrived in camp. They were ordered to fall in with their heavy rifles and equipment. They were marched to the quartermaster's department, and then ordered to lay down their rifles. The Sharps were offered to them, but only one man took one. Seeing that he was alone, he threw it on the ground. They were marched back to their quarters for supper and were told to think about the situation. Again, they were ordered to fall in with arms and equipment. Colonel Griswold gave them a speech and allowed them five minutes to lay down their rifles and accept the new Sharps. When three men complied, the Sharpshooters thought they had disgraced themselves and the entire company. Colonel Griswold then asked the Sharpshooters why they objected to taking the Sharps. Several of the Sharpshooters voiced their reasons, and when the colonel dismissed them they thought the matter was settled.

The brigade commander, Colonel Barnes, appeared in the Sharpshooters' camp and ordered them in formation. He then placed a guard around them. Colonel Barnes addressed them for a considerable time, accusing them of being in a state of mutiny and rebellion against their officers. He told them they were a stigma to themselves and had disgraced the states they came from. He threatened them with court-martial and Dry Tortugas imprisonment. Reminding them that he could order the guard to shoot them as traitors in a time of war, the colonel said, "All those who were willing to obey all lawful orders of their superior officers step six paces forward." As the Sharpshooters had always obeyed such orders and always intended to, there was nothing left to do, and they complied. That released them from arrest and ended the matter for the night. But the Sharpshooters were not satisfied. They were anxious to receive the punishment they were threatened with, which was to be sent to Tortugas on the rip-trap. July 29 was a quiet day. They expected to be arrested over the matter of the Sharps rifles, but nothing happened.[12]

On July 30, the detested Sharps rifles were again offered to the Sharpshooters. They took them under the highest possible protest, and reminded Colonel Barnes that many of the heavy rifles were their own personal property. The two sergeants who distributed the rifles appeared to do it with smug satisfaction. Barnes ordered the quartermaster not to give the Sharpshooters ammunition for the rifles until he ordered them to. The Sharpshooters had just enough time to get some rust from the guns, when they were ordered to fall in with arms and equipment for company drill. Because the Sharpshooters were not trained in Hardee tactics, several sergeants from the regiment were ordered to train them. The Sharpshooters thought these new sergeants acted like tyrants. Their only consolation was that the new sergeants would not always be in charge of them. Thursday, July 31, was a quiet day. They held a short drill in the afternoon and received the ammunition for their new rifles, which they didn't think were fit for duty.[13]

At one in the morning on August 1, the Sharpshooters were awoken by cannonading on the river. They lay awake listening to the balls whistling over their camp. Very few struck in their vicinity, and most went overhead. They expected to get called out, but the firing ended after an hour, and they were not disturbed until daylight, when they learned that a couple of Rebel batteries had planted themselves on a bank across from their camp. The Rebels then amused themselves as they shelled the camp. Union siege guns returned fire and silenced the Rebels. It was reported that three or four Union troops were killed and several wounded. In the morning, gunboats shelled the Rebels and that fire was not returned, so the gunboats ceased firing.

Some of the Union troops crossed the river and burned several buildings the Rebels had used for shelter. The Sharpshooters practiced drill with their bayonets. Their progress went slowly on the first lesson. Sergeants from the regiment drilled them, as none of the officers or sergeants from the Sharpshooters was familiar with the drill. The Sharpshooters thought they had been brought down to infantry standards. Before they got their new arms, they had been promised their duty was to be different. At eight o'clock that night, a sergeant and ten privates from the Sharpshooters were assigned to picket duty. Not knowing where they were going, they left without rations. On August 2, the only duty the Sharpshooters did was bayonet drill. On the 3rd, picket duty returned after twenty-four hours of duty. The pickets had experienced some problems. They thought the officers who commanded them treated them poorly and that they were not provided rations. They thought they would rejoice when Captain Wentworth returned.

On August 4, Nathan Haynes was detailed with ten men to do guard duty at the landing. Starting from their camp at eight o'clock, they arrived at their post at nine. Haynes was stationed with four other men in a shaded area on the riverbank, where they had nothing to do but wait for rations. They amused themselves as they watched the boats on the river. As the river was full of boats, their duty was far from tiresome. In the evening, they were called back to camp and received another two months' pay. They stayed in camp for two hours, and received soft bread, which was rare, as they had not had any for five months. Then they returned to their post at the landing.

On August 5, still at their post, they heard firing in their front; a sharp engagement kept up for an hour and a half, and then ceased. They were curious to know what had happened. Although they heard several rumors, none were authentic. They were on the same post that they had been on the day before, and were to remain there all week. They were satisfied with the arrangement. The men were able to take any amount of vegetables from the commissary stores. They bought their own bread and were not dependent on their company camp for rations. They admitted it was the most pleasant duty they had been called upon to perform since they were in the service. They had made two or three arrests for drunkenness, but there was nothing else to do. Watching the boats on the river, they saw two or three hundred contraband employed by the government unload transports. They swatted some of the millions of greenhead flies around them, thinking they were as bloodthirsty as every living thing in "sesch." At eight o'clock that night they were relieved and returned to their quarters to spend the night undisturbed.

They returned to their post at an early hour on August 6. They cooked potatoes, onions, and coffee, and ate a hearty meal. When one of the Sharpshooters from camp came to their post with rations, they gleaned all the camp news they could from him and sent him back to camp. Lieutenant Stiles started for home at nine in the morning; he had been sick since the Battle of Malvern Hill. Command of the company was turned over to the orderly sergeant. In the afternoon, they heard from the camp that the regiment was under orders to march and everything had been packed. The men had three days' rations in their haversacks. They learned that their knapsacks had been put aboard a transport, which left them with only blankets. Due to their diminished numbers, the regiment had been reported unfit for service, and the men did not think the regiment would be sent to the front. It was a quiet day on post as they made only one arrest; they were relieved at dark. Several exchanged prisoners returned to the regiment that night, and spoke unfavorably of the treatment they received from the Rebels.

The men went back on their post at five thirty in the morning of August 7. They cooked boiled potatoes and coffee for breakfast and settled in the shade. It was a quiet day, and Nathan Haynes requested permission to return to camp, which was granted. The surgeons examined the sick and sent away those who could not march. The majority of the regiment had presented themselves for examination. Realizing that it was more comfortable on the riverbank, Haynes stayed only a short time in camp, then returned to his post. They made two arrests for drunkenness and were relieved for the day. On the 8th, they remained on their post and waited for orders. None came, and they thought they would be there for awhile longer.

Nathan Haynes went on post as usual on August 9, then was ordered off the post to report to the regiment. When he reported, he was promoted to sergeant of the regular guard. His first order as a sergeant was to take a squad of men to the wharf to prevent a steamer from landing there. He had no trouble. The steamer went up the river and was not seen for the rest of the day. The last five days were the warmest they had experienced, but the cool air from the water relieved them.[14]

On August 10, they went to their post and cooked breakfast with the addition of eggs brought to them from the camp. Expecting to be relieved, they packed their blankets about nine in the morning, but no relief came. About noon, they heard a report that the regiment was packed up and that the tents had been struck, and they expected the order to march on a moment's notice. They thought they had been forgotten, as they had no orders to return to camp and pack their gear. They thought there had been some kind of mistake.

Suddenly, a quarter of a mile in front of them, they saw a peculiar sight. A sand spout had formed and was moving slowly toward them. In a few moments, it extended as high as the eye could see. Shaped like an umbrella, it was as large at the base as a molasses hogshead and extended a thousand feet in the air. When its base encountered some gun carriages it broke. The men escaped with only their tents pulled up. The contraband did not work that day. Late in the afternoon a thunderstorm preceded a perfect hurricane, raising a cloud of dust that completely shut out the daylight. Although it rained only a short time, the rain was so intense that it rendered the ground unfit to sleep on. After the storm, the air was so fresh and pure that the men didn't care that they had lost a night of sleep.[15]

The morning of August 11 was bright and clear, as if there had been no change in the weather for some time. The camp sent them their breakfast, and they realized that their regiment had not moved. The vessels were loaded under increased activity, implying that something of importance was about to happen. They heard heavy guns discharged at regular intervals during the day. That night they learned the guns were fired in honor of General McCook, who had been assassinated by guerrillas.

They turned out at an early hour on August 12 and went to the upper landing. There they saw members of the regimental band who had been discharged from the service and had started for home. They returned to camp fatigued, as any small exertion in the heat exhausted them. In the afternoon they had some trouble with the guard, caused by too much whiskey, but it quieted down after the guard sent the offenders back to their camps under guard. It appeared that they would be on that guard post for some time. They made requisitions for rations and equipment to make their quarters more comfortable but then were ordered back to regimental camp. They set up their tents and had everything arranged when they were ordered to strike tents and pack up. They expected to march before morning, but on the 13th, they were still in camp with no signs of moving.

August 14 showed no sign of a movement. It was a quiet day in camp, and they thought they would have a night's sleep on the ground. But at dark, they were ordered to strike their ponchos and pack up. They marched at eleven at night; it was a slow, monotonous march, and on the dawn of the 15th, they were only five miles from camp. All morning, they would march a short distance and then halt, repeatedly. The Sharpshooters thought that this wore the men out more than a continual march. After they passed the village of the Charles City Court House, the pace quickened. The cloudy day relieved the men somewhat from the intense sun, but many of the men fell out, unable to keep up the pace. The column was pushed to the Chickahominy River, where it crossed on a long pontoon bridge just before dark. The men climbed up an embankment and encamped. When the regiment came to a halt, only twenty-seven men were in the ranks, and four of them were Sharpshooters. They learned they had marched twenty-five miles that day, and understood why stragglers came into the camp all night long. They spread their blankets on the ground and went to sleep, too tired to prepare and eat supper.

They marched at seven in the morning on August 16. Strict orders about straggling were given, with the threat of court-martial and a warning that Mosby's men were brutally killing stragglers. Nonetheless, some of the men were unable to keep up. They marched straight through, and at four in the afternoon arrived at Williamsburg, which they marched through and then went two miles beyond where they had been encamped on the battlefield of May 5. As they marched through town, the Sharpshooters were impressed. They thought it was the prettiest place they had seen in Virginia. They saw many public brick buildings, and William and Mary College, with a beautiful edifice pleasantly located. They saw very few of the sort of wooden, worn-out buildings that they had seen throughout Virginia. It had only been three months since the battle, and the field, overgrown with vegetation, looked as though it had never been disturbed. The earthworks and entrenchments had not been disturbed. Viewing those works, they understood why the Federal forces had lost so many men as they had driven the Rebels out. The Union victory spoke volumes of the bravery and endurance of the men who were engaged in that battle. The men did not seek relics, as they usually did on old battlefields. Having just marched fifteen miles, they were so tired they just lay down to sleep. They marched at sunrise on August 17. Their destination was Yorktown, twelve miles from Williamsburg. Extreme heat made it a very difficult march; the dust that rose from the march filled their throats and lungs, and they were frequently halted to catch their breath. Their bodies were stiff and their feet were sore from all the marching they had done. They arrived at Yorktown at five in the afternoon and camped at their old encampment at Wormsley Creek. It had been three months since they left that camp, and they felt as though they were home again. They prepared supper and were so footsore they could hardly move. Unable to resist the temptation, they plunged into the creek for a bath. They felt better and were refreshed before they turned in for the night.[16]

For August 18, Nathan Haynes' journal gives a sense of how the men felt:

> The bugle sounded reveille at half past three o'clock this morning: turned out and cooked our coffee and was soon ready for the march but did not get started until sunrise: got along finely for the first few hours but as the sun got up and grew hot and dusty: the men began to straggle in the rear but think it was more for the purpose of pillaging than for fatigue although there were strict orders prohibiting it: in the course of the day three or four arrests were made which put a stop to it in a measure: before the close of this days march the men had become so worn out with fatigue that they would drop to the ground at every halt: my feet had become so sore that I could not take a firm step on the ground without almost making me cry out in pain but managed to keep in the ranks till about five o'clock P.M. I sat down in the shade beside a clear running brook and rested till the columns had all past then took a bath and hobbled on came up with the Regiment about dark. found it encamped about a mile from Fortress Monroe: laid down my gun and equipment and went in search of water which took me a full hour: cooked some coffee and with the addition of some sweet potatoes and green corn which our men had got I made a hearty meal: then I was willing to rest a while. We have marched twenty-four miles on as dusty a road as could be imagined.[17]

The bugle sounded assembly at seven thirty in the morning on August 19. They were told to march to Newport News and encamp there. They countermarched, filed to the left, and started through the woods toward Newport News. Although they were told it was only five miles to Newport News, they marched more than ten miles to get there. Going down near the earthworks, they halted, made some coffee, and took a look at the inside of the works. They looked at several rough wooden buildings that were formally barracks but now housed sick soldiers. They walked down to the water and viewed the remnants of ill-fated vessels such as the *Cumberland,* the *Congress,* and the *Merrimack.* They watched troops as they embarked and thought they needed to get back to their unit. The regiment had just formed when they returned. They fell in and marched to the wharf to embark, but it was too late, so they marched back to their camp for the night.

The Sharpshooters awoke at daybreak. They went for water to make coffee and learned the regiment had formed, so they left without breakfast. They went aboard the steamer *North America* and waited two hours before they got under way. The steamer was crowded with baggage, boxes, wagons, ambulances, horses, and human beings, but otherwise they had a pleasant journey across the Chesapeake Bay and got some rest. They entered the Potomac River. The steamer kept going until midnight and then dropped anchor.

When they awoke on the morning of August 21, the steamer was under way. At ten

The landing at Aquia Creek, on the Potomac River, near Stafford, Virginia. This photograph was taken circa 1864. U.S. Quartermaster supplies are on the landing, sail ships are seen in the background, and railroad tracks can be seen in the foreground. The Sharpshooters landed on that wharf at ten o'clock on the morning of August 21, 1862 (Library of Congress).

o'clock that morning, they docked at the wharf at Aquia Creek. They immediately disembarked and were loaded on a train that took them to Fredericksburg. Their haversacks were empty and they had not eaten, so they bought whatever they could find that was edible. They did not stay there long, but formed and marched two miles from town, on a very rough hillside, where they cleared the area of rocks and stumps so that they could set up a camp. The Sharpshooters thought their officers were not very wise to select that site for encampment. They also were worn out, hungry, and footsore, and many of the men were not able to march another mile. Nonetheless, they knew that regardless of their condition, they would be thrown into battle as soon as they arrived. They thought that men should not be treated in this manner. They laid down their blankets and tried to sleep their troubles away.[18]

That night it rained all night, and they got up during the night to find rails to lie on, in an effort to get out of the mud. Though they had not gotten much sleep, they arose at an early hour on August 22, made a breakfast of coffee and sweet potatoes and then were ordered to pack up and fall in. They marched about half a mile toward the town and halted in an open field. The regiment was formed in order of encampment. They thought they would be there for a couple of days and would get some needed rest. But while they remained in formation, an officer rode up and ordered them to pack two days' rations in their haversacks, and be ready to march at a moment's notice, dispelling their thoughts of an encampment and rest. They could comply with the latter part of the order, but there were no rations that could be packed in their haversacks. They dared not pitch their tents, as they feared they would be ordered to march at any moment. However, after some time in the sun they decided to pitch them anyway. As soon they finished, they were ordered to fall into formation. They packed up and marched at five in the afternoon. They marched through Falmouth, stopped at three in the morning for a two-hour rest, and then continued. They were not far from Kelly's Ford on the Rappahannock River at daylight on August 23, when they halted for coffee. They resumed their march until five in the afternoon, when they halted and encamped. They had heard cannonading all day, which ended about nine o'clock that evening. They had arrived at that camp with only twenty men in the column. Men who had never left the ranks before had fallen out, unable to keep up with the march. They straggled in throughout the night.

On the morning of August 24, they marched on empty stomachs. Because the wagons had not caught up to the unit, there were no rations. The men learned that they were to backtrack, which excited them as they thought they would meet the wagons and get some food. They marched from noon until sundown, then encamped for the night. But although the wagons were parked in their view, they did not move. The only thing they had was coffee, which often served the soldier as both food and drink.[19]

The bugle sounded at five in the morning on August 25. The men were ordered to fall in, without time to make coffee. They remained there for two hours, then marched for two miles at ten o'clock and halted. They waited for orders for three hours, and then were ordered to about face. They marched back to where they had encamped the night before, pitched their ponchos, and went out and foraged for food. The Sharpshooters were lucky. Not only did they find sweet potatoes and green corn, but also one of the men came in with a carcass of

A Quaker Gun at Centerville, Virginia. This photograph was taken by George Barnard in March 1862. As the Sharpshooters arrived at Centerville, at the end of August 1862, they could not believe the Rebels abandoned it as it was so well fortified. Barnard must have had good relations with the Rebels as he photographed this Rebel soldier igniting the Quaker Gun, which was merely a wooden log painted to look like artillery was there (Library of Congress).

mutton, which they divided up and devoured. They then turned in to get some sleep. Three or four of the Sharpshooters were woken up at ten o'clock and ordered to draw fresh beef for their company.

On the morning of August 26, they were called out at four o'clock in the morning. Hard bread and coffee were issued, but they marched before they could cook the coffee or the beef rations they had been given the night before. Most of the men cut the beef into strips and cooked it on the march. Some of them left the beef on the ground and were later disappointed when they learned that the beef was to be four days' rations, even though they thought there was not enough for one day. They marched at sunrise and continued steadily until four in the afternoon, then camped in a cornfield near a stream. They roasted ears of corn and took baths in the stream. They had marched fifteen miles that day in all directions of the compass. Hearing cannonading to their right, they thought they would be called out, but they were left undisturbed. They marched almost twenty miles under a scorching sun. Men were constantly falling out of the ranks. They followed the Orange and Alexandria Railroad to Warrenton Junction and halted there. The men started fires and put coffee on when they were ordered to fall in; they marched another mile and encamped. Some of the men picked beans on the march and cooked them at camp. The men were so hungry that most of them ate the beans half cooked.

Reveille was sounded at three thirty in the morning on August 28. The men were given two hours to cook breakfast, but they did not need the time, as they had nothing to cook. They marched at five thirty, went a half-mile, and halted to allow Porter's Corps to pass them. As they left Harrison's Landing, they were separated; different brigades took different routes, and they convened at Warrenton Junction. This was the first time they were all together, and they felt confident that they were ready to meet the enemy. They marched slowly along the railroad toward Manassas, obstructed by wagons. It was very hot, dry, and dusty, and many men fell out of the ranks. At Bristoe Station, the Rebels had torn up tracks, cut telegraph lines, destroyed wagons of army stores that they had captured, demolished train cars and locomotives, and blown up bridges. The amount of destroyed property was immense. When the men arrived, they learned their advance had skirmished with the Rebels. The dead were being buried and the wounded were transported to hospitals. The advance had also taken some prisoners. The men were so tired they did not ask about what had happened there. Their march continued until four o'clock, when they encamped. At sundown, it rained, turning the ground from dust to mud. After the rain, cannons could be heard in front of the men until late in the night.

They did not start early on the morning of August 29. They had been issued beef about eleven o'clock the night before and were allotted time to cook it. They were given six pieces of hard bread for the day's rations, and then marched to Manassas Junction. There they were ordered in the direction of Gainesville to reinforce General McDowell. They were hurried at the double quick for three miles, then halted and were ordered to remove their blankets and load their rifles. While they prepared, General McDowell rode by, and they took much notice of him. He was not very well respected by the Sharpshooters. The men advanced and formed a battle line. Rebel artillery opened fire on them, hitting them with such precision that three men in front of them from the 1st Michigan were killed. They were moved out of range, and their 3rd Battery came up and silenced the Rebel artillery. For the rest of the night, they moved forward and retreated, depending on which way the battle had gone. At eight o'clock that night, they moved into a field and encamped. The Sharpshooters had just started fires to prepare supper when they were ordered out on picket duty. It took until midnight to get on their post. They were happy to lie down, even though they could not sleep. Saturday morning, August 30, they were ordered to leave their picket post at daylight.

Returning to the field of encampment, they found it empty. They were ordered to fall in with General Griffin's brigade, until their own brigade could be found. Marching in pursuit of their brigade, they arrived at Manassas Junction at sunrise. Sergeant Haynes felt light-headed, fell out of the ranks, and searched for water. Wandering around, he observed what the Rebels had destroyed. Not a building was left standing, and the place had been made desolate. After a short rest, he caught up with the regiment at Bull Run. They marched to Centreville, where they halted for a short time. They wondered why the Rebels had abandoned it. They had made it almost impregnable: it sat on a hill, fortified, and commanded every point and entrance to the place. The Sharpshooters were not surprised that the Rebels had held the area with Quaker guns (wooden logs painted black to give the appearance that artillery was there) for awhile.

Marching back about a mile, they encamped near a clear stream. The men foraged and came back with green apples, corn, potatoes, and beans, then fortified themselves with a hearty meal. They were out of bread, and Colonel Parker of the 32nd Massachusetts gave them two boxes, which they appreciated. At five o'clock that afternoon, they heard spirited cannons in their rear and were ordered to fall in to assist in the battle. They got to within three miles of the battle and saw that the roads were clogged with wagons and ambulances, which transported the wounded and dying. It was a sad sight to see. Men lay on stretchers, mangled and bleeding. Most were maimed for life. They turned from that sickening sight and asked what happened in the battle, but reports were so conflicted that they could not learn anything. They were ordered back to Centreville, but the march was so slow that they did not arrive until one o'clock that morning.

When they awoke on the morning of August 31, they learned of the great and bloody battle at Bull Run. They did not know which, if either, side had been victorious, but the Rebels held the field and the Federals retreated to Centreville. Ambulances went to the field and brought back many wounded paroled soldiers under a flag of truce. In the afternoon they were issued hard bread and coffee, but no meat, which they desperately needed, although other regiments had received all they wanted. This did not sit well with the Sharpshooters. Stragglers returned to the camp at dark.[20]

On the morning of September 1, troops marched in every direction. The men could not understand what was to happen. They expected to march at any moment. The ambulances went back to the battlefield and returned with more wounded soldiers. At eight o'clock that evening the men were ordered to fall in line, and they stood in the pouring rain for two hours. They did not start their march until midnight. Once they arrived on the streets of Centreville, the march was so slow they did not get out of town until daylight.

On September 2, they marched toward Fairfax, arriving there at ten o'clock in the morning. The regiment turned to the right and avoided going through town. Sergeant Haynes and another Sharpshooter fell out of the ranks and walked through town, expecting to meet the regiment on the other side, but the regiment had gone someplace else and encamped. They searched but could not find the regiment, so they walked toward Alexandria, hearing heavy firing in their rear. At dark they camped on the roadside.

On the morning of September 3, the two Sharpshooters turned out, made coffee, fried a small piece of pork, and proceeded on their way. Both sides of the road were lined with troops, but not their regiment. Arriving at Alexandria at noon, they were provided with a substantial dinner. Although they asked about their regiment's location, they could not learn where it was. They left Alexandria for Fort Albany and arrived there at four o'clock in the afternoon. Meeting a former acquaintance, they stopped to rest and talked of old times. They then learned that their regiment was nearby and searched for it until dark. Unable to find it, they returned to the fort, where they were provided with supper and turned in for the night.

The two Sharpshooters turned out at a late hour on September 4, feeling sore and stiff. Their friend gave them a good breakfast; then they walked around the fort until noon, when they heard that their regiment had returned to Hall's Hill. Going there, they found the regiment camped in a field near their old campground, where they rejoined it. About eight o'clock that evening, they heard that the pickets had engaged the enemy and fell into formation. They marched about a mile but did not find the enemy, and returned to camp. September 5 was a quiet day, as they were not assigned any duty. Captain Wentworth rejoined the company at noon. The men were happy to see him and thought they would fare better, as they now had a company commander.

All was quiet on September 6 until nine o'clock in the morning, when recruits started to pass them, and that continued all day. At noon, they were given rations of beef, pork, beans, rice, and coffee. They thought this was a sure sign they were going to march. At sundown, they were ordered to pack up and, as usual, they left their rations on the ground, as they could not carry them all. At dark, they were reinforced with recruits. They were ready to march at an early hour, but did not get started until midnight, then marched all night.

At daylight on September 7, they arrived at the heights that looked over Alexandria. They marched a short distance further and halted near the Fairfax Seminary, then cooked coffee and ate breakfast. They remained there until noon, then marched in a westerly direction past the Seminary Towers toward Fairfax Courthouse. After marching in several different directions, they halted and encamped at a site that was familiar, as it was always filled with rocks, stumps, and briars, unless it was a swamp. The new recruits complained, but they had kept up fairly well. They had something to eat and fell asleep, and the order was given to fall in under arms. They fell in and waited for orders that did not come until morning.

On the morning of September 8, they were ordered to return to their campsite, where they remained all day. They drew rations and concluded they would move soon. At six o'clock in the evening, they were ordered to be ready to march at seven in the morning. They cooked the meat and filled their haversacks, then threw the rest on the ground as usual. They did not know where they were going, but concluded they would march for another day.

They turned out on the morning of the 9th and cooked breakfast. Although they were ready to march at seven, they did not move until eight o'clock. They marched a few miles, turned to the left, and went past Fort Albany and over the Arlington Heights, where they halted and encamped. For the second time that week, they were mustered for pay. The camp had a large number of visitors, as people took advantage of the opportunity to see acquaintances.

Nothing of importance happened on September 10. They were not assigned any duty, and kept themselves busy while they improved their encampment. The Sharpshooters' camp was on the slope of a very steep hill, and though the men fell asleep in their tents, they woke up in open air as they had slid out of them. They did not hear anything about moving; several Sharpshooters were ordered to bring company stores into camp. They received items they long had been deprived of. They thought if they could remain in camp for several days, they would be as rested as fresh troops.

On September 11, the men re-covered their knapsacks. They were issued new clothing, and their appearance improved markedly, given the worn and tattered clothing they had been wearing. The quartermaster had been able to obtain express boxes that had been sent to them, but they were in deplorable condition. They were issued three days' rations and lost hopes of staying there, as, to them, the rations meant a march.[21]

12. The Rifle or the Cell

Friday, September 12, at an early hour, they were ordered to be ready to march at eight o'clock that morning. The cooks did not have time to boil the meat, which was left on the ground to be brought up by the teams if space was available; if not, it would be left on the ground as usual. Quite a few members of the regiment were left behind, as they were unable to march, and they were ordered to join the regiment as fast as they could. More than half of the Sharpshooters were among that group. They marched at the appointed time. They passed over the Aqueduct Bridge into Georgetown and from there marched to Washington. They halted on a rise south of the capital and had a splendid view of the city. They were ordered to fall into formation. They did not board cars as they thought they would, but marched down the Washington and Baltimore Turnpike until dark and encamped on the slope of a hill as usual. There were more stragglers than usual, as the men carried knapsacks, which they had not done since July 1. They could not find out where they were or what their destination was. (They had encamped outside of Rockville, Maryland.)

Reveille was sounded at four o'clock in the morning on September 13. They were ordered to leave their knapsacks on the ground and take only their blankets. Leaving the knapsacks in a pile, they did not know if they would ever see them again. They marched on a hard road and made good time, with few halts for rest. At noon, they went through the town of Rockville, marched beyond it, and halted, far enough away that men would not straggle back to the village. They halted for an hour to cook coffee, but did not have time to drink it. Continuing their march to Middlebrook, they encamped on the top of a very high hill and pitched their ponchos. Three of the Sharpshooters who were too tired to march went out and foraged, returning with an abundance of green corn, which the men cooked, as their haversacks were empty of rations.

The column began to move at six thirty on the morning of September 14. The hilly terrain and hot, dusty weather made the march extremely difficult. They passed through Clarksburg, Urbana, and Hyattstown, and encamped in the Monocacy Valley. The country and towns they passed through reminded them of New England. The town of Frederick could be seen at a distance, situated in a beautiful valley at the foot of the Blue Ridge Mountains. The Rebels had been there before them and destroyed the Baltimore and Ohio Railroad bridge. They heard cannons all day. Although they had marched more than twenty miles, they appeared to be no closer to the battle. That day the command structure was changed. They remained in the Fifth Corps, First Division, First Brigade, but were commanded by General Barnes of the 18th Massachusetts Volunteer Infantry.[22]

After waiting for and receiving rations at nine in the morning on the 15th, they marched at ten. They passed through the town of Frederick around noon and halted in the streets. The women of Frederick brought them water, bread, and fruit, which they greatly appreciated. They marched up the mountain. It was not difficult, as the road wound around the mountain, and it did not seem that the hills were very steep. They encamped on the banks of a creek near Middletown. Near their camp, a long bridge had been destroyed by the Rebels. In a nearby barn, they were able to get an abundance of straw and made comfortable beds with it.

Reveille was sounded at daybreak of September 16. They continued to march up the mountain, and by mid-morning they reached the battleground of South Mountain. The battle there the day before had been responsible for the cannon fire they had heard then. They saw three or four dead Rebels lying on the side of the road. It appeared the Rebels had held a strong position and had covered Campton and Turner's Gap, but the Federal forces had prevailed. Knapsacks, guns, canteens, and a variety of other things generally carried by soldiers were strewn about. They passed a large number of prisoners. Around noon, they marched through the town of Boonesville and noticed that all of the churches had been turned into hospitals and were filled with wounded Rebels.

View of Antietam Battlefield, September 17, 1862. The Sharpshooters were held in reserve at the Keedysville Road. They held that position in case the Rebels penetrated the Union lines. In front of them was a large hill; they could hear but not see the battle. Several officers climbed that hill to determine which way the battle was going (Library of Congress).

They marched a short distance past Boonesville and halted in a field to eat dinner. While they rested, they heard heavy and rapid firing about two miles in front of them, but it did not last long. They marched toward where they had heard the short battle, and after they had gone a short distance, they passed troops on either side of the road who had stopped to rest or awaited orders. They marched through Keedysville, then halted for a few moments. They were surrounded by troops on all sides, and a cavalry scout told them the Rebels were a short distance in their front. They assumed that was why so many troops had halted. Seeking whatever shelter they could find, they passed the night. As they settled in, they heard the roar of cannons, which lasted until nine o'clock that night. Although their march was only twelve miles, they were very tired. They had been on their feet all day, as the march was slowed by all the troops, wagons, and artillery on the road.

On September 17, 1862, both sides' artillery batteries opened at an early hour. The Sharpshooters were too far from the Antietam battlefield to learn the details. They were ordered to fall in at eight o'clock in the morning. They marched a short distance, and the entire brigade formed en masse, then moved a short distance and took a position under a hill where an artillery battery was stationed. To the right of their position, they could hear the battle raging, with a never-ending roar of artillery and rattle of musketry.

The high hill in front of them made it impossible for them to tell which way the battle was going. One of the officers climbed the hill to view the battle. At noon, they knew the enemy had been driven back. They thought they would be ordered to the front of the battle any moment, but realized they were there to support the battery above them. The Sharpshooters did not know that their brigade was also guarding the main turnpike that led to

Sharpsburg, where their wagons and trains were kept, with a secondary purpose of keeping the enemy from getting behind their lines. At dark, the battle finally ceased and they knew the Union had been victorious. The Sharpshooters heard all kinds of rumors — that General Meagher of the Irish Brigade had been killed and Generals Burnside and Hooker were wounded. They prepared straw beds and hoped they would not be ordered away from their current location.

On the morning of September 18, the men wandered around and went to the top of the large hill to determine where the Rebels were. None could be seen, but an officer with field glasses saw the colors of a Rebel battery far in the distance. The Rebels were falling back, and neither side seemed inclined to fight that day. That morning, they were issued three days' rations of coffee, sugar, and hard bread, and one day's ration of fresh beef. They immediately cooked and ate the beef, as it could not be preserved. At noon, they were ordered to fall in and marched in a southerly direction. Moving slowly under the hills, they passed over the battlefield where General Burnside had fought. The Sharpshooters thought it had been a desperate battle, as the ground was strewn with wounded and dead. They crossed over the Antietam Creek on a stone bridge and proceeded up the creek a short distance, where they relieved the 45th Pennsylvania and went on picket duty. Nearby, a building was filled with Confederate sharpshooters who were firing at them. But they were on a slight rise and hugged the ground, so nobody was injured.[23]

The Sharpshooters turned out of their wet blankets at five o'clock in the morning of September 19, cooked a dish of coffee, and ate their hard bread. Skirmishers went forward and discovered the enemy had retreated. They did not follow the enemy and were ordered back across the stone bridge. When that order was countermanded, they marched back across the bridge and through the streets of Sharpsburg. While in the town, they met families returning to their once-quiet homes to find ghastly scenes: the streets and their front yards were filled with wreckage and wounded soldiers from both armies. The Sharpshooters marched through town and on the outskirts saw hundreds of Rebel prisoners who were guarded by a provost guard. Advancing to the Potomac River, they found the Rebels on the other side, then halted and prepared to reconnoiter.[24]

13

Day of Thanksgiving, but No Food

Captain Wentworth and twelve Sharpshooters were ordered to the riverbank as skirmishers. There, positioning themselves behind trees, they observed the enemy: a large force and two batteries positioned to halt any Union attempt to ford the river. The Sharpshooters were ordered to pick off artillerymen and shoot at any target that moved. The Berdan Sharpshooters assisted the Andrew Sharpshooters, and a twenty-pound battery threw a few shells. The Rebels scattered, leaving their artillery pieces, and it was determined that the Union forces should capture them. The Sharpshooters continued to fire at any man who moved. At dusk, the Berdan Sharpshooters were ordered to the water's edge while two regiments prepared to ford the river. When they were halfway across, a concealed party of Rebels fired at them. The Rebels were driven back by the Andrew Sharpshooters, assisted by an artillery battery. It was so dark that the Andrew Sharpshooters could only locate the enemy position by their muzzle flashes. After they heard the cheers across the river, they knew the enemy batteries had been captured. They went to a wheat stack behind them and spent the night there.[1]

After breakfast on September 20, Sergeant Haynes was sent to camp to receive orders, but none were given. He was told to stay with the regiment until General Porter could be communicated with. The brigade was immediately ordered across the river; Sergeant Haynes did not know what to do with his Sharpshooter squad but decided it would be best if they followed the brigade. They arrived at the river, where the surgeon advised them to take off their socks and roll up their pants. They looked like Scotch Highlanders as they forded the stream. Although the water was not over their knees, the current was strong and the riverbed slippery. They were careful not to fall into the water. They reached the other side and the skirmishers were engaged. Hurrying into line and advancing partway up the hill, they formed in battle formation and advanced to near the hilltop on their hands and knees. As the Rebels exposed themselves at the top of the hill, they were engaged. The right of the brigade, and the left, where the Sharpshooters were, were the hottest spots in the battle. As they were in danger of being hit by their own side's artillery shells, the Sharpshooters were ordered to retreat, which they did in good order until they got to the river. As it was impossible to ford the river in formation, each man had to get across as best he could. Though they were under heavy fire, they crossed without any casualties, except for one man from the 22nd Regiment, who was hit by Union artillery.

On September 21, the Sharpshooters remained on the riverbank. The morning fog was

Depiction of troops firing into Shepherdstown, West Virginia, on September 22, 1862. Sergeant Hanes, with other Sharpshooters, looked through binoculars and noticed Rebel flags hanging on several buildings. They aimed high and fired knowing the ball would drop in elevation over that distance. They were amused as people ran for cover (Library of Congress).

so dense that they could not see fifteen yards in front of them. They moved back into the woods and started a fire to cook coffee, as that was all they had in their haversacks. They found some hard bread on the ground that had been discarded by other regiments and were happy to make a breakfast out of it. After the mist cleared and they could see across the river, they resumed shooting at any man who moved, but then received orders to stop shooting. A party crossed the river under a flag of truce and picked up the wounded and dead. For some time they had nothing to do, and rations were delivered to them from camp. They spent an hour and filled their empty stomachs, then did nothing for the rest of the day. As the *Boston Herald* reported, "All is quiet along the Potomac, the Rebels driven from Maryland soil." At five o'clock the truce ended, and the Union artillery sent over a few shells. As darkness fell, a civilian came upon their post who could not give a good account of himself. Captain Wentworth ordered Sergeant Haynes and another Sharpshooter to take him to General Porter's headquarters. They found headquarters without difficulty, but as they returned through the woods they lost their direction and didn't return to their post until nine o'clock. Nonetheless, they felt rewarded: stumbling through the woods, they had found a set of cooking kettles, which they considered a treasure.

The morning of September 22 saw another heavy fog, which did not clear until nine o'clock. The Sharpshooters expected to hear artillery fire as soon as it lifted and range could be calculated. Sergeant Haynes and three Sharpshooters were sent to a high hill on the right of their post that commanded a view of Shepherdstown, on the opposite side of the river. Viewing the place through field glasses, they observed four churches with another being erected, along with several other buildings. They could see Rebel flags hung on the churches and other buildings. They had no compunctions about shooting at anybody who came from that town. When they saw a person they made him do some "tall walking"—firing at him to make him scramble—which amused the Sharpshooters until they ran out of ammunition. At noon a flag of truce crossed the river; relieved, they returned to camp. Captain Wentworth and Sergeant Leach had each shot a turkey while on post and returned to camp with them. A body of about four hundred Rebels crossed the river under the flag of truce; the Sharpshooters though they were paroled prisoners.[2]

On September 23, the Sharpshooters held their position on the bluff of the riverbank. There was not much for them to do as the flag of truce waved. Captain Wentworth sent Sergeant Haynes and Sergeant Leach to a nearby deserted house on the riverbank, where they would not be disturbed. While there, they filled out the company muster and payrolls. At dark they had finished and returned to their post.

On September 24, they remained on their post and it was reported that Federal forces had taken Richmond. They were told that different regiments had been called on in the night. Believing it was true, they gave three cheers. The two sergeants returned to the deserted house and continued their work on the records, keeping busy all day. They returned to their post at dark and heard no more about Richmond; they thought the report was inaccurate.

After breakfast on September 25, Captain Wentworth and the Sharpshooters were ordered to rejoin the regiment. Sergeants Haynes and Leach returned to the deserted house and completed the records about noon. They brought them to Captain Wentworth, and an examination disclosed several errors. Sergeant Haynes returned to the building and worked on them until dark, then returned to camp and found that the regiment had been sent out on picket duty, leaving the Sharpshooters in camp. He learned that the regiment had crossed and recrossed the river all day. The Sharpshooters told him that their regiment, on picket duty, had crossed the river that night. There was no news of the enemy's location. One rumor stated they were five miles ahead in a large force, but that was doubted.

On September 26, the regiment returned from picket duty at nine o'clock in the morning, having been on picket duty for thirty-six hours. As a company, the Sharpshooters drew and cooked rations, saving the men considerable trouble and time. While they were in camp they spent that time on drill. Captain Wentworth tried to bring the company back to military regularity, but they had been confused for so long they were unable to comply with his wishes. They thought if they persevered and the captain was patient, they would get back to military order again. There was no word of either army's movement. The 27th was a quiet day in camp. In the camp of the 118th Pennsylvania, the Sharpshooters scouted a sutler whom they thought had charged exorbitant and extortionate prices for items which every soldier needed.[3]

After breakfast on September 28, they settled down and cleaned their rifles and equipment. Some wrote letters home, and then they were ordered to fall in with arms and equipment. Surprised, they thought something was up. They soon got in line, prepared for any emergency. They were marched thirty yards and changed camps, then were formed by units in company streets. They stacked arms, cleared the ground, and pitched their tents, pleased to have their canvas homes in line by themselves and not mixed with other companies', as they had been for the past two months. One company could not be distinguished from another until they fell into the ranks. The ground the Sharpshooters were on was healthier and more pleasant, making them appear contented and cheerful. To add to their good fortune, mail arrived. They had been deprived of it for a long time. The duty of the day ended with a dress parade and mounted guards.

The morning of September 29, the regiment went out on picket duty and the Sharpshooters were left in camp. They had very little to do and drilled as a squad in the afternoon.

They had no duty on the 30th, and the regiment returned from picket duty at noon. By October 1, camp conditions had not changed; they still had no duty. President Lincoln had arrived in camp and would remain there a couple of days.

On October 2, part of the regiment went out on picket duty. Not enough men were left to post camp guards or perform other necessary camp duties. It was rumored in camp that a delegation of commissioners from Richmond had gone to Washington to propose peace terms. They thought it would be good news, if true, but they doubted it.

After breakfast on October 3, they were ordered to prepare to be viewed by President Lincoln. They were in line at nine o'clock and marched half a mile to a field large enough for them to be reviewed. Taking their position as a brigade, they waited in the hot sun for two hours before "Old Abe" appeared. A twenty-one-gun salute from Martin's battery and deafening cheers from brigades greeted him as he appeared in front of them. He rode in front and in the rear of each brigade, so each man had a good look at him. They were not required to march in review, as each division was reviewed by the president. They were marched back to their camps and dismissed. That night the Sharpshooters were surprised as sixteen men who had been left behind joined them in camp, including one man they thought they would never see again, as he had deserted the company the past February. They were mystified as to why he was returned to them. They shared rations with the missing men, and then sent them out to find their own lodging. They thought their numbers increased, but did not think their ability had increased as most of the men were wounded. October 4, 5, and 6 were spent in camp with usual camp duties, drill, and dress parade.

On October 7, at nine in the morning, they were ordered to fall in for inspection by Colonel Webb, the inspector general of General Porter's staff. They did not have to wait in line long; they were inspected and dismissed. They had just removed their equipment when they were ordered to fall in at the double quick. They thought something was to happen, but it turned out the drill was to see how long it would take them to get into formation, which they did in four-and a half minutes. While they were in formation, they were read an order about stragglers and then dismissed. Something happened with the picket duty that afternoon, as they were ordered to add more men to each post. At five in the afternoon they were ordered out for dress parade, but it turned into a battalion drill, from which the Sharpshooters were excused but not dismissed. After going through the drill the regiment was dismissed, but the Sharpshooters remained in formation. After some time Sergeant Haynes went to a colonel and explained the oversight. He received permission to dismiss the Sharpshooters. On October 8, the only thing the Sharpshooters did was squad and company drill, followed by a dress parade that evening.

Immediately after breakfast on October 9, they were ordered to fall in without arms or equipment. They were marched thirty yards to the left of their camp and ordered to clear the ground and move their encampment. Their progress was stopped when the major of the Berdan's Sharpshooters came out and claimed the ground. They returned to camp and awaited further orders. They went through squad and company drill, and that afternoon there was a dress parade, as the regiment drilled as a battalion. The Sharpshooters were marched off by staff and drilled as a company. At sunset, Union artillery fired a few shells, but the Rebels did not respond.

On October 10, dress parade and drill were not ordered, as it started to rain. There was a disturbance near headquarters. A sutler had come into camp with a load of bread to sell, but could not sell it fast enough, and the men started to help themselves. Made aware of the commotion, Colonel Barnes, brigade commander, arrived and confiscated the entire load. The 11th and 12th were taken up with fatigue duty around the camp, drill, and dress parade. One corporal and six Sharpshooters were assigned picket duty.[4]

The Shenandoah and Potomac rivers at Harpers Ferry. This photograph was taken by James Gardner in 1865. It is also a very good view of Maryland Heights. The Sharpshooters were amazed at the sight of the mountains above them but were leg weary as they marched up those hills (Library of Congress).

The pickets returned on October 13 and 14. The weather had turned cold and damp in the mornings and during the nights. As the men did not have overcoats, and many were without underwear, they suffered and hoped they would be issued clothing soon. They did not receive orders on the 15th and just did normal camp duty. They were issued new ponchos or shelter tents, which they pitched in the afternoon and made as comfortable as possible. They thought they should have been given "boiled oil" so the tents could be made waterproof. That day, for the first time in a week, they received mail. But there was not much mail, and many of the men were disappointed.

When the Sharpshooters turned out on October 16, a column of troops passed them. They did not know how long they had been passing, but they soon saw the rear of the column. About seven o'clock that morning they heard artillery fire and assumed the advance had passed much earlier. The firing was spirited all day, and they expected to be called up at any time to support the advance. At sundown, they were ordered to prepare one day's ration and be prepared to march at a moment's notice. They were not disturbed on the 17th, and went about their usual camp duties. They did not hear any firing that day. At nine o'clock that night, the advance party passed through their camp. When the men asked what had happened, they were given several different accounts, and could not learn the truth about the skirmish. On October 18, the Sharpshooters were assigned camp guard, and Second Lieutenant Smith returned to the company. He had been sick and had been left in Washington.

Sunday, October 19, was a pleasant day and no duty was required of the Sharpshooters except weekly inspection. The 20th was a cold, raw day and the cold crept into the small tents, making the men suffer. They did not mind drill at the double quick, for it helped to keep them warm. The 21st was a quiet day, and the men performed the usual camp duties. October 22 brought a heavy windstorm. The Sharpshooters woke up and their tent pegs were almost pulled from the ground. The wind continued all day. They went out for an afternoon drill, but were not successful, as the orders could not be heard through the wind. On the 23rd, the wind died down, but it was very cold. Very little was done in camp that day. On the morning of the 24th, they were ordered to be prepared for an inspection at nine in the morning. Although they were prepared, the order was countermanded. They were inspected later in the afternoon and that ended the day.

By October 25, it had gradually grown cold. At seven in the morning, five Sharpshooters were ordered on guard duty. On Sunday the 26th, they were ordered to prepare for inspection at nine in the morning, but when it started to rain the inspection was postponed. They returned to their tents and waited for better weather. They were startled by the sound of artillery, the first they had heard in awhile. One of the Sharpshooters left the tent and found the source. Returning to the tent, he explained that several Rebels had appeared on the side of the river and had attempted to apprehend some stray cattle. Martin's battery had fired a few shells, driving the Rebels back. One of the Sharpshooters was kicked in the face by a horse as he worked with the teams, and his jaw was broken in two places. The Sharpshooters expected to be called during the night as they usually marched in the rain.

The rain stopped on October 27, but it turned cold and windy. The Sharpshooters believed they would soon be moved. The weather eased in the day, but it turned cold at night. It was a quiet day and there was no sign of a movement. The 28th was also quiet, and it appeared that no move was intended. October 29 was a pleasant day. The sick, wounded, and those unable to march were removed from camp. The Sharpshooters thought that was a sure sign of a move.

They were issued rations on October 30. As they cooked beans, they were ordered to pack up. They threw away one of the most delightful dishes of food they had ever cooked. The old Sharpshooters were accustomed to leaving their food on the ground, but the new replacement Sharpshooters thought it was unfair and hard on them. Whenever the order to march was given, if there were rations in the regiment commissary, they were served to the soldiers. It was known that the soldiers could not carry them. The line of march was formed at five o'clock that afternoon. The soldiers marched in the direction of Harpers Ferry. It was a clear, moonlit evening. They marched up some hills and were leg-weary. In total, they marched about ten miles, and then camped about four miles from Harpers Ferry.

The Sharpshooters turned out at an unusually early hour on October 31 and sat by a fire until dawn as their limbs were so numb from the cold that they could not sleep. The march started at ten o'clock in the morning and was of interest to any lover of picturesque scenery. The men expressed wonder, awe, and amazement as each new scene appeared: jagged rocks hundreds of feet above them, and on their left and right the Chesapeake & Ohio Canal and the Potomac River. As they marched short distances and halted for long periods of time, they had time to take in the scenery. It was near dark when they crossed the river at Harpers Ferry. They were amazed at the beautiful scenery at the junction of the Shenandoah and Potomac rivers. After they crossed the Shenandoah River, they marched very fast for three or four miles and encamped with a full view of the Loudon Valley. The Sharpshooters did not think the cold would keep them awake that night after their long, steady march.

On November 1, they stayed encamped and were mustered for pay, which took until nine o'clock that night. They drew new clothing and heard firing ahead of them all day. The bugle sounded at five thirty in the morning of the 2nd. They marched along Loudon Valley. The muddy roads made it a long and tiresome march. Marching eighteen miles to Snickers Gap, they did not have time to eat dinner. The Sharpshooters were tired and sore.

On November 3, they stayed in camp and rested. It was a windblown, cold day, and gathering firewood was their only assignment. In the late afternoon they heard guns ahead of them. At five o'clock in the morning of the 4th, they were ordered to pack up. Turning out, they observed that none of the other companies in the regiment had moved; they thought there had been a mistake. They were ordered not to eat breakfast until they had taken down and rolled up their ponchos. The Sharpshooters then realized that Captain Wentworth had instilled some of his "fine points," and were not pleased. They made breakfast and stayed in camp all day, and at sunset were called out for an inspection. After that, they gathered firewood and set up their ponchos. Troops continually passed them, and the road was cleared. The Sharpshooters thought they would soon be moved, but on November 5 they were not disturbed, and there were no signs of a movement. They remained in camp and waited to march, but all they had that day was a dress parade. The wagon train was made up, and it left camp at five o'clock that evening. That was a sure sign of a move.

The bugle sounded early in the morning on November 6, and they were ordered to pack up and get ready to march. They had breakfast and were ready to march when the 22nd Regiment was ordered to act as rear guard for the division. As a result, they did not start until after eight o'clock that morning. It turned so cold that the water in their canteens froze as soon as they halted. Having no gloves, they wore socks on their hands for protection. Although they marched the longest distance they had for a long time, the Sharpshooters were less fatigued. They passed through Snickersville and into Middleburg about eight o'clock that night. Middleburg was a Rebel haven; as the Union soldiers marched through town, they played and marched to Union music. The blinds on the houses were closed, and the Sharpshooters could feel the inhabitants' scornful, revengeful eyes as they watched the Yanks march through town. They marched a few miles beyond that town and encamped on a hillside, where the wind cut through their garments and their teeth chattered. They gathered firewood, cooked coffee, and hugged the fires so close that some of their pants got scorched. The Sharpshooters stayed by the fires all night, as it was too cold to sleep.[5]

They marched for about an hour on the morning of November 7, and a hard snowstorm set in. About nine o'clock they waded through a stream and their pants froze solid. The men suffered greatly. They were ordered into the woods to encamp at White Plains, near the Manassas Railroad, and were issued rations of quinine and whiskey. Crossing the fields, they obtained straw to place on the ground in their tents, after they pushed the snow away. It was difficult to find any comfort in the severe weather. When the Sharpshooters turned in at nine o'clock that night, the snow continued.

Reveille sounded at five thirty on the morning of November 8. The Sharpshooters turned out quickly and made a dish of coffee before they started. The storm had ended, but it looked as if it would snow or rain again. At daylight they started their march on frozen and slippery roads, and the men's fingers suffered from the cold. Crossing the Manassas Railroad at White Plains, they took the road toward Warrenton. The roads began to thaw and got very slippery, making the march difficult. They passed through New Baltimore and continued. When they came within sight of Warrenton, they changed direction and halted in the woods to encamp at about five o'clock. They had marched thirteen miles sliding in the mud. Details were sent out to get firewood, leaves, and straw to keep them from the cold ground. Fires somewhat aided their comfort. The Sharpshooters thought it would be very difficult to catch the Rebels on the northern side of Richmond, and they would suffer considerably as they tried.

At four o'clock in the morning of November 9, they were called out, packed up, and marched four miles to Warrenton. They encamped in the woods at a healthier site, using hay, leaves, and cedar tips to make their tents as comfortable as possible. It was very blustery and cold. They built fires in front of their tents, which kept them from being frozen. The Sharpshooters learned that men had frozen to death or died from exposure at the encampment of White Plains. When they were ordered out to dress parade, and orders given, the Sharpshooters on the left side of the line could not hear them.

They were called out on the morning of November 10, and it appeared camp would not be broken. They were ordered to fall in for dress parade and listened to orders. They stacked arms and were dismissed, but were ordered to fall in if the bugle sounded, at which point they marched about half a mile and were reviewed by Generals McClellan and Burnside. They cheered loudly for "Little Mac." When the Sharpshooters returned to camp, they learned that General McClellan had been relieved of the command of the Army of the Potomac, which had been given to General Burnside. One of the Sharpshooters who had been taken prisoner at Malvern Hill in July returned to the unit, and said he had seen all of Richmond that he had wanted to see. The Sharpshooters heard artillery fire and thought it was from the generals going down the lines, but learned it was a skirmish that had gone on in their front.

November 11 was a quiet day in camp. They heard cannons in the distance, but were unable to learn any information about those sounds. The weather improved, and they moved about camp comfortably without overcoats. On November 12, the Sharpshooters performed squad and company drills. A divisional formation viewed General Porter as he was relieved of the command of the Fifth Army Corps; that command was given to General Joe Hooker. When the Sharpshooters returned to their camp, they learned that General Pope had prepared charges against General Porter. The 13th and 14th were quiet days in camp. Some of the Sharpshooters complained about the monotony of camp life, but they also complained when they marched.[6]

On November 15, they did their usual squad and company drills. They were ordered into a divisional formation where "Fighting Joe," General Hooker, assumed command. The 16th was a quiet day; some Sharpshooters were assigned as provost guards at brigade headquarters, and they did little but keep the fires stoked.

Reveille was sounded at three o'clock on the morning of November 17, and the men marched at seven o'clock. It rained all day. Marching through the mud, they were covered with it and were unable to get rid of the mud caked on their shoes. It was a difficult march. The wagons had cut up the roads, and some of the mules fell and died, as they could not pull the wagons through the mud. The men marched through Warrenton toward Warrenton Junction, and at noon they marched over the same ground they had been on three months before. They heard firing in front of them all day, and continued their march until dark.

The bugle awakened the Sharpshooters at four in the morning of November 18. They made breakfast and loitered until noon, when the march started. They made good time and did not stop until seven that evening. They heard firing in their rear during the day, but thought everything was all right. When they encamped, the men were so tired they did not pitch tents, but slept out in the open air. The older Sharpshooters thought they were headed for Richmond, and felt they would have to stop soon as the roads were too soft to sustain an army's movement.

On November 19, the bugle sounded "pack up" at noon. The men formed columns and waited an hour for someone or something to pass. The lines straightened, and they marched steadily for eight miles and encamped in the vicinity of Fredericksburg. The Sharpshooters wondered what was to happen as they observed that thousands of troops had arrived before them. It seemed to them that the entire army had amassed at that location. The 20th was spent in camp, mostly in tents, as it continued to rain.

On November 21, Sergeant Haynes woke up in the middle of the night in a pool of water. He got up, as he preferred to walk in the rain than to lie in the water. In the morning, the men turned out voicing general complaints of sore and stiff limbs. When surgeon's call was sounded it was well attended. The older Sharpshooters thought the winter campaign would kill more soldiers than the Rebels' bullets. They were anxious to get into winter quarters before they all got sick. They spent the day drying their clothes and blankets. They heard the Rebels were in their rear.

The November 22 found the roads in terrible condition, yet the order was given to pack up before daylight. The Sharpshooters thought it was to be a wet and miserable march. They pulled up their tents and packed. As they finished, the order was countermanded, so they pitched their tents again to stay dry. But the weather cleared, and at noon the bugle sounded "pack up," so they did. They waited around until night, when the order again was countermanded. They had been kept in a state of excitement all day. They were anxious to get to a place where they could communicate with the North, as they had not received mail for some time, causing them anxiety.

On Sunday, November 23, the bugle sounded at seven thirty. They soon marched in pleasant weather, and the roads were in good condition, considering the recent rain. It was an easy march until dark. When they were within a mile and a half of Fredericksburg, Virginia, they turned into the woods and marched another mile. It was so dark they could not maintain formation, and the group meandered. The Sharpshooters thought they sought to hide from the Rebels. They encamped a mile from Fredericksburg on a damp piece of ground. It was so dark that they could not see anything to lie on, so they stretched their limbs on the cold ground. It was reported that Union forces would shell Fredericksburg in the morning.

The morning of November 24 they were disturbed not by the roar of artillery but the numbness of their feet. It was the coldest morning they had experienced, and they were unable to move. As the men turned out, there was a general complaint of rheumatism. They made fires to warm themselves and tried to stay as comfortable as the conditions permitted. There was little to do in camp that day. The Sharpshooters thought the rations were running low, as they heard the cry for hard bread from the regiments around them. They expected to hear a bombardment, yet not one siege gun was heard.

On November 25, an extremely cold morning, there was no sign of a move. They heard several guns around noon, but they were not shotted, and the Sharpshooters thought they were to honor "Fighting Joe Hooker" as he passed through the camps. It stopped raining on the 26th but remained cold. The Sharpshooters lit fires, but the wood was so damp they did not get hot; instead, the fires sent an acrid smoke through the camp which burned the men's eyes. It was a quiet day spent in camp.

November 27 was the day Governor Andrew appointed as a day of thanksgiving and praise. He recommended that all Massachusetts troops observe it in a becoming manner. Captain Wentworth asked Sergeant Haynes to walk with him. Sergeant Haynes learned that Captain Wentworth's goal was to find something to eat while they observed the countryside. They found plenty of sutler's tents and wagons, but all were empty of goods. They visited Bells Plain Landing, where supplies were landed. They observed few vessels, but plenty of wagons, which waited to be loaded with commissary goods. They looked for a village, but could not even find a house. They returned to camp tired and hungry; their eyes burned from the smoke. Sergeant Haynes's thanksgiving dinner proved to be two hard biscuits he had begged for while he and the captain were on the road. November 28 was a pleasant, quiet day in camp.[7]

On November 29, the Sharpshooters began to think they would be winter quartered at "Camp Smokey." They felt it was a very poor piece of ground for encampment, and thought it would be the final resting place of many of the company if they were to stay there until spring. The damp, swampy ground and freezing conditions made many men sick. They hoped they would be moved soon to more suitable grounds. The only activity for the Sharpshooters on the 30th was a Sunday inspection, which occupied one or two hours.

The Sharpshooters turned out at the usual time on December 1. Captain Wentworth took eight Sharpshooters and went to collect firewood. After they departed, the bugle sounded to pack up and fall in. Amid considerable confusion, the captain and men rushed back, and the Sharpshooters were ready to march with the regiment. When ordered to pack up, soldiers wanted to know what was going to happen but were never told. They had to use their wits and powers of observation. Doing so, they determined that they were going on a reconnaissance. They marched through mud until about three o'clock, when they arrived near their old campground of ten days previous, at Hartwood Church. Moving into the woods, they prepared to encamp. A detail was made up and sent out on picket duty. The remainder of the Sharpshooters pitched their poncho tents and cooked coffee. When they finished, it was about nine o'clock, and all was quiet.

They turned out at the usual hour on December 2. They made breakfast and thought how nice it would be to remain there for the day. That idea was shattered as they were ordered to pack up as fast as possible. Some Sharpshooters remarked that "Old Betty Barnes" (as Colonel Barnes was called) had gotten frightened and wanted to go back to the protection of camp. That proved correct, as they were hurried out of the woods and ordered to march at the double quick for four miles. They then halted, but they marched the rest of the distance to camp without stopping. Although they showered many curses on "Old Betty's" head, he would not stop until he was safely in camp. Soon after noon they arrived in camp, dropping from fatigue. They enjoyed a dish of beans that had been cooked for them while they were gone. Pitching their tents, they huddled around the fire to dry their clothes and attempted to get warm.

December 3 was a cold, unpleasant day. The men seemed to be angry and uncomfortable. The Sharpshooters were assigned different duties; some in the road chopped wood and others cleaned camp. They felt they were given more duties than other companies. On the 4th, there was no drill, and the men worked on their tents. The 5th brought the onset of winter in Virginia. In the morning it started to rain, then turned to snow. The interiors of the men's tents were damp and cold. The Sharpshooters longed for the comforts of home or better quarters but knew that was not possible.

On the morning of December 6, the Sharpshooters awoke to two inches of snow on the ground. It had frozen during the night, but thawed during the day, creating mud that was difficult to move in. There was no drill, and the Sharpshooters went long distances to gather firewood. At three in the afternoon it grew dark and cold. The Sharpshooters had a choice: stand by the fire and get frozen one side at a time or go to their tents and get frozen all over. Sergeant Haynes had raised his tent and built a fireplace in it. He felt he had gained that comfort at the expense of his eyes; the wood was green and damp, and the smoke so burned his eyes that his tears flowed freely.

December 7 was the coldest day of the year. Long before daylight, the Sharpshooters marched up and down the company streets just to keep warm. During the day they learned that three men from other regiments had frozen to death during the night. The Sharpshooters gathered wood all day, but believed they had not gathered as much as was needed to keep the many fires going. On the morning of the 8th, the Sharpshooters learned of another death from exposure in a New York regiment camped near them. The weather began to wear the men down. The surgeon's call was heavily attended. The Sharpshooters gathered wood all day; apparently, wood-gathering had taken the place of drill, as there was none. They were disappointed, as there were no signs of a movement to better quarters. On the 9th, so many Sharpshooters were sick that it took all the rest of the men to gather wood and do fatigue duty in camp.

The morning of December 10, Sergeant Haynes was awakened by a disturbance at his side. His tentmate was in spasms; so Sergeant Haynes got up and summoned the surgeon. They worked on him until daylight before he recovered enough to be left alone. The ever-present "damn rumor" that Fredericksburg was to be assaulted in the morning circulated through camp. The Sharpshooters observed troops who passed them all day and thought it might be true. They prepared for a move, but no orders were issued. They expected the order to come in the middle of the night, but they would be prepared to move on a moment's notice.[8]

Sergeant Haynes was awakened at three in the morning of December 11, as his tent-mate was ill. Haynes took him to the hospital and returned to camp at reveille. They were ordered to make breakfast and prepare to take Fredericksburg. Just before daylight, the cannons roared, and they were ordered to pack up. They marched for about three miles and halted on a level piece of ground, where they remained for the rest of the day. Warming weather thawed the frozen ground. They stood in two inches of mud that day. The cannons continued throughout the day, ending after dark. The Sharpshooters could not learn the results as they were too far back to see anything. After sunset, the brigade was moved about a mile into the woods, where the men encamped for the night. Everybody who came into camp had a different story about what happened. There were as many stories as there were men in the regiment; none could be believed. The men sat by fires and dried their feet. At nine o'clock, they spread their blankets on the ground; they did not pitch their ponchos.

The Sharpshooters awoke in the early morning of December 12 half frozen, as the frost had penetrated their blankets. They got up and sat by the fire until daylight. A boy selling tobacco entered the Sharpshooters' camp, and they asked him if he knew what had happened in the town. They boy told them the town was full of Union troops; the Rebels had retreated a mile and a half from town and entrenched themselves on the heights. This information proved to be true. As the Rebels retreated, they threw large quantities of tobacco in the river, of which the Sharpshooters availed themselves. At ten o'clock in the morning, they marched toward the river and halted underneath their batteries stationed on Stafford Heights. They remained there until sundown, expecting to be ordered to cross the river, but they were ordered to encamp for the night.[9]

December 13, 1862, would prove to be a dark day for the Sharpshooters and the 22nd Regiment. The Sharpshooters rose at daylight, prepared their breakfast, and awaited orders. The first cannon was fired at nine o'clock, and the men were ordered to pack up and be ready to move at a moment's notice. The cannons roared, and they were ordered across the river at noon to take the front. As they advanced through the streets of the town, the Rebels shelled them. Holding a fortified position on Marye's Heights, behind the town, the Rebels had perfect coordinates established to shell the Union as they entered the town. While the Union forces advanced, many men from the 22nd were wounded or killed, four Sharpshooters were wounded, and Sergeant Haynes' leg was broken by artillery fire.

Unable to move and find shelter, Sergeant Haynes lay exposed to artillery and musket fire for three hours, and was fortunate not to be hit again. Under the cover of darkness, some of the Sharpshooters came and took him to the company, where he lay until an ambulance could be obtained to take him to a hospital. He was loaded in an ambulance with a man wounded in the head. By the time they reached the hospital, Sergeant Haynes was accompanied by a corpse. He was taken to the second floor of a building and placed with the dead, dying, and wounded.

The order was given to charge Marye's Heights, and the men tore off their knapsacks and haversacks, with precious food in them, to lighten their load. Stumbling through a railroad cut loaded with hundreds of wounded and dying men, they reached the crest of the railroad bank and the enemy fire on them increased. Dirt and gravel flew all over them as they passed under a hail of iron that rained down on them. Many were wounded, as the enemy's range was perfect. Reaching the foot of Marye's Heights, they were the sixth regiment to attack it that day. They opened fire on the Rebels, who were covered by entrenchments and a stone wall. Behind them were light batteries and above them heavy siege guns, all firing at the regiment. The houses within the Rebel lines were loaded with Rebel sharpshooters who picked off Union soldiers. The Andrew Sharpshooters were in an impossible situation.

The Sharpshooters and the 22nd continued to load and fire, as they picked off artillerymen from the light batteries. The roar and din of the battle were indescribable; smoke clung to their perspiring faces, and the groans of the wounded were heart-sickening. Their cartridge boxes were as exhausted as the men when they were relieved by the 20th Maine. They watched the Maine Regiment be slaughtered by artillery fire as it marched toward the Rebels, just as they themselves had been devastated when they had relieved the 12th Rhode Island. The Sharpshooters and the 22nd crawled on their hands and knees for about twenty feet while the Maine regiment walked over them and took their position under heavy fire.

Falling back along a fence at dusk, they were exposed to enemy fire. Watching the light of muzzle flashes and exploding shells was an eerie sight. Finding themselves in crossfire, they dug into the ground for protection and found their position had been used as a sink — a latrine. Digging into human excrement was nauseating. The firing gradually ceased; a line was formed and roll call was taken.

Many of the men had lost their haversacks and stumbled over the dead and dying. They were oblivious to the moans and groans of the dying as they attempted to find food in the haversacks of those who would no longer need earthly nourishment. Ambulances and stretcher-bearers moved in under the cover of darkness and removed some of the wounded and dead, and the men settled down and lay among the dead of the 12th Rhode Island Regiment.[10]

On the gray morning of December 14, they were aroused after a sleepless night. Roll call was done in whispers, and cartridges were issued. They crept forward a few yards toward the position they had held the previous afternoon. The sun rose and the battle resumed. As they rose up on their elbows from their prostrate position, they saw the enemy protected by the land's natural contour and features. They saw dead and wounded they had passed the night before who had gone unnoticed in the dark. Houses on their front were loaded with Rebel sharpshooters, who attempted to pick them off. They could not move forward or to the rear, unless under the cover of darkness.

Rolling the dead bodies around them, they made a breastwork with them. Rapid decomposition had taken place, so they used a rubber blanket between themselves and the bodies. As horrible as it was, it saved many lives; they heard many hollow thumps, as the corpses absorbed the bullets fired at the living men. They were in a difficult position. The men needed food and water. Several tried to run for provisions, but they drew enemy fire and were wounded or killed. Many others had tried to reach them in the afternoon from the town but had been driven back by enemy fire. After dark they heard trampling of feet and were relieved by the Ninth Corps. They returned to town, and their nerves relaxed somewhat.

Arriving in Fredericksburg, they saw campfires and lit buildings as people moved around. They thought of their Sunday battle and the time they had spent pinned down under fire, unable to move. Though the change was pleasant, it took time to adjust. They marched to an open lot and encamped.

Sergeant Haynes wrote in his journal on December 14:

> Woke up this morning from a short nap, to find myself in a building completely riddled by shells and rifle-balls. Have been very kindly treated by the nurses, but did not get my wound dressed until late this afternoon, because the surgeon had so much to attend to. Still they were very kind and careful of me, and assured me that I would not have to lose my leg. Should like to be present with the company, but as I left them on the ground they occupied yesterday, thought I should not be present with them very soon. There was some firing early this morning, but it soon ceased, and has since been very quiet all day. Many of the wounded died during the day. It is now nearly dark, and I suppose I shall have to pass another sleepless night. Have seen two of my company back here in town.

On the morning of December 15, the men rose early and marched to the river, where they washed the dirt and gunpowder from their faces and cooked coffee. Some of the Sharpshooters wandered into the city and looked around. Wherever they looked, they saw the destruction caused by the Union siege guns. Nothing had escaped destruction. Roofs, walls,

Ruins of houses in Fredericksburg, Virginia, that were destroyed by bombardments, in December 1862. Union artillery continually fired shell into the town prior to the army's ill-advised attack of that town (Library of Congress).

fences, trees, and chimneys were riddled with shot. Houses looked like large pepper boxes, as there were so many holes in them. Union soldiers were frying pancakes on the sidewalks by campfires. At night they fell into formation and marched into the city, stacked arms, and sought shelter for the night. They went into various buildings and lit the fireplaces, which the provost guard ordered them to put out.

Sergeant Haynes wrote in his journal on December 15:

> I was rejoiced to see daylight. Was in distress all night. Another poor fellow died beside me during the night; he died quite calmly. We had orders to leave the hospital in all haste. I was tumbled into an ambulance, and brought to the Falmouth side of the river, and left till they could pitch tents to receive us, when we were taken in and made very comfortable. Were crowded to overflowing, but it was the intention to send off the wounded as fast as possible. It rained during the night, but the tents were of good stock, so we did not get wet. Heard that McClellan had once more taken command, and ordered the troops to recross the river.[11]

At three o'clock in the morning of December 16, they were ordered to fall into formation under arms. As they stood in formation, the rain and wind pelted them and their teeth chattered from the cold. Many rumors were floating around, and they feared they would have to attack the Heights again, but they soon heard an aide ask, "Which bridge?" and they knew they would be leaving. They were at the rear of the formation and acted as rear guard to the Fifth Corps. They marched to their old camp four miles away. General Burnside rode past the Sharpshooters with his hat slouched over his face and a sad look on his face. He realized he had just sacrificed thousands of Union soldiers, and it took its toll on him. When they got to their old camp, the Sharpshooters lay on the damp ground for needed rest.

On December 17 and 18, the Sharpshooters worked around their camp. They cooked meals of various types, as food was limited. They discussed the failure of the battle of Marye's Heights, and the abilities or lack thereof of commanding generals.

Colonel Henry Wilson was present at the inspection on December 19. Many replacement troops had been sent to the regiment, but only about a third of the men he had commanded at Hall's Hill were present; that saddened him. Exposure and disease had thinned the Sharpshooters' ranks. None had died in battle, but many had died from disease.

December 20 was the coldest morning of the season. The Sharpshooters had all they could do to get enough wood to keep warm. Sunday, the 21st, the Sharpshooters celebrated the Sabbath with the regular Sunday morning inspection. They then stacked their arms in the company street, sat and gazed into their fires, and thought of home.

On December 22, they were ordered to pack up and be ready to move at a moment's notice. After the usual delay, they marched about a mile to a new campsite nearer some firewood. The new site was on the side of a hill without a steep slope, and was covered with pine growth. They began to erect their winter quarters. Their tents were six feet by twelve feet, made with small pine logs and covered on the top with the men's rubber blankets. They all built fireplaces in them, and the chimneys, six feet high, were made mostly of sod. On the 23rd, they resumed work on their new houses; as each house reflected the desires of its four occupants, there was little uniformity among the houses. The Sharpshooters finally had comfortable and warm shelters. They made beds out of cedar brush and pine boughs. On December 24, they finished and equipped their houses.

On December 23, Sergeant Haynes dictated this letter to Captain Wentworth:

> *Sir,—After arriving at this hospital, the surgeon found it necessary to amputate my leg. Am very comfortable under the circumstances. It has been very painful, and after an examination, it was found to be much more shattered than was supposed when I left you. Am obliged to lie flat on my back from*

night till morning. It is not a very pleasant condition to write in, but I want to let you know my condition and other matters as soon as possible, not knowing what may happen any day. Any communication that is sent to me at the regiment can be forwarded to me at the hospital. Ezra kept with me till we got to Aquia Creek, where I lost him. I suffered some on board the boat, but am amply repaid in finding such good quarters as have been furnished me. I have suffered terribly since it was amputated. It was taken off three inches below the knee. Is George O. Pond with the company? Please send a list of the wounded in our company. If that box comes, you will please forward it to me. If I can get an envelope large enough, I will send those records. Please send my daguerreotype by the 1st of January. Remember me to all the boys.

Truly yours,
N.W. Haynes[12]

On December 25, Captain Wentworth went to Washington. General Butterfield gave George W. Nichols, one of the original Sharpshooters, a disability discharge for mental disability. It appeared that the horrific experience at Marye's Heights had taken a toll on Nichols. On the 26th, there was no drill, and the men used the time to improve their camp. They prepared for the cold rainy season. On the 27th, Captain Wentworth returned from Washington, and J. W. Faulkner was sent to the hospital. On December 28, all was quiet in the Army of the Potomac. The Sharpshooters were pleased on the 29th to hear that muster rolls were made out and the paymaster would arrive. They had not been paid since June 30.

On December 30, they were ordered to prepare three days' rations and pack the wagons with another ten days' rations. When the Sharpshooters packed, they packed everything. They were surprised. They thought they were to leave their comfortable winter quarters behind. After they left camp, the Sharpshooters learned that they were to go on a reconnaissance up the Rappahannock River. They marched at noon, without dinner, toward Hartwood Church, and marched until dark, when they halted for an hour. They marched about three miles; the regiment in front of them was turned onto another road by a staff officer. The 22nd Regiment followed them, as did the 2nd Maine. The staff officer halted the regiment and galloped away after he had waited awhile.

An aide told Colonel Tilton to move the regiment into the woods to defend a certain hollow. Colonel Tilton realized the regiment was in a dangerous position, as they were miles outside of the pickets in enemy country without artillery support. He ordered the regiment back to the original road, then force-marched them for over an hour, and they caught up with their brigade. They lay on the road in the bitter cold for three hours; after their forced heated march, the men were chilled to their bones.

The Sharpshooters turned out at daylight on December 31 and built a good fire with dry rails. They started to boil coffee and cook breakfast, fearing they would be called to formation before they could eat. They marched about a mile at eight o'clock and were halted at Richards Ferry, where a Rebel picket on the other side of the river was poised to oppose their crossing. But seeing the size of the Union force, the picket offered only a small skirmish. The ice was broken in several places, and the men forded the river in knee-deep frozen water. The slippery river bottom caused several men to fall in the freezing water. Each step chilled them to the bones. Arriving on the other side of the river, they emptied the water out of their boots. It was a cold day, and their wet pants and shoes chilled them; they were anxious for anything to warm them. The brigade threw out skirmishers and flankers. They were unsupported by cavalry or artillery, as they marched seven miles on the Rebel side of the river to Ellis Ford. But they could not escape another drenching and forded the river in waist-deep water. They then encamped in a garden, which afforded them beets, turnips, and cabbage. They made a suitable supper and turned in for the last time in 1862 in their frozen, wet clothes.

The Sharpshooters awoke January 1, 1863, lame and footsore from their wet and cold march. In the morning, they were thrown out as pickets. They skirmished with some Rebels near some houses and captured two prisoners. They learned as a result of their expedition that as a woman had walked up the stairs in her house, a stray bullet went through a transom light above her front door and struck her in the leg. The surgeon offered his services to dress the wound, which was not serious. She accepted, but cursed him for his kindness.

On New Year's Day, they marched back to their old camp twenty miles away. It was a forced, quick march, and they did it in eight hours. The Sharpshooters wondered how the Rebels could go hungry. As they marched, they observed sheep, swine, and cattle all over the Rebels' vast territory across the river. Sergeant Haynes' journal entry for that day quoted a soldier who took part in the march and will give the reader an idea of the Sharpshooters' thoughts.

> How much we thought of home on that toilsome fatiguing march of New Years day! Home Sweet Home!! The festive games and sports, the Grand Ball on New Years Eve. The Greetings and Goodbyes of friends and relatives. What are these to a weary soldier on a march of twenty miles in a day and a thousand miles from home. Well! Only one more New Year in the Army of the U.S. but after all we arrived home at 2 o'clock P.M. Relished a plain supper and appreciated the blessings of a rest and sleep as well as the gayest and happiest of our friends at home in their beds of feather and hair mattresses. It is generally concluded that this has been the severest march that we ever experienced. Our march home was 20 miles in 8 hours.

January 2 was cold and clear, but a fine day for the season. Lame and stiff from their long march, the Sharpshooters were mustered for pay on the morning of the 3rd. They were issued half-rations of whiskey as a cure for the lameness caused by the past reconnaissance. On January 4, Henry F. Colburn, who had enlisted in August 1862, died of typhoid fever at Potomac Creek. His remains were deposited in the "Camp near Falmouth." On the 5th, they had their usual inspection and all was quiet in the Army of the Potomac. On the 6th, the Sharpshooters cut down trees around the officers' tents and the cookhouse. They heard of heavy fighting around Vicksburg from a Rebel source, and also the news that the Federals had captured the city on the 7th. The Sharpshooters felt the news was too good to be true.

At nine o'clock on the morning of January 8, they were ordered to fall in for an inspection. They marched to a selected place, where General Burnside reviewed the Fifth Army Corps. General Meade had assumed command of the Fifth Army Corps. Colonel Tilton of the 22nd Massachusetts was in command of the brigade, and General Barnes was in command of the division. After the debacle at Fredericksburg, the men were not inclined to show any enthusiasm toward General Burnside. Two ladies present at the review attracted far more enthusiasm than General Burnside. The men got back to their camp at two thirty in the afternoon.[13]

On January 9, only two privates were present for duty in the Sharpshooters' camp, as eight had been detailed for picket duty, four were on provost guard, eight were on camp guard, and six were on fatigue duty. The Sharpshooters complained that too much "swine" was given to them for rations. On the 10th, it rained heavily. It had not rained in awhile, and the rain leaked through the worn canvas on their tents.

It stopped raining on January 11. The commissary issued dried apples, molasses, and onions. As it was a Sunday, the Sharpshooters wondered where the chaplains were. They commented on the large amount of labor they performed for the army. The eight pickets returned hungry and covered with mud from the previous day's storm. Tired of the protracted war, the Sharpshooters wanted to go home.

The Sharpshooters were saddened on January 12 as they received word that Sergeant Nathan W. Haynes had died of the wound he received at the battle of Marye's Heights, Fredericksburg. They hoped he would cease his labors and rest in peace. They commented that although Sergeant Haynes had wanted to terminate his participation in the war, they wished it had occurred in another manner.

On Tuesday, January 13, they spent the day in the usual fashion. They did squad drills after breakfast, then company drills. They then had dinner and held battalion drill in the afternoon. The Sharpshooters did not drill with the regiment in battalion drills; they performed fatigue duty instead. On the 14th, the Sharpshooters prepared the cookhouse and encampment for a general camp inspection. At four in the afternoon, it was cloudy and they expected a January thaw. The general inspection took place on the 15th. All equipment, company books, ammunition, rifles, tents, company streets, and everything else in the army were inspected. The usual squad and company drills were called off. Reports circulated in camp that they were on the eve of a move.

The Sharpshooters performed their usual drills on January 16. They heard that they were to break camp at one o'clock the next day. On the 17th, they performed skirmish drills in the morning. They heard that the projected movement, with three days' rations in their haversacks and five men onboard the teams, was deferred until the next day at one o'clock in the afternoon. They did skirmish drills again in the afternoon.

On Sunday, January 18, 1863, the move was deferred to yet another day. They were inspected at eleven o'clock in the morning. The Sharpshooters were discouraged by the action that took place in Fredericksburg, but they would still battle when they were needed. They wondered what General Burnside's next move would be in the unfortunate but remarkably successful rebellion.

Letters and papers that arrived from Massachusetts on January 19 predicted that the great movement was about to take place. The men did squad drills in the morning and skirmish drills for three hours in the afternoon. In the afternoon, they were ordered to a dress parade where orders were read stating that J. Q. A. Sturtevant was reduced to the ranks and that Corporals Madden and Mallory were promoted to sergeants. Preparations were made to move the next day.[14]

The Mud March started on January 20 amid much excitement and confusion. As they prepared, men threw clothes and other items away to lighten their load for the march up the river. George Otis Pond became ill during the excitement of the move; the men sent for a doctor, who gave him medication. He began to vomit and was put in an ambulance. Although the Sharpshooters chased the ambulance, they were ordered to return to the formation, and were forced to leave him in distress and an insensible condition. They had not marched very far when they heard he had died. Pond had joined the Sharpshooters in August of 1862, as a whole, hearty, healthy man, but had been sick for two months. He had waited for his disability discharge papers, which he thought would come any day.

The line of march started at one o'clock. The men marched three miles and halted in a growth of young woods. As they could find no dead or dry branches, they could not keep a good fire. They cooked some coffee and read their mail as it began to rain. They pitched tents and ponchos and turned in for the night, getting thoroughly soaked.

On January 21, reveille sounded at daybreak. The men did not have a fire or coffee, and it was too cold and wet to eat army rations. They were ordered into formation at eight o'clock and stood in the rain until eleven o'clock, as they waited for other divisions to pass them. They then marched for about a mile, halted, built fires, and had coffee and dinner. Resuming their march, they went about a mile when their artillery pieces got stuck in the mud. Twenty horses were unable to drag the pieces out of the bad spots in the road. As no army could go into enemy territory without artillery support, they had no option but to stop the march. They selected a good site for encampment with much dry wood — oak and walnut. Pitching tents and kindling fires, the Sharpshooters found themselves comfortable and in much better condition for a night's rest. Their blankets and clothes were heavy from being wet, and the men were worn down.

The Sharpshooters awoke on January 22 stiff and sore. That morning they were issued a ration of whiskey. Many of the men in the brigade and many of the officers drank too much and got drunk. They chose to fight each other rather than the Rebels, degrading the dignity of field and staff officers. The Sharpshooters' officers and men remained sober. In the afternoon a detail of Sharpshooters was ordered to work on the roads, as supply wagons needed to get to the regiment. It was rumored that the march would continue when the weather cleared. The Sharpshooters were embittered that General Burnside had taken them from their comfortable winter quarters in a long storm and bad weather. It was reported that the Rebels on the other side of the river laughed and taunted the Union troops as they got stuck in the mud. The rations were almost gone.

Reveille was sounded at five o'clock on January 23. It was warm, and there were signs of a January thaw. At seven o'clock, the Sharpshooters were ordered to go on fatigue duty. After daylight, the entire brigade started out to build corduroy roads. The Sharpshooters and the 22nd Massachusetts got within two hundred yards of the road they were to repair, and took a wrong turn. They marched over hill and valley, through briars, brambles, and a dense growth of saplings and shrubs, then halted for an hour. Ordered to go forward before noon, they found themselves an eighth of a mile from where they had left at eight o'clock that morning. They spent the day comfortably and did no work, but sat by campfires for most of the day. It was warm and sunny and the mud dried quickly. In the afternoon, hundreds of pieces of artillery and wagons were sent back to the camp near Falmouth. They returned to their encampment at sunset. Rations of coffee, bread, and sugar were issued to the tired and hungry men, but whiskey rations were not issued, for good reason.

On January 24, Sykes and Humphries' division passed the Sharpshooters' camp on their way to their old quarters. Then on the 22nd, they marched to their winter quarters, through every muddy cornfield that Betty Barnes could find. When they were within two miles of their camp, they were led down a cow path, "right in the wrong direction." They ascended and descended hills, marched through ravines, and waded through brooks, loaded down with their gear on their tired backs, only to find themselves one-half mile closer to camp than where they had left the main road. About four o'clock, they arrived at camp and pitched their tents on the same spot they had been five days earlier. The Sharpshooters thought they would remain in the winter quarters for another three or four weeks.

They had Sunday inspection at eleven o'clock on January 25. It rained from two in the morning until daylight. Orders were read at the dress parade and it was reported that there would be trials by court-martial for the drunkenness of officers. The Sharpshooters commented that whiskey was the most powerful foe of the U.S. Army.

There was no drill ordered on January 26 while the regimental court-martial was in session. The ground was muddy and unfit for drill. The camp was quiet. The men fell in for roll call, were issued rations, and went out and gathered more firewood.

Things started to improve on the 26th, as General Burnside relinquished command of the army to General Joseph Hooker. The army had lost confidence in Burnside; rations were poor and insufficient, and there were desertions. Hooker changed things. Vegetables were issued, soft bread replaced hard bread, and furloughs were allowed. In a short time, the men began to live more comfortably, and their morale improved.[15]

January 27 was a quiet day. There was very little drill. The Sharpshooters were ordered to be ready for picket duty in the morning.

On the morning of January 28, the Sharpshooters went on picket duty with the regiment. They started in the rain and had marched two or three miles when a lieutenant of the 22nd Massachusetts fell into the mud, drunk, and was unable to get up. The Sharpshooters thought it was a ludicrous sight. The rain turned to snow, and it ended with a foot of snow on the ground. At about eleven that morning, they arrived at their picket site, built fires, and ate dinner. Some of the Sharpshooters pitched tents. Others built shelters with boughs, while others got behind the rocks for shelter. The men lay down in their rain-soaked clothes on the wet ground while it stormed furiously. On the 29th and 30th, they remained on picket duty. There was a sufficient supply of oak and hickory and the men passed the time sitting quietly by campfires. They were comfortable, and discussed the war, politics, and religion.

They were relieved of picket duty on January 31 at eleven in the morning. They marched back to their encampment, where they arrived at three o'clock and enjoyed a dish of baked beans. They learned that Paymaster Holman had started to pay the regiment. They fell in and were paid at midnight. On February 1, the men were anxious to spend their money. The sutlers showed up and were asked the same question a thousand times that day: "Have you got anything good to eat?" They had their usual Sunday inspection.

On the morning of February 2, the Sharpshooters had squad drill and at ten-thirty did company drill. They fell in for a beefsteak dinner at noon. February 3 was cold and windy. Only three men did company drill; the rest were assigned to guard and fatigue duty. The Sharpshooters were disappointed that they had not received mail for some time.

The morning of February 4 was so intensely cold that the ground had frozen hard. Some of the Sharpshooters had stayed by the fires all night. They heard good news about the navy. An English vessel had been captured which had carried eight Whitworth guns, a set of brass field artillery, and a host of other articles destined for the Rebels. None of that equipment would fall into enemy hands. They also heard a spurious rumor that the cruiser *Florida* had been captured; in actuality, she was herself capturing ships in the West Indies. The army correspondent of the *Philadelphia Inquirer* told the Sharpshooters that the right and left Grand Divisions were to go west, and the Central Division would retire to Washington.

A storm raged on February 5. On the 6th, the weather turned more pleasant and the Sharpshooters did their usual squad and company drills. The 7th saw an extreme change in the weather, turning from very cold to very warm. As the men sat on the cold ground and shed their jackets, they caught colds at an alarming rate. The Sharpshooters talked about General Sigel's Grand Reserve being sent from their army to the south and west; General Sigel was to command the Eleventh Army Corps.

On February 8, some of the Sharpshooters went on a pass to the New York Mozart Regiment. Talking to the men of the Mozart Regiment, they found them to be discouraged at the length of the war. They learned that the 38th New York Regiment and the Mozarts had been consolidated, and only about a dozen men were fit for duty. As they walked around, the Sharpshooters noticed that just about all of the wood in the area had been cut down and burned. That knew that they would soon have to travel two or three miles for wood, and that the muddy roads would make it impossible to haul heavy loads. They thought the encampment would be moved closer to a better supply of firewood.

On February 9, a lieutenant colonel from the 4th Michigan Volunteers conducted a general inspection. An order was read to the 18th Massachusetts Volunteer Infantry that had been issued by the army's chief medical director. He ordered that soldiers must have better fare or they would get sick, and that they must have four rations of flour or soft bread each week, and vegetables and potatoes more often. The Sharpshooters thought this was a step in the right direction. They talked about how men of feeble health were unable to eat hard bread and pork strips. Many starved themselves into the hospital and sometimes into an early grave. They felt it would be more economical for the government to feed its men more generously.

February 10 was as warm as a June day, and the sun burned the Sharpshooters. Their camp was quite dry, though only a mile away, others were encamped in mud. They heard that two or three of the Sharpshooters at the hospital had been given disability discharges. Their numbers were going down. All was quiet on the 11th. They were issued two rations of flour and tried to determine the best way to cook them to make them palatable. The Sharpshooters were assigned fatigue duty on the 13th. Along with others, they drained surface water, repaired bridges, built a guardhouse, and built a log house for the colonel, among other tasks.

February 14 was another very warm day. Four Sharpshooters were on provost guard at brigade headquarters, ten on camp guard, and the few that remained were assigned fatigue duty as usual. The Sharpshooters felt life in winter quarters had grown monotonous. Reflecting on the year before at the same time, they noted that Fort Donelson had been captured with eighteen thousand prisoners, New Orleans had been taken, and the cry, "On to Richmond!" had created enthusiasm. Discouraged, the men saw only bleak prospects.

A warm rain set in at daybreak on February 15. Anything that was unnecessary was not done; the usual Sunday inspection was canceled. The Sharpshooters commented that Sundays in the army were so very unlike the Sabbath in good old New England. The 16th was a very pleasant day. The Sharpshooters attended dress parade at four o'clock that afternoon. Extracts of army regulations were read regarding saluting officers, and other orders said they would receive four rations of soft bread or flour with more onions and potatoes each week.

A severe snowstorm set in on February 17, muddying the roads. Unlike other camps in the area, the Sharpshooters' camp remained free of mud. On the 18th, the marriage of General Tom Thumb to Miss Lavinia Warren of Middleboro, Massachusetts, by Reverend Riley of New York City created more excitement than the movement of their own generals. The Sharpshooters commented that the men worshipped General Heyman. The snow turned into rain, forcing its way into the Sharpshooters' tents and putting out their fires, which made them very uncomfortable. On February 19, the Sharpshooters heard big guns in the direction of the picket line, but could not determine the reason, as there was too much mud for the Rebels to move their artillery.[16]

Some of the Sharpshooters visited General Sickles' division on February 20. They noted how muddy the roads were, and that all of the trees had been cut down and used for firewood. They thought that if the Rebels attacked, it would be an open field battle. At seven in the morning of the 21st, the Sharpshooters marched to Stafford's Corner for picket duty. It began to snow at about ten that evening.

On February 22, the Sharpshooters found themselves covered with snow. The squad built a bough house, conical in shape, that accommodated twenty men. They then waded through ten inches of snow and obtained firewood. At midnight, they heard cannons and concluded it was a salute to Washington's Birthday.[17]

The snowstorm ended on February 23. They commented that they had not seen as much snow since the winter of 1860. The Sharpshooters yearned for a merry New England sleigh ride to the juvenile tune of "Jingle, jingle, clear the way." They noted that nothing in Virginia kept harmony with winter. There were no sleighs, coaches, runners, or sleds. The only "winter conveyances" they observed were a citizen cart dragged through the snow by a skeleton of a beast and army wagons dragged by a half dozen lanky, shivering, half-starved, and much-abused mules. Some of the hungry men bought hoe cake at twenty-five cents, even though they contained a cent's worth of dough. They were issued a half-ration of whiskey as the storm cleared.

On February 24, they were issued another half-ration of whiskey and were relieved of picket duty at ten that morning. Marching back to camp on frozen roads, they made good time and arrived in their camp around noon. On the 25th, the Sharpshooters removed snow from the camp. They attended dress parade at four that afternoon and were ordered to be ready to move at a moment's notice. At midnight, they were awoken and ordered to be ready for anything.

On February 26, it rained heavily, flooding everything and melting the snow. The Sharpshooters heard that the Confederate cavalry general Stuart had captured sixty U.S. Cavalry members. That raid indicated a forward movement by the Rebels, which was why the Sharpshooters had been aroused at midnight. It was rumored that the Federals had captured Confederate general Fitzhugh Lee, but the Sharpshooters doubted it. They commented that they preferred to be attacked where they were, rather than in another location.

On February 27 the muster rolls were made out. Due to the rainy season there had been no drills. At dress parade, General Griffin announced that Stuart had been driven back across the river, and that he had captured seventy Union cavalrymen. The Sharpshooters were mustered for pay on the morning of the 28th. They received news of promotions in the Sharpshooters Company: 2nd Lieutenant Robert Smith to 1st lieutenant, and 1st Sergeant Ivory Leach was promoted to 2nd lieutenant. Lieutenant Robert Smith left camp that day and went home on ten days' furlough.

March 1, 1863, was the first day of spring, and it was warm but rainy. There was no Sunday inspection, and all was quiet. The Sharpshooters wondered where the chaplains were. On the 2nd, four Sharpshooters were detailed on provost guard at brigade headquarters. The rest of the company was assigned fatigue duty. The fatigue party was also at brigade headquarters, and some went to a fort not far from there which commanded the high bridge of the railroad to Aquia Creek. They learned it was more than one hundred feet high. Close by was another fort. The men commented that in a short time, all of the high hills would be covered with forts.

One of the old men from the company returned from the hospital on March 3. Corporals Newell Swett and George Munn were promoted to sergeants. The promotions of Lieutenant Smith and Sergeant Leach were read at dress parade. On the 4th, two Sharpshooters were detailed to provost guard at division headquarters for ten days. They heard that Vicksburg had been evacuated. The Sharpshooters received mail on March 5, and no drill was ordered, so the men were assigned guard or fatigue duty. There was a cold wind on the 6th.

This was the last entry of Sergeant Haynes' journal. Someone in the company continued to keep the journal after Sergeant Haynes was wounded at the Battle of Fredericksburg December 13, 1862, until March 6, 1863. Company records suggest a number of possibilities for the identity of the person who could have maintained the journal. John Faulkner was given a disability discharge on March 24, 1863; Aaron Neal died of disease on April 21, 1863; and John Newmarch was discharged from the company to accept a promotion with the 22nd Massachusetts. Samuel Stillman died of disease on March 27, 1863. John Sturtevant was given a disability discharge on March 10, 1863. John Welch was given a disability discharge on March 17, 1863.[18]

On March 8, at dress parade, orders were read which named their camp Camp Gove, in honor of Colonel Gove. Dress coats were issued on the 13th. The men did not want them, as they would throw them away when they marched in order to lighten the load. March 15 saw heavy rain and snow, and all unnecessary duties were suspended. On the 17th, most of the men visited the 9th Massachusetts Irish Regiment to watch them celebrate Saint Patrick's Day. They were amused as they watched greased-pig races and hurdle races. They later learned that an officer from the 9th was killed in a hurdle race.[19]

14

Seventy-Seven Held Longstreet

On March 20, they were again assigned picket duty. It snowed all day and night, and the Sharpshooters thought they were selected for all of the stormy details. On the 26th, they were ordered out for a review as it started to snow. Returning to camp, they were ordered back out at eleven thirty and were reviewed by General Meade. On April 5, General Meade conducted another division review, with General Hooker present.

On April 8, President Lincoln reviewed the army. Each corps was reviewed separately; it was a magnificent sight. Column after column marched in review as the sun gleamed off the bayonets and shiny rifles. This was all done in full view of the Rebel camps. The Articles of War were read to the men on the 12th at Sunday inspection. On April 16, Henry Wilson visited the 22nd Regiment and the Sharpshooters. He never lost an opportunity to show his thoughtfulness toward them. On the 14th, they were ordered to be ready to march on a moment's notice. On the 21st, ambulances carried the sick men from camp; the Sharpshooters thought that was a sure sign of a movement.[1]

The spring campaign started April 27, 1863, as the men marched out of Camp Gove. The Sharpshooters were ordered to have three days' rations in their haversacks and another five in their knapsacks. The wagons had been cut to a minimum. Officers were required to carry their blankets and baggage on pack-mules, which were led by buglers and drummers. It was warm, and the roads were muddy. After each halt, the men left overcoats and surplus comforts on the side of the road. The Sharpshooters were not in condition for a hard march. They marched eight miles and encamped near Hartwood Church. On the 28th, they marched at one o'clock in the afternoon. It started to rain, and the roads turned to mud, making it a long and difficult march. They marched eighteen miles and arrived at Kelly's Ford. At each halt, they disposed of more clothing and gear.

They started to march at seven in the morning on April 29. They crossed the Rappahannock River at Kelly's Ford about eight o'clock. Griffin's Division had the advance and Barnes's Brigade led the division. They marched on Ellis Ford Road, followed the river, and crossed Mountain Run soon after. Their clothes were now wet and heavy, the roads were muddy, and with each step more mud stuck to their shoes. As the pace quickened to near double-quick, there were no more halts. This took a toll on the men, who began to fall out in high numbers. Word was sent to Barnes that many straggled. Barnes sent word back that the march was necessary, and that his objective was to seize the bluffs on the opposite bank before the Rebels could. That would save a battle and lives.[2]

The men continued marching and reached the ford at about four o'clock. They had marched sixteen miles at a rapid pace. There were small skirmishes ahead of them, and several Rebels were captured. The Union men stripped off their clothes and tied them to their rifles, held them over their heads, and forded the river with water up to their armpits. The bottom of the Rapidan River was very rocky and slippery. Cavalry was placed downriver to rescue men who lost their footing in the swift current, but there were very few accidents.

Once they crossed the river, they climbed up the slippery, mud-covered banks. They made fires and dried themselves, thankful they were dry, then settled in for a comfortable night's sleep. But it began to rain heavily, and they and their blankets got soaked. They knew their load in the morning would be doubly heavy, as everything would be waterlogged.

At seven in the morning of April 30, they fell into formation. They were in deep mud and some men threw their haversacks and wet blankets on the ground, only to have them trampled on by others and buried under the mud. After marching a few miles, they threw out skirmishers and flankers to feel for the enemy. The cavalry went in advance and encountered a small force of Rebel infantry. General Barnes ordered the Sharpshooters forward in support, but the Rebels had retreated, and there was nothing to be done. They marched along Ellis Ford Road and found an enemy earthwork which faced the road. Marching up a slight hill, they could see the Chancellor House, a cleared farm of about one hundred acres; but at a distance of a few hundred yards in all directions, they could see only dense forest and thickets.

At about eleven o'clock that morning, they marched into that clearing, stacked arms, and made coffee. There were no other troops around, and they were the advance of the army at Chancellorsville. At one thirty, they were ordered to fall in. They marched on the Fredericksburg Turnpike about three miles and saw the enemy's works near the Zion Church. They moved off the road, halted, formed a battle line, and threw out skirmishers. General Griffin rode down the road, returned, and talked about a battery. The Sharpshooters expected their batteries to move to the front. They could see the Rebel batteries as they moved into position and the sun reflected off the brass pieces. The Sharpshooters moved to the rear by the same road, crossed Mott Run, and encamped at Ellis Ford Road. They passed many troops in front of the Chancellor House. The entire 11th, 12th, and 5th Corps were there.[3] On May 1, orders were given: "The Fifth Corps, including three batteries, will be thrown on the river-road, by the most direct route. The head of it [is] to advance near midway between Mott and Golin Runs. The movement to be made by small parties thrown out in advance and [is] to be completed by two o'clock."

Similar orders were given to the 12th and 3rd Corps. Hooker's plan was to get beyond the woods around Chancellorsville, form a battle line, and force the Confederates to attack a defended position. General Lee had his eye on the same piece of ground, and during the night moved his men into that position.

The three corps moved out in the morning. Sykes made first contact with the enemy and skirmished, taking a number of prisoners. The Sharpshooters could hear the battle roar to their right and rear, and it appeared that their brigade had advanced too far. Cautious, they halted more often. They passed through deserted Rebel camps whose campfires were still hot, a sign that the enemy had just departed. General Hooker issued an order to retreat and wanted a defensive line formed near the Chancellorsville House.

As the Sharpshooters retraced their earlier steps, they did not meet the enemy. The Sharpshooters thought they were a reconnaissance force. At the intersection of the old mine road and the turnpike to United States Ford, they met a squad of prisoners who had been captured by General Sykes and were being sent back to United States Ford. It was getting dark, and the Sharpshooters were marching at near the double-quick. From the river road they moved off to the left into a dense forest, traveling diagonally between the mine road and the turnpike.

They quickly formed a battle line, as the enemy had followed up on their retreat. If they had not moved at near the double-quick, their brigade would have been caught off the river road and separated from its division.

The enemy pushed so close to their line that the Sharpshooters could hear Rebel commands reverberating through the dense woods, as clearly as if the speakers had been in their own company. Only a few hundred yards away, pushed up the road, was the Rebel artillery, with which the Rebels vigorously shelled the Sharpshooters. The Sharpshooters hugged the ground. The division sent out skirmishers and a pioneer detail; both groups included Sharpshooters. The skirmishers kept up a sharp fire while the pioneers worked with their axes and felled trees to create a barricade. They were in a desperate situation as the shells glared, shrieked, and burst against the huge pine trees; they could hear the screaming of the shells through the thickets in their rear. The surgeon, Dr. Stearns, had a little boy with him who could not be safely moved to the rear and was stuck in the battle. The boy experienced the full horror of what was happening around him, and lost control. He started screaming hysterically. His screams could be heard over the roar of the artillery, and only stopped when he was exhausted. The Rebels did not advance, as the forest was so dense, and they were as much confused as the Union troops, so they just kept shelling.

The moon rose, and it was a bright night. Not a man slept. No one knew what his fate would be. All night, the men could hear the rumble of Rebel batteries and the Rebel infantry stomping their feet. Each time it got quiet and the men felt secure, the batteries would open up on them again. Private Osgood of the Sharpshooters was ten to fifteen yards in front of the regiment on pioneer duty, exposed to the Rebels one hundred yards away. He was cutting down a large pine tree when it was struck by a shell that exploded. Fragments of it broke both of his hips, and he died May 27.[4]

A little after midnight, the men were cautioned not to make any noise, and in particular not to let their bayonets or dippers clank. The command to creep and crawl to the rear was whispered through the lines. Doing so, the men thus gradually got out of their desperate situation. They marched until four in the morning, when they reached the clearing at the Chancellor House, making camp there. They were kept busy, building strong barricades and log breastworks with slashing, until the afternoon of May 2. When they were done, they felt secure.

Around six o'clock that evening, they heard cannonading on their right, which grew in intensity. They thought they would be called up at any time. In the midst of the sound of battle, Sykes' division's band started to play "Hail Columbia" and "The Star-Spangled Banner." It seemed strange to hear the song amidst the roar of battle, but it inspired the troops and calmed their fears.

They were ordered on picket duty at midnight. They went over their barricades and into the dense forest in front of them. Soon after, artillery and musketry could be heard some distance from them. Stonewall Jackson was attacking Berry's division of the Third Corps, which had been cut off from the main army as it traveled on the plank road to rejoin the larger force. The battle raged, roared, and resonated through the thick forest. They heard a party coming through the woods in front of them from the Rebels' direction. They challenged the party, did not get a response, and opened fire. No line appeared, and they were ordered to cease fire. They learned that the party was made up of stragglers from the 11th Corps who had spent the night trying to find their way back to their unit. The Sharpshooters were relieved of picket duty on the morning of May 3.

They passed over the barricades they had built, only to find them abandoned. As they passed through a group of wounded men, they learned their brigade had been sent to the

In the afternoon of May 5, 1863, under a flag of truce, the wounded were removed across the Rappahannock River following the Battle of Chancellorsville (Library of Congress).

center of the battlefield, and joined their corps. When they reached their brigade, they came under heavy fire and were ordered to lie down. The fire was so intense that they were moved into the woods near a field hospital, which flew the yellow flag. The Rebels thought it was a ruse and that the Federals were attempting to shield themselves under color of the hospital. The Rebels vigorously shelled them with artillery. The shot and shells went through the hospital and further harmed the wounded men. The surgeon moved the hospital further to the rear.

Their position was now on the Ellis Ford Road, in the center, near the small, white house (Bullock's) which they had passed on April 29 on their way to the Chancellor House. The thick woods in front of them were on fire, filled with dead and wounded men. It was spine-chilling to hear the screams of the wounded as they were consumed by the fires. In range of Rebel sharpshooters, they hugged the ground, but the occasional dull thud told of another man hit. A captain of Berdan's Sharpshooters jumped over the log breastworks and concealed himself with his telescopic rifle. A puff of smoke from a location in a tree and a groan from one of the Federal troops told the story. He watched as the Rebel sharpshooter fired three times, but could not see him in the tree. Finally, when the Rebel sharpshooter moved to ease his cramped body, the Berdan captain saw him and fired. The Rebel fell out of the tree.

In the afternoon, General Lee sent a reconnaissance party to determine whether the Union position was strong or weak. The battle was sharp and short. Seventy-two Union artillery pieces opened on General Lee. The Sharpshooters hugged the ground as the shells screamed over their heads.

At dusk, the regiment was ordered to the front. They climbed over the breastworks and moved to the edge of the woods, where they were ordered on picket duty. It was a bright, moonlit night — another sleepless one, as they were on alert. Heavy cannonading could be heard in the direction of Fredericksburg. About midnight, shots were fired on their front and right. The Sharpshooters sprang to their feet, ready to repulse the enemy, but the firing died out. Union batteries opened along the line with grape and canister shot. Again, the Sharpshooters hugged the ground as they were fired over. Their little regiment made as much noise as a corps, and the Rebels retreated. They were relieved of picket duty at seven in the morning, climbed over the breastworks, and settled into their rifle pits.

In the afternoon of May 5, a truce flag was raised and permission was sought to bury the dead. No firing took place except for small skirmish or picket lines. The men were visibly astonished at the lack of action. The Sharpshooters learned from an officer attached to headquarters that they would withdraw that night.

Later in the afternoon, it started to rain heavily and the ground turned to mud. The Sharpshooters could not get comfortable. They could not see much, but all night long they could hear troops sloshing past them and artillery being moved out. They didn't understand why they had not received an order to move. The Sharpshooters were exhausted, as they had not slept for three nights after a period of constant movement. At three o'clock in the morning of May 6, they were ordered to move out. They marched a mile or two and halted at United States Ford. They were ordered behind newly constructed breastworks and thrown out as skirmishers. Just as their brigade had been appointed the vanguard for the opening of the Battle of Chancellorsville, they were now appointed rear guard for the Army of the Potomac. As then, the Sharpshooters were the first in and last out.

About seven-thirty on the morning of May 6, they marched about two miles in knee-deep mud to the river and crossed over the pontoons, under the cover of about thirty-two guns. They were ordered to assist the 50th New York Engineer Regiment to take up the bridges. Though they didn't like it, they obeyed the order. The road was a sheer bluff. Taking up planks and stringers and loading the wagons, they then lowered ropes and pulled the teams up. In mud over their knees, they almost slept on their feet as they pulled the ropes up the bluff. They labored until late afternoon, then were ordered to escort the wagons inside the picket lines at Hartwood Church. Exhausted, they headed for their old camp at Stoneman's Switch, which they had stripped, as they had never thought they would return there. Without the benefit of any commands, they struggled through fields and dense woods. By nightfall, the woods had become so dense and dark that the men lit matches to see lost paths and cart

50th New York Engineers pontoon bridge pulled up and assembled in a train, May 6, 1863. The Sharpshooters were exhausted from the previous Battle of Chancellorsville. They were in constant motion and had not slept for three days; they marched two miles through knee deep mud. They were then ordered to break down and load that pontoon bridge (Library of Congress).

roads. Only about forty men had reached the camp by eleven o'clock that night. Late that night, while men still straggled in, they were ordered to return to the river at once and escort the pontoon train to safety. At nine in the morning they moved out, passing many men nursing their blistered feet and drying their drenched clothes. Finding the train safe, they returned to camp at eleven o'clock that morning.[5]

On May 21, the officers of the 5th Corps presented General Barnes with a sword, equipment valued at three hundred dollars, a horse valued at four hundred dollars, and a saddle valued at two hundred dollars, all as a token of respect for their commander. It was a brilliant affair, and all men not on duty attended. Nonetheless, the Sharpshooters were not as impressed as some of the other men were.

On May 28, the Sharpshooters were on picket duty and were ordered to pack up. The regiment returned from picket duty on May 29, made a long march of eighteen miles, and encamped at Wykoff's Mine. On May 30, at six in the morning, they marched to Morrisville, four miles away, and on May 31 marched two miles back to Grove Church, where they encamped. Learning that the Federals had taken Vicksburg, the men cheered. They were covering the Fords Banks, United States Ford, and Kelly's Ford until General Hooker could determine what General Lee's army was doing.

They expected to remain in the camp at Grove Church for several days. The camp was like a field in New England, and commanded a view of the region with a gentle slope which led to a valuable clean stream. They were on a high, level piece of ground, and some of the men were camped in the woods. When the men finished laying out company streets and pitching their tents, they all agreed it was the best camp location they had ever had.

On May 31, a chaplain from a Michigan regiment was murdered by guerrillas. His throat had been slashed from ear to ear, even though his uniform identified him as a chaplain. In response to this atrocity, the Sharpshooters were put on constant guard and picket duty. Guards were placed around all Rebel properties, as their owners and occupants were believed to be Rebel spies harboring guerrillas. On June 5, nine members of the regiment, along with one officer, scouted a house in which they thought guerrillas were present. Though they surrounded the house and rushed in, they only found an older couple. Some slaves told them where the guerrillas were, and they raided some brush, but all they found were three horses. The guerrillas had escaped. After that, stricter orders were issued for guard and picket duty.

On June 6, the men were ordered to be ready to march on five minutes' notice, and every conceivable rumor floated through the camp. The only thing the Sharpshooters knew for sure was that they were to leave the best camp they had to date. They were on picket duty on the 8th, and observed corps flags approaching, which turned out to be two brigades of infantry going to support the cavalry at Beverly Ford. The brigades carried the corps flag to make the enemy think it was the entire Army of the Potomac. On the 9th, the Sharpshooters heard heavy booming all day, which indicated a sharp cavalry fight. On the 10th, they were marched to Kelly's Ford to support the cavalry, but they were not needed and returned to camp, traveling over six miles of dusty roads to do so.

On June 11, they again received orders to be ready to move on a moment's notice. That night they broke camp and marched two miles to Morrisville, where they encamped for the night. On June 14, they marched early and went twenty miles through Bristersburg, camping near Catlett's Station on Deep Run. The hot, dusty weather made it a difficult march; their lungs filled with dust, and there was very little water. Orders were given to go to Bristoe Station but then were countermanded, bringing a large cheer from the men.

At five-thirty in the morning on June 15, they marched through Catlett's to near Bristoe

Station. As on the previous day, it was terribly hot and dusty, and now there was no water at all. The men suffered, reaching camp at eleven o'clock. There they were mustered and paid, remaining in that miserable and unattractive encampment through June 16. They marched twenty miles on June 17, passing through Manassas Junction, crossing Bull Run Stream, and striking the Gum Stream Road. They encamped near Gum Spring.[6]

After they left Bull Run Stream, there was nothing but slimy mud holes to drink from, and the men suffered terribly. Several men got sunstroke. In the afternoon, they gained some relief as they marched on wooded roads, sheltered from the sun, and slowed their pace. General Gleason of the 25th New York died of exhaustion and heatstroke that day. The regiment gathered its stragglers and went into camp. Men continued to enter camp during the night in deplorable conditions.

During this march, all of the sutlers were ordered out of the trains and back to Washington. Sutler Hackett, who had a good relationship with the Sharpshooters and the 22nd, was entrusted to take a great deal of money from the men to Washington, which would then be sent home to their families. He was warned that the countryside was filled with many guerrillas, who would strip sutlers, and that he would probably be caught. Leaving camp, he kept a sharp eye out. As he camped that night, a sorry-looking wagon carrying five or six men approached. It sported two different wheels, and was pulled by two broken-down mules. The men were sutlers from other regiments. Mosby's guerrillas had captured them and cleaned them out of everything — horses, wagons, goods, money, and in some cases, the coats from their backs. Hackett fed the men, and in the morning continued to Washington, all the while thinking his turn might be next. He made it safely to Washington, sent the money, and returned to the regiment with receipts. The regiment greeted him with cheers. At first, Hackett

Edwin Forbes' drawing of Gum Spring, Virginia, June 18, 1863. The Sharpshooters were nearly felled by heat stroke from their arduous twenty mile march to Gum Spring. There was nothing but mud holes to drink from. (Library of Congress).

did not know why, but he learned that word had gone out that he had been captured and that the men had lost their money.

On June 18, the men remained at Gum Spring, a pleasant camp with good water. On June 19, at three in the afternoon, they marched five miles to Aldie and supported the cavalry. The Sharpshooters visited the camp of the 1st Massachusetts Cavalry, whose men complained that the Rebels were fighting from behind stone walls with dismounted cavalry, and that a Rhode Island cavalry unit was shot up by those methods.

The cavalry fight continued at Aldie, where the Sharpshooters remained. On June 21, General Pleasanton of the U.S., Cavalry requested that General Griffin's division, including the Sharpshooters, come to the cavalry's aid. At three o'clock in the morning, the division marched to just beyond Middleburg. Looking out over open, rolling countryside, they formed a battle line behind the cavalry. The Sharpshooters, commanded by Colonel Tilton, threw out skirmishers ahead of the cavalry, then were ordered to relieve the cavalry pickets, which took about an hour. No sooner had they done so when another cavalry picket relieved them.

As they withdrew, they were hidden by a grove of trees on a knoll, directly behind the 1st Massachusetts Cavalry. The Rebels opened fire on them from mounted batteries. Skirmishers were thrown out ahead of the 1st Massachusetts Cavalry and moved forward. The brigade followed, and they gained the ridge. As the cavalry charged, it was a sight to behold, starting out in a slow trot until the formation was made, and then charging at full gallop. The crack of carbines and pistols was sharp for a few moments, then gradually died down. Men reeled in the saddle when shot. Riderless horses ran past the Sharpshooters toward town, pursued by dismounted cavalrymen trying to catch them. The Rebels scattered in every direction. Some went behind barns or haystacks, only to be dislodged by the Federal cavalry. Vast and moving, the battle raged on, and observers had an unobstructed view that extended in all directions.

At two o'clock, the men were ordered to fall in and marched toward Ashby's Gap. Their rest the day before had refreshed them. While they marched, Colonel Tilton received an order to go directly into battle when they arrived at Ashby's Gap. Passing Rector's Crossroads and Upperville, they encamped near Ashby's Gap late in the afternoon, but found that the Rebels had fled. They were ordered to return and marched at three in the morning of June 22., At six in the morning, they arrived at Middleburg, where they halted until one in the afternoon, when they marched to Aldie and encamped.

The men remained at Aldie until June 25, their time taken up by squad, company, and brigade drill. The Sharpshooters and the 22nd Massachusetts were detached from the brigade and ordered to go with the corps wagons to Fairfax Station to load wagons and then rejoin the army. Taking the Little River Road, they passed through Chantilly and by Fairfax Courthouse, loaded the wagons with rations, and then destroyed what was left. They left Fairfax, passed through Germantown, and camped near Frying Pan. After the men had left Fairfax, the Rebels entered and shelled the town, capturing a few stragglers who were not with the command when it left the town.

On the night of June 26, the men camped near Dranesville, then marched at four thirty on the morning of June 27. It was an easy march, and the men took ample time to eat cherries along the way, as they were ripe and plentiful. Arriving at Edward's Ferry, they waited until a division crossed, then crossed themselves at ten o'clock. That night they camped at Bennett's Creek. On July 28, they passed through Poolesville, Barnesville, and Buckeystown, and went on to Frederick, where they rejoined the brigade. They marched with their brigade on a turnpike road and crossed the Monocacy River, then encamped near the cemetery at Ballinger's Creek. They awoke on June 29 to a beautiful morning, with a vista of Frederick, Maryland,

and the Monocacy Valley, surrounded by grain fields and green trees with a mountainous background.

It was here that General Hooker requested the use of the Harpers Ferry garrison and was refused. At his own request, he was relieved of command of the army, which was given to General Meade. The army was spared a grand review, as General Butterfield thought there were more important matters at hand.[7]

On June 29, the men marched through Frederick, Harmony Grove, Mount Pleasant, and Liberty, Maryland, and encamped two miles outside of Liberty. The Sharpshooters had marched great distances — twenty-two miles to Fairfax Station, twenty miles to Edward's Ferry, thirty miles to Frederick, and twenty-two miles on June 29. They had a rapid march of twenty-five miles on June 30, passing through Johnsonville, Union Bridge, and Union, and to Union Mills, where they encamped in a nearby meadow. They were immediately ordered out on picket duty.

Early on the morning of July 1, in the dark, they started a long march. They had no time to cook coffee. As they marched along, they munched on hard bread and drank water lightly tinged with coffee and sugar. They were in marching shape, but as they passed through Frizzleburg, more men than usual straggled. It was reported that whiskey was on tap there. In the afternoon, they marched into Pennsylvania, and were elated to be in a Northern free state. Various regimental bands played patriotic music as they entered the free state. Late in the afternoon, they arrived in Hanover and encamped in a meadow west of town. They saw dead horses all around the town, as there had been a cavalry battle there the day before. The wounded were treated in a schoolhouse. The citizens of the town tended to the wounded, and supplied the incoming troops with bread and fruit.

They men tried to get some needed rest from the long march of the day, but orders were issued to fall in. They marched through McSherrytown, Prussia, and other small hamlets, and about one o'clock in the morning, encamped near Bonaughtown. Throwing themselves on the ground, they slept after the demanding, all-day march. Stragglers came into camp all night long. The men marched again at four thirty on the morning of July 2. They left the Hanover Road, marched on the low ground to Rock Creek, crossed the creek, and halted on the high ground at Power's Hill. They were held in reserve at the rear center of the battlefield, to be available to move in either direction as needed.

By the time they reached Power's Hill, the men were exhausted, Many were without shoes or hats after their long day and night march to reach the battlefield. Lying on the ground, they used rocks for pillows. Even the din of cannonading and the rattle of musketry from the battle raging in front of them did not keep them awake.

At four in the afternoon, they were awakened and ordered to fall in. Descending Power's Hill, they marched about a mile and three quarters to the right of the Round Tops. The Rebel artillery zeroed in on them and vigorously shelled them. Moving to the left, they came upon a lane that led to the Emmettsburg Road. They entered the woods south of Trostle's House and halted at the edge of a dry ravine which emptied into Plum Run. Fifty yards to their right was an open field, and one thousand yards to their right front was Sherfy's peach orchard. Directly to their front, at about four hundred yards, was the Rose House, which they could see clearly when the smoke lifted.[8]

At this point, the skirmishers ran in and yelled, "Fix bayonets!" Before any commands could be given, firing commenced. The Sharpshooters stacked cartridges on the ground in front of them and engaged the enemy. The 22nd and the Sharpshooters entered the battle with sixty-seven rifles. The Rebels screamed their rebel yell, and the Sharpshooters responded by cheering. Though their nerves were strained, their resolve grew stronger. Hearing the groans

Trostle's barnyard, seen by the Sharpshooters July 2, 1863, where the 9th Massachusetts Battery was cut up. This photograph was taken by Timothy O'Sullivan probably July 4 or 5. The Ninth Massachusetts Artillery lost eleven men killed, sixteen wounded, and fifty horses killed on July 2, 1863. The men killed have been removed along with the artillery. All that remains in this photograph are partially bloated horses (Library of Congress).

of the wounded men, they were determined not to be pushed over the ridge behind them. They had no time to dwell on their apprehensions or fears, as they could clearly see a stand of Rebel colors in front of them.

Discovering a gap in the battle line between the 5th and 3rd Corps, the Rebels charged toward it. In an attempt to close the gap, a brigade from the 3rd Corps moved through the woods and through the 22nd and the Sharpshooters. Under a full charge by the enemy, that brigade changed fronts without being given commands. They were intertwined with the 22nd and Sharpshooters, which created much confusion. The 22nd and the Sharpshooters picked up their cartridges from the ground and moved one hundred yards to the rear with the wounded men.

As they turned around, the company viewed the carnage. The Rebels were pouring through the woods from behind the Trostle House. The din of cannonading and musketry was so loud that bugles or commands could not be heard. The men now faced the gap between the divisions toward the peach orchard. Their lines were broken, but they all kept their eyes on the company colors and followed them. The 5th and 9th Batteries shelled the Rebels to

Rock defenses built at Round Top, Gettysburg, Pennsylvania. On July 3, 1863, the Sharpshooters built rock defenses in front of Little Round Top. It was fortunate they did, as they soon were under fire from Rebel sharpshooters located in front of them at Devil's Den. This photograph was taken by Alexander Gardner in July 1863 (Library of Congress).

try to stem their flow. The company fired and retreated and fired again. Nonetheless, it was overrun, losing three officers, twenty-eight men, and seventy horses. The Rebels gained control of the guns, but Union troops retrieved the guns and brought them off the field by hand.[9]

The key strategic features of this battlefield were the Round Tops, two high hills that commanded it, and, in particular, the smaller of them, Little Round Top. The Confederates wanted the advantage of that position, but the Union would not grant it to them at any cost. The Sharpshooters slowly moved back until they held a position at the foot of a slope on the right side of Little Round Top. They repelled Rebels at the left and center. The Rebels tried to move around to the right and rear of the hill but were repulsed and driven back in a fierce hand-to-hand battle with the 20th Maine, led by Colonel Chamberlain. At dusk, the Pennsylvanian Reserves charged through the wheat field and beyond, and the enemy retired in all directions. The area in front of the Sharpshooters was now clear of Rebels.[10]

There were no plans or strategy at Gettysburg. Rather, the armies met there and clashed.

The courage and intelligence of the rank and file of the Army of the Potomac saved the day. The 22nd and the Sharpshooters were determined to do their jobs, as were all the other units.

When the battle had ceased, it was learned that the Confederate general Longstreet had reconnoitered the position of the 22nd and Sharpshooters. He had led an expedition to attack that point, but seeing the stands of colors of the 6th Corps behind him, he gave up hopes of capturing Little Round Top.

Early on the morning of July 3, the Sharpshooters were moved a few hundred yards to protect the ravine between the two Round Tops. They piled up stones in an effort to protect themselves, waiting to see what the day would bring. They did not have to wait long, as Rebel sharpshooters were lodged behind the rocky cover of Devil's Den. The Rebels were picking off the cannoneers who were on top of Little Round Top. The Andrew Sharpshooters could not expose any part of their bodies without being fired at by the Rebel sharpshooters.

Lookouts were shielded in the rocky crevices and warned when the Rebel sharpshooters were going to fire, at which point the Andrew Sharpshooters would rise and fire at the Rebels. Hiram Berdan's Sharpshooters were called in and sought cover in the rocks and trees but could not dislodge the Rebel sharpshooters. That night, the Rebel sharpshooters were captured by a division which moved into the Rebels' rear. The Rebel sharpshooters were the 3rd Arkansas of Hood's old division. Tattered and dirty, they were a pretty ragged group of men who used long, old-fashioned squirrel rifles that fired a small pea ball.

On the evening of July 3, the men were ordered on picket duty. By the soft light of the moon, they could see the dead and dying all around them. At midnight, they were relieved and started on an errand of mercy. Moving among the wounded and dying, they gave them water and any other comfort they could. They could not believe the sights around them. Hundreds of wounded could not be taken off the field. Every conceivable piece of equipment was strewn over the ground among the dead and dying. The Sharpshooters went as far as Devil's Den, but the situation was the same all over the battlefield.[11]

15

"Stuck in the Mud March"

On the afternoon of July 4, the 22nd and Sharpshooters were thrown out as skirmishers through the woods, to the extreme left of Little Round Top. Ordered to probe carefully for the Rebels, they met and pushed back some Rebel skirmishers in a brisk encounter, but a skirmish line of battle was never formed, as the Rebels fell back. The 22nd and the Sharpshooters had the distinction of being the last to fire at the Confederates at Gettysburg. As they returned to Little Round Top, they saw Confederate bodies lying all through the woods in every imaginable position. The Confederates had crawled or been carried, but unable to keep up, they had lain down and died.

At Gettysburg, not a man of the Andrew Sharpshooters was killed in battle, but Lieutenant Winsor Ward and Sergeants William Madden and Private George Munn were wounded. *The War of the Rebellion: A Compilation of the Official Records of the Union and Confederate Armies*, reports that Lieutenant Ward was cited for his bravery in assisting wounded from the battlefield.[1]

On July 5, the Sharpshooters were detailed to a burial party. It was repulsive work. Many of the bodies were decomposed and broke apart as the Sharpshooters moved them. The men used rails to support the bodies as they slid them into the graves. As many as ninety bodies were buried in one grave. In the afternoon, the men marched in pursuit of the enemy. They moved on the crossroad to the rear of the Round Tops until they reached the Emmitsburg Road. Marching seven miles, they encamped near Marsh Creek.[2]

On July 6, they marched slowly on the blocked-up road for three miles to Moritz Crossroads. It was a difficult march, as sharp stones under the mud cut through their boots. Many men had blistered feet from the long march from Fredericksburg, so they removed their boots and marched in stocking feet.

They started their march on the morning of July 7. As the rain continued, they marched to Emmittsburg over the muddy roads, which had been cut up by wagon trains. As the dark arrived and the rain poured down, nothing could be distinguished. Many men fell out, unable to keep up. They marched and sought shelter wherever they could. By the time the men encamped at Utica, the ranks were greatly thinned.

On July 8, the rain continued and the Sharpshooters led the division on the march. One benefit of their doing so was that they did not have to march through mud that had been trampled on by thousands of men. At about noon, the rain ended and the sun came out. The men marched through Utica and Creagerstown, over the High Knob of the Catoctin Mountains and into the valley of Frederick. After a long day's march, they encamped at Middletown.

They dried their clothes, and when rations were issued, they filled their stomachs, then got some much-needed sleep.

They started to march at nine in the morning of July 9, on the Boonesborough Road. Passing through South Mountain at Fox's Gap, they marched past pickets on the side of the road. They went down the mountain and encamped near Boonesborough and Springvale about a mile and a half from Keedysville, where they had encamped during the Antietam campaign.

On July 10, they marched, commencing once again at nine in the morning, on the Keedysville Road. They crossed the Antietam River on a bridge above the battlefield. Marching for a few miles, they encamped in a battle line near Delaware Mills. On the 11th, they marched in a battle line and advanced in the area of Jones Crossroad and Bakersville. They then marched about two miles and occupied a position between the Antietam River and Sharpsburg.

On July 12 they marched closer to St. James College, and all of the divisions closed ranks. Their battle line was almost seven miles long. They were on the other side of Sharpsburg Road, which led to Hagerstown. The Rebels had just evacuated Hagerstown, and Marsh Run was in their front. The Sharpshooters and the 22nd were moved to the front on a skirmish line and probed for the enemy. Senator Wilson visited them on the picket line and collected their mail to send home; he had to be whisked to the safety of the rear as bullets flew out of the woods in front of him.

They remained in the line of battle at Bakersville on July 13. They slowly worked their way toward Williamsport, expecting a great battle at any time and building breastworks with logs to prepare for it. General Humphreys, chief of staff, rode past the Sharpshooters' camp and told them to stop building fortifications, as they would not be needed. General Meade also passed their camp that day. At Funkstown, as the Sharpshooters looked at the entire Army of the Potomac in battle formation, they were amazed at its size. As far as the eye could see in both directions, cavalry moved about, batteries unlimbered and got ready for action, and staff officers and orderlies rode around as the infantry moved slowly forward through the fields. The entire might of the Army of the Potomac could be seen. The Sharpshooters thought the army had never been used to its potential, and thought if it went forward and used all of its abilities, Lee's army would be crushed.

That night they were assigned picket duty in the rain. They caught several prisoners and deserters. One of the prisoners told them that Lee's army was huddled up on the riverbank and had left a double line of pickets to keep up a heavy line of fire in order to deceive the Union troops. Though word was sent to headquarters, it was not followed up on. There would be no assault on Lee's broken and disorganized army.[3]

On July 15, they endured a long and exhausting march, going twenty miles over South Mountain and encamping near Burkittsville. That march was so difficult that men fell out by the scores. From there, they marched on July 16 through Petersville to the river at Berlin, where they encamped. On the 17th, they crossed the river on pontoons and marched six miles to the other side of Lovettsville, where they made camp. On the 18th, they marched to Purcellsville, making frequent stops and resting. On this day, the Sharpshooters learned of the draft riots in Boston and New York. They were angry that the Copperheads had organized these armed riots, which gave encouragement to the Rebels. They had fought hard and defeated the Rebels at Gettysburg, and now the Rebels were on the run. The Army of the Potomac felt as one man: enraged that the loyalty of the devoted North was in question. They learned that some units would be detached and returned to Boston and New York to quell the riots.

July 19 found the Sharpshooters in a valley opening from the mountains near Philemont. It was the height of blackberry season, and the berries were everywhere. After the men had encamped, they filled themselves up with the luscious fruit. On July 20, they marched on the Philemont Road via Union and encamped near Panther Skin Creek. There they spent the day and got some much-needed rest, as well as an opportunity to clean themselves and their equipment. They continued to enjoy the abundant blackberries.

On July 21, they marched fourteen miles, ending at Uniontown. They encamped at the same site where they had been a month before when they had supported the cavalry at Aldie. On July 22, they marched about five miles to Rector's Crossroads near Goose Creek. On July 23, they marched through Markham's Station, Farrowsville, and Linden to Manassas Gap, where they collided with the Rebel army. General French's division of the 3rd Corps engaged the Rebels and drove them away. General Meade was disappointed that General French had not attacked more vigorously, as he had intended to engage both Union armies against the Rebels, but General Lee had slipped away again.

On July 24, the Sharpshooters' division was ordered to take a certain hill. Moving over ground that was rough, rocky, and entangled with thickets, they did not find the enemy, and returned. In the afternoon, the Sharpshooters' brigade was ordered back through a gap about two miles and became the army's rear guard. The men marched through Farrowsville and Barber's Crossing to Orleans on July 25. They arrived at Warrenton on the 26th, very tired as they had been left near Manassas Gap for two days as reserve for the 3rd Corps.

The morning of July 27, they marched about six miles through Warrenton and encamped at a very pleasant site three and a half miles past Warrenton. On the 29th, five deserters were executed in the presence of the 5th Corps. The five condemned men, preceded by four men who carried their coffins, marched to the dirge played by the provost marshal's band. Arriving at the place of execution, they sat on their coffins beside their future gravesite. Prayers were said, and they made their goodbyes to each other. They were blindfolded, and the execution squad was given the command to fire. When shot, their riddled bodies fell lifeless to the ground. The Sharpshooters wondered what went through the condemned men's minds as they marched to their own funeral, and saw their own future coffins and graves. The Sharpshooters reflected on the fairness of the rules: an enlisted man who deserted was executed, yet an officer was only dismissed from the service.

The men remained encamped near Warrenton until August 3, when the order was given to pack up. That day they marched on the Warrenton Turnpike to Bealton Station and encamped. On August 4, they moved and encamped on top of a hill, where they stayed until the 8th. On August 8, they marched to Beverly Ford, where they encamped and rested until September 16.

While encamped at Beverly Ford, the Sharpshooters heard rumors that Governor Andrews wanted the Sharpshooters, the 22nd Massachusetts Volunteer Infantry, and the 2nd Massachusetts Volunteer Infantry to return to Boston to quell the draft riots, but this never happened.

They made a very healthy and comfortable encampment at Beverly Ford. The Rappahannock River was a short distance away, so they enjoyed the privilege of frequent baths and lived very well for a change. They resumed drill. The Sharpshooters drilled as a squad and participated in company drill for two hours in the morning and two hours in the afternoon, with an occasional battalion drill thrown in. They resumed the usual parades and inspections at that camp.

On August 31 and September 1, they were under orders to move but did not. Two hundred conscripts arrived around September 9. Although the Sharpshooters thought they were a rough bunch of men who had to be watched — one of them deserted his first night in camp — the overall group turned out well. On the 13th, they were ordered to move out to support a reconnaissance force that had moved toward Culpepper, but the order was countermanded. Hearing gunfire, they thought they would be moved at any time.

On September 16, they packed up. They moved across the river to Culpepper, marched about twelve miles, and encamped. The day was hot, and the new conscripts had a hard time as they were not accustomed to long marches. As they fell out of the ranks, the conscripts lined the sides of the roads.

On September 17, 1863, the Sharpshooters passed through Culpepper Courthouse and encamped two miles from the town, which was itself about five miles from the Rapidan River. Cedar Mountain could clearly be seen in the foreground. General Banks had fought a fierce battle on the site of their camp in August of 1862. They remained at that camp for four weeks, which was an unusually long stay for that time of year. In this comfortable and healthy camp, they resumed their usual drills, inspections, and parades. Brigade headquarters was in a house just behind the Sharpshooters. The parade ground was sufficient in size for all of their drills. There were some cold spells, and on October 2, a severe storm blew down some tents. The cold spells alternated with warmer days when the men went for a swim or a bath in the river.[4]

On the evening of October 9, they were ordered to pack eight days' rations, all their gear, and be ready to move at two in the morning. At five in the morning, they marched to Raccoon Ford on the Rapidan River, where they remained all day, and then returned to their

John Minor Botts' residence at Culpepper, Virginia. This photograph was taken by Timothy O'Sullivan in September 1863. Botts and his family are visible on the porch. The Sharpshooters marched past Botts' home on October 11, 1863. They learned Botts was a Virginian that remained loyal to the Union. The Rebels followed the Sharpshooters closely, and as they passed Botts' residence on October 12, 1863, they burned his house and outbuildings to the ground (Library of Congress).

encampment at about six o'clock that same day. It appeared that a flank movement across the Rapidan River was planned, but orders from Washington cancelled it. There were indications that General Lee's army was on the move, and the Sharpshooters were not surprised to be given orders to move the next day.

Sunday, October 11, was a beautiful day, and the march began with no signs of panic, confusion, or haste. As the Sharpshooters passed through Culpepper, they made up the rear guard. Culpepper was a quaint town with its courthouse, churches, and stores. The sutlers and camp followers were disappointed as they watched the troops slip away from them. The provost guard went through all of the buildings to ensure that all those assigned to the army went with the army. At noon, they marched past the plantation of John Minor Botts, a famed Virginian who had remained loyal to the Union.

The Rebels followed the march closely, and there were some minor skirmishes. General Meade sent orders to march to Warrenton, but General Pleasanton reported that General Lee was closely following and had moved his army closer to the Union troops. That night, the Sharpshooters encamped near Beverly Ford.

On October 12, the Sharpshooters crossed Beverly Ford with the 5th, 2nd, and 6th Corps. They advanced in line and drove the Rebels back to Brandy Station, encamping nearby. That night, General Gregg reported that General Lee, whose advance guard he had fought near Warrenton, had crossed the Rappahannock at Sulphur Springs. That night, after the Sharpshooters passed Mr. Bott's plantation, they learned that the Rebels had burned his house and outbuildings to the ground.

On October 13, at three in the morning, the Sharpshooters marched at the double-quick back to their old camp at Beverly Ford. They halted long enough to have breakfast, and then marched to Catlett's Station, which they did not reach until long after dark. The men were so tired that they had no energy to cook coffee or food, and simply threw themselves on the open ground. Their encampment was on Stone's Farm, about two miles from Catlett's on the Walnut Branch.

On October 14, the Sharpshooters marched along a road which ran parallel to the railroad. Though they moved along quite peacefully, they heard the skirmishes of the rear guard, as the Rebels closely followed them. At around noon, they halted at Bristoe Station and cooked dinner. All of a sudden, the Rebels shelled them from a hill they had just passed over. The Union batteries were quick to respond and drove the Rebels back. The Sharpshooters and the 5th Corps waited at Bristoe Station for the 2nd Corps. General Heth, of Lee's army, attacked; he saw the gap in the Corps and felt it was an opening he could penetrate. The Battle of Bristoe Station was fought through the afternoon and early evening. While this battle raged Generals Meade and Lee raced to capture Centreville with their respective forces. General Meade was successful. The Sharpshooters crossed the Bull Run at Blackburn's Ford about midnight, marched up the hill to Centreville, and encamped about three in the morning on October 15. Having marched twenty-six miles and fought a battle that day, the Sharpshooters had suffered greatly.

At eight in the morning of October 15, the Sharpshooters marched toward Fairfax Courthouse and encamped about a mile from the town. It had rained all day, and the men were completely worn out after the march. On the 16th and 17th, they made two short marches to gain better positions. They marched to Fox's Mill on the 18th. On the 19th, they marched over Bull Run, which was covered with many graves where the bodies were only half-buried from the Second Battle of Bull Run. The men quickly assembled a detail and covered the bodies thoroughly. The Sharpshooters went into Groveton and encamped on Benjamin Chinn's farm, and from there marched to Gainesville on October 20.

Catlett's Station, Virginia. This photograph was taken by Timothy O'Sullivan in August 1862. United States Military and railroad boxcars can be seen. The Sharpshooters spent much of October 13, 1863, marching to Catlett's Station. They did not arrive until long after dark. They were so exhausted they could not cook food or make coffee, and they threw themselves on the ground to sleep (Library of Congress).

Marching out of Gainesville through Buckland and Broad Run, they encamped near New Baltimore on a high hill off the road. They remained encamped for five days and got some much-needed rest. Persimmons were in season, and the men enjoyed the fresh fruit. On the afternoon of October 24, they were ordered to pack up, and they marched to Auburn, where they arrived about nine o'clock that night. Auburn was a post office and the estate of Stephen McCormick, inventor of the McCormick plough and a cousin of the McCormick who invented the reaper. At this fine country home and estate, several of the officers stayed in the house. The men were marched about a mile away on October 25, and encamped until October 30.[5]

The Sharpshooters then marched to Three Mile Station, on the Warren Branch. They encamped in an oak grove, which was not a healthy campsite. The railroad passed by the camp, and supplies were brought in. They remained at that camp until November 7.

At six in the morning, they marched to Rappahannock Station, reaching it at about noon. Marching on dried mud raised dust, making the march unpleasant. The Sharpshooters marched on the left side of the railroad, on the north bank of the river. They saw some Rebel earthworks which could only be attacked with a frontal assault. The ground in front of the earthworks was low, and the men were swept by Rebel artillery. The Union artillery opened on the earthworks, sparking a lively exchange of shells.

Divisions of the 6th Corps reconnoitered at dark; they decided to assault and were supported by heavy artillery. The Sharpshooters went in with the 22nd Massachusetts. The Rebels were unable to stop the advance and lost over sixteen hundred men, four guns, and eight

15. "Stuck in the Mud March"

Rappahannock Station, Virginia, in August of 1862. On the morning of November 7, 1863, the Sharpshooters marched along the left side of the railroad tracks, on the north bank of the river. They reached the Rappahannock Station early in the afternoon. It was a difficult march as it was hot and dry. All those men walking on the dried mud raised a lot of dust to be inhaled (Library of Congress).

stands of colors. The 22nd Massachusetts had seven men wounded, but the Sharpshooters were unharmed. The Sharpshooters encamped by the river that night.

On the morning of November 8, the Sharpshooters learned that the Rebels had slipped away during the night. They then marched about six miles to Brandy Station, and on the 9th, they marched about three miles to Kelly's Ford. During the night of the 9th, the Sharpshooters re-crossed the Rappahannock River and encamped on the Washington side. Lacking proper shelter, they suffered through the cold night.

The Sharpshooters were ordered out on picket duty, which they considered to be a desirable assignment. Despite Kelly's reportedly questionable loyalty to the Union, they were detailed to guard Kelly's Mills and Kelly's property.

Even though the Sharpshooters, along with the 22nd Massachusetts, had long sought such duty, much grumbling ensued. There was constant demand for river guards, camp guards, and fatigue duties, and they also had to provide their quotas for brigade picket duty, even though they were isolated and five miles from the picket line. They toiled away building winter quarters — huts with fireplaces, as they tried to make themselves comfortable. It was all in vain, as they were ordered to cross the river and go to Mountain Run on November 19. On November 20, the paymaster arrived and paid them. On November 21, the 22nd Massachusetts and the Sharpshooters were assigned picket duty. They had a pleasant camp and light picket action. They remained there until they were relieved on the 23rd, when they returned to their camp at Kelly's Ford.

On the morning of November 24, the Sharpshooters marched in an early morning rain. It was not long before the march resembled the Burnside Mud March, and General Meade ordered them back to camp. Though they were drenched to their skin, they soon dried off at large campfires.

On November 26, the roads had dried enough to travel on. The Sharpshooters marched toward Ellis' Ford at six o'clock that morning, crossing at Mountain Run and halting within a mile of the river. Hearing gunfire from Culpepper Ford, they started in that direction. They soon learned they had taken the wrong road and cut across the country to get to the ford. When they arrived at one thirty, they learned that the cannon fire they had heard was a Union battery which had fired on Union cavalry in error — fortunately doing little damage, as the cavalry quickly got out of range. The Sharpshooters then marched several miles on a small dirt road through the Wilderness. Running into the road from Germania Ford, they marched several more miles, then encamped.

As they encamped, their leaders ordered them into a battle line, which took three attempts to get correct. Already tired, the men questioned their leaders' competence. It was Thanksgiving Day, and the Sharpshooters reflected on the previous Thanksgiving Day, when food had not been available. At least things had improved enough that the supply lines delivered rations to the men. It was nonetheless cold, and the men started fires in an attempt to get warm.

The men marched at six in the morning of November 27, as the rear guard of the 5th Corps. They wanted to march toward New Verdiersville. They marched on the plank road toward the Old Wilderness Tavern, and then moved in a southeasterly direction, arriving at Parker's Store about ten o'clock. The cavalry skirmished in front of them, and forward progress was slow. While the men were on the plank road, a party of the 6th Virginia Cavalry had hidden themselves in the woods. After the Sharpshooters had passed, the Rebels rushed to the supply wagon and captured the general headquarters team and several munitions wagons, running them down the plank road toward Fredericksburg. Colonel Sherwin took a rifle from one of the Sharpshooters and shot one of the raiders. Fifteen wagons were taken and set ablaze, and as the munitions wagons exploded, they made things quite lively. General Bartlett ordered the Sharpshooters to act as a special guard for the trains and the 22nd Massachusetts to act as flankers on each side of the trains.

Early that afternoon, the Sharpshooters and the 22nd Massachusetts came upon the enemy's entrenchments at the New Hope Church. They were ordered to the front. As no fires were allowed, they passed the night cold, uncomfortable, and without coffee. The Rebels occasionally shelled them, and there was some minor picket fire. At seven in the morning on the 28th, they marched at the quick step on a crossroad to Robertson's Tavern, and massed behind breastworks. There, they were able to make coffee and cook food, and they encamped there for the night. Some skirmishing took place in a heavy rain, adding to their discomfort.

At daybreak on November 29, the Sharpshooters marched on the Orange Courthouse Turnpike for about four miles and took up a position two thousand yards in front of the enemy, who were entrenched on a hill. The field between the Sharpshooters and the Rebels was entirely open, and Mine Run, a waist-deep stream, was between them. They formed a battle line, and there was some minor skirmishing. As it grew dark, it also grew extremely cold; it was difficult for the men because fires were not allowed. The men encamped there under arms, ready to move at a moment's notice.

General French's failure to engage General Lee meant that Lee had been able to move his army and choose a defensive position. Lee had a full twenty-four hours to fortify a very strong natural position on the west side of Mine Run. Nonetheless, General Meade decided to attack General Lee's position.

15. "Stuck in the Mud March"

The Sharpshooters remained concealed in the woods all day. The Rebel and Union pickets had agreed that they would not fire at each other. Some Union pickets had crossed the stream of Mine Run and had conversations with the Rebel pickets. Each side moved about freely while gathering wood and water.

At two o'clock in the morning of November 30, the Sharpshooters were moved about a mile to the right, into the woods. They piled up their knapsacks. The Sharpshooters and the 22nd Mass. were in the first battle line. An open field in front of them sloped to the run, a small stand of pines, another open field, and then the enemy lines. The Sharpshooters could see the enemy's campfires in the rear of their lines and thought there were not enough fires for a large Rebel force. Through their carelessness, the Union forces gave their position away to the enemy, who worked like beavers to strengthen their defenses even more.

General Warren had orders to begin artillery fire at eight in the morning and continue until nine o'clock; he did so. As they lay and waited for the order to attack, the Sharpshooters shivered. They considered the attack to be instant death, as they were to be the first to assault the Rebels' impregnable position while in an open field.

General Warren sent word to General Meade that the enemy had been reinforced with troops and artillery. General Warren advised that it would take eight minutes for Union troops to cross the open fields and the run, and that they would be exposed to terrible fire from the Rebels. Warren believed there would be no chance for success, and that the assault should be suspended. General Sedgwick took a gun, walked out to the picket line, and assessed the situation. He returned to General Meade, and told him the assault should be suspended.

Not knowing this, the Sharpshooters had a terrible night. With the temperature below zero, water froze in their canteens, and the bitter, cold wind took a terrible toll on them. It seemed to them that the assault would be worse than that of Fredericksburg, and that it would be madness to attack such a highly fortified position without any cover. They were so sure of instant death that they wrote their names on paper and attached the paper to their bodies so they could be identified after they were killed. That night took years from their lives.

As morning arrived on November 31, they found various ways to try to warm up, as fires still were not allowed. Some stamped their feet, walked, ran, and jumped, while others joined hands around a tree and went around and around it. As their rations had run out, they were also so hungry that they ate raw corn found on the ground that was meant as fodder for the horses. They were greatly relieved when General Meade gave the order to suspend the assault. General Meade "did not wish to charge his conscience with the burden of a needless exposure of his men to death, for the sake of an advanced and a great battle."

The Sharpshooters remained in that position all day; at night, they returned to their first position. They feared another rainstorm would make all but the planked roads impassable. On December 1, they were told their rations were to last them until the 4th. Most of them did not have any rations anymore. At six o'clock that evening, they had a very difficult march, because they halted frequently. They marched on the Germanna plank road through the night, and crossed the Rapidan River at Germanna Ford at four in the morning of December 2. Marching three miles beyond the river, they halted and slept until eight o'clock. They then marched until noon and halted at Stevensburg, four miles from Brandy Station; altogether, they had marched about twenty miles.

They were entirely out of rations and were willing to pay a dollar for two small pieces of hard bread. One of the men went into a house near a mill which had been used as a bakery. Finding some crumbs that were as hard as flint, he soaked them in water until they were soft enough to eat, and then filled his stomach. One of the members of the 22nd Massachusetts had an uncle who served with an artillery battery, and he went to his uncle and looked for food. His uncle filled his haversack with coffee, sugar, pork, and hard bread, which the soldier shared with other men.[6]

On the morning of December 3, the Sharpshooters marched at seven in the morning. They passed through Brandy and Rappahannock stations, crossing the river at Beverly Ford and encamping in the woods for the night after they had marched for ten miles. At this location they received rations. They learned that the Confederates had closely followed their movements, and in one day had captured two hundred stragglers, then another three hundred. It must have been difficult for all of the men, sleepless and out of rations, to keep up with the long marches.

On December 4, they moved about a half of a mile to an open field that was formerly the encampment of the 9th Massachusetts. The Sharpshooters' brigade picket extended from the river along the railroad to Bealton Station, and outposts stretched from Fant's Mill to Liberty, a distance of three and one half miles.

In the bitter cold, they started to prepare for winter quarters of 1863–64 at Beverly Ford, as General Meade directed. They laid out company streets and were ordered to construct log houses at an inside dimension of ten by six feet. The houses were to be uniform; all had to be above ground and to include a fireplace. The encampment, about half a mile from the Rappahannock Station, was named Camp Barnes. Colonel Tilton boarded in a house located on Merry Hill that was owned by a Mr. Jennings.

On December 6, the Sharpshooters went on picket with the 22nd Massachusetts and relieved the 18th Massachusetts, which had been fired on the previous night. Some of the 18th had been wounded. The Sharpshooters were ordered to constantly patrol the ground between the picket sentinels and were not to have fires except in the reserve area. The men on duty at picket and in camp were in a state of constant alert. Disloyal citizens aided the guerrillas and Rebel scouts, keeping them informed of the Federal positions at all times. Only the brigade's vigilance kept the enemy from penetrating them. During this time, boxes arrived from home, furloughs were granted as men went home on leave, and officers' wives arrived at Camp Barnes.[7]

16

Breakfast with Rebels

At this time, General Order 191 was issued, allowing men to go home on a thirty-five day furlough if they re-enlisted. Re-enlistment fever started. Men were cold and lonely and had been away from home for a very long time at the seat of war. Nonetheless, only thirty from the 22nd Massachusetts and one of the Sharpshooters re-enlisted.

Those who remained faced difficult times, as the brigade was required to provide four hundred men for picket duty, another three hundred to corduroy roads three miles from camp, and the usual camp duties and camp guards. Although few in the 22nd Massachusetts or Sharpshooters re-enlisted or took furloughs, members of other units in the brigade were more avid to do so. When so many men went on furlough, it put a strain on those soldiers who remained, as fewer men were available to perform duties. In addition, the Official Records include correspondence from General Meade that indicates his fear of the Rebels' proximity, given that so many men had left on furlough. He felt vulnerable if the Rebels decided to attack and ordered some units to be merged during that thirty-five day period that started on January 8.

The cold had become intense, and the Sharpshooters' camp was on a hill without protection from the wind. On January 4, an intense snowstorm lasted all day. To their displeasure, the Sharpshooters were ordered to move their encampment across the river. They had spent so much time building their huts and fireplaces, and the little comfort they had created was dashed. Fortunately, that order was countermanded.

About this time, Mrs. Tilton, Mrs. Field, and Mrs. Perkins arrived and stayed until March 21. Chaplain Tyler arrived on January 15. The Christian Commission provided a large fly tent for services that was improved in February, as it was built with logs and covered with canvas. The building also was used as a Masonic lodge and named Warren Army Lodge No. 1. The building had multiple functions and aided in the soldiers' general morale. At this time a letter that was written home said,

> It does seem so good to catch a view of the ladies occasionally. It is a variety that softens the harsh, coarse, every-day life in the army, so full of everything hostile to society, and evils that blunt the finer sensibilities and feelings.... To see something a little different from this continual separation from all that is good at home, is most gratifying to anyone accustomed to better things.

On February 18, the Rappahannock River was completely frozen over. The Sharpshooters would have liked to have had skates, but there were none within a hundred miles. On the

Colonel John R. Coxe with a lady seated in front of his log-cabin winter quarters, at Headquarters of the Army of the Potomac. This photograph was taken February 1864 at Brandy Station, Virginia. Women were allowed to join their husbands in winter quarters. It was more common among officers, but occasionally enlisted men's wives would join them (Library of Congress).

20th, re-enlistment fever broke out again, and complete regiments went home on furlough. On February 28, Chaplain Tyler delivered a sermon, "Ask and it shall be given to you." A wife of one of the enlisted men arrived at camp, and the Sharpshooters thought it a novelty in those surroundings.

On March 2, another terrible snowstorm dumped about eight inches on them. The huts which the Sharpshooters had built did not stop the snow from gusting through the cracks and landing on their blankets. It was a bitterly cold night. The Blue Ridge Mountains showed the presence of snow for some time.

On March 9, General Grant was appointed lieutenant general and was given command of the armies. On the 10th, he visited the headquarters near Brandy Station and announced that he would stay there for awhile. He gave his reasons: Virginia was important in the campaign, Lee's army was the best-led of all of the Confederates, and there was the matter of "the political and personal influences of various sorts and of various individuals, which centered in Washington, having thwarted and interfered with all who had commanded the Army of the Potomac during the war." The Sharpshooters welcomed him near their camp. The ground was so muddy that there would be no general reviews.[1]

The Sharpshooters continued their monotonous winter encampment at Beverly Ford. On March 21, they were notified that the Rebel cavalry had driven in the Union cavalry vedettes and the enemy hovered near the Union lines. All of the ladies were sent out of camp, which the men regretted, as their presence had a civilizing effect on the soldiers. General

2nd Corps Hospital at Brandy Station, Virginia, February 1864. This was the hospital unit used by the Sharpshooters during their last winter at war (Library of Congress).

Sykes ordered out several squads, but they returned on the 22nd without encountering the enemy.

On March 22, the Sharpshooters were ordered on a scouting expedition. The 22nd Massachusetts thought they would be ordered to follow the Sharpshooters. On the 23rd, no further passes were allowed; officers escorted their wives home. All noncombatants were moved out of the encampment, and the army was reorganized. General Warren was placed in command of the 5th Corps, to which the Sharpshooters were assigned. The reorganization upset some of the men, as each unit had had its own distinct history and identity. Pride was lost, and the esprit de corps suffered.

On March 26, arms were stacked in company streets and the Sharpshooters were on heightened alert. Expecting an enemy cavalry raid at any time, the Sharpshooters slept with one eye open and one foot on the ground. They were ordered to move in three days. However, on the 29th, a violent rainstorm flooded the rivers and the ground, making a review by General Grant impossible. On the 30th, Chaplain Tyler gave a sermon on "Outward appearances and the inward heart." The Sharpshooters were pleased they finally had a chaplain. The soldiers had had a much heightened interest in religion, and Chaplain Tyler had a good effect on them.

On April 2, General Griffin returned and took command of the brigade, which was reorganized again. Colonel Tilton again was given command of the 22nd Massachusetts and the Sharpshooters. The weather turned cold, with much rain, and many men got sick. About April 23, the weather improved, and the men resumed drill. The Sharpshooters took part in squad, company, and occasionally brigade drill; they also resumed target practice. On the 24th, Chaplain Tyler gave his last sermon in the lodge, entitled, "Be grateful to God for all He has done and is doing in our behalf," and picturing the effects of the victory at Gettysburg on the country as well as on the North.

On April 27, the sun's warm rays reached the ground, and the smell of peach and apple blossoms permeated the air. The encampment was calm. Birds could be heard chirping and frogs croaking, and the river flowed. All this reminded the Sharpshooters of New England.

On April 30, the Sharpshooters received orders to be ready to march on a moment's notice. Black troops had arrived and relieved the pickets along the railroad, and the pickets returned to their brigades. The Sharpshooters looked at all of the low campfires around them in a marching formation, and thought it would be difficult to sleep on the ground again.

They marched on May 1, at eight o'clock in the morning. Crossing the Rappahannock, they went about five miles to Rappahannock Station, and encamped at about one thirty that afternoon. They talked about the scene as they had broken winter encampment. They had been in winter quarters so long that they had left behind a great deal of public and personal property which they could not take with them on the march. They thought twenty families could have set up housekeeping from the remnants left by the Sharpshooters and the 22nd Massachusetts alone, and wished there were a way to send the remnants home to poor and needy families. They believed their old camp would soon be occupied by contraband, and that the items left behind would be used by them.

The Sharpshooters moved forward to Brandy Station; they were a quarter of a mile to the left of Ingall's Station, and the corps were all together. The Army of Northern Virginia lay along the entrenchments of the Rapidan from Barnett's Ford to the vicinity of Morton's Ford, a distance of about eighteen miles. General Lee's headquarters was at the Orange Courthouse. General Lee's army had a decided advantage, as it was entrenched.[2]

On May 2, in the afternoon, while the Sharpshooters were on dress parade, a heavy gale blew in from the south and raised a lot of dust. The Sharpshooters broke ranks, moved at the double-quick to their camp, and secured their tents.

As night approached on May 3, the Sharpshooters left their camp at Brandy Station, marched rapidly toward Culpepper, and encamped near that town. They placed pontoons across the river and marched at one o'clock in the morning of the 4th. Taking a direct route on Germanna Ford Road, they crossed the river about daylight, then rested for an hour as they cooked coffee. They then marched on the Germanna Plank Road to Orange Grove near Spottswood. Continuing their march, they passed the Wilderness Tavern and the Tannery on the right side of the road, then intersected the Orange Turnpike, turned right, and crossed a branch of Wilderness Run. They moved down the pike about a mile and passed the Lacy house, then, at about four o'clock that afternoon, encamped in a dense forest for the night.

They had marched twenty miles that day. Though it was a long and tedious march for the first of the campaign, very few men straggled. The rapid march proved to be successful, misleading General Lee and his generals. It seemed impossible to them that an army could cross rivers and move its artillery and supply trains such long distances while in the face of a hostile foe.

At five o'clock in the morning of May 5, the Sharpshooters were in the rear of the division which moved toward the Old Wilderness Tavern. They then learned that the enemy's infantry was in force on the Orange and Fredericksburg Turnpike, about two miles from the Old Wilderness tavern. The Sharpshooters' brigade was ordered to attack Confederate general Ewell on the turnpike road. It took a slow two or three hours to form the battle line as the men felt out the enemy. It was nearly two o'clock in the afternoon when the Sharpshooters moved in support of the first line.

Moving through a dense forest, the ground covered with impenetrable thickets, the Sharpshooters went slowly. While moving laboriously through the obstructions, they came face to face with Confederate general Jones's brigade and drove them back in confusion. General Jones was killed while he attempted to rally his lines. Confederate general Early came up and supported Jones's brigade, steadying the enemy's lines.

The Sharpshooters' brigade could not be supported, as their reinforcements could not move quickly enough through the dense obstructions. They were driven back across the pike and avoided being flanked. They enemy followed and entrenched their first line. As the Sharpshooters' brigade retreated, it lost two pieces of artillery. The team horses were killed, and the enemy took the guns.

General Wadsworth had been ordered to move to the left of the Sharpshooters' brigade. He became entangled in the thickets and lost his direction, exposing his flank to a deadly fire. Falling back, he took severe losses in killed, wounded, and prisoners taken. The Rebels faced the same entangling thickets and also fell back. The Union and Confederate lines were now each entrenched about three to four hundred yards apart.

The order was given to attack the enemy at five o'clock in the morning of May 6. Confederate general Ewell anticipated the attack and attacked the 6th Corps but was repulsed. The Sharpshooters' position was in the edge of the woods; the woods fronted a small, open plain, and beyond was another piece of woods, behind which the enemy was strongly entrenched. Attacking the 6th Corps on the flank, the Confederates forced it back; the Sharpshooters also fell back to avoid the same fate. The battle was horrific, as the dense brush had caught on fire. The wounded of both armies were burned to death in those fires.

General Griffin had succeeded in bringing up two pieces of artillery, which shelled the Rebels intensely and accurately. The Rebels fell back with great loss of life. The Sharpshooters lay entrenched all day as the enemy was in a defensive position. Both sides were happy to rest from the exhausting battles they had fought over the past two days. The Sharpshooters' brigade was always on the front line and under fire. On May 6, they were not heavily engaged. The

Soldiers attempt to remove the wounded from burning brush during the Wilderness Battle, Virginia. The artist who drew this picture between May 5 and 7, 1864 was Alfred R. Waud. It was horrific as the screams of wounded from both sides could be heard as they were consumed by the fires (Library of Congress).

casualties to the Sharpshooters at the Battle of the Wilderness were Privates Edward Newhall and David Jeffrey, and Corporal Daniel Wares. All were wounded; the latter lost a leg.

On the morning of May 7, reconnaissance of the enemy's line found them to be quite strong. General Grant felt an attack would be unsuccessful, and determined that a flank movement to General Lee's left was more promising. The Sharpshooters' brigade followed the second division and attempted to gain control of Spotsylvania Courthouse. At ten o'clock that night, the Sharpshooters moved silently from their breastworks in the Wilderness over the Brock Road toward Spotsylvania. It was the first in a series of slow, tedious marches. The men marched on the Orange Courthouse Turnpike to the intersection of the Germanna Plank Road, traversed that road a little over a mile, and arrived at the Brock Road. They crossed the Orange Plank Road and the unfinished railroad, then marched through the woods on a narrow road in the extreme dark. General Sheridan and his cavalry protected their right flank from enemy attack.

About eleven o'clock that night, the Sharpshooters came upon the mounted provost guard which followed headquarters' wagon train; they would not move to allow passage. In addition, at Todd's Tavern, Confederate general Fitzhugh Lee had felled trees in the road in an attempt to impede the march. At about three-thirty that morning, the Sharpshooters arrived at General Merritt's headquarters about one mile east of Todd's Tavern. Here, they halted and rested from the difficult all-night march, and waited for the road to be cleared. The Sharpshooters thought that if it had not been for General Fitzhugh Lee's roadblock, they would have been at the courthouse by daylight on the 8th.[3]

General John Robinson, in command of the 2nd Division of the 5th Corps, led the move to Spotsylvania Court House. He emerged from the woods into an open field at Allsop's Farm, which was about two and one half miles from Spotsylvania Court House, with the Sharpshooters following behind. At this point the Brock Road forked and re-merged in another half mile. General Robinson moved on the left-hand fork in a battle formation. As the division moved along this road in open ground, they were suddenly attacked with musketry and artillery fire from the enemy's entrenchment just inside the woods. This forced the 2nd Division to fall back to the woods at their rear for shelter.

The Sharpshooters followed closely, taking the right-hand fork. As they entered open ground, they also came under musket and artillery attack. At the double-quick, they formed a battle line. Their skirmishers were driven in, and they immediately commenced firing. The Rebels charged, and their center was repulsed and scattered in every direction. To the Sharpshooters' left, a line of Rebels came through the woods and threatened to capture Martin's battery of the 22nd Massachusetts. Colonel Tilton ordered the 22nd and the Sharpshooters to the right of the battery, which they protected until it could limber up and move to the rear. There was no doubt that they had saved the battery. The battle raged all day as they moved forward and backward. Each inch of ground was hotly contested, and the losses were great on both sides.

That night, the Sharpshooters' pickets occupied a rail fence by the peach orchard between Spindler's Farm and Allsop's. There, the Sharpshooters slept on their arms behind breastworks they had thrown up. On the morning of May 9, the Sharpshooters were about five hundred and fifty yards from the entrenched enemy on the other side of Po Run. The 5th and 6th Corps were ordered to advance skirmishers and determine if the enemy was vulnerable at any point. The Sharpshooters' corps was joined by the 2nd Corps on the right and by the 6th Corps on the left. They adjusted their lines, moved forward, and gained the ground in front of the peach orchard of Spindler's Farm. The pioneers were ordered to dig rifle pits, which the pickets were ordered to occupy and hold. A small second line of pits was dug near Spindler's buildings. At ten o'clock that night, the enemy attacked as the pioneers worked, driving them out of the advanced rifle pits.

On the morning of May 10, the Sharpshooters, the 22nd Massachusetts, and the 4th Michigan were ordered to advance and take back those rifle pits at all costs. They were ordered to, if possible, hold the edge of the woods, where the enemy rifle pits were located. At nine o'clock that morning, they advanced as skirmishers, at the double-quick. They carried the rifle pits and only stopped as they reached the edge of the woods in the face of the enemy's own pits. Many men were killed and wounded as they charged. The wounded crawled into the rifle pits. The Rebels were driven out of some of their rifle pits. In the thin woods, the skirmishers were exposed to a deadly, grueling Rebel fire. They hugged the ground under fire but held onto their terrritory. Many played dead so they would not be shot. Some of the skirmishers were relieved in the afternoon, but others were not relieved until ten o'clock at night.

At the end of the day, they had recaptured their own rifle pits and driven the enemy from their hold on the edge of the woods. But driving the enemy from their rifle pits imposed a heavy cost on the 22nd Massachusetts and the Sharpshooters. On May 11, there was not much fighting in front of the Sharpshooters, but on their left and right, fighting continued without much success. At three o'clock that day, General Grant ordered a major assault on the enemy lines at four o'clock on the following morning. There was a heavy fog at four o'clock, but it lifted at four thirty, and units advanced to the left and right of the Sharpshooters. At about nine o'clock, General Grant thought the center in front of the Sharpshooters was vulnerable, and ordered them to attack. Moving forward over open ground, they got within fifty yards of Confederate general Longstreet's entrenchments but were driven back by heavy artillery and musket fire. General Humphreys gave the order to cease the assault when he saw that it could not succeed. The Federals returned in a disordered state, and the Sharpshooters, 22nd Massachusetts, and 4th Michigan were ordered to occupy and hold the rifle pits, where they lay all day long. At dusk, the brigade was moved out of the entrenchment lines and left the 22nd Massachusetts and Sharpshooters alone to hold the rifle pits. They were relieved during the night and moved back two miles, near the corps headquarters.[4]

They now had a chance to rest as they prepared some food. But before they had a chance to taste the food, at ten o'clock that night, they were ordered to move at once, and within five minutes were a part of a flank movement to the left. They had spent more than thirty-six hours in the mud and rain, in cramped positions in the rifle pits. Having been exposed to deadly fire while in full view of their unburied dead a hundred yards in front of them, the tired, stiff, and cramped men were in no condition for an all-night march.

At the battle of Spotsylvania, the Sharpshooters killed were John McKenzie, Zenas Truel, Herman Parlin, John Morrison, Isaac H. Lewis, and Cyrus Osgood. Wounded were Newell Swett, John Sturtevant, Charles Swett, Charles Herrick, and Henry Adams.[5]

Early in the morning of May 13, they learned that the enemy had withdrawn from the salient. General Grant's plan was to left flank General Lee's right before it could be reinforced. That was the reason the Sharpshooters were not allowed to recover from their arduous thirty-six hours. They marched by Shelton's and Landron's, and then to Landron's Ford on the Ny River. Marching another half mile, they crossed the Ny River, marched across the country through fields to get to the Fredericksburg and Spotsylvania Court House Road near the Harris house, and then re-crossed the Ny River.

All night, they marched through three feet of soft mud, through dark forests, over stumps, and across creeks, and forded the Ny where it was three feet deep. Precautions had been taken to mark the route with small fires, but the rain extinguished them. The Sharpshooters floundered about through the woods, unable to see an arm's length in front of them. Men lost their way and lit matches in an attempt to find their way. Some fell to the ground totally exhausted. Even under those conditions, they reached the point of attack at six o'clock in the morning. It was considered impractical to attack, as the lines were broken and men were scattered all over the land. As they could not attack, the opportunity was lost, and General Lee was able to reinforce his position.

On the afternoon of May 14, General Longstreet advanced into the breastworks abandoned by the Sharpshooters and 22nd Massachusetts near Allsop's and Spindler's Farm. During the 15th, 16th, and 17th, the Sharpshooters advanced their lines and entrenched. They set up batteries and opened roads. They prepared for a battle on the 18th, and got some much-needed rest. The Sharpshooters were told the enemy was hemmed in and would have to come through the Union lines to get away. Thinking back to General Hooker's proclamation at Chancellorsville, they were not convinced. On the night of May 17, they advanced another five hundred yards and constructed excellent breastworks about a thousand yards in front of the enemy.

At five thirty on the morning of May 18, Union artillery opened on the enemy, who returned the fire. A heavy artillery duel lasted all morning, and the Sharpshooters hugged the ground to stay alive. Artillery shells from both armies flew over their heads. The 2nd, 6th, and 9th Corps made several attempts to take the enemy's position, but the Rebels repelled them all. The 19th was a quiet day, and the pickets of both lines agreed not to fire at each

The scene of General Ewell's attack at Allsop's Farm, May 19, 1864. A dead soldier can be seen on a stretcher from the previous day battle. Mrs. Allsop's farm was very near the Spottsylvania Courthouse in Virginia (Library of Congress).

other. They talked to each other and were very friendly. The Sharpshooters were now on the right side of the battle lines. Confederate general Ewell attacked at the extreme right of the Sharpshooters near the Harris house in an attempt to capture the Union wagon trains and cut off communications but was driven back. On the night of the 20th, the 22nd Massachusetts and the Sharpshooters were relieved. They enjoyed music that night as bands from both armies played.

On the morning of May 21, Union skirmishers moved close to the enemy lines to determine whether the enemy had withdrawn. They learned that Confederate general Ewell had been detached to hold the crossing at Telegraph Road and Stannard's Mill. The Sharpshooters received orders to be ready to move at once. At one fifteen that afternoon, without dinner, the Sharpshooters left their breastworks in full view of the enemy. Observing that movement, the Rebels attempted to drive in the Union pickets, but were stopped by the 6th Corps.[6]

The Sharpshooters crossed the Ny River and marched on the Fredericksburg and Richmond Railroad for two miles, then marched on a road parallel with the Telegraph Road, passing near Guiney's Station. Crossing the Mattapony River below the junction of the Po and Ny, they continued on runs southwest to Madison's Store by Catlett's, where another road from Mud Tavern came in. They then encamped, but as soon as they were settled, they were ordered out on picket duty and marched ten miles to their post.

On the night of May 21, cavalry outposts at Lebanon Church heard Confederate troops moving on Telegraph Road, at about a mile's distance. It appeared that the Union troops' withdrawal from Spotsylvania had set General Lee in motion, causing him to position his troops between the Federals and Richmond. Word of this was sent to General Warren.

Sunday, May 22, was a warm and comfortable day. The Sharpshooters were relieved early in the morning. They were then assigned to the lead division and marched on the road by Madison's Store and Nancy Wright's. That night they encamped near Harris's Store, which was near the Telegraph Road. As they marched in the lead, they skirmished quite often and took several prisoners. They were about three miles away from the main body of Confederates. The country became more open and highly cultivated, as neither army had trampled through that area.

On the morning of May 23, the Sharpshooters continued their march on the Telegraph Road and soon found themselves within a few miles of the North Anna River, on high, advantageous ground. It was a long march, as they had incorrect maps, and they changed directions several times. They reached Mount Carmel Church, three miles from Jericho, at eleven that morning, then scouted up and down the river until three o'clock that afternoon as they looked for a place to cross.

The Sharpshooters and the 22nd Massachusetts led the crossing at Jericho Ford. It is no wonder that the 22nd Massachusetts and the Sharpshooters were in the advance, as they had earned a reputation for gallantry under fire second to none in the Army of the Potomac. This was amply proven during the battles at Spotsylvania. There, they were used as skirmishers, because the number of men in the unit was so depleted that they did not have enough to make up a regiment.

General Griffin posted artillery to cover them as they crossed the river. As the banks were very high and rocky, it was a difficult crossing, and the roads on both sides were in poor condition. Needing to get across quickly and secure the river banks on the other side, the Sharpshooters and 22nd Massachusetts jumped in the river and crossed as quickly as possible.

As soon as they reached the other side, they deployed as skirmishers and advanced nearly a mile beyond the river. Veering to the left, they approached a section of woods where Rebels came out and fired on them. They fired back, and the Rebels quickly retired back into the

The mill at Jericho Ford; this view is looking up the North Anna River from the southern banks. The Sharpshooters crossed here on May 24, 1864, and led the battle. This photograph was taken by Timothy O'Sullivan on that date (Library of Congress).

woods. Going further into the woods, the Sharpshooters and 22nd Massachusetts shortly came into contact with Confederate general A. P. Hill's full advance line of skirmishers. The Sharpshooters and 22nd Massachusetts opened fire on the Rebel skirmishers and drove them back, then followed them to a rail fence where they were in full view of the Virginia Central Railroad. Halting there, the men were reinforced by other skirmishers, then threw up some breastworks and waited for orders.

While they waited, they could plainly hear the Confederates giving orders to form a battle formation. Although it was now reinforced, the skirmish line remained weak, as the Rebels had captured the right side. The Rebels knew their exact location. The order was given for the Sharpshooters and 22nd Massachusetts to hold the enemy back as long as they could. At five thirty that afternoon, they observed Rebel flankers who came toward them, parallel to their line and in back of them. Also seeing a heavy column of dust which came from their rear and from the direction of Hanover Junction, they knew that a large body of Rebels was moving on them.

The Rebel flankers halted, faced the Sharpshooters and 22nd Massachusetts, and advanced on them. Then the battle line of Hill's entire division moved toward them in battle formation. While the Union troops who had just crossed the river got into their own battle formation, the 22nd Massachusetts and the Sharpshooters exchanged shots with the Rebels. They held on as long as they could, and then fell back to the Union lines. The battle over open ground started. The enemy attacked toward the right center of the Union lines, where the Sharpshooters and 22nd Massachusetts were located. The Union artillery was on a crest near the river. It swept the lines of Confederates with shell, shrapnel, and canister over the Sharpshooters' heads. The battle raged for two hours, and the 22nd and Sharpshooters held the center firmly. The Rebels retreated across the railroad, heavily repulsed. The casualties on both sides were about equal, except that about one thousand Rebels were taken as prisoners.

Mile-and-a-quarter-long breastworks were built, crossing the road from Jericho Ford to Noell's Station and through the farm of Fountainon on the left. The battle was over, and Colonel Tilton was ordered to take the Sharpshooters and 22nd Massachusetts in front of the breastworks to capture what prisoners they could. This was a dangerous mission for such a small body of men. While they were undertaking it, a Rebel pointed a musket at the unarmed Colonel Tilton. The colonel grabbed the barrel of the rifle and the two wrestled on the ground. Hearing the commotion, some of the 22nd Massachusetts rescued him. The men returned to the lines with four prisoners.

The Sharpshooters remained in the breastworks until they were relieved on the afternoon of May 24. They then marched two miles to the right and encamped at Noell's Station on the Central Railroad. On the 25th, the division destroyed the railroad; the Sharpshooters and the 22nd Massachusetts were ordered on picket duty. They went about five-and-a-half miles out toward Hanover Junction, and heard heavy firing in that direction. There was frequent skirmishing, and Ezra Chapman of the Sharpshooters was killed. Moving another three miles, they took a position at Anderson's Plantation. Little River was directly in their front. A heavy shower started and continued through the night and into the 26th.[7]

General Lee's army was now well fortified and concentrated along the North Anna, from Little River on his left to Ox Ford and south to Morris's Bridge. General Lee could reinforce any part of his lines if attacked. General Grant realized that, and continued his left flank movement. General Lee was at a loss as to which side Grant would flank.

On May 26, at seven o'clock in the evening, the Sharpshooters were relieved by the 18th Massachusetts. They then marched to the river and at about nine o'clock, re-crossed the North Anna at Quarle's Ford, about two miles from Jericho Mills, and rejoined their brigade. They halted for an hour and drew rations, then marched by the river all night and halted at six in the morning of the 27th. They cooked breakfast, then continued their march through St. Paul. Since neither army had marched on the country, it was full of vegetable gardens, flocks of sheep, pigs, and plenty of poultry. Under no orders to limit foraging, they did more foraging than had been done in months. Over the entire route they marched over, they cleared the area of any living livestock, making no discrimination between rich and poor inhabitants.

They encamped on John B. Floyd's estate, about one mile from the Monogohick Church. Stragglers came into camp as they had marched a total of thirty miles in twenty-one and a half hours. They cooked fried pork, chicken, coffee, and hard bread. On May 27, they continued in the direction of Hanover Courthouse, by Little Page's Bridge, and moved in a southerly direction. They were to cross the river at New Castle Ferry, but orders were changed. As the Sharpshooters and 22nd Massachusetts approached a farm, its owner came out and complained some of his garden had been confiscated and three of his hens had been killed. Asking for protection, he said that he was a Union man. But the Sharpshooters and 22nd Massachusetts learned that he was a Rebel commissary. Finding one hundred and fifty bushels of corn in his barn and a cellar filled with smoked sides of bacon, they took all his butter, milk, meat, and anything else that was edible, then burned down his house and outbuildings.

On the morning of May 28, they crossed on pontoons over the Pamunkey River at Dabney's Ford near Hanover Town. Orders were given that prohibited foraging, and that stragglers

Quarles' Mill Ford, where Sharpshooters crossed the North Anna River about two miles from Jericho Mills, May 26, 1864, to rejoin their brigade (Library of Congress).

would be shot by the marching columns. Refreshed and invigorated after a good night's rest and the absence of cannonading and musketry fire, the men were in good spirits. Reflecting on the blood-soaked fields they had left behind at the Wilderness, Spotsylvania, and North Anna, they mused over what terrible fate waited for them in the future.

The Sharpshooters were now seventeen miles from Richmond, eight from Hanover Courthouse, and seventeen from White House. General Lee had followed them since they left the North Anna River. The entire Confederate army was well entrenched in their front. At noon battle formations were formed. The 22nd Massachusetts and Sharpshooters were posted to the left of the 2nd Corps. The road to Richmond was on their right and the Tolopotomy River on their left. They then built breastworks. On the morning of May 28, General Sheridan pushed his cavalry in the direction of Hawes's shop and encountered the enemy's dismounted cavalry about a mile beyond Hawes's shop to Old Church. Hearing firing in their front all day and into the evening, the men learned that General Sheridan's cavalry had driven the enemy all along the Sharpshooters' front.

On the morning of May 29, the Sharpshooters and 22nd were ordered out on reconnaissance. They left their breastworks and crossed the Tolopotomy. As skirmishers advanced on the Shady Grove Church Road, they encountered the enemy's outpost pickets and drove them in. The enemy was in a strong position behind that road, and a reinforcement division was sent to back them up. The Sharpshooters and 22nd Massachusetts had advanced about one and a half miles on the Dry Road to Mechanicsville. They halted in a battle line and encamped for the night at Talley's plantation, raiding it for sweet potatoes and bacon, and enjoying fresh strawberries that were in season.

On the morning of May 30, the Sharpshooters' division was massed in columns of brigades and ordered forward. The Sharpshooters and 22nd Massachusetts received great praise for their gallant skirmishing at North Anna, and were ordered to be the advance skirmishers for the division. Moving rapidly, they encountered the enemy and drove them back about two miles, as they charged across open fields. The Confederates entrenched themselves in houses and behind rail fences, slowing the Union advance so that it made little progress. General Griffin sent orders to them to push forward rapidly. The Sharpshooters and 22nd Massachusetts fixed bayonets, screamed, yelled, and charged across the open fields toward the entrenched enemy, who became confused and retreated from their entrenchments. The Sharpshooters and 22nd Massachusetts captured a number of prisoners.

However, their success was not without cost, as the first five men who charged the field were shot down one after another. It was a hard day, as the Sharpshooters skirmished constantly for seven hours straight. They were out of ammunition and were relieved. The Sharpshooters' casualties were Patrick Lawler and Moses Deland (killed) and John Hooper (wounded). Returning, the Sharpshooters and 22nd Massachusetts received many congratulations on the gallant and successful manner in which they repelled the enemy's advance. The reputation of the Sharpshooters and the 22nd Massachusetts as a fighting unit was fully forged. General Warren said, "Griffin's division would go into Richmond, if left alone, and they were not all killed before they got there."[8]

June 1 found the Sharpshooters and 22nd Massachusetts resting in the rear for the first time since the campaign began. They were encamped near Bethesda Church on swampy wooded ground of the Tolopotomy and Matahdequin creeks in a shaded, cool piece of ground. There was firing along the lines all day long. General Grant had decided to seize Cold Harbor. General Lee had the same idea. The Sharpshooters' rest did not last long as they were ordered to move up and support their first and third brigade. On the morning of the 2nd, they advanced toward Bethesda Church on the Old Church Turnpike. They were now in reserve for any emergency.

Though they were ordered to march to Cold Harbor at midnight, they waited until four o'clock in the afternoon and were still not relieved. They were suddenly ordered to move to the right to repel an attack of the Rebels amassed in front of General Burnside. At five o'clock a hard rain stopped all operations and drenched the Sharpshooters through to their skin. On the extremely hot morning of June 3, the Sharpshooters were at Bethesda Church. At five o'clock in the morning, they were awakened by picket firing, and while they ate breakfast minieballs flew into their encampment. At six o'clock, General Burnside began to push the enemy. Again, the 22nd Massachusetts and Sharpshooters, along with some men from the 4th Michigan, were ordered out as skirmishers to lead the brigade.

Jumping over the breastworks on the run, they charged across an open field to the woods in front of them about six hundred yards away. They drove back all of the Rebels in front of them and stopped only when they had lost one-fourth of their own men. About one hundred and fifty yards in front of the enemy's breastworks, they drove the Confederates back to the road into their second line of breastworks. They had accomplished all that was asked of them. The Sharpshooters and 22nd Massachusetts line was in the shape of a bow, which allowed the enemy to crossfire on the rear of their line. However, artillery support enabled them to hold the line of woods until dark. Shortly after dark, they were relieved. The Sharpshooters' casualties were Thomas Neal (killed) and Sewell Richardson and James Gardner (wounded).[9]

That night, the Rebels abandoned their position. On the morning of June 4, the Sharpshooters and 22nd Massachusetts were ordered on a reconnaissance expedition. They counted twenty-two dead artillery horses, proving the accuracy of the 3rd, 5th, and 9th artillery batteries, which had silenced the enemy's artillery when the enemy fired on the advance of the Sharpshooters and 22nd Massachusetts.

On Sunday, June 5, at three in the afternoon, the Sharpshooters and 22nd Massachusetts were ordered on the Shady Grove Church Road, where they were deployed as skirmishers. Just beyond the Union pickets they encountered the Rebel skirmishers, whom they charged and drove back a half a mile. The Rebels concealed themselves under heavy brush, and were strongly reinforced. The Sharpshooters and 22nd Massachusetts were ordered to charge, but before they reached the Rebels' works they were ordered back. Retiring to a wood line, they remained there and exchanged fire until dark, then returned to the Union lines exhausted. During the night, the enemy made two attacks on the Sharpshooters and 22nd Massachusetts, but all were alert and drove the enemy back.

At midnight on June 5, they marched all night for about five miles to near Allen's Mill in the rear of Cold Harbor and rejoined the 5th Corps. They were exhausted and short of rations, blankets, and all the other basic equipment. As they passed, General Griffin said, "Poor fellows, they ought to have four days' rest, but I can give them only one." On the 6th, the wagon supply train arrived for the first time since they had left the Rapidan. They drew rations, ate, and were issued new clothing and equipment. They reflected on the day before as they had plodded along in worn-out shoes, filth, vermin-infested clothes, and empty stomachs. Now, a day later, they had full stomachs, new clothes and shoes, and clean socks. What a difference a day had made. They rested there all day on the 6th.

At three o'clock in the morning of June 7, they marched a few miles as far as the Chickahominy, near Sumner's Lower Bridge and three miles from Despatch Station, where they rested. They built breastworks facing Gaines's Mills, where two years before they had experienced a bloody encounter with the Confederate generals Jackson and Hood. Here, the army was partially reorganized again. Orders were given to clean guns, draw rations, and get all the sleep possible, but be ready to move on a moment's notice. An officer, out of sheer stupidity, woke up his cook and ordered him to get all of the sleep possible. On June 10, the 9th Massachusetts started for home, as their enlistment term was over. The Sharpshooters knew their own time was nearer. On that day, the Rebels threw a few shells into their lines, hitting the 5th Massachusetts battery, killing three men, and wounding five. Nothing much happened on June 11.

On June 12, some of the Sharpshooters visited the 2nd Corps, on their right. The Union and Confederate pickets had agreed that they would not fire on each other, and they exchanged some newspapers. Farther down the line on the right, a Virginian unit would not agree to a truce, and exchanged fire constantly. At nightfall on the 12th, the Sharpshooters and the 22nd Massachusetts were ordered to pack up. They moved out in twenty minutes.

They marched until two in the morning of June 13, halting in a large wheat field, where they rested for two hours. Continuing their march, they crossed the Chickahominy River at Long Bridge at four that morning. Then they continued their march to White Oak Bridge and halted. They stayed there all day, while the rest of the army passed them. That night, they were again on the march. From three in the morning until five they halted near St. Mary's Church. It was an arduous march, and they only were able to march seven miles that night.

That morning, General Lee learned that General Grant had withdrawn troops from Cold Harbor. General Lee quickly moved his army to block the roads leading to Richmond, then built entrenchments and held a line from Malvern Hill to White Oak Swamp. At five in the afternoon on June 14th, the Sharpshooters started their march on the Charles City Courthouse

Road. The day was hot, and the dust from all the marching troops baked on them and entered their lungs, making it a difficult march. Halting, they rested from ten thirty that night until two in the morning of the 15th. They reached Charles City Courthouse about three that afternoon, and rested until nightfall.

They continued their march to Wilcox's Landing and encamped there five miles below Harrison's Landing and two miles from the river. Their encampment was on the former Buckland plantation, which extended about a mile from Westover's to Harrison's Landing. The land was beautiful and fertile, with all kinds of vegetation. They started out at three in the morning. After some delay, they crossed the river in the transport *Star*. They encamped for about four hours on a plantation and waited for the rest of the corps to cross. They were ordered to bathe in the river, which they enjoyed after being caked with dust on their difficult marches.

At three that afternoon, they were ordered to pack up. The refreshing bath seemed to have been a waste of time as they marched through the torrid heat in a fine dust that once

Wilcox Landing Telegraph Station, June 1864. The Sharpshooters marched through heat and dust to reach Charles City, Virginia. General Lee had learned General Grant had removed troops from Cold Harbor and sent his own troops to block all access to Richmond. The Sharpshooters were immediately sent to Wilcox Landing where a telegraph station was being erected for communications (Library of Congress).

more choked them and caked on them. They reached Prince George Courthouse about nine that evening and halted for an hour to make coffee. As they continued, their march proved more painful with every step. They could find no water, and suffered as the march continued until midnight, when they arrived near Petersburg.

On June 12, the 18th Corps had been withdrawn from Cold Harbor and sent by boat to White House. They reported to General Butler on the 14th and were ordered to assault Petersburg on the morning of the 15th. Fearing that the Union objective was Petersburg, Confederate general Beauregard asked General Lee to send him troops, which arrived at five o'clock in the afternoon of the 15th.

The 18th Corps assaulted Petersburg on the morning of June 15 and succeeded in overtaking five redans, about a mile and a half of infantry entrenchments, and sixteen cannons. The Confederates had only twenty-four hundred infantrymen and one brigade of cavalry to protect Petersburg at the time of the assault. Had another division followed up on the assault, the Union probably would have taken Petersburg. On June 16, three corps attacked but were repulsed with heavy losses. General Beauregard had an additional fourteen thousand infantrymen supported by artillery. On the 16th and 17th, the Sharpshooters were in reserve support for the 9th Corps. The 9th Corps made several assaults on those two days, but with a disastrous effect and great losses to the Union forces.

Late at night on June 17, an order was issued to attack at four o'clock in the morning. The Sharpshooters were on the left side of the barrel formation. A deep cut in the ground in front of them proved difficult to pass. The Sharpshooters moved out at three in the morning and passed over the ground which had been fought over on the 17th. Dead bodies and other evidence of destruction were strewn all around them, and they felt very uneasy. Learning that the Rebels had moved back and fortified themselves, they made breakfast and waited for orders.

The Sharpshooters and 22nd were again ordered out as skirmishers in front of the brigade. Their orders were to move across an open field in their front at the double-quick and occupy a ravine directly in front of the Norfolk Railroad. They rushed forward under heavy artillery fire and a group of Rebel skirmishers on a steep hill which overlooked the ravine. Reaching the ravine, they drove the Rebel skirmishers from the top of the hill and stopped. The Rebels re-grouped and rushed over a fence, raking fire down on them. They evacuated that ravine and ran into another one, where they found themselves under direct artillery fire from their front.

They evacuated again to the other side of the road in a safe position but then were ordered to return to the ravine and to hold that position. Hollering, they charged into the ravine and drove the Rebels, with a steady and relentless forward movement, back into their breastworks. They then held a position within one hundred yards of the entrenched Rebels. The brigade followed them and assaulted the breastworks. Joining the brigade, the Sharpshooters got within twenty yards of the enemy's position, but as their left side was not supported, they took heavy artillery fire and had to retreat. They left their dead closer to the enemy than any other brigade.

Bringing back as many dead and wounded as they could, they reformed their battle line. The Sharpshooters and 22nd Massachusetts were ordered to dig rifle pits and hold the picket line. During that grueling night, any movement at all would incur enemy fire. They lay in their rifle pits as they hugged the ground all night long. In the morning, under a brisk battle, they were relieved.[10]

On June 19, they were under fire all day. On the 20th, they encamped for the night in the battle line. That night, they were relieved and moved about a mile back from the railroad, where they encamped for the rest of the night. Telling them he was very pleased with all they

The Sharpshooters and the 20th Massachusetts Volunteer Infantry referred to this 200-pound shell artillery piece as the Petersburg Express; it is listed in the Library of Congress as the Dictator. Mounted on a flatbed railcar, it could easily be moved to different locations during the long siege of Petersburg, Virginia (Library of Congress).

had done, General Grant ordered them to a safe area for some needed rest. The entire campaign had been all-night marching and daily fighting, with frequent assaults on strong enemy works in the face of artillery and musketry. Their officers and men had been slaughtered, and they were exhausted.

On June 21, they moved to their left and encamped in the woods near the Jerusalem plank road. On the 22nd, they enjoyed a quiet and needed rest. During the night, the enemy made an assault, and the 22nd Massachusetts and the Sharpshooters were called on to help defend the 2nd Corps. It was a difficult night, and Charles Oviatt of the Sharpshooters was wounded.

On the night of June 23, they returned to their encampment at the Jerusalem Plank Road. Then they were moved to support the flank of the 6th Corps. It proved to be a difficult march, in extreme heat and ankle-deep dust like a fine powder that clogged their lungs, with no water to be had. Men constantly fell out, some with heat exhaustion and sunstroke. On the 25th, they marched back to their old position in reserve. The 12th Massachusetts left the seat of war and returned home that day as their enlistment term had expired.

On June 26, Chaplain Tyler came to the men and preached a sermon. Only forty men were present, a far cry from the number who had been at Brandy Station. At that time, a staff officer from another division came in and said the pickets were playing cards and swapping hard bread for tobacco. The exchange rate in the card games was twenty-five cents of Federal money for a dollar of Confederate money. He also reported that the Confederates were hungry and only had cornmeal cob-cakes to eat. The Rebels in front of the Sharpshooters and 22nd were quite friendly, and the two sides agreed not to fire on each other. On June 27, a Confederate fired at the Union pickets. His officer disarmed him and made him march around for several hours in the scorching sun with a wood fence rail on his shoulder. The wagon trains came up and supplied the men with goods. The Sanitary Commission also supplied the men with extras, which they appreciated. The temperature that day exceeded one hundred and five degrees.

On June 30, muster-rolls, returns, and reports were made out. The men laid out company streets and removed brush and debris. Major Burt was put in command of the 22nd Massachusetts and Sharpshooters. The major consolidated the battalion into four companies: Companies A, B, and C and the Sharpshooters. It was rumored that the entire unit was to be consolidated as Sharpshooters for the division, but that never happened.

On July 1, the temperature was recorded at one hundred and five degrees in the shade, and the heat was intolerable. On July 3, three Rebels came across the picket lines and stated that Petersburg had a large enough food supply for a year, but they really came in for something to eat. On July 4, the bands on both sides played. Life during the month of July consisted of

Bomb enclosures at Petersburg. The small mounds with chimneys are soldiers' quarters under the ground. This photograph was taken April 3, 1865 (Library of Congress).

pioneer work, as the men built redans and bomb enclosures as they laid in the siege of Petersburg. The Rebel lines were about one hundred yards in front of the Sharpshooters, and the Rebel pickets about fifty yards. Both sides moved safely in full view of each other, as neither side would fire at the other. But occasionally, the Rebels shelled the pioneer crews working on the redans, at which time all sought shelter.

Rebel deserters continued to come across to the Union lines in droves. One group of deserters said the 5th Corps was to be attacked, and a great deal of excitement ensued as the lines were fortified, but the attack never came, and all calmed down again. As the temperatures soared, it did not rain from June 2 until July 19. Water sources dried up, and the dust was unbearable. As drills had started again, the dust made by the troop movements made things very uncomfortable. The rain of July 19 was welcomed. The artillery mounted on train tracks roved Petersburg and shelled the city at will.

The men received a letter from Senator Wilson stating that their muster-out date would be October 5. The men were upset, as many had enlisted in September of 1861. Not a company except for the Sharpshooters was mustered as late as October 5. But they calmed down and continued the siege of Petersburg, waiting for the legal date when they could return home.[13]

Pioneer parties were everywhere. They constructed covered ways to ensure the safety of their supply trains. The men dug and made shelters for their own use and set their tents inside them. Both sides engaged in constant shelling and attempts to mine each other's redans.

On August 6, 1864, Major Burt received a notice from Massachusetts that the time for the regiment to muster out would be September 5. That notice was sent to headquarters. On

In August 1864 the Sharpshooters were ordered to City Point, Virginia, used to store supplies, make repairs, and organize distribution of materials. General Grant wanted additional security to protect those valuable resources. He wanted a combat experienced unit with little time left to serve for that operation. He selected the 22nd Massachusetts Volunteer Infantry and the 2nd Company of Andrew Sharpshooters for that detail (Library of Congress).

General Grant's headquarters at City Point. It appears General Grant resided in the house, and other buildings were erected for his staff. This photograph was taken in 1865 (Library of Congress).

August 7, the Sharpshooters and 22nd Massachusetts were ordered to City Point to provide guard duty at the government machine repair shops. Having sought to fill that duty with a unit that was diminished in numbers and close to their discharge date, General Meade selected them. The order came as a surprise to them. They had one more night to spend in front of the enemy lines. If nothing occurred, they would be out of the reach of the enemy artillery and musketry fire.

The morning of August 9, they marched nine miles to City Point, then encamped on the left bank of the railroad near General Grant's headquarters. The Appomattox River was close, as were the corps hospitals. They drew rations from the Post Commissary and the Sanitary Commission, and obtained water from a fifty-foot deep well until they were able to dig their own well. At night, they bathed in the river and listened to the music of the bands. They laid out company streets and with all military discipline had a very good encampment.

On August 9, a munitions barge at the landing blew up and killed seventy men and wounded one hundred and thirty. They watched in horror as the charred remains of those killed were shoveled into bags. Colonel Sherwin returned from the front and told the men that per the War Department their time would not be up until October 8. The men were up

16. Breakfast with Rebels

City Point, Virginia, August 9, 1864. A munitions barge at the landing blew up and killed seventy men and wounded one hundred and thirty. The Sharpshooters thought they had seen the last of horror when they were removed from combat. They watched in revulsion as the remains of those charred bodies were shoveled into bags. This photo was quoted as being taken on August 4, 1864, but the Sharpshooters indicated it was on the 9th (Library of Congress).

in arms, and not being in the danger of the front all started to yell at the same time. On August 24, Colonel Tilton returned and took command of the regiment.

The Sharpshooters and 22nd Massachusetts thought their fighting days were over, but on September 16, Colonel Gates, post commander, ordered them under arms to repel an enemy attack. When he asked if they could skirmish, the men responded with much laughter and explained the regiment's history as skirmishers. They were ordered to defend the railroad until reinforcements could be sent in. They sent out a reconnaissance party and determined that the danger had passed. It appeared that about twelve hundred Rebels had driven off three thousand head of cattle, but were overtaken by the Union cavalry and had given up the cattle.[14]

The weather had grown cooler. The health of the Sharpshooters and 22nd Massachusetts had improved greatly. A steady change of diet and the prospect of going home soon had a positive effect on their morale.

On October 1, General Meade ordered the Sharpshooters and 22nd Massachusetts to turn in their rifles and go home. General Tilton sent to General Meade a dispatch which stated that the men would be mortified to return home unarmed. On October 3, General Griffin sent a letter which reported how they were regarded.

Headquarters First Division, Fifth Army Corps,
Before Petersburg, Va., Oct. 3, 1864

General:- As your regiment leaves the army on the 5th inst. By reason of expiration of term of service, I desire to express to you, your officers and men, my satisfaction at the manner you have conducted yourselves since I have commanded the division, in every circumstance of trial and danger. The valuable and efficient service you have rendered your country during the past three years of its eventful history is deserving of its gratitude and praise.

You leave the army with an enviable record, and with the regrets of your comrades at parting with you.

Sincerely yours,

Charles Griffin

Brigadier-General Com'd'g

Brig-Gen. W. S. Tilton, Com'd'g' Twenty-Second Mass. Vol.

General Tilton's request that the men's arms remain with them was denied by General Meade. On October 4, the Sharpshooters and the 22nd Massachusetts turned in their arms. On the 5th, they embarked on the dilapidated transport steamer *Kennebec*. They stopped at Hampton Roads and arrived in Washington on the afternoon of the 6th, happy to be on firm ground after having crossed the Chesapeake on that old hulk. On the 7th, they resumed their journey, arriving in Boston at one o'clock in the morning of the 10th. They were marched to the Beach Street Barracks. Of the more than eleven hundred who had marched to war three years before, only one hundred and twenty-four men remained. They had left in the field one hundred and eighty one men who had re-enlisted, or were replacement troops added to the regiment. Those men were assigned to the 32nd Massachusetts Volunteer Infantry.

At the barracks, they had time to clean up from the trip and prepared to meet their old comrades and friends at eight o'clock in the morning. At that time, they marched to the United States Hotel, where a fine breakfast was served. There they met old comrades who had been previously discharged because of wounds or sickness. These men almost outnumbered the returned men, but reinforced them, leaving a respectable number of men. The returned men were offered a banquet at Faneuil Hall and an escort by the First Company of the Independent Corps of Cadets, which they accepted.

A line was formed with the Sharpshooters, 22nd Massachusetts, discharged veterans, and the Cadets. They marched through Beach, Washington, Boylston, Beacon, Tremont, Winter, Washington, State, and Merchants Row Streets to Faneuil Hall. As they passed Boston Common, a national salute was fired. Cheered and welcomed all along the route, the men enjoyed a glorious last march. A splendid dinner was served, and Boston's mayor Lincoln gave a welcome home speech.

Speeches were given by Adjutant General Schouler, General Tilton, Lieutenant Colonel Sherwin, Captain A. P. Martin, Captain J. Henry Symonds, Chaplain Tyler, and Dr. Stearns. The elegant speeches talked of the men's service and sacrifice, and recognized their great contributions, which helped crush the rebellion. The speeches from the officers of the regiment thanked the citizens for their support and for the great reception they gave the returning regiment. It was noted that on October 17, 1864, the regiment passed into history as the only regiment that had been organized by a senator and accompanied by artillery and a company of sharpshooters.[15]

First Company Biographical Roster

Sources are abbreviated and can be found in the Bibliography.

Abbott, James D., enlisted for three years as a private at age 23 into the 1st Company September 3, 1861, at Camp Saunders in Lynnfield. He was single. He was a moulder. He was born in 1838 and his service was credited to Lowell. His service and discharge dates are unknown, as there was no further information found regarding his service. Sources: Adjutant General Vol. 1–7 & Vol. 1–2

Abbott, Samuel D., enlisted for three years as a private at age 23 into the 1st Company September 2, 1861, at Camp Saunders in Lynnfield. He was a moulder. He was born December 2, 1837, at Andover, Maine, and his service was credited to Lowell. He was wounded at the Battle of Antietam on September 17, 1862, and died from those wounds September 20, 1862, at Bolivar, Virginia. His parents' names were Farnum and Mary (Chapman). Sources: Adjutant General Vol. 1–7 & Vol. 1–2. Abbott, Lemuel Abijah.

Abbott, Wesley, enlisted for three years as a private at age 27 into the 1st Company September 2, 1861, at Camp Saunders in Lynnfield. He was a sailor. He was born March 9, 1834, at Andover-Lawrence. He received a disability discharge December 10, 1862 at Newark, New Jersey. He was married to Roxanne B. Grave. Records indicate he is interred at Woodlawn Cemetery. His parents' names were Orlando and Lydia (Kimball). Sources: Adjutant General Vol. 1–7 & Vol. 1–2. Microfilm Collection. Harnwell.

Adams, Albion A., enlisted for three years as a private at age 22 into the 1st Company August 15, 1862, at Camp Wightman, Long Island, Boston. He was a student. He was born August 30, 1840, at Carlisle and his service was credited to Carlisle-Boston. He received a disability discharge on February 13, 1863, probably from a wound he received in 1862. On December 27, 1864, he received a bounty of $123.33 for enlisting in Company A, First Battalion, Massachusetts Volunteer Cavalry for one year; Concord was credited. He was promoted to sergeant January 1, 1865. He was discharged from the Cavalry June 30, 1865. This unit was known as the 26th New York Cavalry Frontier Cavalry. It served along the northern border of New York and Vermont to resist Confederate raids from Canada. His parents' names were Samuel Jr. and Dorcas (Heald). Sources: Adjutant General Vol. 1–7 & Vol. 1–2. Stokinger; Essex, *Carlisle*.

Adams, Charles Putman, enlisted for three years as a private at age 22 into the 1st Company March 17, 1862, at Washington, D.C. He was a lather. He was born September 17, 1838, at Salem and his service was credited to Salem. He received a disability discharge September 16, 1862, probably from a wound received in 1862. He also served for three months in the 5th Massachusetts Infantry from April 16, 1861, to July 31, 1861. He was single and an only child. His parents' names were Joseph and Rebecca (Putman). Sources: Adjutant General Vol. 1–7 & Vol. 1–2. Harnwell.

Adams, George Sumner, enlisted for three years as a private at age 21 into the 1st Company September 2, 1861 at Camp Saunders in Lynnfield. He was a shoemaker. He was born February 8, 1840, at Littleton, New Hampshire, and his service was credited to Lowell-Reading. He reenlisted February 16, 1864, and received a $325.00 bounty. He was wounded near Cold Harbor, Virginia, on May 31, 1864, and died from those wounds the following day. He was not married and his parents were his dependents. His parents' names were Nathan and Almyra (Lumer). Sources: Adjutant General Vol. 1–7 & Vol. 1–2; Furber, George C., *Littleton, N.H.*

Adams, John Q., enlisted for three years as a private at age 36 into the 1st Company August 15,

1862, at Camp Wightman, Long Island, Boston. He was a farmer. He was born March 22, 1826, at Carlisle and his service was credited to Carlisle-Boston. He was killed in action September 17, 1862, at the Battle of Antietam. His brother Albion was also in the 1st Company His parents' names were Samuel Jr. and Dorcas (Heald). Sources: Adjutant General Vol. 1–7 & Vol. 1–2; Stokinger; Essex, *Carlisle*.

Ainsworth, Samuel A., was transferred as a private at age 20 into the 1st Company November 3, 1862. His original enlistment was in the 51st Massachusetts Volunteer Infantry Company E at Camp Wool in Worcester on September 9, 1862. He received a $25.00 bounty. He was a gunsmith. He was born July 11, 1842, at Millbury and his service was credited to Millbury-Cambridge. He was given a disability discharge February 18, 1863. His skills as a gunsmith could have been the reason for his transfer. His brother Henry was killed in action at the Battle of Antietam while serving with the 15th Massachusetts Volunteer Infantry Company H. His parents' names were Elam W. and Candice (Allen). Sources: Adjutant General Vol. 1–7 & Vol. 1–2; Stokinger; Systematic Fund, *Millbury*; Coco, Gregory.

Allen, Edward A., enlisted for three years as a private at age 35 into the 1st Company September 2, 1861, at Camp Saunders in Lynnfield. He was a shoemaker. He was born January 20, 1827, at Lynn and his service was credited to Lynn. He was given a disability discharge April 2, 1862, at Falmouth, Virginia. He was married to Olive Carroll and had four children. His parents' names were Edward and Sarah (Alley). Sources: Adjutant General Vol. 1–7 & Vol. 1–2; Essex, *Lynn*.

Allen, John H., enlisted for three years as a private at age 19 into the 1st Company October 29, 1862, at Camp Wightman, Long Island, Boston, and received a $25.00 bounty. He was an engineer. He was born in 1843 at New York, New York, and his service was credited to Boston. His service and discharge dates are unknown as there was no further information found regarding his service. Source: Adjutant General Vol. 1–7.

Ambrose, John B., enlisted for three years as a private at age 23 into the 1st Company September 2, 1861, at Camp Saunders in Lynnfield. He was a moulder. He was born in 1838 in Boston and his service was credited to Newburyport. He deserted September 17, 1862, at the Battle of Antietam. He first enlisted August 1, 1861 in the 8th Massachusetts Volunteer Infantry Company A (3 month) and was discharged from the 8th on August 1, 1861. He was married. His parents' names were Richard and Anne. Sources: Adjutant General Vol. 1–7 & Vol. 1–2. Creasey, George W.

Andrews, Edward A. enlisted for three years as a private at age 25 into the 1st Company September 2, 1861, at Camp Saunders in Lynnfield. He was a farmer. He was born December 28, 1834 in Lee and his service was credited to Shrewsbury. He died of disease on March 1, 1862, at Pawpaw, Virginia. He was single. His parents' names were Austin and Mary (Fairbanks). Sources: Adjutant General Vol. 1–7 & Vol. 1–2.

Andrews, John Lloyd enlisted for three years as a private at age 35 into the 1st Company on September 11, 1862 at Camp Wightman Long Island, Boston and received a $25.00 bounty. He was a shoe cutter. He was born May 21, 1827 at Foxcraft, Maine and his service was credited to Saugus. One reference states he was absent without leave from his enlistment date until January 16, 1864. Correspondence at the Natick Archives says he was captured as a deserter December 11, 1863 and sent by provost marshal Captain Shaw to provost at Washington, D.C. A $30.00 reward was paid for his arrest. His discharge date was September 8, 1864. He was married and had two children. His parents' names were Lloyd and Lovina (Steadman). Sources: Adjutant General Vol. 1–7 & Vol. 1–2; Stokinger.

Archer, James M., enlisted for three years as a private at age 18 into the 1st Company September 2, 1861, at Camp Saunders in Lynnfield. He was a teamster. He was born May 26, 1843, at Bath, New Hampshire, and his service was credited to Lynn. He was discharged September 8, 1864. O.R.'s I, 21 report him missing near Fredericksburg, Virginia. His parents' names were Addison and Melissa (Merrill). Sources: Adjutant General Vol. 1–7 & Vol. 1–2; Root, Elihu; Harwell.

Arnold, Marcus Palmer, enlisted for three years as a private at age 23 into the 1st Company October 29, 1862, at Camp Wightman, Long Island, Boston, and received a $25.00 enlistment bonus. He was a bookmaker. He was born December 13, 1839, in Braintree and his service was credited to Boston-Reading. He reenlisted on February 16, 1864, and received a $325.00 reenlistment bonus. He was transferred to the 19th Massachusetts Volunteer Infantry Company K October 21, 1864, to complete his reenlistment commitment. That tour of duty was credited to Reading, where he could have resided or collected the bounty from there. He was discharged June 30, 1865. He was single and his parents' names were John and Mehitable (Holbrook). His mother's middle name was Allen and he was also known as Mark. Sources: Adjutant General Vol. 1–7 & Vol. 1–2; Stokinger; Microfilm collection.

Arnott, John, enlisted for three years as a private at age 32 into the 1st Company November 19, 1862, at Camp Wightman Long Island, Boston, and received a $25.00 bounty. He was a sailor. He was born March 11, 1831, at Elmira, New York, and his service was credited to Boston. He received a disability discharge April 25, 1863, at Falmouth, Virginia. His parents' names were John and Harriet (Tuttle). One source indicates this name was an alias, his other name being John G. Whitney. Sources: Adjutant General Vol. 1–7 & Vol. 1–2; Stokinger; Microfilm collection; Harnwell.

Atwood, Otis W., enlisted for three years as a private at age 22 into the 1st Company September 2, 1861, at Camp Saunders in Lynnfield. He was a shoemaker. He was born in February 6, 1840, at Lynn and his service was credited to South Reading. He deserted September 17, 1862, at the Battle of Antietam. He was married and had two children. His parents' names were Samuel and Sarah (Sparks). Sources: Adjutant General Vol. 1–7 & Vol. 1–2; Topsfield Historical Society, *Vitals*; Harnwell.

Averill, Trask Woodbury, enlisted for three years as a private at age 21 into the 1st Company October 25, 1862, at Camp Wightman, Long Island, Boston, and received a $25.00 bounty. He was a trader. He was born in March 20, 1841, at Vernon, New Hampshire, and his service was credited to Boston. He received a disability discharge April 17, 1864. He was single and his parents' names were John and Anna (Woodbury). Sources: Adjutant General Vol. 1–7 & Vol. 1–2; Stokinger; Smith, Charles J., *History*.

Ayer, John H., enlisted for three years as a private at age 31 into the 1st Company September 2, 1861, at Camp Saunders in Lynnfield. He was a mason. He was born December 20, 1829, at Underhill, New Hampshire, and his service was credited to South Danvers. He deserted January 13, 1863. He was captured as a prisoner of war September 3, 1862, and paroled September 9, 1862. He was married and had three children; his parents' names were James and Dorcas (Clough). Sources: Adjutant General Vol. 1–7 & Vol. 1–2; Essex, *Danvers*.

Bancroft, George Washington, enlisted for three years as a private at age 21 into the 1st Company September 13, 1862, at Camp Wightman, Long Island, Boston, and received a $25.00 bounty. He was a mason. He was born in July 28, 1841, in Danvers and his service was credited to South Danvers. He was wounded at Mine Run, Virginia, on November 27, 1863, and was discharged September 8, 1864. He was single and his parents' names were Alpheus Woodbury and Charity (Galeucia). His brother was Robert B. of the same company. Sources: Adjutant General Vol. 1–7 & Vol. 1–2; Stokinger; Essex, *Danvers*.

Bancroft, Robert B., enlisted for three years as a sergeant at age 26 into the 1st Company September 13, 1862, at Camp Wightman, Long Island, Boston, and received a $25.00 bounty. He was a mason. He was born May 7, 1836, in Salem and his service was credited to South Danvers. He was discharged September 3, 1864, as a private, indicating that at some point he was reduced in rank. His parents' names were Alpheus Woodbury and Charity (Galeucia). His brother was George W. of the same company. Sources: Adjutant General Vol. 1–7 & Vol. 1–2; Stokinger; Essex, *Danvers*.

Barker, Samuel S., enlisted for three years as a private at age 22 into the 1st Company September 2, 1861, at Camp Saunders in Lynnfield. He was a sailor. He was born in 1839 and his service was credited to Andover. He deserted September 17, 1862, at the Battle of Antietam. He first enlisted April 16, 1861, in the 5th Massachusetts Volunteer Infantry Company B (3 month) and was discharged from the 8th on July 31, 1861. He later enlisted in the 1st Regiment Potomac Home Brigade Cavalry (Cole's Cavalry) August 19, 1864, as Samuel Sprague and was discharged from that unit June 28, 1865. He was single and his parents were his dependents, and their names were Asa and Mary G. Sources: Adjutant General Vol. 1–7 & Vol. 1–2; Harnwell.

Baron, Morris, enlisted for three years as a private at age 21 into the 1st Company October 4, 1862, at Camp Wightman, Long Island, Boston, and received a $25.00 bounty. He was a blacksmith. He was born in 1841 at Boston and his service was credited to Cambridge. He deserted October 10, 1862, just six days after he enlisted. Sources: Adjutant General Vol. 1–7 & Vol. 1–2; Stokinger.

Bartlett, Alonzo W. enlisted for three years as a private at age 20 into the 1st Company September 2, 1861 at Camp Saunders in Lynnfield. He was a shoemaker. He was born 1840–1841 in Newton and his service was credited to Lynn. He first enlisted April 15, 1861 in the 8th Massachusetts Volunteer Infantry Company "D" (3 month) and was discharged August 1, 1861. While serving with the Sharpshooters he was wounded twice, once at the Battle of Antietam, Maryland September 17, 1862, and again at the Battle of Cold Harbor, Virginia, June 6, 1864. He was discharged September 2, 1864. Regarding his wounds at Cold Harbor, Captain John B. Adams, of the 19th Regiment Massachusetts Volunteer writes in his *Reminiscences of the 19th Regiment Massachusetts Volunteers*, ... (Patriot Files) found Alonzo W. Bartlett of Andrews, Mass. Sharpshooter. Bart. Had come out after the body of a colonel of the 8th New York, who fell at the foot of the rebel works. He managed to get a rope around the body, but the rebels made it so hot that he was forced to entrench, which he did with his dipper, and was fighting the war on his own hook. His face was cut and bleeding from the gravel stones which had struck him, but he held his own, and having a good rifle with plenty of ammunition thought he could hold out as long as they." His parents' names were Robert and Mary (Tate). Sources: Adjutant General Vol. 1–7 & Vol. 1–2; Harnwell.

Batchelder, Alfred A., was transferred into the 1st Company October 23, 1862. He was a wheelwright.

He was born July 10, 1843, in Millbury and his service was credited to Worcester. At age 19, he enlisted on July 31, 1861, in the 15th Massachusetts Volunteer Infantry and received a $25.00 bounty at Camp Scott in Worcester. He was unassigned and transferred to the Sharpshooters. He was wounded July 3, 1863, at the Battle of Gettysburg and died from those wounds July 10, 1863, in Baltimore, Maryland. His parents' names were Ebenezer and Elizabeth. It appears his father was born in Sutton January 30, 1809, to Josiah and Susanna. Vital statistics give his name as Batcheller. Sources: Adjutant General Vol. 1–7 & Vol. 1–2; Stokinger; Systematic Fund, *Millbury*.

Benham, Winfield H., enlisted for three years as a private at age 25 into the 1st Company August 14, 1861, at Camp Saunders in Lynnfield. He was a carpenter. He was born August 17, 1836, in Luisville, NewYork and his service was credited to Stow. He died of disease May 18, 1863. Muster in rolls indicate he was transferred to the 26th Massachusetts Volunteer Infantry on July 22, 1862. *Soldiers and Sailors* indicates he enlisted in the 26th Company I on October 9, 1861, was promoted to sergeant November 1, 1861, was promoted to 2nd lieutenant July 22, 1862, and was promoted to 1st lieutenant on February 11, 1863. He was single and his parents' names were Harvey and Orrilla. Sources: Adjutant General Vol. 1–7; Adjutant First Company; N.E.H.G.S., *Stow*.

Bently, Noah, enlisted for three years as a private at age 35 into the 1st Company March 24, 1862, at Camp Wightman, Long Island, Boston. He was a farmer. He was born in 1827 at Stewiacke, Colchester County, Nova Scotia, and his service was credited to Andover. He was transferred to 19th Massachusetts Volunteer Infantry Company K and was discharged in March of 1865. He was married and his father's name was James. Sources: Adjutant General Vol. 1–7 & Vol. 1–2; Stokinger; Microfilm Collection.

Berkley, John, enlisted for three years as a private at age 22 into the 1st Company September 3, 1861, at Camp Saunders in Lynnfield. He was a farmer. He was born in either 1838 or 1839 at St. Andrews, New Brunswick, Canada, and his service was credited to North Andover. He was discharged from the Sharpshooters October 29, 1862, to enlist in the United States Engineers. He died in service February 13, 1863, presumably of disease. He was married. His parents' names were Joseph and Mary. Sources: Adjutant General Vol. 1–7 & Vol. 1–2. Harnwell.

Berry, William Burges, enlisted for three years as a sergeant at age 36 into the 1st Company August 19, 1861, at Camp Saunders in Lynnfield. He was a publisher. He was born August 10, 1825, in Cambridge and his service was credited to Somerville. He was killed in action September 17, 1862, at the Battle of Antietam. He was promoted to 2nd lieutenant date unknown, 1st lieutenant April 4, 1862. He was among the total casualty list of 384 under the command of Col. John W. Kimball, of the 15th Massachusetts Volunteer Infantry. The 15th entered the battle with 582 men and left the field with 234 men and a stand of Confederate colors (Ref. #4 O.R. I, 19). In Bicknell's journal he was said to be a close friend of Captain Saunders before his service in the Sharpshooters. His parents' names were Samuel and Abigail (Burges). Sources: Adjutant General Vol. 1–7 & Vol. 1–2; Root Elihu; Adjutant First Company; Bicknell, Luke; Microfilm Collection.

Bestwick, Frederick Litchfield, enlisted for three years as a private at age 39 into the 1st Company October 10, 1862, at Camp Wightman, Long Island, Boston, and received a $25.00 bounty. He was a carriage maker. He was discharged September 3, 1864. He was born March 23, 1823, in Medway and his service was credited to Dedham. He was married and his parents' names were John and Mary. Sources: Adjutant General Vol. 1–7 & Vol. 1–2; Stokinger; N.E.H.G.S., *Medway*.

Bicknell, Emerson Luke, enlisted for 3 years as a private at age 21 into the 1st Company August 19, 1861, at Camp Saunders in Lynnfield. He was a student. He was born October 29, 1839, in Windsor and his service was credited to Boston-Chelsea, (Reference #4-O.R. I, 27). He first enlisted April 15, 1861, in the 8th Massachusetts Volunteer Infantry Company A (3 month) and was discharged August 1, 1861. He was wounded at the Battle of Antietam September 17, 1862, and was given a disability discharge September 19, 1863. He was promoted to sergeant July 19, 1862, and was commissioned 2nd lieutenant. He married Lucretia T. Peirce. They had a son, Benjamin Humphrey, on August 8, 1873, and daughter, Sarah Gertrude, born March 19, 1876. He died April 19, 1888, of laryngeal phthisis. His parents' names were Loren and Mary E. (Cady). Sources: Adjutant General Vol. 1–7 & Vol. 1–2; Root, Elihu; Streeter, William.

Blaisdell, Josiah Coleman, enlisted for three years as a private at age 22 into the 1st Company September 2, 1861, at Camp Saunders in Lynnfield. He was a shoemaker. He was born February 25, 1840, in Compton, New Hampshire, and his service was credited to Lynn. He was given a disability discharge December 10, 1861. He was single and his parents' names were Charles and Phippen (Webber). Sources: Adjutant General Vol. 1–7 & Vol. 1–2; Microfilm Collection.

Blodgett, William E., enlisted for three years as a private at age 34 into the 1st Company September 2, 1861, at Camp Saunders in Lynnfield. He was a shoemaker. He was born in either 1826 or 1827 in Topsfield and his service was credited to Lynn-Middleton. He was wounded September 17, 1862, at the Battle of Antietam and given a disability discharge November 19, 1862. He reenlisted August 13, 1864, in the Veteran Reserve Corps and received a $325.00

bounty. He was discharged November 13, 1865 from the Veteran Reserve Corps at Concord, New Hampshire He resided in Lynn with his wife Mary (Porter) and his four children. His parents' names were Isaac and Cynthia (Peabody). Sources: Adjutant General Vol. 1–7 & Vol. 1–2; Adjutant First Company; Harnwell.

Bradford, Luther T., enlisted for three years as a private at age 21 into the 1st Company September 2, 1861, at Camp Saunders in Lynnfield. He was an engineer. He was born November 17, 1839, in Massachusetts and his service was credited to North Reading. He was given a disability discharge January 22, 1862, at Potter's Creek, Virginia, for chronic hepatitis. He was married and his parents' names were Dana and Harriet (Jones). Sources: Adjutant General Vol. 1–7 & Vol. 1–2; Microfilm Collection; Harnwell.

Brooks, David, enlisted for three years as a private at age 29 into the 1st Company October 29, 1862, at Camp Wightman, Long Island, Boston, and received a $25.00 bounty. He was a farmer. He was born in 1834, at Cumberland, New Jersey, and his service was credited to Boston. His service and discharge date are unknown as there was no further information found. He was single and his parents' names were Samuel and Ketura (Gilman). Sources: Adjutant General Vol. 1–7 & Vol. 1–2; Microfilm Collection.

Brown, John H., enlisted for three years as a private at age 19 into the 1st Company September 3, 1861, at Camp Saunders in Lynnfield. He was a storekeeper. He was born August 12, 1842, in Stoneham and his service was credited to Stoneham. He was wounded September 17, 1862, at the Battle of Antietam. He was transferred to the United States Engineers Corps October 25, 1862. While on long marches and when illness threatened to overtake the men, the men were given whiskey rations. John gave his word to his mother that he would not drink. He was greatly teased by the men of the unit for not drinking. He was discharged September 3, 1864. He was single and his parents' names were John and Mary (Taft) Sources: Adjutant General Vol. 1–7 & Vol. 1–2; Microfilm Collection; Essex, *Stoneham*; Bicknell, Luke.

Bryant, Frank W., enlisted for three years as a musician at age 20 into the 1st Company September 2, 1861, at Camp Saunders in Lynnfield. He was a farmer. He was born March 2, 1841, in Dorchester, and his service was credited to East Lexington. He deserted September 17, 1862, at the Battle of Antietam. He was single and his parents were his dependents, and their names were Nathaniel and Mary (Gardener). Sources: Adjutant General Vol. 1–7 & Vol. 1–2; Harnwell.

Burbank, James S., enlisted for three years as a corporal at age 34 into the 1st Company September 2, 1861, at Camp Saunders in Lynnfield. He was a carpenter. He was born in 1827 and his service was credited to Providence, Rhode Island. He deserted January 15, 1862. Sources: Adjutant General Vol. 1–7 & Vol. 1–2.

Burnham, Ansel, enlisted for three years as a private at age 35 into the 1st Company March 19, 1862, at Camp Wightman, Long Island, Boston. He was a farmer. He was born September 12, 1822, in Essex and his service was credited to Andover. He died of disease January 23, 1863, at Washington, D.C. and was interred at Military Asylum Cemetery in Washington, D.C., He was married and his parents' names were Zebulon and Judith (Andrews). Sources: Adjutant General Vol. 1–7 & Vol. 1–2; Stokinger; U.S. Quartermaster's Department.

Burrows, John A., enlisted for three years as a private at age 21 into the 1st Company September 2, 1861, at Camp Saunders in Lynnfield. He was a farmer. He was born April 24, 1840, in Chelmsford and his service was credited to Lowell-Billerica. He was given a disability discharge December 15, 1862, at Newark, New Jersey. He first enlisted in the 8th Massachusetts Volunteer Infantry Company A April 15, 1861 (3 month), and was discharged from that unit August 1, 1861. His parents' names were William and Louisa (Eastman). Sources: Adjutant General Vol. 1–7 & Vol. 1–2; Essex, *Lowell*; Microfilm Collection. Harnwell.

Butters, Daniel H., enlisted for three years as a sergeant at age 44 into the 1st Company September 19, 1862, at Camp Wightman, Long Island, Boston, and received a $25.00 bounty. He was a trader. He was born in June 17, 1819, at Bedford and his service was credited to Bedford. He was discharged September 8, 1864. He married Mary Bailey and they had three sons. His parents' names were Daniel and Susan (Goodwin). Sources: Adjutant General Vol. 1–7 & Vol. 1–2; N.E.H.G.S., *Bedford*; Microfilm Collection.

Buzzell, Albert P., enlisted for three years as a private at age 27 into the 1st Company September 15, 1862, at Camp Wightman, Long Island, Boston, and received a $25.00 bounty. He was a scale maker. He was born September 15, 1834, at Vassalborough, Maine, and his service was credited to Boston. He was given a disability discharge February 17, 1863, at Falmouth, Virginia. He was single. His parents' names were Stephen and Sarah (Hawes). Sources: Adjutant General Vol. 1–7 & Vol. 1–2; Stokinger; Harnwell.

Cameron, Charles, enlisted for three years as a private at age 22 into the 1st Company November 11, 1862, at Camp Wightman, Long Island, Boston, and received a $25.00 bounty. He was a cigar maker. He was born in 1840 at Madison, Maine, and his service was credited to Boston. His service and discharge date are unknown as there was no further information found. He was single. Sources: Adjutant General Vol. 1–7 & Vol. 1–2.

Campbell, Samuel Grimes, enlisted for three years as a private at age 31 into the 1st Company September 2, 1861, at Camp Saunders in Lynnfield. He was a shoemaker. He was born in Reading October 20, 1830, and his service was credited to Reading. He was discharged September 2, 1864. He was missing at the Battle of Antietam. He was transferred to the 14th Veterans Reserve Corps Company "B" July 24, 1863. He was baptized May 22, 1831, at the Congregational Church, Reading. He was married and had four children. His parents' names were Robert and Sally (Nichols). Sources: Adjutant General Vol. 1–7 & Vol. 1–2; Baldwin, Thomas, *Reading*; Harnwell.

Carter, E. B., enlisted for three years in the 1st Company. It is unknown when or where. He was captured by the Confederates June 2, 1864, near Cold Harbor, Virginia, and was released near Vicksburg April 2, 1865. He was discharged by Special Order of the War Department May 1, 1865. Sources: Adjutant General Vol. 1–7 & Vol. 1–2.

Champney, John H., enlisted for three years as a private at age 25 into the 1st Company March 24, 1862, at Camp Wightman, Long Island, Boston. He was a farmer. He was born November 8, 1836, in Lowell and his service was credited to Carlisle. He received a disability discharge January 26, 1864, at Stevensburg, Virginia. He was married. His parents' names were Ebenezer and Sarah (Nichols). Sources: Adjutant General Vol. 1–7 & Vol. 1–2; Stokinger; Harwell

Chase, Samuel E., enlisted for three years as a private at age 19 into the 1st Company October 29, 1862, at Camp Wightman, Long Island, Boston, and received a $25.00 bounty. He was a bootmaker. He was born December 17, 1842, at Grafton and his service was credited to Boston-Braintree. He reenlisted February 16, 1864, and received a $325.00 bounty. He was transferred October 21, 1864, to 19th Massachusetts Volunteer Infantry Company K and was discharged June 30, 1865. His parents' names were Samuel and Lydia (Savory). Sources: Adjutant General Vol. 1–7 & Vol. 1–2; Stokinger; Microfilm Collection.

Chenery, James Parkman, enlisted for three years as a private at age 19 into the 1st Company March 18, 1862, at Camp Wightman, Long Island, Boston. He was a student. He was born September 28, 1842, at Medfield and his service was credited to Northampton. He was discharged from the Sharpshooters on November 28, 1862, by Special Order # 367 to enable him to receive a commission in the Volunteer Militia Service. He died March 2, 1863, but there are no details of his death. The *History of Medfield* states he was killed in action at Gettysburg. That battle was fought July 3, 1863; a typo could be the answer. His parents' names were Seth and Sophia (Fairbanks). Sources: Adjutant General Vol. 1–7 & Vol. 1–2; Stokinger; Microfilm Collection.

Clapp, Philo, enlisted for three years as a private at age 40 into the 1st Company September 20, 1862, at Camp Wightman, Long Island, Boston, and received a $25.00 bounty. He was a pump maker. He was born May 26, 1806, at Deerfield and his service was credited to Stow. He was given a disability discharge February 6, 1863, at Boston. He married Flora Wheterbee of Bolton and had three children. His parents' names were Seth and Anna (Cantral). His father was from Deerfield and his mother was from Sunderland. It appears he was older than he stated. Sources: Adjutant General Vol. 1–7 & Vol. 1–2; Stokinger; N.E.H.G.S., *Stow*; Sheldon, George.

Clement, Oscar H., enlisted for three years as a private at age 22 into the 1st Company September 2, 1861, at Camp Saunders in Lynnfield. He was a shoemaker. He was born in 1839 at Holderness, New Hampshire, and his service was credited to Stoneham. He was discharged September 27, 1863. He first enlisted the 8th Massachusetts Volunteer Infantry Company D April 15, 1861 (3 month), and was discharged from that unit August 1, 1861. He was promoted to 1st sergeant and then commissioned 1st lieutenant May 30, 1863. He was cashiered September 27, 1863 by General Court Martial. His parents' names were Simeon and Mary. Sources: Adjutant General Vol. 1–7 & Vol. 1–2. Root, Elihu. Baldwin Thomas, *Reading*. Harnwell

Coburn, Horace G., enlisted for three years as a private at age 42 into the 1st Company September 25, 1862, at Camp Wightman, Long Island, Boston and received a $25.00 bounty. He was a teamster. He was born in either 1819 or 1820 in Boston, and his service was credited to Boston. He was given a disability discharge March 11, 1863, at Falmouth, Virginia. He also served in the Veterans Reserve Corps; credit for that service was to the state of New Hampshire. One source indicates his name as Colburn. He was married and had four children. His parents' names were John and Bethia (Wyman). Sources: Adjutant General Vol. 1–7 & Vol. 1–2; Stokinger; Harnwell.

Cole, Alvin, enlisted for three years as a private at age 21 into the 1st Company September 2, 1861, at Camp Saunders in Lynnfield. He was a carpenter. He was born July 30, 1840, in Charlestown and his service was credited to East Lexington. He was wounded in September 1862; although the day was not given, one would assume he was wounded at the Battle of Antietam on the 17th. At some point in time he was promoted to corporal. He was given a disability discharge December 22, 1862, at Falmouth, Virginia. His parents' names were Simeon and Jerusha (Pitkin). He was also known as Alvan. Sources: Adjutant General Vol. 1–7 & Vol. 1–2.

Coleman, George M., enlisted for three years as a private at age 27 into the 1st Company September 2, 1861, at Camp Saunders in Lynnfield. He was a shoemaker. He was born in 1834 and his service was credited to Lynn. He was given a disability discharge July

11, 1863 at Washington, D.C. Sources: Adjutant General Vol. 1–7 & Vol. 1–2.

Conners, John, enlisted for three years as a private at age 25 into the 1st Company November 24, 1862, at Camp Wightman, Long Island, Boston, and received a $25.00 bounty. He was a painter. He was born in 1837 at Lowell and his service was credited to Boston. His service and discharge dates are unknown as there was no further information found regarding his service. His parents' names were John and Ann (Lockwood). Sources: Adjutant General Vol. 1–7 & Vol. 1–2; Microfilm Collection.

Cookson, Edward, enlisted for three years as a private at age 20 into the 1st Company September 2, 1861, at Camp Saunders in Lynnfield. He was a sailor. He was born in 1841 and his service was credited to Gloucester. He was given a disability discharge August 8, 1862. He first enlisted in the 8th Massachusetts Volunteer Infantry Company G (3 months) April 15, 1861, and was discharged from that unit August 1, 1861. Sources: Adjutant General Vol. 1–7 & Vol. 1–2.

Courier, Charles, enlisted for three years as a private at age 21 into the 1st Company October 22, 1862, at Camp Wightman, Long Island, Boston. He was born in 1841 and his service was credited to Boston. His service and discharge dates are unknown as there was no further information found regarding his service. Sources: Adjutant General Vol. 1–7 & Vol. 1–2; Stokinger.

Crane, Robert T., enlisted for three years as a private at age 28 into the 1st Company September 2, 1862, at Camp Wightman, Long Island, Boston, and received a $25.00 bounty. He was a farmer. He was born in 1834 in Franklin, New Hampshire, and his service was credited to Boston. He received a disability discharge February 13, 1863, at Falmouth, Virginia. He was married and had one child. Sources: Adjutant General Vol. 1–7 & Vol. 1–2; Stokinger.

Crossman, Ferdinand J. F., enlisted for three years as a private at age 28 into the 1st Company August 10, 1862, at Camp Wightman, Long Island, Boston, and received a $25.00 bounty. He was a farmer. He was born April 21, 1834, at Sutton and his service was credited to Sutton. He was taken prisoner at Spotsylvania, Virginia, May 12, 1864 and sent to Andersonville Prison. He died of disease August 9, 1864. He was married and had two children. His parents' names were Martin and Experience (Robbins). Sources: Adjutant General Vol. 1–7 & Vol. 1–2; Stokinger; Harnwell.

Curtis, George, enlisted for three years as a private at age 22 into the 1st Company September 2, 1861, at Camp Saunders in Lynnfield. He was a shoemaker. He was born June 29, 1839, at Leeds, England, and his service was credited to Chelmsford and Bedford. He reenlisted February 16, 1864, and received $325.00 and $60.00 bounties. He was wounded September 17, 1862, at the Battle of Antietam and again May 18, 1864, at Spotsylvania, Virginia. He died from that wound May 28, 1864. He was promoted to corporal and then to sergeant. He, as a corporal, designed and implemented a plan at Bristoe, Virginia, October 17, 1863, to capture two pieces of Confederate artillery. He was commended for his bravery in that action in the O.R.'s I-19. He was single and his mother was his dependent. His parents' names were James and Jane (Morgan). Sources: Adjutant General Vol. 1–7 & Vol. 1–2; Root, Elihu; Harnwell.

Davis, William M., enlisted for three years as a private at age 25 into the 1st Company November 29, 1862, at Camp Wightman, Long Island, Boston, and received a $25.00 bounty. He was a farmer. He was born September 24, 1838, at New Market, New Hampshire, and his service was credited to Cambridge. His service and discharge dates are unknown as there was no further information found regarding his service. His parents' names were Stephen and Clara (Demeritt). Sources: Adjutant General Vol. 1–7 & Vol. 1–2; Harnwell.

Dike, Henry, enlisted for three years as a private at age 23 into the 1st Company September 2, 1861, at Camp Saunders in Lynnfield. He was a clerk. He was born March 3, 1838, at Stoneham and his service was credited to Stoneham. He first enlisted in 6th Massachusetts Volunteer Infantry Company L April 22, 1861 (3 months), and was discharged from that unit August 2, 1861. While passing through Baltimore, his unit was attacked by a mob and he was wounded. He was wounded again September 17, 1862, at the Battle of Antietam and received a disability discharge December 8, 1862, as a result of that wound. He was single and his parents' names were Alfred and Sara (Jones). Sources: Adjutant General Vol. 1–7 & Vol. 1–2. Root; Elihu; Essex, *Stoneham*.

Dobbyn, Caesar H., enlisted for three years as a private at age 26 into the 1st Company October 29, 1862, at Camp Wightman, Long Island, Boston, and received a $25.00 bounty. He was a grocer. He was born in 1836 in Ireland and his service was credited to Boston. Company muster rolls indicate he left camp without leave February 13, 1863. He was taken prisoner June 20, 1863, at Dumfries, Virginia. He was paroled July 2, 1863 and reported to parole camp at Annapolis, Maryland, July 3, 1863. He was married. Sources: Adjutant General Vol. 1–7 & Vol. 1–2; Adjutant First Company.

Dodge, Moses G., was transferred to the 1st Company September 30, 1861. His original enlistment was in the 13th Massachusetts Volunteer Infantry Company G July 10, 1861, at Fort Independence, Castle Island, Boston, as a private for three years at 45 years of age. He was a teamster. He was born August 23, 1816, at Francistown, New Hampshire, and his service was credited to Stoneham. He was given a disability discharge on December 16, 1861. He was married. His parents' names were Dimon and Anna (Wilson). Sources: Adjutant General Vol. 1–7 & Vol. 1–2; Stokinger; Harnwell.

Dodge, Orrin A., enlisted for three years as a private at age 20 into the 1st Company September 2, 1861, at Camp Saunders in Lynnfield. He was a shoemaker. He was born July 25, 1841, in Stoneham and his service was credited to Stoneham. He was wounded during 1862, date and location unknown. He was given a disability discharge November 17, 1863. He reenlisted July 25, 1864, in the 13th Veteran Reserve Corps, Company A, and received a $325.00 bounty. He was discharged November 17, 1865, from the Veteran Reserve Corps. He was the son of Moses Dodge, also in the 1st Company. He returned to Stoneham as a fireman and worked his way to chief engineer. In about 1890 his brother offered him the position of chief engineer in the city of Lynn. To the displeasure of Stoneham, he accepted that position. There is a picture of Orrin in the *History of Stoneham*. His parents' names were Moses and Elizabeth (Bryant). Sources: Adjutant General Vol. 1–7 & Vol. 1–2; Essex, *Stoneham*; Stevens, William.

Dodge, Samuel L., enlisted for three years as a private at age 23 into the 1st Company September 2, 1861, at Camp Saunders in Lynnfield. He was a shoemaker. He was born February 28, 1838, at Francistown, New Hampshire, and his service was credited to Stoneham. He was given a disability discharge September 24, 1862. He died of disease October 19, 1862. His parents' names were Moses and Elizabeth (Bryant). Sources: Adjutant General Vol. 1–7; Lynnfield Heritage; *Civil War Papers*, Stoneham; Harnwell.

Durand, Joseph, enlisted for three years as a private at age 33 into the 1st Company October 25, 1862, at Camp Wightman, Long Island, Boston, and received a $25.00 bounty. He was a tailor. He was born in 1829 at Montreal, Canada, and his service was credited to Boston. He deserted, at a date not indicated in the muster rolls. He was single. Sources: Adjutant General Vol. 1–7 & Vol. 1–2; Stokinger.

Eaton, Daniel W., enlisted for three years as a private at age 21 into the 1st Company September 2, 1861, at Camp Saunders in Lynnfield. He was a shoemaker. He was born February 17, 1840, in Wilton, Maine, and his service was credited to North Reading. He was wounded August 25, 1864, at Ream's Station, Virginia. He was discharged September 8, 1864. He was single and his parents' names were Osgood and Hanna (Wentworth). Sources: Adjutant General Vol. 1–7 & Vol. 1–2; Microfilm Collection.

Ellis, Nathan Basset, was transferred into the 1st Company prior to December 2, 1862. His original enlistment was in the 25th Massachusetts Volunteer Infantry unassigned August 12, 1863, at age 27 as a private. He was born March 19, 1835, in Sandwich and his service was credited to Framingham. He was promoted to sergeant, was commissioned lieutenant and was wounded October 14, 1863, at Bristoe Station, Virginia, while serving with the Sharpshooters. He was also wounded May 6, 1864 at Wilderness, Virginia while serving with the 20th Massachusetts and received a disability discharge July 29, 1864. He reenlisted December 20, 1863 in the 25th Massachusetts Volunteer Infantry Company and received a $325.00 bounty. He was transferred January 29, 1864 to the 20th Massachusetts Volunteer Infantry Company F and K. He also received a $25.00 bounty at some other time. He was married; his parents' names were Nathan and Sabrina (Nickerson). His mother's first married name was Crowell. Sources: Adjutant General Vol. 1–7 & Vol. 1–2; Stokinger; Ellis, Harry H.

Emerson, Stephen D. B., enlisted for three years as a private at age 23 into the 1st Company September 2, 1861, at Camp Saunders in Lynnfield. He was a shoemaker. He was born October 22, 1837, in Chester, New Hampshire, and his service was credited to Stoneham-Dorchester. He was given a disability discharge February 16, 1863. He reenlisted July 29, 1864, in the 13th Veteran Reserve Corps Company G and received a $325.00 bounty. He was discharged November 21, 1865, from the Veteran Reserve Corps. He was married and had one child. His parents' names were William and Mary J. Sources: Adjutant General Vol. 1–7 & Vol. 1–2; *Civil War Papers,* Stoneham; Harnwell.

Evans, Robert, enlisted for three years as a private at age 23 into the 1st Company September 3, 1861, at Camp Saunders in Lynnfield. He was a shoemaker. He was born in either 1837 or 1838 in Ireland and his service was credited to Haverhill. He was given a disability discharge September 24, 1862. He was single. His parents' names were David and Agnes (Fergusson). Sources: Adjutant General Vol. 1–7 & Vol. 1–2; Harnwell.

Everest, Henry Martin, enlisted for three years as a private at age 25 into the 1st Company March 10, 1862, at Camp Wightman, Long Island, Boston. He was a spinner. He was born February 2, 1836, at Meriden, New Hampshire, and his service was credited to Dracut-Lowell. He was wounded in 1862, with no date or location indicated. He was given a disability discharge September 28, 1862, in Boston as a result of that wound. One source indicates his name as Everett. He was married, and his parents' names were Joseph W. and Eleanor (Hunt). Sources: Adjutant General Vol. 1–7 & Vol. 1–2; Stokinger; Microfilm Collection.

Fletcher, Asa, enlisted for three years as a private at age 41 into the 1st Company August 2, 1862, at Camp Wightman, Long Island, Boston. He was a carpenter. He was born in 1821 at Westford and his service was credited to Winchester. He was wounded at the Battle of Antietam on September 17, 1862. He was given a disability discharge October 27, 1862, at Boston, as a result of that wound. He was instrumental in setting up the public water system in Winchester and sat on its board of directors. At his death, about 1893, the Asa Fletcher Fund was established and funded with some $54,000. The income from that fund was to be devoted to the poor. His parents' names were Asa and Hanna (Brown). Sources: Adjutant General Vol. 1–7 & Vol. 1–2; Stokinger; Microfilm Collection.

Flint, Henry E., enlisted for three years as a private at age 23 into the 1st Company September 2, 1861 at Camp Saunders in Lynnfield. He was a shoemaker. He was born December 5, 1837, in North Reading, and his service was credited to North Reading. He was given a disability discharge September 10, 1862. He was married. His parents' names were Henry and Susan (Swain). Sources: Adjutant General Vol. 1–7 & Vol. 1–2; Harnwell.

Forbes, William C., enlisted for three years as a private at age 18 into the 1st Company September 2, 1861, at Camp Saunders in Lynnfield. He was a shoemaker. He was born June 16, 1843, in Newburyport and his service was credited to Newburyport. He was given a disability discharge February 17, 1862, at Poolesville, Maryland. He reenlisted November 13, 1863, in the 3rd Massachusetts Volunteer Heavy Artillery Company H and received a $402.00 bounty. He died of disease November 9, 1864, at Newburyport. His first enlistment was in the 8th Massachusetts Volunteer Infantry Company A April 15, 1861 (3 month). and he was discharged from that unit August 1, 1861. He was single and his parents' names were Lyman and Hanna (March). Sources: Adjutant General Vol. 1–7 & Vol. 1–2; Essex, *Newburyport*.

Franklin, George E., enlisted for three years as a private at age 31 into the 1st Company January 4, 1864, at Camp Wightman, Long Island, Boston, and received $325.00 and $60.00 bounties. He was a mechanic. He was born in 1833 at Lyme, New Hampshire, and his service was credited to Natick. He reenlisted February 16, 1864, and received a $325.00 bounty. He was transferred October 21, 1864, to the 19th Massachusetts Volunteer Infantry Company K to complete his enlistment as the Sharpshooters were mustered. He was discharged June 30, 1865. He was married to Mariah M. and his parents' names were Asahel and Margaret. Sources: Adjutant General Vol. 1–7 & Vol. 1–2; Stokinger; Lainhart, Ann.

Fuller, Sanford K., enlisted for three years as a private at age 31 into the 1st Company September 2, 1861, at Camp Saunders in Lynnfield. He was a blacksmith. He was born in 1830 in Maine, and his service was credited to Lynn. He was wounded September 17, 1862, at the Battle of Antietam. He was also wounded at the Battle of Gettysburg and died from that wound July 18, 1863. Correspondence at the Worcester Archives indicates he died of "secondary amputation" at McKim's Mansion, Baltimore, Maryland, and had $24.05 cash with him. He was married and had three children. His parents' names were William and Hannah (Brock). Sources: Adjutant General Vol. 1–7 & Vol. 1–2; Harnwell.

Gardner, Charles A., enlisted for three years as a private at age 44 into the 1st Company September 2, 1861, at Camp Saunders in Lynnfield. He was a manufacturer. He was born November 3, 1812, in Nantucket, and his service was credited to South Danvers. He was given a disability discharge April 29, 1864, at Washington, D.C. He married Mary Ann West in Salem October 18, 1835, and they had four children. His parents' names were Hezekiah and Rebecca (Bartlett). Sources: Adjutant General Vol. 1–7 & Vol. 1–2; Essex, *Danvers*; Harnwell.

Gay, Charles, enlisted for three years as a private at age 29 into the 1st Company November 11, 1862, at Camp Wightman, Long Island, Boston, and received a $25.00 bounty. He was a spinner. He was born February 16, 1834, in Groton and his service was credited to Boston. He received a disability discharge January 27, 1863. He was married and his parents' names were Timothy and Julia (Barden). Sources: Adjutant General Vol. 1–7 & Vol. 1–2; Microfilm Collection.

Gifford, Charles P., enlisted for three years as a private at age 19 into the 1st Company March 24, 1862, at Camp Wightman, Long Island, Boston. He was a carpenter. He was born in 1843 and his service was credited to Salem. He died of disease July 1, 1862, at Nelson's Farm, Virginia. He was single. Sources: Adjutant General Vol. 1–7 & Vol. 1–2; Stokinger.

Gilbreth, John T., enlisted for three years as a private at age 20 into the 1st Company September 2, 1861, at Camp Saunders in Lynnfield. He was a farmer. He was born in 1841 at Belfast, Maine, and his service was credited to Belfast, Maine. He died of disease March 17, 1863, at Chester, Pennsylvania. He was single and his parents' names were Samuel and Emily (Tagart). His brother Samuel was in the same company. Sources: Adjutant General Vol. 1–7 & Vol. 1–2. Bicknell, Luke; Williamson, Joseph, *Belfast*; Microfilm Collection.

Gilbreth, Samuel Gordon, enlisted for three years as a private at age 31 into the 1st Company September 2, 1861, at Camp Saunders in Lynnfield. He was a sailor. He was born March 8, 1830, at Belfast, Maine and his service was credited to Belfast, Maine. He was wounded in May 1864. He was commissioned 1st lieutenant September 22, 1863. He was killed in action June 18, 1864, at Petersburg, Virginia (Ref. O.R.'s I-29, 33, 36, 40, organizational). He first enlisted in the

8th Massachusetts Volunteer Infantry Company A (3 months). He was single and his parents' names were Samuel and Emily (Tagart). His brother John was in the same company. Sources: Adjutant General *Vol. I–7* & Vol. 1–2; Root, Elihu; Bicknell, Luke; Williamson, Joseph, *Belfast*; Microfilm Collection.

Gleason, William, was commissioned as an officer, 1st lieutenant, at age 54 into the 1st Company August 1, 1861, at Camp Saunders in Lynnfield. He was a farmer. He was born November 18, 1807, in Salem, Maine, and his service was credited to Lexington. He was discharged from the Sharpshooters April 3, 1862, when he resigned his commission. He married Charlotte Brown October 9, 1832, and they had a daughter, Abbie Louisa. His parents' names were William and Laura (Pratt). William Gleason died in Lexington October 16, 1881. Sources: Adjutant General Vol. 1–7 & Vol. 1–2; Town of Lexington, *Vital Records*; Microfilm Collection.

Goodwin, Stephen H., enlisted for three years as a private at age 22 into the 1st Company September 2, 1861, at Camp Saunders in Lynnfield. He was a shoemaker. He was born October 31, 1839, in Exeter, New Hampshire, and his service was credited to Newburyport. He was given a disability discharge April 2, 1862. He reenlisted July 26, 1862, in the 9th Massachusetts Battery Volunteer Light Artillery and was discharged from that unit June 6, 1865. His first enlistment was in the 8th Massachusetts Volunteer Infantry Company "A" April 15, 1861 (3 month), and was discharged from that unit August 1, 1861. He was single and his parents' names were Stephen and Nancy (Prescott). His mother was his dependent. He died in Newburyport January 24, 1873. Sources: Adjutant General Vol. 1–7 & Vol. 1–2; Creasey, George, *Newburyport*; Microfilm Collection.

Grasus, Peter, enlisted for three years as a private at age 30 into the 1st Company September 11, 1862 at Camp Wightman, Long Island, Boston, and received a $25.00 bounty. He was a laborer. He was born in 1832 in Germany and his service was credited to Boston He was transferred to the 2nd Massachusetts Volunteer Cavalry Company B October 28, 1862. He deserted February 18, 1863, at Baltimore, Maryland. He was married and had two children. Sources: Adjutant General Vol. 1–7 & Vol. 1–2; Essex, *Lynn*.

Gray, George C., was commissioned as an officer, 2nd lieutenant, at age 25 into the 1st Company September 3, 1861, at Camp Saunders in Lynnfield. He was a carpenter. He was born April 26, 1836, in Salem and his service was credited to Salem. He first enlisted in 8th Massachusetts Volunteer Infantry Company I (known as the Salem Light Infantry) April 15, 1861 (3 months), and was discharged from that unit August 1, 1861. He was discharged from the Sharpshooters May 30, 1862, when he resigned his commission. Sources indicate he also served as a captain in the 178th New York Volunteers. His parents' names were Benjamin Archer and Martha Ann (Agge). Sources: Adjutant General Vol. 1–7 & Vol. 1–2; Essex, *Salem*.

Gray, Joseph Jr., enlisted for three years as a private at age 39 into the 1st Company September 3, 1861, at Camp Saunders in Lynnfield. He was a currier. He was born August 18, 1822, in Hiram, Maine, and his service was credited to Salem. He was wounded September 17, 1862, at the Battle of Antietam and received a disability discharge January 27, 1863, as a result of that wound. He married Clara H. Bassett of Salem on June 30, 1847, and had five children. The family lived at House #177 Boston in Salem. His parents' names were Joseph and Susan (Brown). Sources: Adjutant General Vol. 1–7 & Vol. 1–2; Salem Street Directory; Harnwell.

Hall, Ammi, enlisted for three years as a private at age 28 into the 1st Company September 3, 1861, at Camp Saunders in Lynnfield. He was a carpenter. He was born March 28, 1833, in Arlington, and his service was credited to West Cambridge. He was given a disability discharge September 26, 1862, from the Sharpshooters. His name was listed as Amoni on the Muster Rolls. His father was born in West Cambridge and his mother was from Salem; they lived in Lexington. His parents' names were Ammi and Elizabeth (Crandall). Sources: Adjutant General Vol. 1–7 & Vol. 1–2; Adjutant First Company; Cambridge Historical, *History*; Harnwell.

Hammond, Anselm C., enlisted for three years as a private at age 36 into the 1st Company November 26, 1862, at Camp Wightman, Long Island, Boston. He was a soldier by profession. He was born in 1826 at Kent, England, and his service was credited to Cambridge. He was promoted to sergeant July 18, 1863. He was taken prisoner at Spotsylvania, Virginia, during the Battle of the Wilderness, on May 12, 1864. One source states he was killed in that battle; the source is probably unaware he was taken prisoner. At some point he was exchanged and returned to his unit on a date not stated. He was discharged October 12, 1864. His fathers' name was Charles. Sources: Adjutant General Vol. 1–7 & Vol. 1–2; Stokinger; Harnwell.

Hanson, Charles, enlisted for three years as a private at age 24 into the 1st Company September 3, 1861, at Camp Saunders in Lynnfield. He was a painter. He was born March 17, 1836, in Danvers and his service was credited to Andover. His first enlistment was in the 4th Massachusetts Volunteer Infantry Company B (known as the Easton Light Infantry) April 16, 1861 (3 month), and was discharged from that unit July 22, 1861. He was discharged from the Sharpshooters September 24, 1864. He was single and his parents' names were Tobias and Margaret (Pert). Sources: Adjutant General Vol. 1–7 & Vol. 1–2; Microfilm Collection.

Harkness, Matthew, enlisted for three years as a private at age 22 into the 1st Company October 14, 1862, at Camp Wightman, Long Island, Boston, and received a $25.00 bounty. He was a tailor. He was born in 1840 at Scotland and his service was credited to Cambridge. He deserted six days after he enlisted. He was married. Sources: Adjutant General Vol. 1–7 & 1–2; Stokinger.

Harrington, Charles F., enlisted for three years as a private at age 18 into the 1st Company October 21, 1862, at Camp Wightman, Long Island, Boston, and received a $25.00 bounty. He was a clerk. He was born August 10, 1843, in Waltham and his service was credited to Boston. He was promoted to 1st sergeant July 15, 1864. He was wounded at the Battle of Ream's Station, Virginia, on August 25, 1864. He was discharged December 13, 1864. His parents' names were Charles and Mary Ann (Seaver). Sources: Adjutant General Vol. 1–7 & 1–2; Stokinger.

Hart, Charles N. (A)., enlisted for three years as a private at age 35 into the 1st Company October 25, 1862, at Camp Wightman, Long Island, Boston, and received a $25.00 bounty. He was single and a farmer. He was born in Castle, Maine, in 1827 and his service was credited to Boston. His service and discharge dates are unknown as there was no further information found regarding his service. Sources: Adjutant General Vol. 1–7 & 1–2; Stokinger.

Hatch, Cyrus K., enlisted for three years as a private at age 30 into the 1st Company September 2, 1861, at Camp Saunders in Lynnfield. He was a shoe maker. He was born in 1831 at Wilton, Maine, and his service was credited to Middleton. He was wounded October 14, 1863, at the Battle of Bristoe Station, Virginia. He was discharged September 3, 1864. He was single and his parents' names were Cyrus and Abigail (Teague). His brother Edwin B. also served in the same company. Sources: Adjutant General Vol. 1–7 & 1–2; Microfilm collection.

Hatch, Edwin B., enlisted for three years as a private at age 24 into the 1st Company October 29, 1862, at Camp Wightman, Long Island, Boston, and received a $25.00 bounty. He was a fireman. He was born in August of 1842 in Wilton, Maine, and his service was credited to Boston. He was wounded at the Battle of Gettysburg July 3, 1863. He was taken prisoner at the Battle of Cold Harbor, Virginia, June 2, 1864, and was released April 2, 1865. He was discharged June 24, 1865, by order of the War Department. He was single and his parents' names were Cyrus and Abigail (Teague). His brother Cyrus also served in the same company. He is interred at the Wilton Cemetery, third driveway, old part. Sources: Adjutant General Vol. 1–7 & 1–2; Stokinger; Microfilm Collection.

Heald, Austin M., enlisted for three years as a private at age 18 into the 1st Company August 15, 1862, at Camp Wightman, Long Island, Boston. He was a farmer. He was born January 6, 1844, in Carlisle and his service was credited to Boston-Carlisle. He died of disease January 30, 1863, at Windmill Point Hospital, Virginia. His brothers Thomas H. and Timothy W. also served in the same company. His parents' names were Benjamin Franklin and Susan Philbrook (Kimball). His mother was from Lowell. Sources: Adjutant General Vol. 1–7 & 1–2; Stokinger; Essex, *Carlisle*.

Heald, Thomas H., enlisted for three years as a private at age 23 into the 1st Company September 2, 1861, at Camp Saunders in Lynnfield. He was a tradesman. He was born April 7, 1838, in Carlisle and his service was credited to Lowell. He was promoted to sergeant. He was wounded June 30, 1862, at Nelson's Farm, Virginia, and received a disability discharge September 28, 1862, as a result of that wound. He was married and his parents' names were Benjamin Franklin and Susan Philbrook (Kimball). His mother was from Lowell. His brothers Austin M. and Timothy W. also served in the same company. Sources: Adjutant General Vol. 1–7 & 1–2; Essex, *Lowell;* Essex *Carlisle*.

Heald, Timothy W., enlisted for three years as a private at age 20 into the 1st Company March 24, 1863, at Camp Wightman, Long Island, Boston. He was a manufacturer. He was born July 16, 1842, in Carlisle and his service was credited to Carlisle. He first enlisted in 6th Massachusetts Volunteer Infantry Company B (known as the Groton Artillery) April 15, 1861 (3 months), and was discharged from that unit August 2, 1861. He was wounded May 4, 1862, at Yorktown, Virginia, and was given a disability discharge October 31, 1862, as a result of that wound. His brothers Thomas H. and Austin M. also served in the same company. His parents' names were Benjamin Franklin and Susan Philbrook (Kimball). His mother was from Lowell. Sources: Adjutant General Vol. 1–7 & 1–2; Stokinger; Essex, *Carlisle*.

Hetzel, Frederick, enlisted for three years as a private at age 31 into the 1st Company October 22, 1862, at Camp Wightman, Long Island, Boston, and received a $25.00 bounty. He was a saddler. He was born in 1830 in Russia and his service was credited to Boston. His service and discharge dates are unknown as there was no further information found regarding his service. He was single. Sources: Adjutant General Vol. 1–7 & 1–2; Stokinger.

Hill, Henry H., enlisted for three years as a private at age 40 into the 1st Company September 3, 1861, at Camp Saunders in Lynnfield. He was a shoemaker. He was born July 14, 1820, at Lyme, New Hampshire, and his service was credited to Stoneham. He was given a disability discharge April 26, 1862. He was single. Sources: Adjutant General Vol. 1–7 & 1–2; *Civil War Papers,* Stoneham.

Hill, Moses, enlisted for three years as a private at

age 38 into the 1st Company September 3, 1861, at Camp Saunders in Lynnfield. He was a stonemason. He was born March 22, 1823, in Bellingham and his service was credited to Medway. He was given a disability discharge October 13, 1862, at Washington, D.C. He died of disease October 29, 1862. He was married and had two children. His parents' names were Moses and Peris (Phipps). Sources: Adjutant General Vol. 1–7 & 1–2; Jameson, E. O., *Medway*.

Hills, Edwin T., enlisted for three years as a private at age 18 into the 1st Company September 3, 1861, at Camp Saunders in Lynnfield. He was born February 23, 1843, in Boston and his service was credited to Lynnfield-Boston. He first enlisted in 8th Massachusetts Volunteer Infantry Company D (known as the Lynn Light Infantry) April 15, 1861 (3 months), and was discharged from that unit August 1, 1861. He was listed as missing September 17, 1862, at the Battle of Antietam and "supposed killed." Sources indicate he received a disability discharge October 31, 1862. His parents' names were Joseph and Harriet (Robbins). Sources: Adjutant General Vol. 1–7 & 1–2; Lynnfield; Heritage, *Lynnfield*. Microfilm Collection.

Hixon, Egbert Oswell, enlisted for three years as a private at age 35 into the 1st Company September 4, 1861, at Camp Saunders in Lynnfield. He was a bootmaker. He was born August 1, 1824, in Medway and his service was credited to Medway. He first enlisted in 8th Massachusetts Volunteer Infantry Company D (known as the Lynn Light Infantry) April 30, 1861 (3 months), and was discharged from that unit August 1, 1861. He deserted from the Sharpshooters September 4, 1862. He then enlisted in the 124th Ohio Infantry Company "C" December 21, 1863, for three years under the name of Hicks and died of disease (malaria) November 22, 1864, at Nashville, Tennessee. He was married and had four children. His parents' names were Isaac and Persis (Adams). Sources: Adjutant General Vol. 1–7 & 1–2; Jameson, E. O., *Medway*.

Holston, John C., enlisted for three years as a private at age 34 into the 1st Company March 10, 1862, at Camp Wightman, Long Island, Boston. He was a manufacturer. He was born June 5, 1822, at Portland, Maine, and his service was credited to Lowell-Boston. He was wounded September 17, 1862, at the Battle of Antietam and was transferred to the 13th Veterans Reserve Corps Co. F in June of 1863. He reenlisted April 25, 1864, and received a $325.00 bounty. He was discharged from that unit in Maine November 13, 1865. He was married. His name was also identified as Holstein. Sources: Adjutant General Vol. 1–7 & 1–2; Adjutant First Company; Harnwell.

Houghton, Chilon, enlisted for three years as a private at age 23 into the 1st Company August 19, 1862, at Camp Wightman, Long Island, Boston, and received a $25.00 bounty. He was a gunsmith. He was born February 11, 1839, at Northbridge, and his service was credited to Sutton. He received a disability discharge March 9, 1863, at Falmouth, Virginia. He was single. His parents' names were Lysander and Lydia (White). Sources: Adjutant General Vol. 1–7 & 1–2; Stokinger; Harnwell.

Hudson, James L., enlisted for three years as a private at age 21 into the 1st Company September 2, 1861, at Camp Saunders in Lynnfield. He was a clerk. He was born in 1840 at New York, and his service was credited to Newburyport. He received a disability discharge May 9, 1862. He first enlisted in 8th Massachusetts Volunteer Infantry Company A (known as the Cushing Guards) April 15, 1861 (3 months), and was discharged from that unit August 1, 1861. He was single. Sources: Adjutant General Vol. 1–7 & 1–2; Harnwell.

Hunt, Josiah Harrison, enlisted for three years as a private at age 28 into the 1st Company October 31, 1862, at Camp Wightman, Long Island, Boston, and received a $25.00 bounty. He was a farmer. He was born September 14, 1839, at Braintree and his service was credited to Braintree. He was transferred to the 24th Veteran Reserve Corps Company E March 16, 1864, and received a disability discharge September 14, 1864. He was single and his parents' names were Josiah and Lucinda (Lane). Sources: Adjutant General Vol. 1–7 & 1–2; Stokinger.

Huse, David Scoby, enlisted for three years as a private at age 18 into the 1st Company September 3, 1861, at Camp Saunders in Lynnfield. He was a carpenter. He was born September 28, 1844, in Lowell and his service was credited to Danvers. He was given a disability discharge January 11, 1862, at Cumberland, Maryland. He was single and his parent' names were Thomas and Elizabeth (Scolby). Sources: Adjutant General Vol. 1–7 & 1–2; Microfilm Collection.

Hutchins, Edward, enlisted for three years as a private at age 36 into the 1st Company October 12, 1862, at Camp Wightman, Long Island, Boston, and received a $25.00 bounty. He was a printer. He was born January 3, 1828, at Dedham and his service was credited to Dedham. He was promoted to sergeant at some point. He was killed in action July 3, 1863, at the Battle of Gettysburg. His parents' names were Joseph and Sally (White). Sources: Adjutant General Vol. 1–7 & 1–2; Stokinger; Microfilm Collection. Harnwell.

Ingalls, Albert Pierce, enlisted for three years as a private at age 20 into the 1st Company March 17, 1862, at Camp Wightman, Long Island, Boston. He was a currier. He was born May 23, 1842, at Tyngsborough and his service was credited to Boston. He deserted August 29, 1862, and was captured by the Confederates and made a prisoner of war at Fairfax Court House, Virginia, September 23, 1862. He was paroled and sent to Alexandria, Virginia, in November

1862. There were no later records of his service found. He was single and his parents' names were Joel and Laura Ann (Wright); they were married in Westford. Sources: Adjutant General Vol. 1–7 & 1–2; Stokinger; Microfilm Collection.

Ingalls, Charles N., enlisted for three years as a sergeant at age 40 into the 1st Company August 19, 1861, at Camp Saunders in Lynnfield. He was a carpenter. He was born July 19, 1820, at North Andover and his service was credited to Danvers. He received a disability discharge December 15, 1862. He first married Hannah Judith Abbott of Andover. They had four children, but she died December 29, 1868. He then married Mary Jane Morse of Portland, Maine. He had settled in Danvers in 1851. His parents' names were Francis and Elizabeth (Foster). Sources: Adjutant General Vol. 1–7 & 1–2; Putnam, Eben, *Report of the Committee.*

Ingalls, Joseph S., enlisted for three years as a private at age 36 into the 1st Company September 2, 1861, at Camp Saunders in Lynnfield. He was a stonemason. He was born February 12, 1825, in Lynn and his service was credited to Danvers. He was shot through the body and killed at the Battle of Antietam September 17, 1862. His parents' names were Charles and Hannah (Shaw); they were married at Providence, Rhode Island, August 5, 1818. Joseph married Lydia Fowler (Eaton) and they had two children. Sources: Adjutant General Vol. 1–7 & 1–2; Essex, *Danvers.*

Jenkins, Henry, enlisted for three years as a sergeant at age 52 into the 1st Company September 2, 1861, at Camp Saunders in Lynnfield. He was a miller. He was born May 1, 1809, in Andover and his service was credited to Reading. He was given a disability discharge October 2, 1863, at Boston. He was married and had eight children, and his parents' names were Joel and Phebe (Gray). Sources: Adjutant General Vol. 1–7 & 1–2; Eaton, Lilley, *Reading;* Microfilm Collection.

Johnson, Alonzo, enlisted for three years as a private at age 22 into the 1st Company September 2, 1861, at Camp Saunders in Lynnfield. He was a hostler. He was born in 1839 at Manchester, New Hampshire, and his service was credited to Manchester, New Hampshire. He was single. His service and discharge dates are unknown as there was no further information found regarding his service. Sources: Adjutant General Vol. 1–7 & 1–2.

Kelly, Richard, enlisted for three years as a private at age 25 into the 1st Company October 6, 1862, at Camp Wightman, Long Island, Boston, and received a $25.00 bounty. He was a clerk. He was born in 1837 at Boston and his service was credited to Cambridge. He deserted four days after he enlisted. He was single. Sources: Adjutant General Vol. 1–7 & 1–2; Stokinger.

Kendall, Frank, enlisted for three years as a private at age 26 into the 1st Company October 22, 1862, at Camp Wightman, Long Island, Boston, and received a $25.00 bounty. He was a trader. He was born in 1836 at Boston and his service was credited to Boston. His service and discharge dates are unknown as there was no further information found regarding his service. He was single. Sources: Adjutant General Vol. 1–7 & 1–2

Kimball, Horace, enlisted for three years as a private at age 34 into the 1st Company September 2, 1861, at Camp Saunders in Lynnfield. He was a mason. He was born July 23, 1826, in Beverly, and his service was credited to Danvers. He was transferred to the 24th Veteran Reserve Corps Company F January 16, 1864, and was discharged September 5, 1864. His parents' names were Caleb and Mary (Pousland). He married Elizabeth Gray and had two children; she was the daughter of Josiah and Eunice. Sources: Adjutant General Vol. 1–7 & 1–2; Putnam, Eben, *Report of the Committee*; Harnwell.

King, James L., enlisted for three years as a private at age 36 into the 1st Company October 31, 1862, at Camp Wightman, Long Island, Boston, and received a $25.00 bounty. He was a harness maker. He was born April 26, 1826, at East Medway and his service was credited to Hopkinton. He received a disability discharge April 12, 1863, at Falmouth, Virginia. He resided in Boston prior to the Civil War. He died April 17, 1876, in Hopkinton and was interred at Mt. Auburn Cemetery. His death notice listed him serving in the 21st Regiment Company F. His wife, Angline, was from Worcester. They had two children, Herbert M. (also a harness maker) and Ella C. His parents' names were James H. and Nancy (Tileston). Sources: Adjutant General Vol. 1–7 & 1–2; Stokinger; Jameson, E. O., *Medway*; N.E.H. G.S. *Medway.*

Lawrence, Sayles, enlisted for three years as a private at age 30 into the 1st Company October 15, 1862, at Camp Wightman, Long Island, Boston, and received a $25.00 bounty. He was a farmer. He was born in 1832 at Portsmouth, New Hampshire, and his service was credited to Lexington. His service and discharge dates are unknown as there was no further information found regarding his service. He was married. Sources: Adjutant General Vol. 1–7 & 1–2; Stokinger.

Leavitt, Jerome, enlisted for three years as a private at age 27 into the 1st Company September 3, 1861, at Camp Saunders in Lynnfield. He was a shoemaker. He was born March 14, 1833, and his service was credited to Middleton-Buckland. He was given a disability discharge November 30, 1862. He reenlisted January 13, 1865, in the 13th Veterans Reserve Corps Co. F and received a $325.00 bounty. He was discharged from that unit December 15, 1865. He was married and had two children. His parents' names were Rouse and Anne. Sources: Adjutant General Vol. 1–7 & 1–2; Harnwell.

Leroy, Charles, enlisted for three years as a private at age 31 into the 1st Company October 25, 1862, at Camp Wightman, Long Island, Boston, and received a $25.00 bounty. He was a printer. He was born in 1831 in Montreal, Canada, and his service was credited to Boston. His service and discharge dates are unknown, as there was no further information found regarding his service. He was single. Sources: Adjutant General Vol. 1–7 & 1–2

Littlefield, David M., enlisted for three years as a private at age 23 into the 1st Company September 2, 1861, at Camp Saunders in Lynnfield. He was a farmer. He was born March 18, 1840, at Dexter, Maine, and his service was credited to Lowell. He first enlisted in 8th Massachusetts Volunteer Infantry Company A (known as the Cushing Guards) April 15, 1861 (3 months), and was discharged from that unit August 1, 1861. He was wounded at Yorktown, Virginia, in April or May 1862 and again at the Battle of Antietam on September 17, 1862. He was given a disability discharge December 12, 1862, as a result of those wounds. During his service in the Sharpshooters he was promoted to sergeant. Bicknell, in his journal, identifies him as his assistant, counselor, and advisor. His parents' names were Tobias and Lucy (Allen). Sources: Adjutant General Vol. 1–7 & 1–2; Bicknell. Luke; Harnwell.

Martin, Henry L., enlisted for three years as a sergeant at age 24 into the 1st Company August 19, 1861, at Camp Saunders in Lynnfield. He was a carpenter. He was born September 6, 1836, in Pawtucket, Rhode Island, and his service was credited to Newburyport. His first enlistment was in the 8th Massachusetts Volunteer Infantry Company A (known as the Cushing Guards) April 15, 1861 (3 month), and was discharged from that unit August 11, 1861. He then enlisted in the Sharpshooters; he was commissioned 1st lieutenant September 19, 1862. He was wounded in April or May 1862, at Yorktown, Virginia. He accompanied the body of General Landers to Massachusetts from Ball's Bluff, Virginia, on October 21, 1861. He was given a disability discharge from the Sharpshooters July 30, 1863. His parents' names were Calvin and Candis (Wade). Sources: Adjutant General Vol. 1–7 & 1–2; Creasey, George, *Newburyport.*

Martin, John M., enlisted for three years as a private at age 24 into the 1st Company September 3, 1861, at Camp Saunders in Lynnfield. He was a shoemaker. He was born in 1838 at Maine, and his service was credited to Lynn. He first enlisted in 8th Massachusetts Volunteer Infantry Company D (known as the Lynn Light Infantry) April 15, 1861 (3 months), and was discharged from that unit August 1, 1861. He then enlisted in the Sharpshooters and was given a disability discharge December 26, 1862. He reenlisted in the 56th Massachusetts Volunteer Infantry Company C December 28, 1863, and received a $325.00 bounty. He was promoted to hospital steward June 22, 1865, and was discharged July 12, 1865. He was married and had two children. Sources: Adjutant General Vol. 1–7 & 1–2; Harnwell.

Martin, Lysander, enlisted for three years as a private at age 26 into the 1st Company August 9, 1862, at Camp Wightman, Long Island, Boston, and received a $25.00 bounty. He was a farmer. He was born August 5, 1836, in Sutton and his service was credited to Sutton. He was wounded June 10, 1863, at Fredericksburg, Virginia, and died from that wound June 19, 1863, at Washington, D.C. His parents' names were Timothy and Rachel (Darling) and they were his dependents. Sources: Adjutant General Vol. 1–7 & 1–2; Rice, Franklin, *Sutton.*

Mason, Josiah, enlisted for three years as a private at age 39 into the 1st Company September 2, 1861, at Camp Wightman, Long Island, Boston. He was a farmer. He was born May 20, 1822, in Andover, and his service was credited to Andover. He received a disability discharge April 28, 1862, at Hampton, Virginia. He married Harriet L. Cahoon on September 7, 1843, and had four children. His parents' names were Thomas and Phebe (Wardwell). Sources: Adjutant General Vol. 1–7 & 1–2; Stokinger; Topsfield Historical Society, *Andover*; Topsfield Historical Society, *Middleton*; Harnwell.

Matt, Frank enlisted for three years as a private at age 38 into the 1st Company on September 8, 1862, at Camp Wightman, Long Island, Boston and received a $25.00 bounty. He was a shoemaker. He was born in 1824 in Austria and his service was credited to Boston, He reenlisted December 20, 1863, and received $60.00 and $325.00 bounties. He was transferred October 21, 1864, to 19th Massachusetts Volunteer Infantry Company K to complete his enlistment when the Sharpshooters were mustered out. He was discharged June 30, 1865. He was married and had two children. His name could have been Matts. Sources: Adjutant General Vol. 1–7 & 1–2; Stokinger.

Mattoon, Eleazer, enlisted for three years as a private at age 34 into the 1st Company September 2, 1861, at Camp Saunders in Lynnfield. He was a farmer. He was born in 1827 at Illinois and his service was credited to Bunker Hill, Illinois. He was given a disability discharge February 5, 1863, at Washington, D.C. Sources: Adjutant General Vol. 1–7 & 1–2; Bicknell, Luke.

Maxfield, Joseph B., enlisted for three years as a private at age 23 into the 1st Company September 2, 1861, at Camp Saunders in Lynnfield. He was a shoemaker. He was born in either 1837 or 1838 and his service was credited to South Danvers. He died of disease November 10, 1862, at Bolivar, Virginia. He was married and had two children. His exact cause of death was not indicated, but is believed by the author to be disease. Sources: Adjutant General Vol. 1–7 & 1–2; Harnwell.

Mayberry, Benjamin B., enlisted for three years as a private at age 36 into the 1st Company April 4, 1862, at Camp Wightman, Long Island, Boston. He was a trader. He was born March 16, 1825, at Windham, Maine, and his service was credited to Lowell. His first enlistment was in the 3rd Massachusetts Volunteer Cavalry Company M and he was discharged from that unit September 19, 1861. He then enlisted in the Sharpshooters and was given a disability discharge November 23, 1862, at Washington, D.C. He reenlisted December 29, 1863, in the 15th Battery Massachusetts Volunteer Light Artillery and received a $325.00 bounty. He was discharged from that unit August 4, 1865. He was married and his parents' names were Francis and Susannah (Stuart). Sources: Adjutant General Vol. 1–7 & 1–2; Stokinger; Dole, Samuel.

Mayers, Henry, enlisted for three years as a private at age 44 into the 1st Company September 9, 1862, at Camp Wightman, Long Island, Boston, and received a $25.00 bounty. He was a painter. He was born in 1818 at Dresden, Maine, and his service was credited to Charlestown. He was transferred to the 118th Veterans Reserve Corps 2nd Battalion January 26, 1864. He was discharged from that unit November 16, 1864. He was married and had two children. Sources: Adjutant General Vol. 1–7 & 1–2; Stokinger.

McDermott, Michael, enlisted for three years as a private at age 23 into the 1st Company October 25, 1862, at Camp Wightman, Long Island, Boston, and received a $25.00 bounty. He was an iron moulder. He was born in 1839 at Brandon, Vermont, and his service was credited to Boston. His service and discharge dates are unknown, as there was no further information found regarding his service. He was single. Sources: Adjutant General Vol. 1–7 & 1–2

McDonald, William, enlisted for three years as a private at age 40 into the 1st Company October 4, 1862, at Camp Wightman, Long Island, Boston, and received a $25.00 bounty. He was a laborer. He was born in 1822 at St. John, New Brunswick, Canada, and his service was credited to Cambridge. His service and discharge dates are unknown, as there was no further information found regarding his service. He was married. Sources: Adjutant General Vol. 1–7 & 1–2.

McLaughlin, Benjamin L., enlisted for three years as a private at age 22 into the 1st Company March 17, 1862, at Camp Wightman, Long Island, Boston. He was a farmer. He was born May 24, 1839, in Georgetown and his service was credited to Newburyport. He was wounded May 30, 1864, near Cold Harbor, Virginia. He became ill and died from that wound June 23, 1864, at David's Island, New York Harbor, where his right arm had been amputated. He was interred at New York Harbor. His remains were claimed by family or friends and were returned to Georgetown. He was single and his parents' names were Benjamin and Abigail S. (Tyler). Sources: Adjutant General Vol. 1–7 & 1–2; Stokinger; Essex, *Georgetown;* Essex, *Rowely*; Creasey, George, *Newburyport*; U.S. Quartermaster's Department.

Miller, James, enlisted for three years as a private at age 22 into the 1st Company October 4, 1862, at Camp Wightman, Long Island, Boston, and received a $25.00 bounty. He was a boilermaker. He was born in 1840 at New York, New York, and his service was credited to Cambridge. He deserted October 10, 1862, six days after he enlisted. He was single. Sources: Adjutant General Vol. 1–7 & 1–2.

Montague, John F., enlisted for three years as a private at age 21 into the 1st Company October 4, 1862, at Camp Wightman, Long Island, Boston, and received a $25.00 bounty. He was a watchmaker. He was born in 1841 in Ireland and his service was credited to Cambridge. He deserted October 10, 1862, six days after he enlisted. He was single. Sources: Adjutant General Vol. 1–7 & 1–2; Stokinger.

Moody, James S., enlisted for three years as a private at age 28 into the 1st Company September 2, 1861, at Camp Saunders in Lynnfield. He was a shoemaker. He was born in 1833 at Landaff, New Hampshire, and his service was credited to Stoneham. He first enlisted in 6th Massachusetts Volunteer Infantry Company L (known as the Stoneham Light Infantry) April 16, 1861, (3 months), and was discharged from that unit August 2, 1861. He was wounded April 19, 1861, while trapped in a train car at Baltimore, Maryland, during the riots. He then enlisted in the Sharpshooters and received a disability discharge February 17, 1862, at Poolesville, Maryland. He then enlisted in the 50th Massachusetts Volunteer Infantry Company C (9 months) September 16, 1862, and was discharged from that unit August 24, 1863. He reenlisted on January 11, 1864, in the 3rd Massachusetts Heavy Artillery Company E, received a $325.00 bounty, and deserted from that unit April 28, 1864. He was married and had two children. His parents' name were Moses and Betsy. Sources: Adjutant General Vol. 1–7 & 1–2; Harnwell.

Moore, William, enlisted for three years as a private at age 30 into the 1st Company March 7, 1862, at Camp Wightman, Long Island, Boston. He was a farmer. He was born in 1832 at Boxborough and his service was credited to Carlisle. He died of disease September 9, 1862, at Fort McHenry Hospital, Maryland. He was married. The Company muster rolls indicate his name as More. His parents' names were Sampson and Mary H. Sources: Adjutant General Vol. 1–7 & 1–2; Harnwell.

Morris, Louis, enlisted for three years as a private at age 24 into the 1st Company October 28, 1862, at Camp Wightman, Long Island, Boston. He was a butcher. He was born in 1838 and his service was credited to Boston. He was transferred to the 2nd Massachusetts Volunteer Cavalry Company B. He deserted February 18, 1863, and was captured April 30, 1864. He again deserted July 8, 1864, while in confinement. At the time of his second desertion, he is recorded as having attained the rank of sergeant. Sources: Adjutant General Vol. 1–7 & 1–2; Stokinger.

Morse, Henry, enlisted for three years as a private at age 18 into the 1st Company October 29, 1862, at Camp Wightman, Long Island, Boston, and received a $25.00 bounty. He was a clerk. He was born in 1844 at Detroit, Michigan, and his service was credited to Boston. He reenlisted as a Sharpshooter and received $325.00 and $60.00 bounties. He was missing in action and captured by the Confederates at the Spotsylvania Court House. He was held in Florence and Andersonville prisons. He was exchanged as a prisoner of war March 8, 1865. He was discharged from that unit June 12, 1865. He was single. Sources: Adjutant General Vol. 1–7 & 1–2; Stokinger.

Mudgett, Isaac Newton, enlisted for three years as a private at age 23 into the 1st Company September 2, 1861, at Camp Saunders in Lynnfield. He was a shoemaker. He was born May 30, 1838, in Tamworth, New Hampshire, and his service was credited to Lynn. His first enlistment was in the 8th Massachusetts Volunteer Infantry Company D (known as the Lynn Light Infantry) April 15, 1861 (3 month), and was discharged from that unit August 11, 1861. He then enlisted in the Sharpshooters. He was promoted to sergeant October 22, 1863, and was commissioned captain July 5, 1864. He was taken prisoner of war on August 25, 1864, at Ream's Station, Virginia, and parole date was not indicated. He was transferred to the 19th Massachusetts Volunteer Infantry Company F at the time the Sharpshooters were mustered out (Ref. O.R.'s I 40, 42). He was discharged May 17, 1865. He was married and had two children; his parents' names were Isaac and Mercy (Hobbs). His brother Jacob also served in the same company. Sources: Adjutant General Vol. 1–7 & 1–2; Root, Elihu; Mudgett, Mildred, *Descendents*.

Mudgett, Jacob Hobbs, enlisted for three years as a private at age 20 into the 1st Company September 2, 1861, at Camp Saunders in Lynnfield. He was a machinist. He was born February 19, 1842, in Tamworth, New Hampshire, and his service was credited to Dover, New Hampshire. He was transferred to the U.S. Engineers October 26, 1862, and discharged September 24, 1864. He also served in the 1st New Hampshire Infantry Company "A." He was single and his parents' names were Isaac and Mercy (Hobbs). His brother Isaac also served in the same company. Sources: Adjutant General Vol. 1–7 & 1–2; Mudgett, Mildred, *Descendents*.

Orcutt, Joseph C., enlisted for three years as a private at age 23 into the 1st Company September 2, 1861, at Camp Saunders in Lynnfield. He was a shoemaker. He was born in 1838 at Tewksbury, and his service was credited to North Reading. He deserted September 17, 1862, at the Battle of Antietam. He was married and had one child. His parents' names were Charles and Jennet T. Sources: Adjutant General Vol. 1–7 & 1–2; Harnwell.

Packard, William H., enlisted for three years as a private at age 22 into the 1st Company September 2, 1861, at Camp Saunders in Lynnfield. He was a manufacturer. He was born January 20, 1840, at Kerryfield, Maine, and his service was credited to Lowell. He first enlisted in 6th Massachusetts Volunteer Infantry Company A (known as the National Greys) on April 15, 1861 (3 months), and was discharged from that unit August 2, 1861. While his unit was passing through Baltimore it was attacked by a mob. He was promoted to sergeant in July of 1863 while with the Sharpshooters. He reenlisted December 29, 1863, and received $60.00 and $325.00 bounties. He was taken prisoner of war August 19, 1864, at Weldon Railroad, Virginia, and released March 1, 1865. He received an additional three months' pay due to the hardships he encountered in Confederate prisons. He was discharged June 29, 1865. He was single. He was also identified as Packham. His parents' names were Simon and Nancy (Jordan). Sources: Adjutant General Vol. 1–7 & 1–2; Harnwell.

Parmenter, Marcus Morton, enlisted for three years as a private at age 22 into the 1st Company March 10, 1862, at Camp Wightman, Long Island, Boston. He was a farmer. He was born February 5, 1839, in Holden and his service was credited to Shirley. He was killed in action September 17, 1862, at the Battle of Antietam. His parents' names were Joshua and Julia (Lapling). His mother was from Leominster. Sources: Adjutant General Vol. 1–7 & 1–2; Stokinger; Microfilm collection.

Pendergast, William I., enlisted for three years as a private at age 30 into the 1st Company September 2, 1861, at Camp Saunders in Lynnfield. He was a clerk. He was born in 1831 and his service was credited to Boston. He was given a disability discharge February 26, 1863, near Falmouth, Virginia. He was single. Sources: Adjutant General Vol. 1–7 & 1–2.

Penniman, Nathaniel W., enlisted for three years as a private at age 40 into the 1st Company October 11, 1862, at Camp Wightman, Long Island, Boston, and received a $25.00 bounty. He was a music teacher. He was born March 16, 1822, at Braintree and his service was credited to Reading. He reenlisted as a Sharpshooter February 16, 1864, and received $325.00 and $60.00 bounties. He was wounded May 12, 1864, at the Spotsylvania Court House and was given a disability discharge July 12, 1864. He was single. His parents' names were Nathaniel and Elizabeth (Hollis). Sources: Adjutant General Vol. 1–7 & 1–2; Stokinger; Eaton, Lilley, *Reading*; Harnwell.

Perley, John L., enlisted for three years as 1st sergeant at age 24 into the 1st Company August 19, 1861, at Camp Saunders in Lynnfield. He was a baker. He was born December 21, 1837, in Georgetown and his service was credited to Georgetown. His first enlistment was in the 8th Massachusetts Volunteer Infantry Company A (known as the Cushing Guards) April 15, 1861 (3 month), and was discharged from that unit August 1, 1861. He then enlisted in the Sharpshooters. He was commissioned 2nd lieutenant May 21, 1862. He resigned that commission and was discharged July 12, 1862. He was commissioned 1st lieutenant in the 4th Massachusetts Volunteer Cavalry Company D January 5, 1864. He was taken prisoner of war August 5, 1864, at Palatka, Florida. He died of disease as a prisoner November 16, 1864, while at Charleston, South Carolina. He was married and had one child; his parents' names were Gilman and Mary (Picket). Sources: Adjutant General Vol. 1–7 & 1–2; Essex, *Georgetown*.

Perry, Joseph L., enlisted for three years as a private at age 24 into the 1st Company March 7, 1862, at Camp Wightman, Long Island, Boston. He was a farmer. He was born December 12, 1837, at Litchfield, Maine, and his service was credited to Concord. He was given a disability discharge November 13, 1862. He was married and his parents' names were Otis and Poly (Masoon). Sources: Adjutant General Vol. 1–7 & 1–2; Stokinger.

Pingree, Walter W. enlisted for three years as a private at age 30 into the 1st Company March 17, 1862, at Camp Wightman, Long Island, Boston. He was a farmer. He was born February 27, 1832, in Rowley and his service was credited to Newburyport. He died of disease September 16, 1864, at Harwood Hospital, Washington, D.C., and was interred at Arlington National Cemetery. He was single and his parents' names were John and Elizabeth (Herrick). Sources: Adjutant General Vol. 1–7 & 1–2; Stokinger; U.S. Quartermaster's Department.

Plimpton, Amos G., enlisted for three years as a private at age 19 into the 1st Company July 31, 1862, at Camp Wightman, Long Island, Boston, and received a $25.00 bounty. He was a yeoman. He was born September 27, 1842, at Wardsboro, Vermont, and his service was credited to Northbridge. He reenlisted as a Sharpshooter February 16, 1864 and received $325.00 and $60.00 bounties. He was wounded May 13, 1864, at the Spotsylvania Court House, Virginia. He was transferred to the 19th Massachusetts Volunteer Infantry Company K September 18, 1864, and given a disability discharge from that unit July 6, 1865. Company muster rolls indicate his name as Plympton and that he was born in Wardsborough, Vermont. He was single and his parents' names were Gardener and Hannah (Whitney). Sources: Adjutant General Vol. 1–7 & 1–2; Stokinger; Adjutant First Company; Baldwin, Thomas, *Northbridge*; Harnwell.

Plummer, William, was commissioned as a captain at age 39 into the 1st Company October 19, 1862, at Camp Wightman, Long Island, Boston. He was a lawyer. He was born November 29, 1823, in New Market, New Hampshire, and his service was credited to Cambridge. He was wounded July 3, 1863, at the Battle of Gettysburg. He was given a disability discharge September 26, 1863, by Special Order of the War Department (Ref. O.R.'s I, 25, "Report of men going to the front to silence Confederates"). It was done in such a manner that Plummer complimented his men. He graduated from Holy Cross in 1845 and was admitted to the bar in 1848. He married Emily J. Lord of Cambridge; they lived in Lexington and had seven children. His grandfather was a leading lawyer, statesman, U.S. senator and governor of New Hampshire. His father was a congressman. His parents' names were William and Margaret (Mead). Sources: Adjutant General Vol. 1–7 & 1–2; Root, Elihu; Baldwin, Thomas, *Cambridge*; Hudson, Charles, *Lexington*.

Potter, Joseph M., enlisted for three years as a private at age 36 into the 1st Company October 22, 1862, at Camp Wightman, Long Island, Boston, and received a $25.00 bounty. He was a carpenter. He was born in 1826 at Providence, Rhode Island, and his service was credited to Boston. His service and discharge dates are unknown as there was no further information found regarding his service. He was married. Sources: Adjutant General Vol. 1–7 & 1–2.

Pray, Joseph L., enlisted for three years as a private at age 24 into the 1st Company March 7, 1862, at Camp Wightman, Long Island, Boston. He was born in 1838 and his service was credited to Lowell. There is little known of his service. In the Company muster rolls, he is listed as having died of disease sometime in 1862. Sources: Adjutant General Vol. 1–7 & 1–2.

Pray, Otis, R., enlisted for three years as a private at age 18 into the 1st Company September 2, 1861, at Camp Saunders in Lynnfield. He was a farmer. He was born in 1843 and his service was credited to Great Falls, New Hampshire. He deserted September 17, 1862, at the Battle of Antietam. He was single. Sources: Adjutant General Vol. 1–7 & 1–2.

Price, John, III, enlisted for three years as a private at age 31 into the 1st Company September 2, 1861, at Camp Saunders in Lynnfield. He was a carpenter. He was born in 1831 at Salem and his service was credited to South Danvers. He died of disease February 16, 1862. He was married and his parents' names were John and Susan (Fillebrown). His birth is not found in Salem's Vital Records; his father was born there in 1803. Sources: Adjutant General Vol. 1–7 & 1–2; Essex, *Salem*; Essex, *Danvers*.

Randall, Lot J., enlisted for three years as a private at age 21 into the 1st Company November 7, 1862, at Camp Wightman, Long Island, Boston, and received a $25.00 bounty. He was a farmer. He was born in 1841 at Wilton, Maine, and his service was credited to Boston-Reading. He reenlisted as a Sharpshooter February 16, 1864, and received $325.00 and $60.00 bounties. He was transferred to the 19th Massachusetts Volunteer Infantry Company K October 21, 1864, as the Sharpshooters were being mustered out and he had time yet to serve. He was single. Brooks could have been a town or village in Maine where he lived. His parents' names were Jacob and Sally. Sources: Adjutant General Vol. 1–7 & 1–2; Stokinger; Harnwell.

Reed, Leonard S., enlisted for three years as a private at age 41 into the 1st Company September 2, 1861, at Camp Saunders in Lynnfield. He was a morocco dresser. He was born March 12, 1821, at Westford and his service was credited to Danvers. According to one source he died of disease August 5, 1862, while on a steamer near Harrison's Landing, Virginia. According to another, he died of disease August 7, 1862, while at Camp Parley, Maryland. He was married and had three children; his parents' names were Joel and Joanna (Chandler). Sources: Adjutant General Vol. 1–7 & 1–2; Microfilm Collection..

Reynolds, William Francis, enlisted for three years as a private at age 21 into the 1st Company August 19, 1861, at Camp Saunders in Lynnfield. He was born May 31, 1837, at Smithfield, Rhode Island, and his service was credited to Lynnfield. He received a disability discharge February 17, 1862, due to fever while at Poolesville, Maryland. His parents' names were Samuel E. and Lydia A. (Sholes). Sources: Adjutant General Vol. 1–7 & 1–2; Microfilm Collection..

Rhoades, William W., enlisted for three years as a private at age 28 into the 1st Company September 2, 1861, at Camp Saunders in Lynnfield. He was a butcher. He was born in 1833 at Lynn, and his service was credited to Saugus. He died of disease November 14, 1862, as a paroled prisoner of war at Annapolis, Maryland. There is no indication where he was taken prisoner or paroled. He was married and had two children. His parents' names were William and Miriam (Burrill). Sources: Adjutant General Vol. 1–7 & 1–2; Harnwell.

Rice, Cortis N., enlisted for three years as a private at age 24 into the 1st Company March 24, 1862, at Camp Wightman, Long Island, Boston. He was a manufacturer. He was born September 30, 1837, at Sheldon, Vermont, and his service was credited to Lowell. He was given a disability discharge December 23, 1862, at Providence, Rhode Island. He was single. His parents' names were Willis and Marancy (Davis). Sources: Adjutant General Vol. 1–7 & 1–2; Stokinger. Harnwell.

Rines, Jason S., enlisted for three years as a private at age 28 into the 1st Company September 2, 1861, at Camp Saunders in Lynnfield. He was a caulker. He was born August 27, 1834, at Washington, Maine, and his service was credited to Newburyport. He first enlisted in 8th Massachusetts Volunteer Infantry Company A (known as the Cushing Guards) April 15, 1861 (3 months), and was discharged from that unit August 2, 1861. He reenlisted while with the Sharpshooters December 30, 1863, and received $60.00 and $325.00 bounties. He was promoted to corporal, date not indicated. He was killed in action September 24, 1864, at the Battle of Petersburg, Virginia. He was married and had two children, and his parents' names were Isaac and Nancy. Sources: Adjutant General Vol. 1–7 & 1–2.

Roach, William, enlisted for three years as a private at age 28 into the 1st Company September 9, 1862, at Camp Wightman, Long Island, Boston, and received a $25.00 bounty. He was a carpenter. He was born May 15, 1834, at Wilton, Maine, and his service was credited to Boston. He was given a disability discharge January 20, 1864, at Washington, D.C. His parents' names were Selmen and Rebecca Jones. Sources: Adjutant General Vol. 1–7 & 1–2. Harnwell.

Roundy, George Pickering, enlisted for three years as a private at age 28 into the 1st Company September 2, 1861, at Camp Saunders in Lynnfield. He was a miner. He was born July 12, 1835, at Marblehead and his service was credited to Lynn. He was killed in action July 3, 1863, at the Battle of Gettysburg. He was single and his parents' names were George and Tabitha (Calhoon). Sources: Adjutant General Vol. 1–7 & 1–2; Essex, *Marblehead.*

Runnels, William F., enlisted for three years as a private at age 21 into the 1st Company September 2, 1861, at Camp Saunders in Lynnfield. He was a riverman. He was born February 18, 1842, at Pittsfield, Maine, and his service was credited to Pittsfield, Massachusetts. He received a disability discharge February 17, 1862, while at Poolesville, Maryland. He was single. His parents' names were Greenwood and Louisa (Mahoney). Sources: Adjutant General Vol. 1–7 & 1–2; Harnwell.

Saunders, John, was commissioned as an officer, captain at age 38 into the 1st Company September 2, 1861, at Camp Saunders in Lynnfield. He was a carpenter. He was born June 17, 1825, in Ashburton, England, and his service was credited to Salem. He was killed in action September 17, 1862, at the Battle of Antietam. Camp Saunders was named for him (Ref. O.R.'s I, 19 organizational, battle position September 17, 1862, and casualty list). His parents' names were William and Elizabeth (Butchers). Sources: Adjutant General Vol. 1–7 & 1–2; Root, Elihu; Harnwell.

Schmitt, Jacob, enlisted for three years as a private at age 38 into the 1st Company October 22, 1862, at Camp Wightman, Long Island, Boston, and received a $25.00 bounty. He was a saddler. He was born in

1824 in Germany and his service was credited to Boston. His service and discharge dates are unknown as there was no further information found regarding his service. He was single. Sources: Adjutant General Vol. 1–7 & 1–2.

Seavey, William H., enlisted for three years as a private at age 20 into the 1st Company September 2, 1861, at Camp Saunders in Lynnfield. He was a farmer. He was born in 1844 and his service was credited to Litchfield, New Hampshire. He was discharged September 2, 1864. Sources: Adjutant General Vol. 1–7 & 1–2.

Severance, Joshua, enlisted for three years as a private at age 37 into the 1st Company September 3, 1861, at Camp Saunders in Lynnfield. He was a painter. He was born March 15, 1822, at Orrington, Maine, and his service was credited to Danvers. He was given a disability discharge July 11, 1863, at Washington, D.C. He was married to Martha and had one child. His parents' names were Rueben and Sally. Sources: Adjutant General Vol. 1–7 & 1–2; Putman, Eben, *Report of the Committee*.

Shattuck, Oramel C., enlisted for three years as a corporal at age 20 into the 1st Company September 3, 1861, at Camp Saunders in Lynnfield. He was an artist. He was born January 11, 1841, at Rockford, Illinois, and his service was credited to Lowell. He deserted May 3, 1862, while at Fredericksburg, Maryland. He surrendered May 8, 1865, under the President's Amnesty Proclamation, and he was mustered out of the service May 15, 1865. He was single, and his parents' names were Obil and Martha (Conant). Sources: Adjutant General Vol. 1–7 & 1–2; Microfilm Collection; Harnwell.

Shepard, James W., enlisted for three years as a private at age 21 into the 1st Company March 17, 1862, at Camp Wightman, Long Island, Boston. He was a brakeman. He was born in 1841 at Hanover and his service was credited to Charlestown. He was last seen fighting guerrillas at Germania Ford, Virginia, on November 27, 1863, where he was taken as a prisoner of war. The Confederates returned him March 16, 1865, and he was discharged the same day. Sources: Adjutant General Vol. 1–7 & 1–2.

Shepard, Lewis C., enlisted for three years as a private at age 25 into the 7th Massachusetts Volunteer Infantry Band June 15, 1861, at Camp Old Colony in Taunton. He was a machinist. He was born March 19, 1838, at Mansfield and his service was credited to Milford. He was discharged August 11, 1862, from the 7th Massachusetts. He reenlisted in the 1st Company Sharpshooters February 29, 1864, and received a $325.00 bounty. He was transferred to the 19th Massachusetts Volunteer Infantry Unassigned (no date indicated), probably as the Sharpshooters were mustering out and he had time yet to serve. He was discharged May 6, 1865. One source indicates he was killed in action June 13, 1864, at the Battle of Cold Harbor, Virginia. Company muster rolls do not indicate this. His parents' names were Seth and Ann J. (Wetherell). Sources: Adjutant General Vol. 1–7 & 1–2; Stokinger; Essex, *Mansfield*; Ballou, Adin, *Milford*.

Simonds, Joel H., enlisted for three years as a private at age 22 into the 1st Company September 2, 1861, at Camp Saunders in Lynnfield. He was a clerk. He was born in 1839 and his service was credited to Charlestown. He was given a disability discharge March 6, 1863, at Philadelphia, Pennsylvania. He was single, and his parents' names were Joel and Emeline (Blodgett). Sources: Adjutant General Vol. 1–7 & 1–2.

Sleeper, Solomon, enlisted for three years as a private at age 30 into the 1st Company September 2, 1861, at Camp Saunders in Lynnfield. He was an operative. He was born in 1831 at New Hampshire, and his service was credited to Lowell. He was given a disability discharge January 20, 1864, at Washington, D.C. He was married. Sources: Adjutant General Vol. 1–7 & 1–2; Harnwell.

Smart, Joseph T., enlisted for three years as a private at age 30 into the 1st Company September 2, 1861, at Camp Saunders in Lynnfield. He was a carpenter. He was born in 1831 and his service was credited to Danvers. He was taken prisoner of war August 25, 1864, at Ream's Station, Virginia. He died of disease as a prisoner October 23, 1864, while at Salisbury, North Carolina. He was single. Sources: Adjutant General Vol. 1–7 & 1–2.

Smith, James, enlisted for three years as a private at age 26 into the 1st Company October 25, 1862, at Camp Wightman, Long Island, Boston. He was a tinsmith. He was born in 1836 and his service was credited to Boston. His service and discharge dates are unknown as there was no further information found regarding his service. He was married. Sources: Adjutant General Vol. 1–7 & 1–2.

Smith, John, enlisted for three years as a private at age 35 into the 1st Company November 29, 1862, at Camp Wightman, Long Island, Boston, and received a $25.00 bounty. He was a mechanic. He was born in 1827 at Philadelphia, Pennsylvania, and his service was credited to Boston. He deserted January 11, 1863, near Falmouth, Virginia. He was caught, tried by a general court–martial and shot to death September 29, 1863, at Munsonville, Virginia. He was married. Sources: Adjutant *General* Vol. 1–7 & 1–2; Stokinger.

Smith, Thomas Cook, enlisted for three years as a private at age 41 into the 1st Company December 12, 1863, at Camp Wightman, Long Island, Boston, and received $325.00 and $60.00 bounties. He was a butcher. He was born September 9, 1822, at Brighton and his service was credited to Brighton. He was wounded June 18, 1864, at Spotsylvania, Virginia. He was transferred to the 19th Massachusetts Volunteer Infantry Company K October 21, 1864, as the Sharpshooters were being mustered out and he had time yet to serve. He was married, and his parents' names were Isaac and Ann B. (Baker). Sources: Adjutant General Vol. 1–7 & 1–2; Stokinger; Microfilm Collection.

Snow, Charles H., enlisted for three years as a private at age 22 into the 1st Company November 24, 1862, at Camp Wightman, Long Island, Boston, and received a $25.00 bounty. He was a farmer. He was born in 1840 at China, Maine, and his service was credited to Cambridge. He deserted, date and location not indicated. Sources: Adjutant General Vol. 1–7 & 1–2; Stokinger.

Snow, Edwin A., enlisted for three years as a private at age 22 into the 1st Company September 2, 1861, at Camp Saunders in Lynnfield. He was a clerk. He was born in 1839 and his service was credited to Boston. He was taken prisoner September 17, 1862, at the Battle of Antietam. He was paroled as a prisoner of war October 6, 1862, and sent to Alexandria, Virginia, in November of 1862. There was no further record of his service found after he was paroled. Sources: Adjutant General Vol. 1–7 & 1–2.

Snow, Warren, enlisted for three years as a private at age 27 into the 1st Company September 2, 1861, at Camp Saunders in Lynnfield. He was a storekeeper. He was born December 7, 1834, at Danvers and his service was credited to Lynn. He first enlisted in 8th Massachusetts Volunteer Infantry Company F (known as the City Guards) April 15, 1861 (3 months), and was discharged from that unit August 1, 1861. He then enlisted in the Sharpshooters. He was killed in action September 17, 1862, at the Battle of Antietam. He was single, and his parents' names were Joseph and Elenor (Carroll). Sources: Adjutant General Vol. 1–7 & 1–2; Essex, *Danvers*.

Stetson, Reuben, enlisted for three years as a private at age 52 into the 1st Company March 10, 1862, at Camp Wightman, Long Island, Boston. He was a farmer. He was born October 31, 1810, and his service was credited to Hanover. He was given a disability discharge December 13, 1862, at Washington, D.C. Then, as a blacksmith, he enlisted in the 2nd Massachusetts Volunteer Cavalry Company K and received a $325.00 bounty. He was transferred to the 72nd Company 2nd Battalion Veterans Reserve Corps and was discharged from that unit March 13, 1865. There appears to be some misinformation regarding his age. Sources indicate ages 35 and 43 at enlistment, yet *Hanover* indicates his age at 52. He was married, and his parents' names were Samuel and Abigail (Monroe). Sources: Adjutant General Vol. 1–7 & 1–2; Stokinger; Dwelley, Jedediah, *Hanover*.

Stone, Charles, enlisted for three years as a wagoner at age 21 into the 1st Company September 2, 1861, at Camp Saunders in Lynnfield. He was a tanner. He was born October 30, 1839, at Beverly and his service was credited to Salem. He reenlisted while with the Sharpshooters on February 16, 1864, and received $60.00 and $325.00 bounties. He was promoted to corporal July 1, 1864. He was captured by the Confederates on August 25, 1864, at the Battle of Ream's Station, Virginia. He was held in prison camps at Salisbury, Libby and Belle Island. He was paroled as a prisoner of war March 10, 1865. He was single, and his parents' names were William and Hannah (Evans). His mother was his dependent. Sources: Adjutant General Vol. 1–7; N.E.H.G.S., *Stow*; Essex, *Danvers*.

Strong, Martin V., enlisted for three years as a private at age 25 into the 1st Company September 2, 1861, at Camp Saunders in Lynnfield. He was a machinist. He was born in 1836 and his service was credited to Lowell. He first enlisted in 6th Massachusetts Volunteer Infantry Company H (known as the Watson Light Guards) April 16, 1861 (3 months), and was discharged from that unit August 2, 1861. He then enlisted in the Sharpshooters. He was killed September 17, 1862, at the Battle of Antietam. He was single. Sources: Adjutant General Vol. 1–7 & 1–2.

Sturtevant, Daniel Green, enlisted for three years as a private at age 39 into the 1st Company September 2, 1861, at Camp Saunders in Lynnfield. He was a shoemaker. He was born April 1, 1822, in Stoneham and his service was credited to Stoneham. He was given a disability discharge January 31, 1863, from the Sharpshooters. He reenlisted July 25, 1864, in the 13th Veterans Reserve Corps Company A and received a $325.00 bounty. He was discharged from that unit November 17, 1865. He married Laura G. Young, and his parents' names were Heman and Sarah (Green). His brother, John, also served in the 2nd Company of Sharpshooters and Veteran Reserve Corps. Sources: Adjutant General Vol. 1–7 & 1–2; Essex, *Stoneham*; *Civil War Papers*.

Temple, David H., enlisted for three years as a private at age 33 into the 1st Company September 2, 1861, at Camp Saunders Lynnfield. He was a sportsman. He was born August 3, 1826, at Southborough and his service was credited to Marlborough. He was discharged September 8, 1864. He was married, and his parents' names were David and Elizabeth (Guard). Sources: Adjutant General Vol. 1–7 & 1–2; Lainhart, Ann, *Census*; Coco, Gregory, *Ball's Bluff*; Microfilm Collection.

Tenny, Whitney, enlisted for three years as a private at age 25 into the 1st Company October 23, 1862, at Camp Wightman, Long Island, Boston, and received a $25.00 bounty. He was a weaver. He was born September 23, 1835, at Windham, Vermont, and his service was credited to Boston. His service and discharge dates are unknown as there was no further information found regarding his service with the

Sharpshooters. It appears he was drafted at Londonderry May 5, 1864, into the 2nd Vermont Regiment Company I and served in that unit until July 15, 1865, when he was discharged. He was married, and his parents' names were Jonathan and Anna (Laughton). Sources: Adjutant General Vol. 1-7 & 1-2; Stokinger; Microfilm Collection; Peck, Theodore, *Vermont.*

Thompson, Edward, enlisted for three years as a private at age 21 into the 1st Company October 22, 1862, at Camp Wightman, Long Island, Boston, and received a $25.00 bounty. He was a clerk. He was born in 1841 in Maine and his service was credited to Boston. His service and discharge dates are unknown as there was no further information found regarding his service. He was single. Sources: Adjutant General Vol. 1-7 & 1-2.

Townsend, Thaddeus J., enlisted for three years as a private at age 44 into the 1st Company September 29, 1862, at Camp Wightman, Long Island, Boston, and received a $25.00 bounty. He was a butcher. He was born April 18, 1818, in Brighton and his service was credited to Brookline. He was discharged September 8, 1864. He was single, and his parents' names were Samuel and Esther (Jackson). His father was his dependent. Sources: Adjutant General Vol. 1-7 & 1-2; Stokinger; Harnwell.

Trask, Alfred M., enlisted for three years as a private at age 21 into the 1st Company September 2, 1861, at Camp Saunders in Lynnfield. He was a butcher. He was born January 25, 1840, at Danvers and his service was credited to Danvers. He was given a disability discharge November 13, 1862, at Washington, D.C. He married Mary K. Griffith of South Danvers, and his parents' names were Alfred and Mary (Blackley). His father was from Wendell, New Hampshire, and mother from Sandwich, New Hampshire. Sources: Adjutant General Vol. 1-7 & 1-2; Putman, Eben, *Report of the Committee.*

Travis, Nathan F., enlisted for three years as a private at age 30 into the 1st Company September 2, 1861, at Camp Saunders in Lynnfield. He was a farmer. He was born in 1831 at Hopkinton, New Hampshire, and his service was credited to North Reading. He died of disease October 4, 1861, while at Poolesville, Maryland. He was married and had three children. His parents' names were James and Nancy (Foster). Sources: Adjutant General Vol. 1-7 & 1-2; Harnwell.

Upton, Austin, enlisted for three years as a private at age 35 into the 1st Company September 2, 1861, at Camp Saunders in Lynnfield. He was a shoemaker. He was born June 28, 1825, at Danvers and his service was credited to Danvers. He reenlisted while with the Sharpshooters February 16, 1864, and received $60.00 and $325.00 bounties. He was promoted to corporal. He was wounded and captured by the Confederates May 12, 1864, at the Battle of Spotsylvania Court House, Virginia. He died from that wound. He was married, and his parents' names were Captain Eli and Matilda (Parker). His mother was his dependent. Sources: Adjutant General Vol. 1-7 & 1-2; Stokinger; Putman, Eben, *Report of the Committee*; Essex, *Danvers.*

Van Moll, Richard A., enlisted for three years as a private at age 21 into the 1st Company September 2, 1861, at Camp Saunders in Lynnfield. He was a shoemaker. He was born November 27, 1840, at Newburyport and his service was credited to Newburyport. He first enlisted in 8th Massachusetts Volunteer Infantry Company A (known as the Cushing Guards) April 15, 1861 (3 months), and was discharged from that unit August 1, 1861. He then enlisted in the Sharpshooters and was killed in action September 17, 1862, at the Battle of Antietam. He was single and his parents' names were Augustine and Hannah (Broderick). His mother was his dependent. He had two brothers also serving in the Union Army, George in the 40th New York Frontier Cavalry and John in the 11th Massachusetts Volunteer Infantry Company B. Sources: Adjutant General Vol. 1-7 & 1-2; Creasey, George, *Newburyport.*

Varrell, John P., enlisted for three years as a private at age 41 into the 1st Company October 25, 1862, at Camp Wightman, Long Island, Boston, and received a $25.00 bounty. He was a marble worker. He was born in 1821 at Portsmouth, New Hampshire, and his service was credited to Chelsea. He was wounded July 3, 1863, at the Battle of Gettysburg. He reported to the unit from the hospital at Gettysburg August 17, 1863. He deserted February 11, 1864. The adjutant general's report gives his name as Vanill. His parents' names were Nathaniel and Nancy. Sources: Adjutant General Vol. 1-7 & 1-2; Stokinger; Harnwell.

Wadleigh, Joseph, enlisted for three years as a private at age 30 into the 1st Company September 2, 1861, at Camp Saunders in Lynnfield. He was a shoemaker. He was born in 1831 at Windham, New Hampshire, and his service was credited to Lowell. He was given a disability discharge May 28, 1862. He was married. His parents' names were Newell and Sarah (Patten). Sources: Adjutant General Vol. 1-7 & 1-2; Harnwell.

Waitt, Samuel A., enlisted for three years as a private at age 28 into the 1st Company September 2, 1861, at Camp Saunders in Lynnfield. He was a storekeeper. He was born June 27, 1833, at Danvers and his service was credited to Danvers. He was given a disability discharge February 17, 1862, at Poolesville, Maryland, for consumption (tuberculosis). He married Elizabeth Dodge of Hamilton, and his parents' names were Samuel and Lydia (Woodbury). His father was from Danvers and mother from Gloucester. Sources: Adjutant General Vol. 1-7 & 1-2; Lynnfield Heritage, *Lynnfield.*

Walcott, Charles O., enlisted for three years as a private at age 31 into the 1st Company November 26,

1862, at Camp Wightman, Long Island, Boston, and received a $25.00 bounty. He was a carriage painter. He was born in 1830 at Rumford, Maine and his service was credited to Lowell. He was wounded May 30, 1864 near Cold Harbor, Virginia. He was discharged September 2, 1864. Sources: Adjutant General Vol. 1–7 & 1–2; Stokinger.

Warner, William H., enlisted for three years as a private at age 22 into the 1st Company November 1, 1862, at Camp Wightman, Long Island, Boston, and received a $25.00 bounty. He was a mariner. He was born in 1840 at Salisbury, Connecticut, and his service was credited to Boston and Connecticut. He was wounded July 3, 1863, at the Battle of Gettysburg. He was discharged September 2, 1864. Sources: Adjutant General Vol. 1–7 & 1–2.

Wheelock, Frederick E., enlisted for three years as a private at age 21 into the 1st Company September 2, 1861, at Camp Saunders Lynnfield. He was a farmer. He was born August 10, 1840, at Shrewsbury and his service was credited to Shrewsbury. He was wounded September 17, 1862, at the Battle of Antietam and was given a disability discharge May 23, 1863, at Falmouth, Virginia, as a result of that wound. He was single, and his parents' names were Abraham and Mary Elizabeth (Bradley). His mother was from Smithfield, Rhode Island. Sources: Adjutant General Vol. 1–7 & 1–2; Rice, Franklin, *Shrewsbury*.

Wheelock, Henry Lincoln, enlisted for three years as a private at age 29 into the 1st Company October 10, 1862, at Camp Wightman, Long Island, Boston, and received a $25.00 bounty. He was a farmer. He was born January 14, 1833, at Shrewsbury and his service was credited to Lexington. He was wounded July 3, 1863, at the Battle of Gettysburg. He was discharged September 3, 1864. He was single and his parents' names were Abraham and Catherine (Pratt). Sources: Adjutant General Vol. 1–7 & 1–2; Stokinger; Franklin, *Shrewsbury*.

White, David, enlisted for three years as a private at age 42 into the 1st Company October 24, 1862, at Camp Wightman, Long Island, Boston, and received a $25.00 bounty. He was a shoemaker. He was born in 1820 at Northbridge and his service was credited to Boston. He deserted prior to November 1862. He was married. Sources: Adjutant General Vol. 1–7 & 1–2; Stokinger.

White, Frederick, enlisted for three years as a private at age 25 into the 1st Company September 2, 1861, at Camp Saunders in Lynnfield. He was a shoemaker. He was born January 1, 1836, at Lawrence, and his service was credited to Middleton. He was wounded September 17, 1862, at the Battle of Antietam. He was given a discharge from the Sharpshooters January 5, 1863, to enlist in the United States Army Regular 1st U.S. Artillery, Company K. He was discharged from the Army August 3, 1864, at Camp Barry, Washington, D.C. He was single. Sources: Adjutant General Vol. 1–7 & 1–2; Harnwell.

Whittemore, George, enlisted for three years as a private at age 24 into the 1st Company September 2, 1861, at Camp Saunders in Lynnfield. He was a lawyer. He was born in 1837 and his service was credited to Gloucester. He was killed in action September 17, 1862, at the Battle of Antietam as a corporal. While traveling on a train he met Luke Emerson Bicknell and they became good friends. George had poor eyesight and joined the Sharpshooters because of the telescopic rifles. The aid of the telescopes allowed him to serve the Union. He was single. Sources: Adjutant General Vol. 1–7 & 1–2; Bicknell, Luke.

Whittier, Leonard S., enlisted for three years as a private at age 19 into the 1st Company September 2, 1861, at Camp Saunders in Lynnfield. He was a clerk. He was born March 20, 1842, at Deerfield, New Hampshire, and his service was credited to Stoneham. He was given a disability discharge May 25, 1863. He then enlisted November 14, 1863, in the 59th Massachusetts Volunteer Infantry Company A and received a $325.00 bounty. He was killed in action May 12, 1864, in the Battle of Spotsylvania. He was single and his parents' names were Edward and Elizabeth J. (Young). They were married in Malden. Sources: Adjutant General Vol. 1–7 & 1–2; Essex, *Stoneham*; *Civil War Papers*.

Wildes, Solomon, enlisted for three years as a private at age 37 into the 1st Company September 2, 1862, at Camp Wightman, Long Island, Boston, and received a $25.00 bounty. He was a painter. He was born February 16, 1825, at Topsfield and his service was credited to Charlestown. He was transferred, as a corporal, to the Veterans Reserve Corps February 15, 1864. He reenlisted in the 1st Veterans Reserve Corps Company G May 17, 1864, and received a $415.33 bounty. He was discharged November 14, 1865. He married Lucretia Ellis of Charlestown, and they had two children. His parents' names were Thomas and Eunice (Foster). His mother was from Ipswich. Sources: Adjutant General Vol. 1–7 & 1–2; Stokinger; Joslyn, Roger, *Charlestown*.

Williams, George, enlisted for three years as a private at age 24 into the 1st Company October 29, 1862, at Camp Wightman, Long Island, Boston, and received a $25.00 bounty. He was a farmer. He was born November 17, 1839, at Brookfield, Vermont and his service was credited to Boston. His service and discharge dates are unknown as there was no further information found regarding his service. He was single, and his parents' names were Anaziah and Eunice (Fiske). Sources: Adjutant General Vol. 1–7 & 1–2; Stokinger; Microfilm Collection.

Williams, Samuel W., enlisted for three years as a private at age 30 into the 1st Company September 2,

1861, at Camp Saunders Lynnfield. He was a shoemaker. He was born April 18, 1831, in Danvers and his service was credited to South Danvers. He first enlisted in 5th Massachusetts Volunteer Infantry Company H April 19, 1861 (3 months) (known as the Salem City Guards), and was discharged from that unit July 31, 1861. He was wounded September 17, 1862, at the Battle of Antietam. He was given a disability discharge May 16, 1863, as a result of that wound. His parents' names were Samuel and Lydia (Newhall). Sources: Adjutant General Vol. 1–7 & 1–2; Essex, *Danvers*.

Williams, Theodore, enlisted for three years as a private at age 19 into the 1st Company August 9, 1862, at Camp Wightman, Long Island, Boston. He was a naturalist. He was born October 19, 1842, at Raynham, and his service was credited to South Boston. He was captured as a prisoner of war July 18, 1863, near Harpers Ferry, Virginia. He was returned by the Confederates October 15, 1863. He was wounded May 5, 1864, at the Battle of the Wilderness, Virginia. He was discharged September 2, 1864. Sources: Adjutant General Vol. 1–7 & 1–2; Stokinger; Harnwell.

Willis, Henry, enlisted for three years as a private at age 33 into the 1st Company September 23, 1862, at Camp Wightman, Long Island, Boston, and received a $25.00 bounty. He was a painter. He was born in 1829 at Portland, Maine, and his service was credited to Roxbury. He deserted July 9, 1863. He was married and had three children. Sources: Adjutant General Vol. 1–7 & 1–2; Stokinger.

Wilson, James H., enlisted for three years as a private at age 21 into the 1st Company October 22, 1862, at Camp Wightman, Long Island, Boston, and received a $25.00 bounty. He was a washer. He was born in 1841 at Hillsborough, New York, and his service was credited to Boston. His service and discharge dates are unknown as there was no further information found regarding his service. He was single. Sources: Adjutant General Vol. 1–7 & 1–2; Stokinger.

Wilson, Robert A., enlisted for three years as a private at age 35 into the 1st Company September 16, 1862, at Camp Wightman, Long Island, Boston, and received a $25.00 bounty. He was a mason. He was born in 1827 at Derby, Vermont, and his service was credited to Boston. He was wounded December 13, 1862, at the Battle of Fredericksburg, Virginia. He was discharged September 15, 1864. He was married and had one child. Sources: Adjutant General Vol. 1–7 & 1–2; Stokinger.

Wood, Ephraim, enlisted for three years as a private at age 21 into the 1st Company September 2, 1861, at Camp Saunders in Lynnfield. He was a weaver. He was born April 19, 1840, at Nova Scotia, Canada, and his service was credited to Lowell. Official Records state he was wounded but do not indicate which battle or date. There is a note in the Company muster rolls which indicates he was wounded while dueling. He was given a disability discharge November 22, 1862, as a result of that wound. His parents' names were Nelson and Sarah (Wood). Sources: Adjutant General Vol. 1–7 & 1–2; Harnwell.

Wood, Joseph L., enlisted for three years as a private at age 18 into the 1st Company September 2, 1861, at Camp Saunders Lynnfield. He was a weaver. He was born in 1842 at Nova Scotia, Canada, and his service was credited to Lowell. He first enlisted in 6th Massachusetts Volunteer Infantry Company D (known as the Lowell City Guards) April 16, 1861 (3 months), as a corporal and was discharged from that unit August 2, 1861. He then enlisted in the Sharpshooters and was promoted to corporal. He was wounded September 17, 1862, at the Battle of Antietam and again November 28, 1863, at the Battle of Mine Run, Virginia. He was discharged September 12, 1864. He was single. His parents' names were Nelson and Sarah (Wood). Sources: Adjutant General Vol. 1–7 & 1–2; Harnwell.

Woodruff, James Francis, enlisted for three years as a private at age 27 into the 1st Company January 4, 1864, at Camp Wightman, Long Island, Boston, and received $325.00 and $60.00 bounties. He was a carpenter. He was born January 23, 1836, at West Stockbridge and his service was credited to West Stockbridge. He was transferred to the 19th Massachusetts Volunteer Infantry Company K September 8, 1864, as the Sharpshooters were mustered out and he had time yet to serve. He was discharged June 30, 1865, from the 19th. He was married and his parents' names were Isaac and Huldah (Van Horn). Sources: Adjutant General Vol. 1–7 & 1–2; Stokinger; Microfilm Collection.

Young, J Albert, enlisted for three years as a private at age 36 into the 1st Company October 28, 1862, at Camp Wightman, Long Island, Boston, and received a $25.00 bounty. He was a carpenter. He was born in 1826 at Roxbury, Vermont, and his service was credited to North Bridgewater. He was wounded May 30, 1864, at the Battle of Cold Harbor, Virginia. He was discharged September 2, 1864. He was married to Aurilla Dodge and had a son born August 15, 1850, at Montpelier, Vermont. His parents' names were Aaron and Elizabeth. Sources: Adjutant General Vol. 1–7 & 1–2; Stokinger; Microfilm Collection. Harnwell.

Second Company Biographical Roster

Sources are abbreviated and can be found in the Bibliography.

Adams, Henry J., was drafted for three years as a private at age 25 into the 2nd Company at Camp Wightman Long Island, Boston. He was a farmer. He was born October 3, 1837, at Harvard and his service was credited to Harvard-Salem. He was wounded at Laurel Hill, Virginia, on May 10, 1864. He was transferred to the Veteran Reserve Corps Company B as a result of that wound. He was also in battles at Rappahannock Station, Mine Run and The Wilderness. He was discharged August 7, 1865. His parents' names were Joseph and Sarah (Wetherbee). Sources: Adjutant General Vol. 1–7 & 1–2; Stokinger; Baldwin, Thomas, *Harvard*; Adjutant Second Company.

Adams, William Jones, enlisted for three years as a private at age 34 into the 2nd Company September 11, 1861, at Camp Saunders in Lynnfield. He was a painter. He was born October 22, 1827, at Buxton, Maine and his service was credited to Danvers. He was given a disability discharge February 18, 1863, at Alexandria, Virginia. He was married to Mary L. Mayberry of Windham, Maine. His parents' names were William and Esther (Warren). Sources: Adjutant General Vol. 1–7 & 1–2; Stokinger; Putman, Eben, *Report of the Committee*; Meserve, Charles, *Buxton*.

Allen, Sherman, enlisted for three years as a private at age 42 into the 2nd Company September 25, 1861, at Camp Saunders in Lynnfield. He was a shoemaker. He was born in 1819 and his service was credited to Plymouth. He was given a disability discharge November 29, 1862. He first enlisted April 16, 1861, in the 3rd Massachusetts Volunteer Infantry Company "B" (3 month) Sources: Adjutant General Vol. 1–7 & 1–2.

Allen, William H., enlisted for three years as a private at age 32 into the 2nd Company October 3, 1861, at Camp Saunders in Lynnfield. He was a mariner. He was born December 30, 1827, at Lynn and his service was credited to Salem. He was given a disability discharge October 1, 1862. He married Susan Nelson in Salem on October 13, 1849. His parents' names were Ezra Jr. and Mary (Moulton). Sources: Adjutant General Vol. 1–7 & 1–2; Essex, *Lynn*; Essex, *Salem*.

Archer, Benjamin H., enlisted for three years as a private at age 18 into the 2nd Company August 13, 1862, at Camp Wightman Long Island, Boston. He was a clerk. He was born in November of 1846 in Salem and his service was credited to Salem. He received a disability discharge January 30, 1863, at Boston. His parents' names were William and Charlotte (Phippen). Sources: Adjutant General Vol. 1–7 & 1–2; Stokinger; Essex, *Salem*.

Archer, William H., enlisted for three years as a corporal at age 40 into the 2nd Company September 14, 1861, at Camp Saunders in Lynnfield. He was a carpenter. He was born July 27, 1816, at Salem and his service was credited to Salem. He was given a disability discharge December 29, 1862, at Washington, D.C. He was married. His parents' names were William and Eliza (Daniels). There is some question as to the accuracy of his age; it appears it should be listed as 45. Sources: Adjutant General Vol. 1–7 & 1–2; Essex, *Salem*.

Baron, Frederick A., enlisted for three years as a private at age 16 into the 2nd Company August 13, 1861, at Camp Saunders in Lynnfield. He was a manufacturer. He was born June 17, 1845, in Lowell and his service was credited to Lowell. He first enlisted April 15, 1861, in the 6th Massachusetts Volunteer Infantry Company A (known as the National Grays) (3 months) and was discharged August 2, 1861. He had deserted from the Sharpshooters on October 3, 1862.

He again enlisted July 7, 1864, in the 6th Massachusetts Volunteer Infantry Company G (100 days), received $68.66 bounty, and was discharged from that unit October 27, 1864. His parents were from Lowell and his father was a carpenter; their names were Jacob and Cynthia (Merriam). Sources: Adjutant General Vol. 1–7 & 1–2; Essex, *Lowell*.

Bartlett, Sylvanus, enlisted for three years as a private at age 35 into the 2nd Company August 14, 1861, at Camp Saunders in Lynnfield. He was a farmer. He was born December 21, 1823, in Shrewsbury and his service was credited to Lowell. He was given a disability discharge October 1, 1862. His parents' names were Alexander and Lucy (Jones). Sources: Adjutant General Vol. 1–7 & 1–2; Microfilm Collection.

Batchelder, John H., enlisted for three years as a corporal at age 43 into the 2nd Company September 13, 1861, at Camp Saunders in Lynnfield. He was a sash maker. He was born January 16, 1817, in Beverly and his service was credited to Salem. He was given a disability discharge November 29, 1862, at Providence, Rhode Island. He married Emma Eaton Dodge on March 19, 1846. His parents' names were Henry and Abigail (Mann). Sources: Adjutant General Vol. 1–7 & 1–2; Essex, *Salem*; Topsfield Historical Society, *Beverly*.

Beard, George, enlisted for three years as a private at age 35 into the 2nd Company August 16, 1861, at Camp Saunders in Lynnfield. He was a shoemaker. He was born April 6, 1826, in Windsor, Vermont, and his service was credited to Danvers. He was given a disability discharge October 21, 1862, at Boston. He was single and lived in Quincy. Sources: Adjutant General Vol. 1–7 & 1–2; Putman, Eben, *Report of the Committee*; Microfilm Collection.

Berry, Israel Augustus, enlisted for three years as a private at age 34 into the 2nd Company August 29, 1861, at Camp Saunders in Lynnfield. He was a farmer. He was born June 16, 1827, in Middleton and his service was credited to Andover. He was given a disability discharge on August 8, 1862, at Fort McHenry, Maryland. His parents' names were Israel and Serena (Town). Sources: Adjutant General Vol. 1–7 & 1–2; Topsfield Historical Society, *Andover*; Microfilm Collection.

Brown, George Gillman, enlisted for three years as a private at age 16 into the 2nd Company August 27, 1862, at Camp Wightman Long Island, Boston. He was a farmer. He was born April 6, 1846, in West Newbury and his service was credited to Boston. He was given a disability discharge November 26, 1862, at Falmouth. It appears he lied about his age and was later found out and discharged for being under age without parental consent. His father's name was Francis and his mother was Susan C. B. (George) from Salisbury. Sources: Adjutant General Vol. 1–7 & 1–2; Stokinger; Microfilm Collection.

Burdett, George, enlisted for three years as a corporal at age 43 into the 2nd Company September 5, 1861, at Camp Saunders in Lynnfield. He was a shoe cutter. He was born August 15, 1819, in Wakefield and his service was credited to South Reading. He was given a disability discharge October 1, 1862. One source lists his name as Burdett. He was engaged to Martha Stone of Stoneham but withdrew that intention October 8, 1840. His parents' names were Michael and Polly (Dix). Sources: Adjutant General Vol. 1–7 & 1–2; Baldwin, Thomas, *Wakefield*.

Burdick, Benjamin J., enlisted for three years as a private at age 27 into the 2nd Company September 25, 1861, at Camp Saunders in Lynnfield. He was a farmer. He was born June 5, 1834, in Boston and his service was credited to Stoneham-Beverly. He was given a disability discharge February 12, 1863. He reenlisted July 18, 1864, in the 13th Veteran Reserve Corps Company E at Boston and received a $325.00 bounty. He was discharged November 15, 1865, from the Veteran Reserve Corps. Sources: Adjutant General Vol. 1–7 & 1–2.

Burrill, Alden, enlisted for three years as a private at age 49 into the 2nd Company September 16, 1861, at Camp Saunders in Lynnfield. He was a shoemaker. He was born October 9, 1811, in Lynn and his service was credited to Lynn. He was given a disability discharge January 23, 1863, at Washington, D.C. He married Mary Ann Palmer June 4, 1832, and she died of consumption (tuberculosis) July 14, 1847; he then married Martha Riley, who had been previously married. Alden and Mary Ann had 4 daughters, Harriet Ann, Henrietta, Margaretta and Maria Ellen. His parents' names were Theophis and Eunice (Newhall). Sources: Adjutant General Vol. 1–7 & 1–2; Essex, *Lynn*.

Burrill, Edward Atwill, enlisted for three years as a private at age 19 into the 2nd Company September 1, 1861, at Camp Saunders in Lynnfield. He was a shoemaker. He was born January 9, 1844, in Lynn and his service was credited to Lynn. He died of typhoid at 5:30 a.m. on January 29, 1862, in Halls' Hill, Virginia, after two or three days in the hospital. It was early on in the war, and the men had not experienced much death. His comrades thought of him highly, so they took a vote to raise the money to ship his body home; money enough was raised. He was single and his parents' names were Richard and Almira (Atwill). Sources: Adjutant General Vol. 1–7 & 1–2; Haynes, Nathan, *Journal of the 2nd Company*; Microfilm Collection.

Cahoon, John S., enlisted for three years as a private at age 32 into the 2nd Company September 5, 1861 at Camp Saunders in Lynnfield. He was a boot cutter. He was born in 1819 at Raccoon, Ohio, and his service was credited to Holliston-Bragville. He was given a disability discharge October 29, 1862, at

Boston. His parents' names were William and Evaline (Wood). It must be noted that he is the only John S. Cahoon found born in North America during this time period and there is a possibility that these are not his parents. Sources: Adjutant General Vol. 1–7 & 1–2; Massachusetts Registry, *A Very Complete Account*; Microfilm Collection.

Carter, James B., enlisted for three years as a private at age 18 into the 2nd Company October 5, 1861, at Camp Saunders in Lynnfield. He was a shoemaker. He was born August 11, 1839, in Danvers and his service was credited to Lynn. He was given a disability discharge January 11, 1863, at Alexandria, Virginia. His parents' names were Richard and Mary Lou (Mead). Sources: Adjutant General Vol. 1–7 & 1–2; Essex, *Danvers*.

Chapman, Ezra, enlisted for three years as a private at age 25 into the 2nd Company September 3, 1861, at Camp Saunders in Lynnfield. He was a laborer. He was born January 2, 1836, at Portland, Connecticut, and his service was credited to Sterling. He was wounded December 13, 1862, at Fredericksburg, Virginia. He was killed in action May 25, 1864, at North Anna River, Virginia. His parents' names were Ralph and Louisa (Alger). Sources: Adjutant General Vol. 1–7 & 1–2; Microfilm Collection.

Clark, Ozro E., enlisted for three years as a private at age 19 into the 2nd Company September 5, 1861, at Camp Saunders in Lynnfield. He was a bootmaker. He was born in 1842 and his service was credited to Holliston-Bragville. He was given a disability discharge September 26, 1862, at Washington, D.C. He lived on Howard Street in Milford from 1869 to 1880 and possibly longer. Sources: Adjutant General Vol. 1–7 & 1–2; Microfilm Collection; Ballou, Adin, *Milford*.

Clements, Charles H., enlisted for three years as a private at age 18 into the 2nd Company August 28, 1861, at Camp Saunders in Lynnfield. He was a farmer. He was born August 9, 1842, in Danvers and his service was credited to Salem-Lynn-Woburn. He was given a disability discharge September 22, 1862. He enlisted in the 8th Massachusetts Volunteer Infantry Company D (100 days) on July 11, 1864 (3 months), received a $75.32 bounty, and was discharged from that unit November 10, 1864. He enlisted in the 2nd Regiment Massachusetts Volunteer Cavalry Company A (three years) on February 25, 1865, received a $95.99 bounty, and was discharged from that unit July 20, 1865. 2nd Massachusetts Cavalry indicates his residence as Granville and occupation as a currier. His parents' names were Samuel and Laura Matilda (Allen). Sources: Adjutant General Vol. 1–7 & 1–2; Topsfield Historical Society, *Beverly*.

Clemons, Charles E., enlisted for three years as a private at age 19 into the 2nd Company September 19, 1861, at Camp Saunders in Lynnfield. He was a shoemaker. He was born in 1842 at Andover and his service was credited to South Reading. He was given a disability discharge April 15, 1862. He reenlisted in the 19th Massachusetts Volunteer Infantry Company B August 20, 1862 (3 years), indicating Lynn as his residence. He was wounded December 13, 1862, at Fredericksburg, Virginia and received a disability discharge from that unit February 7, 1863, at Alexandria Virginia. His parents' names were Robert M. and Olive (Gardner). His brother was born in Deerfield, New Hampshire, and his mother was from Boston. Sources: Adjutant General Vol. 1–7 & 1–2; Eaton, Lilley, *Reading*.

Clemons William H., enlisted for three years as a private at age 21 into the 2nd Company August 11, 1862, at Camp Wightman Long Island, Boston. He was a glue maker. He was born in 1841 and his service was credited to Salem. He was discharged October 17, 1864. He first enlisted in the 5th Massachusetts Volunteer Infantry Company A (3 months) (known as the Mechanic Light Infantry) on April 18, 1861, and was discharged from that unit July 31, 1861. Sources: Adjutant General Vol. 1–7 & 1–2; Stokinger.

Clifford, Wells Webster, enlisted for three years as a private at age 26 into the 2nd Company August 13, 1862, at Camp Wightman Long Island, Boston. He was a carpenter. He was born in 1836 at Caledonia, Vermont, and his service was credited to Chelsea. He was given a disability discharge November 3, 1862. His parents' names were Wells and Phebe. Sources: Adjutant General Vol. 1–7 & 1–2; Stokinger; Microfilm Collection.

Colburn, Henry F., enlisted for three years as a private at age 36 into the 2nd Company August 22, 1862, at Camp Wightman Long Island, Boston. He was a driver. He was born in 1826 and his service was credited to Boston. He died of typhoid on January 4, 1863, at Potomac Creek, Virginia. His remains were deposited in the camp near Falmouth, Virginia. Sources: Adjutant General Vol. 1–7 & 1–2; Stokinger; Haynes, Nathan, *Journal of the Second Company*.

Cowdrey, Isaac B., enlisted for three years as a private at age 18 into the 2nd Company September 18, 1861, at Camp Saunders in Lynnfield. He was a shoemaker. He was born July 1, 1846, in Stoneham and his service was credited to Stoneham. He died of typhoid on April 20, 1862, at Yorktown, Virginia after being in the hospital four days. His friends made a coffin for him and buried him in the vicinity. They were saddened they could not ship his body home. His parents' names were Warren and Sarah (Williams). Sources: Adjutant General Vol. 1–7 & 1–2; Haynes, Nathan, *Journal of the Second Company*; Microfilm Collection.

Crafts, Walter S., enlisted for three years as a private at age 21 into the 2nd Company October 14,

1862, at Camp Wightman, Long Island, Boston. He was a machinist. He was born January 21, 1839, at Newton and his service was credited to Boston. He was wounded at the Battle of Fredericksburg, Virginia, on December 13, 1862. He was transferred to the 166th Veteran Reserve Corps 2nd Battalion on April 24, 1864. His parents' names were Nathan and Relief (Witherby). Sources: Adjutant General Vol. 1–7 & 1–2; Stokinger; Microfilm Collection.

Crane, Albert J., enlisted for three years as a private at age 26 into the 2nd Company September 20, 1861, at Camp Saunders in Lynnfield. He was a currier. He was born in 1835 and his service was credited to South Danvers. He was discharged October 5, 1864. He first enlisted in the 5th Massachusetts Volunteer Infantry Company A (known as the Mechanic Light Infantry) April 16, 1861 (3 months) and was discharged from that unit July 31, 1861. Sources: Adjutant General Vol. 1–7 & 1–2.

Currier, Charles W., was drafted for three years as a private at age 33 into the 2nd Company July 13, 1863, at Camp Wightman Long Island, Boston and received a $25.00 bounty. He was a teamster. He was born in 1830 at Boston and his service was credited to Lynn. He was discharged from the Sharpshooters June 19, 1865. While on a march on May 4, 1864, he was taken prisoner. He was exchanged as a prisoner the same day. He was single. Sources: Adjutant General Vol. 1–7 & 1–2; Stokinger.

Dearborn, William H., enlisted for three years as a private at age 23 into the 2nd Company September 10, 1861, at Camp Saunders in Lynnfield. He was a wheelwright. He was born February 8, 1838, at Lynn and his service was credited to Lynn. He was given a disability discharge September 30, 1862, at Providence, Rhode Island. His parents' names were John and Harriet (Frothington) and his father was from Guilford, New Hampshire. Sources: Adjutant General Vol. 1–7 & 1–2; Essex, *Lynn*; Essex, *Salem*.

Deland, Moses, enlisted for three years as a private at age 22 into the 2nd Company August 22, 1861, at Camp Saunders in Lynnfield. He was a farmer. He was born in 1839 at Danvers and his service was credited to Danvers. He was killed in action May 30, 1864, at Bethesda Church, Virginia. He was single and his family was from Peabody. His father was also named Moses Deland; his father's last name had an alternative spelling of Daland. Moses Deland, Sr., was born March 6, 1811, to Joseph and Phebe (Guilford) at Danvers. Sources: Adjutant General Vol. 1–7 & 1–2; Putnam, Eben, *Report of the Committee*.

Donnelly, James E., enlisted for three years as a private at age 19 into the 2nd Company August 29, 1861, at Camp Saunders in Lynnfield. He was a painter. He was born in 1838 and his service was credited to Lynn. He first enlisted in 8th Massachusetts Volunteer Infantry Company F (known as the City Guards) April 15, 1861 (3 months), and was discharged from that unit August 1, 1861. He was discharged from the Sharpshooters October 17, 1864, as a corporal. Sources: Adjutant General Vol. 1–7 & 1–2.

Durgin, Erastus A., enlisted for three years as a private at age 23 into the 2nd Company September 14, 1861, at Camp Saunders in Lynnfield. He was a shoemaker. He was born July 9, 1836 in Reading and his service was credited to Stoneham-Beverly. He was given a disability discharge November 5, 1862. He reenlisted July 18, 1864, in the Veteran Reserve Corps and received a $325.00 bounty. He was single. Records at the Congregational Church in North Reading indicate his father could have been from Newfield, Maine. Sources: Adjutant General Vol. 1–7 & 1–2; Baldwin, Thomas, *Reading*.

Eastman, John F., was drafted for three years as a private at age 28 into the 2nd Company July 10, 1863, at Camp Wightman Long Island, Boston. He was a baker. He was born in 1835 at Conway, New Hampshire, and his service was credited to Lawrence. The 2nd Company was mustered out October 21, 1864, and men with time left to serve were transferred to the 32nd Massachusetts Volunteer Infantry. Eastman was with that group of men assigned to Company M and was discharged June 29, 1865. Sources: Adjutant General Vol. 1–7 & 1–2; Stokinger; Adjutant Second Company.

Evans, Alvan Augustus, was commissioned as an officer (2nd lieutenant) at age 21 into the 2nd Company September 2, 1861, at Camp Saunders in Lynnfield. He was a currier. He was born August 14, 1840, in Salem and his service was credited to Salem. He first enlisted in 8th Massachusetts Volunteer Infantry Company I (known as the Salem Light Infantry) as a corporal April 15, 1861 (3 months), and was discharged from that unit July 5, 1861. He was discharged from the Sharpshooters on July 5, 1862, when he resigned his commission. He lived at 9–11 Mason Street in Salem. He later supplied Jonathan G. Day as a substitute on September 17, 1864. That same day, Jonathan enlisted in the 1st Massachusetts Mounted Rifles, Company D, and served as a private until discharged June 25, 1865 (Ref. O.R.'s III, 5). Sources: Adjutant General Vol. 1–7 & 1–2; Root, Elihu; Essex, *Salem*; Salem Street Directory.

Faulkner, John W., enlisted for three years as a private at age 16 into the 2nd Company September 16, 1861, at Camp Saunders in Lynnfield. He was a farmer. He was born May 27, 1845, at Andover and his service was credited to North Andover. He was given a disability discharge March 24, 1863, as a corporal at Potomac Creek, Virginia. His parents' names were Eldridge C. and Martha (Town). Sources: Adjutant General Vol. 1–7 & 1–2; Topsfield Historical Society, *Andover*; Microfilm Collection.

Fenno, George F., enlisted for three years as a private at age 26 into the 2nd Company September 4, 1861, at Camp Saunders in Lynnfield. He was a carriage maker. He was born in 1835 and his service was credited to Dorchester. He was discharged October 17, 1864. Sources: Adjutant General Vol. 1–7 & 1–2.

Gage, Andrew Jr., enlisted for three years as a private at age 41 into the 2nd Company September 19, 1861, at Camp Saunders in Lynnfield. He was a painter. He was born July 2, 1820, in Salem and his service was credited to Salem. He was given a disability discharge October 1, 1862. He lived at 54 Derby House, 18 Hardy. His father's name was Andrew, Sr., and he was born in Beverly on February 19, 1798. Sources: Adjutant General Vol. 1–7 & 1–2; Essex, *Salem;* Topsfield Historical Society, *Beverly.*

Gardner, Abel, enlisted for three years as a private at age 24 into the 2nd Company September 26, 1861, at Camp Saunders in Lynnfield. He was an upholsterer. He was born January 16, 1837, in Somerville and his service was credited to Salem. He was given a disability discharge September 22, 1862, at Boston. He reenlisted January 6, 1863, in the 1st Battalion Massachusetts Volunteer Heavy Artillery Company and was promoted to corporal September 8, 1863; he was discharged from that unit June 29, 1865. His first enlistment was in the 5th Massachusetts Volunteer Infantry Company A April 16, 1861 (3 months), and was discharged from that unit July 31, 1861. He was the brother of James in the same company. His parents' names were Benjamin and Betsy (Nichols). Sources: Adjutant General Vol. 1–7 & 1–2; Microfilm Collection.

Gardner, James W., enlisted for three years as a private at age 35 into the 2nd Company August 27, 1862, at Camp Wightman, Long Island, Boston. He was a carpenter. He was born in 1829 at Salem and his service was credited to Salem. He was wounded June 3, 1864, at the Battle of Bethesda Church, Virginia. He was discharged October 17, 1864. He lived at House 114, Derby Wharf. He was the brother of Abel in the same company. His parents' names were Benjamin and Betsy (Nichols). Sources: Adjutant General Vol. 1–7 & 1–2; Stokinger; Salem Street Directory; Microfilm Collection.

Goldthwait, Ebenezer G., enlisted for three years as a private at age 40 into the 2nd Company August 31, 1861, at Camp Saunders in Lynnfield. He was a cordwainer. He was born August 12, 1821, in Salem and his service was credited to Reading. He was given a disability discharge February 16, 1863, at Alexandria, Virginia. He married Harriet Augusta Pervere, filing those intentions July 6, 1845, in the town of Reading. His parents' names were Eben and Rebecca (Allen). Sources: Adjutant General Vol. 1–7 & 1–2; Essex, *Salem.*

Goss, Richard, enlisted for three years as a private at age 40 into the 2nd Company September 26, 1861, at Camp Saunders in Lynnfield. He was a farmer. He was born April 17, 1821, in Mendon and his service was credited to Danvers. He was given a disability discharge November 13, 1862, at Boston. He married Hannah Jane Tedford and the family lived in Beverly. His parents' names were William and Abigail (Fairbanks). Sources: Adjutant General Vol. 1–7 & 1–2; Putnam, Eben, *Report of the Committee;* Microfilm Collection.

Graham, James, enlisted for three years as a private at age 21 into the 2nd Company September 2, 1861, at Camp Saunders in Lynnfield. He was a painter. He was born in 1840 and his service was credited to Lynn. He was wounded July 1, 1862, at the Battle of Malvern Hill, Virginia. He was not heard from after that date and he was dropped from the rolls July 13, 1862, as a deserter. Sources: Adjutant General Vol. 1–7 & 1–2.

Graham, Samuel, enlisted for three years as a private at age 28 into the 2nd Company September 13, 1861, at Camp Saunders in Lynnfield. He was a morocco dresser. He was born September 16, 1834, in Lynn and his service was credited to Lynn. He was given a disability discharge October 1, 1862. His parents' names were John and Hannah (Hutchins). Sources: Adjutant General Vol. 1–7 & 1–2; Essex, *Lynn.*

Green, Henry W., enlisted for three years as a private at age 27 into the 2nd Company September 18, 1861, at Camp Saunders in Lynnfield. He was a teamster. He was born December 7, 1834, in Stoneham and his service was credited to Stoneham. He first enlisted in 6th Massachusetts Volunteer Infantry Company L April 16, 1861 (3 months), known as the Stoneham Light Infantry, and was discharged from that unit August 2, 1861. While passing through Baltimore, his unit was attacked by a mob. He was given a disability discharge February 11, 1863, from the Sharpshooters at Washington, D.C. His parents' names were Henry and Abigail (Geary). His brother Joshua was also in the company. Sources: Adjutant General Vol. 1–7 & 1–2; Essex, *Stoneham.*

Green, Isaac E., enlisted for three years as a private at age 30 into the 2nd Company September 9, 1861, at Camp Saunders in Lynnfield. He was a shoemaker. He was born August 18, 1830, in Wakefield and his service was credited to South Reading. He was taken prisoner July 2, 1863, at the Battle of Gettysburg. He was returned to the Sharpshooters May 24, 1864, from his prisoner status. He was discharged October 17, 1864. His parents' names were Isaac and Lucinda (Kinerson). Sources: Adjutant General Vol. 1–7 & 1–2; Baldwin, Thomas, *Wakefield.*

Green, Joshua G., enlisted for three years as a private at age 24 into the 2nd Company August 30, 1861, at Camp Saunders in Lynnfield. He was a shoemaker. He was born March 9, 1837, in Stoneham and his service was credited to Stoneham. He was discharged from the Sharpshooters August 24, 1863. He was transferred to the 3rd Veteran Reserve Corps Company F September 7, 1863. His brother Henry was also in the same company. He was married and his parents' names were Henry and Abigail (Geary). Sources: Adjutant General Vol. 1–7 & 1–2; *Civil War Papers*, Stoneham.

Green, Orrin A., enlisted for three years as a private at age 20 into the 2nd Company August 27, 1861, at Camp Saunders in Lynnfield. He was a farmer. He was born May 14, 1841, in Stoneham and his service was credited to Stoneham. He first enlisted in 6th Massachusetts Volunteer Infantry Company L April 16, 1861 (3 months), known as the Stoneham Light Infantry and was discharged from that unit August 2, 1861. While his unit passed through Baltimore, it was attacked by a mob. He was transferred to the 1st Veterans Reserve Corps, Company D, August 19, 1863, and was discharged from that unit October 6, 1864, as a corporal. His parents' names were Benjamin and Martha (Geary). Sources: Adjutant General Vol. 1–7 & 1–2; Essex, *Stoneham*.

Green, Stephen H., enlisted for three years as a private at age 18 into the 2nd Company September 5, 1861, at Camp Saunders in Lynnfield. He was a shoemaker. He was born April 30, 1846, in Stoneham and his service was credited to Stoneham. He was transferred to the 3rd Veterans Reserve Corps, Company B, July 1, 1863. He reenlisted May 9, 1864, and received a $325.00 bounty. As a corporal he was discharged from that unit at Augusta, Maine, on November 20, 1865, as a corporal. His parents' names were Elijah and Elizabeth (Tuttle). Sources: Adjutant General Vol. 1–7 & 1–2; Essex, *Stoneham*.

Grover, Benjamin P., enlisted for three years as a corporal at age 25 into the 2nd Company September 11, 1861, at Camp Saunders in Lynnfield. He was a teamster. He was born April 23, 1838, in Harvard and his service was credited to Lynn. His first enlistment was in the 8th Massachusetts Volunteer Infantry Company F (known as the City Guards) April 15, 1861 (3 months), and he was discharged from that unit August 11, 1861. He was given a disability discharge from the Sharpshooters on November 1, 1862. He reenlisted on July 21, 1864, in the 13th Veteran Reserve Corps, Company G, and received a $325.00 bounty. He was promoted to corporal October 1, 1864, and discharged from that unit January 18, 1865. His parents' names were Charles and Mary (Sawyer). Sources: Adjutant General Vol. 1–7 & 1–2; Microfilm Collection.

Hardback, Horace P. enlisted for three years as a private at age 24 into the 2nd Company July 11, 1863, at Camp Wightman Long Island, Boston. He was an armorer. He was born October 17, 1838, in Grafton and his service was credited to Worcester. He was taken prisoner at the Battle of the Wilderness, Virginia May 5, 1864, and sent to Andersonville Prison. He died of disease while there in 1864. His name is not listed among the interred at Andersonville; he could be in an unmarked grave. His parents' names were Rufus and Susan S. (Keith). His mother was from Uxbridge. Sources: Adjutant General Vol. 1–7 & 1–2; Stokinger; U.S. Quartermaster's Department.

Hawkes, Francis, enlisted for three years as a private at age 25 into the 2nd Company September 14, 1861, at Camp Saunders in Lynnfield. He was a teamster. He was born July 24, 1836, in Wakefield and his service was credited to Stoneham. He was discharged October 17, 1864. His parents' names were Davis and Lucretia (Tweed). Sources: Adjutant General Vol. 1–7 & 1–2; Baldwin, Thomas, *Wakefield*.

Hay, John Francis, enlisted for three years as a private at age 18 into the 2nd Company September 16, 1861, at Camp Saunders in Lynnfield. He was a teamster. He was born April 30, 1842, in Reading and his service was credited to Stoneham. He was wounded July 1, 1862, at the Battle of Malvern Hill, Virginia and received a disability discharge in New York City January 4, 1863, as a result of that wound. He was single and his parents' names were Jonathan and Rebecca. Sources: Adjutant General Vol. 1–7 & 1–2; Microfilm Collection.

Hayes, Nathaniel, was drafted for three years as a private at age 34 into the 2nd Company on July 10, 1863, at Camp Wightman Long Island, Boston. He was a farmer. He was born in 1829 and his service was credited to Ipswich. He died of disease July 2, 1864, at Petersburg, Virginia. He was single. Sources: Adjutant General Vol. 1–7 & 1–2; Stokinger.

Haynes, Nathan Wheeler, enlisted for three years as a corporal at age 37 into the 2nd Company September 5, 1861, at Camp Saunders in Lynnfield. He was a carpenter. He was born October 5, 1833, in Concord and his service was credited to Haverhill. He was promoted to sergeant September 30, 1862. He was wounded December 13, 1862, at the Battle of Fredericksburg, Virginia, and died from that wound January 3, 1863, at Washington, D.C. His parents' names were Elnathan and Sarah (Wheeler). He had nine siblings, including brother George H. of Shirley, who died while serving in the 26th Massachusetts Volunteer Infantry. Sources: Adjutant General Vol. 1–7 & 1–2; Haynes, Francis, *Walter Haynes*.

Herrick, Charles Greeley, enlisted for three years as a private at age 36 into the 2nd Company December 2, 1863, at Camp Wightman Long Island, Boston and received a $325.00 bounty. He was a painter. He was born in 1830 at Haverhill and his service was credited to Lynn. He first enlisted in 8th Massachusetts Volunteer Infantry, Company F, September 19, 1862

(9 months), and was discharged from that unit August 7, 1863. He was wounded May 10, 1864, at Laurel Hill, Virginia. He was transferred to the 32nd Massachusetts Volunteer Infantry, Company M, to complete his enlistment commitment as the Sharpshooters were mustered out. His parents' names were Greeley and Elizabeth (Noyes). Sources: Adjutant General Vol. 1–7 & 1–2; Stokinger. Adjutant Second Company; Microfilm Collection.

Herring, Edwin James, enlisted for three years as a private at age 28 into the 2nd Company October 1, 1861, at Camp Saunders in Lynnfield. He was a shoemaker. He was born in 1833 at Dedham and his service was credited to Lynn. He received a disability discharge March 1, 1863, at Potomac Creek, Virginia. He was baptized at Saint Paul's Church in Dedham January 1, 1836. Sources: Adjutant General Vol. 1–7 & 1–2; Hill, Don Gleason, *Record*.

Holden, William, enlisted for three years as a private at age 29 into the 2nd Company August 27, 1861, at Camp Saunders in Lynnfield. He was a shoemaker. He was born March 16, 1832, in Stoneham and his service was credited to Stoneham. He was given a disability discharge October 1, 1862. He died of disease September 19, 1863, at Baton Rouge, Louisiana. He was single and his parents' names were Joseph and Sally (Crocker). Sources: Adjutant General Vol. 1–7 & 1–2; Essex, *Stoneham*; Stoneham, *Civil War Papers*.

Holt, Edwin, enlisted for three years as a private at age 20 into the 2nd Company August 19, 1861, at Camp Saunders in Lynnfield. He was a clerk. He was born in 1841 and his service was credited to Lowell. He was wounded in 1862 and received a disability discharge November 23, 1862, as a result of that wound at Falmouth, Virginia. Sources: Adjutant General Vol. 1–7 & 1–2.

Hone, John H., enlisted for three years as a private at age 18 into the 2nd Company September 10, 1861, at Camp Saunders in Lynnfield. He was a teamster. He was born April 28, 1844, in Saugus and his service was credited to Saugus. He was discharged as a corporal from the Sharpshooters October 17, 1864. His parents' names were Henry and Lydia (Jacobs). Company muster rolls indicate his name as Horri. Sources: Adjutant General Vol. 1–7 & 1–2; Essex, *Saugus*.

Hooper, John, enlisted for three years as a private at age 36 into the 2nd Company September 2, 1862, at Camp Wightman Long Island, Boston. He was a brickmaker. He was born July 31, 1825, at Marblehead and his service was credited to Lynn. He was wounded May 30, 1864, at Bethesda Church, Virginia. He was discharged from the Sharpshooters October 17, 1864. He reenlisted in Hancock's Corps (U.S. Veteran Volunteers) 8th Regiment, Company C on April 10, 1865, and received a $240.00 bounty. He was discharged from that unit November 9, 1865. His parents' names were John and Lydia (Blackler). Sources: Adjutant General Vol. 1–7 & 1–2; Stokinger; Microfilm Collection

Howlett, John W., enlisted for three years as a private at age 21 into the 2nd Company September 16, 1861, at Camp Saunders in Lynnfield. He was a shoemaker. He was born in 1840 and his service was credited to Saugus. As a result of a wound, he received a disability discharge December 23, 1863, at Convalescent Camp, Virginia. Sources: Adjutant General Vol. 1–7 & 1–2.

Hutchinson, George C., enlisted for three years as a private at age 38 into the 2nd Company August 26, 1862, at Camp Wightman, Long Island, Boston. He was a joiner. He was born May 3, 1824, at Salem and his service was credited to Salem. He was transferred to the 6th Veteran Reserve Corps, Company H, March 1, 1864, and was discharged January 10, 1865, at Johnson's Island, Ohio. His parents' names were Ruben M. and Ann (Gilson). He lived at House #30 Turner and his parents were married in Lowell. Sources: Adjutant General Vol. 1–7 & 1–2; Stokinger; Essex, *Salem*; Salem Street Directory; Microfilm Collection.

Ingalls, Nathan B. M., enlisted for three years as a private at age 32 into the 2nd Company September 2, 1861, at Camp Saunders in Lynnfield. He was a trader. He was born October 6, 1829, in Lynn and his service was credited to Lynn. He received a disability discharge July 24, 1862, at Harrison's Landing, Virginia. He reenlisted June 10, 1863, into the 1st Massachusetts Volunteer Heavy Artillery, Company G and received a $50.00 bounty. He was discharged from that unit August 6, 1865. He was taken prisoner by the Confederates June 1, 1864, at Cold Harbor, Virginia. He was married and his parents' names were Nathan Benjamin Moulten III and Lydia (Fern); they were married June 7, 1824. Sources: Adjutant General Vol. 1–7 & 1–2; Essex, *Lynn*.

Jeffery, David N., enlisted for three years as a sergeant at age 29 into the 2nd Company September 18, 1861, at Camp Saunders in Lynnfield. He was a tanner. He was born November 25, 1831, in Danvers and his service was credited to South Danvers. He first enlisted in 5th Massachusetts Volunteer Infantry Company A (known as the Mechanic Light Infantry) as a sergeant May 16, 1861 (3 months), and was discharged from that unit July 31, 1861. He was wounded May 5, 1864, at the Battle of the Wilderness in Virginia and was given a disability discharge October 17, 1864. Sources: Adjutant General Vol. 1–7 & 1–2; Essex, *Danvers*.

Jewett, George Horace, was drafted for three years as a private at age 24 into the 2nd Company July 11, 1863, at Camp Wightman Long Island, Boston. He was a railroad repairman. He was born May 1, 1837, at Sterling and his service was credited to Clinton-Worcester. He first enlisted in 36th Massachusetts Volunteer Infantry, Company G August 16, 1862, and was given a disability discharge February 28, 1863. He was discharged from the Sharpshooters July 3, 1864, by declaration of the illegality of his being drafted. His parents' names were Horace and Jane (Churchill). Sources: Adjutant General Vol. 1–7 & 1–2; Stokinger; Ford, Andrew, *Clinton*; Microfilm Collection.

Kenniston, Hiram B., enlisted for three years as a private at age 36 into the 2nd Company September 27, 1861, at Camp Saunders in Lynnfield. He was a shoemaker. He was born September 13, 1827, in Alton, New Hampshire, and his service was credited to Danvers. He was given a disability discharge January 30, 1863, at Fort Monroe, Virginia. He married Lucinda Meader. Sources: Adjutant General Vol. 1–7 & 1–2; Putnam, Eben, *Report of the Committee*.

Kidder, Henry K., enlisted for three years as a private at age 42 into the 2nd Company September 9, 1861, at Camp Saunders in Lynnfield. He was a teamster. He was born in 1819 and his service was credited to Saugus. He was given a disability discharge October 27, 1862. Sources: Adjutant General Vol. 1–7 & 1–2.

Kingman, Orlando Pope, enlisted for three years as a sergeant at age 23 into the 2nd Company August 9, 1862, at Camp Wightman Long Island, Boston. He was a machinist. He was born May 8, 1839, at Wakefield and his service was credited to Boston. He received a disability discharge September 29, 1863. His parents' names were John and Miriam (Isbell). Sources: Adjutant General Vol. 1–7 & 1–2; Stokinger; Microfilm Collection

Knapp, George Washington, enlisted for three years as a private at age 32 into the 2nd Company August 30, 1861, at Camp Saunders in Lynnfield. He was a carpenter. He was born August 27, 1827, in Danvers and his service was credited to South Danvers. He was wounded at some time in 1864 and was discharged October 17, 1864. He was married. Sources: Adjutant General Vol. 1–7 & 1–2; Essex, *Danvers*.

Knowlton, George W., enlisted for three years as a private at age 23 into the 2nd Company August 11, 1862, at Camp Wightman Long Island, Boston. He was a stonecutter. He was born July 16, 1840, at Rockport and his service was credited to Salem. He received a disability discharge December 30, 1862, at Falmouth, Virginia. His parents' names were George and Mary (Murphy). He lived at House #35 Charter and was listed as a blacksmith. Sources: Adjutant General Vol. 1–7 & 1–2; Stokinger; Salem Street Directory; Microfilm Collection.

Lawler, Patrick, enlisted for three years as a private at age 21 into the 2nd Company August 28, 1863, at Camp Wightman Long Island, Boston. He was a circus rider. He was born in 1842 at Sarasota Springs, New York, and his service was credited to South Danvers. He was killed in action May 30, 1864, at Spotsylvania, Virginia. (One source indicates Bethesda Church, Virginia.) Sources: Adjutant General Vol. 1–7 & 1–2; Stokinger.

Lawrence, Eben B., enlisted for three years as a private at age 28 into the 2nd Company August 3, 1861, at Camp Saunders in Lynnfield. He was a carpenter. He was born November 13, 1832, at Lynnfield and his service was credited to Stoneham-Dorchester. He was given a disability discharge October 3, 1862, at Georgetown, D.C. He reenlisted July 29, 1864, in the 13th Veterans Reserve Corps Company G, and received a $325.00 bounty. He was discharged from that unit November 21, 1865. He was married, and his parents' names were Ebenezer and Joan (Perkins). Sources: Adjutant General Vol. 1–7 & 1–2; Stoneham, *Civil War Papers*; Essex, *Lynnfield*.

Leach, Ivory Lowe, enlisted for three years as a sergeant at age 29 into the 2nd Company August 19, 1861, at Camp Saunders in Lynnfield. He was a carriage maker. He was born November 5, 1831, at Somerset, Maine and his service was credited to Lowell. He was commissioned 2nd lieutenant January 30, 1863; prior to that, he was 1st sergeant. He was given a disability discharge June 20, 1863, by Special Order No. 274 of the War Department. His parents' names were Henry and Nancy (Stevens). Sources: Adjutant General Vol. 1–7 & 1–2; Microfilm Collection.

Lewis, Charles, enlisted for three years as a private at age 32 into the 2nd Company August 21, 1861, at Camp Saunders in Lynnfield. He was a shoemaker. He was born September 2, 1828, at Windham, New Hampshire, and his service was credited to South Danvers. He was given a disability discharge January 6, 1863, at Annapolis, Maryland. His parents' names were Ebenezer and Mary (Hamblet). He married Esther Ellen Taylor at Danvers. Sources: Adjutant General Vol. 1–7 & 1–2; Essex, *Danvers*; Lewis, George, *Edmund Lewis*.

Lewis, George B., was drafted for three years as a private at age 26 into the 2nd Company July 13, 1863, at Camp Wightman Long Island, Boston. He was a baker. He was born October 6, 1839, at Salem and his service was credited to Salem. He received a disability discharge May 4, 1864. His parents' names were William and Betsy (Goldthwaite). His father, a tinsmith, was born in Newburyport; his mother was born in Peabody. Sources: Adjutant General Vol. 1–7 & 1–2; Stokinger; Essex, *Salem*.

Lewis, Isaac H., enlisted for three years as a private at age 31 into the 2nd Company September 20, 1861, at Camp Saunders in Lynnfield. He was a shoemaker. He was born in 1830 and his service was credited to Lawrence. He was wounded May 8, 1864, at the Battle of Laurel Hill, Virginia, and died from that wound four days later at Fredericksburg, Virginia. Sources: Adjutant General Vol. 1–7 & 1–2.

Madden, William H., enlisted for three years as a corporal at age 18 into the 2nd Company September 17, 1861, at Camp Saunders in Lynnfield. He was a farmer. He was born in 1843 and his service was credited to Stoneham. He first enlisted in 6th Massachusetts Volunteer Infantry, Company L (known as the Stoneham Light Infantry), April 16, 1861 (3 months), and was discharged from that unit August 2, 1861. In all likelihood, he was among those in the trapped train cars attacked in Baltimore, Maryland, during the riots. While with the Sharpshooters, he was promoted to 1st sergeant. He was wounded July 2, 1863, at the Battle of Gettysburg (Ref. O.R's I 34, 40), cited for bravery while silencing artillery at the Rapidan River. Stoneham Historical Society indicates his name as Marden. Sources: Adjutant General Vol. 1–7 & 1–2; Root, Elihu; Stoneham, *Civil War Papers*.

Mallory, William Henry Harrison, enlisted for three years as a private at age 21 into the 2nd Company August 30, 1861, at Camp Saunders in Lynnfield. He was a machinist. He was born February 9, 1841, in Cambridge and his service was credited to Cambridgeport. He first enlisted in 6th Massachusetts Volunteer Infantry, Company K (known as the Washington Light Guard), April 16, 1861 (3 months), and was discharged from that unit on August 2, 1861. While passing through Baltimore, his unit was attacked by a mob. He was promoted to corporal while with the Sharpshooters and discharged October 17, 1864. His parents' names were Richard P. and Mary A. D. (Bott). Sources: Adjutant General Vol. 1–7 & 1–2; Root, Elihu; Essex, *Stoneham*.

May, Henry E., enlisted for three years as a private at age 44 into the 2nd Company August 30, 1862, at Camp Wightman Long Island, Boston. He was a hackman. He was born in 1818 and his service was credited to Salem. He was transferred to the 13th Veterans Reserve Corps, Company C, September 11, 1863. He was discharged from that unit February 6, 1864. He was married and had two children. Sources: Adjutant General Vol. 1–7 & 1–2; Stokinger.

McCragin, John H., enlisted for three years as a private at age 32 into the 2nd Company September 27, 1861, at Camp Saunders in Lynnfield. He was a painter. He was born in 1829 and his service was credited to Lawrence. He was given disability discharge April 18, 1862. In August of 1862, he reenlisted in the 40th Massachusetts Volunteer Infantry, Company C, and received a disability discharge March 10, 1863. He then reenlisted in the 1st Battalion Massachusetts Volunteer Heavy Artillery November 24, 1863, and was transferred to the U.S. Navy April 21, 1864. His navy service was credited to Springfield; he was discharged from the Navy October 24, 1865, as Seaman McCrakin. Sources: Adjutant General Vol. 1–7 & 1–2.

McDuffee, Daniel N., enlisted for three years as a private at age 35 into the 2nd Company September 30, 1861, at Camp Saunders in Lynnfield. He was a farmer. He was born in 1826 and his service was credited to Lynnfield. He was given disability discharge July 24, 1862, at Harrison's Landing, Virginia. He was single and his parents' names were David and Elizabeth (Newhall). Sources: Adjutant General Vol. 1–7 & 1–2; Lynnfield Heritage Associates, *Lynnfield*.

McKenzie, John W.; was drafted for three years as a private at age 40 into the 2nd Company July 13, 1863, at Camp Wightman Long Island, Boston. He was a tailor. He was born in 1823 and his service was credited to Salem. He was killed in action May 10, 1864, at Spotsylvania, Virginia. (One source indicates Laurel Hill, Virginia.) It appears he boarded at 249 Essex and worked at 114 Derby. Sources: Adjutant General Vol. 1–7 & 1–2; Stokinger; Salem Street Directory.

Meady, Daniel F., enlisted for three years as a private at age 34 into the 2nd Company September 7, 1861, at Camp Saunders in Lynnfield. He was a confectioner. He was born in 1827 at Salem and his service was credited to Salem. He was discharged October 4, 1864. He married Tabitha Roberts March 25, 1849. He lived at House 10 Carton. Sources: Adjutant General Vol. 1–7 & 1–2; Salem Street Directory; Microfilm Collection.

Melcher, Levi L., enlisted for three years as a private at age 25 into the 2nd Company September 13, 1861, at Camp Saunders in Lynnfield. He was a mason. He was born in 1836 and his service was credited to Salem. He first enlisted in 5th Massachusetts Volunteer Infantry, Company A (known as the Mechanic Light Infantry), April 16, 1861 (3 months), and was discharged from that unit July 31, 1861. He then enlisted in the Sharpshooters and was given a disability discharge May 1, 1862. He reenlisted in the 7th Regiment Massachusetts Volunteer Militia, Company B, (6 months), and was discharged from that unit December 31, 1862. He lived at House 44 Buffum. Sources: Adjutant General Vol. 1–7 & 1–2; Salem Street Directory.

Morris, George E., enlisted for three years as a private at age 25 into the 2nd Company September 12, 1861, at Camp Saunders in Lynnfield. He was a mariner. He was born in Prussia and his service was credited to Lynn. He was given disability discharge October 7, 1862, at Providence, Rhode Island. He was single. Sources: Adjutant General Vol. 1–7 & 1–2.

Morrison, John, was drafted for three years as a private at age 20 into the 2nd Company August 28, 1863, at Camp Wightman Long Island, Boston. He was a linen packer. He was born in 1843 in Ireland

and his service was credited to Salem. He was killed in action May 10, 1864, at Spotsylvania, Virginia. (One source indicates Laurel Hill, Virginia.) He was interred at the Battlefield Cemetery of Wilderness or Spotsylvania. There are two cemeteries there: one at Orange Court Turnpike about two miles from the Wilderness Tavern, and Orange Court House Plank Road, about two and one half miles from Orange Court House Turnpike. Sources: Adjutant General Vol. 1–7 & 1–2; Stokinger; U.S. Quartermaster's Department.

Munn, George, enlisted for three years as a private at age 42 into the 2nd Company September 16, 1862, at Camp Wightman Long Island, Boston. He was a soldier. He was born in 1820 and his service was credited to Charlestown. He was wounded July 2, 1863, at the Battle of Gettysburg. He was transferred to the 24th Veterans Reserve Corps, Company I, May 11, 1864, and was discharged October 5, 1864. He married Catherine E. Maloy; they both were from Charlestown. Sources: Adjutant General Vol. 1–7 & 1–2; Stokinger.

Neal, Aaron D., enlisted for three years as a private at age 27 into the 2nd Company August 22, 1861, at Camp Saunders in Lynnfield. He was a painter. He was born in 1834 and his service was credited to Lynn. He was wounded December 13, 1862, at Fredericksburg, Virginia. He died of disease April 21, 1863, at Convalescent Camp, Virginia. Sources: Adjutant General Vol. 1–7 & 1–2.

Neal, Henry, enlisted for three years as a private at age 40 into the 2nd Company September 19, 1862, at Camp Saunders in Lynnfield. He was a sailmaker. He was born in 1821 and his service was credited to Lynn. He was transferred to the 3rd Veterans Reserve Corps, Company A, July 27, 1863, and was dishonorably discharged October 5, 1863. Sources: Adjutant General Vol. 1–7 & 1–2.

Neil, Thomas J., enlisted for three years as a private at age 28 into the 2nd Company August 13, 1862, at Camp Wightman Long Island, Boston. He was a tin man. He was born in 1834 and his service was credited to Boston. He was taken prisoner of war May 3, 1863, at Chancellorsville, Virginia and was returned in October of 1863. He was killed in action June 5, 1864, at Shady Grove Church, Virginia. Sources: Adjutant General Vol. 1–7 & 1–2; Stokinger.

Newhall, Edward E., enlisted for three years as a private at age 25 into the 2nd Company October 5, 1861, at Camp Saunders in Lynnfield. He was a shoemaker. He was born May 29, 1836, in Lynn and his service was credited to Lynn. He was promoted to corporal September 22, 1863. He was wounded May 5, 1864, at the Battle of the Wilderness, Virginia, and also was taken prisoner of war the same day. He died as a prisoner of war November 15, 1864, at Millen, Georgia. His parents' names were Otis Jr. and Sarah (Pool). He had two brothers serving in the same company, Herman C. and Henry A. They all enlisted on the same day. Sources: Adjutant General Vol. 1–7 & 1–2; Essex, *Lynn*.

Newhall, Herman C., enlisted for three years as a private at age 23 into the 2nd Company October 5, 1861, at Camp Saunders in Lynnfield. He was a farmer. He was born May 13, 1838, in Lynn and his service was credited to Lynn. He was discharged October 17, 1864. His parents' names were Otis Jr. and Sarah (Pool). He had two brothers serving in the same company, Edward C. and Henry A. They all enlisted on the same day. Sources: Adjutant General Vol. 1–7 & 1–2; Essex, *Lynn*.

Newhall, Henry A., enlisted for three years as a private at age 21 into the 2nd Company October 5, 1861, at Camp Saunders in Lynnfield. He was a teamster. He was born August 14, 1840, in Lynn and his service was credited to Lynn. His first enlistment was in the 8th Massachusetts Volunteer Infantry, Company D (known as the Lynn Light Infantry), on April 15, 1861 (3 months), and was discharged from that unit August 11, 1861. He was discharged from the Sharpshooters on October 17, 1864. His parents' names were Otis Jr. and Sarah (Pool). He had two brothers serving in the same company, Herman C. and Edward E. They all enlisted on the same day. Sources: Adjutant General Vol. 1–7 & 1–2; Essex, *Lynn*.

Newhall, Henry W., enlisted for three years as a private at age 37 into the 2nd Company September 19, 1861, at Camp Saunders in Lynnfield. He was a cordwainer. He was born in 1824 at Lynn and his service was credited to Lynn. He was given a disability discharge November 4, 1862, at Newark, New Jersey. He reenlisted August 18, 1864, in the 4th Massachusetts Volunteer Heavy Artillery, Company B, and received a $199.99 bounty. He was discharged from that unit June 17, 1865. His parents' names were Isaiah and Selina (Bailey). He married Susan Henry Lewis December 15, 1844. Adjutant General Vol. 1–7 & 1–2; Microfilm Collection.

Newmarch, John, enlisted for three years as a private at age 31 into the 2nd Company August 18, 1861, at Camp Saunders in Lynnfield. He was a shoemaker. He was born November 25, 1824, in Newburyport and his service was credited to Lynn. He was discharged from the Sharpshooters April 21, 1863, to accept a promotion to the Noncommissioned Officers' Staff of the 22nd Massachusetts Volunteer Infantry and was appointed hospital steward. He was given a disability discharge April 26, 1864. His parents' names were John and Sarah (Johnson). His age or his parents could be incorrect, but he was the only one found by this name in this area. Sources: Sources: Adjutant General Vol. 1–7 & 1–2; Microfilm Collection.

Newton, John F., enlisted for three years as a private at age 29 into the 2nd Company August 20, 1862, at Camp Wightman Long Island, Boston. He was a carpenter. He was born in 1833 and his service was credited to Southborough. He was promoted to sergeant, date not indicated. He was discharged October 8, 1864. Sources: Sources: Adjutant General Vol. 1–7 & 1–2; Stokinger.

Nichols, George Whitefield, enlisted for three years as a private at age 23 into the 2nd Company August 30, 1861, at Camp Saunders in Lynnfield. He was a farmer. He was born in April 1840 at Reading and his service was credited to Reading. He was given a disability discharge December 25, 1862. He enlisted July 14, 1864, in the 8th Massachusetts Volunteer Infantry, Company E (100 days), and received a $74.66 bounty. He was mustered out of that unit November 10, 1864. He then enlisted in the 62nd Massachusetts Volunteer Infantry, Company C, April 30, 1865 (1 year), received a $24.00 bounty, and was discharged from that unit May 5, 1865. His parents' names were Samuel and Achsah. Sources: Adjutant General Vol. 1–7 & 1–2; Baldwin, Thomas, *Reading*.

Osgood, Cyrus M., was drafted for three years as a private at age 28 into the 2nd Company September 2, 1862, at Camp Wightman Long Island, Boston. He was a peddler. He was born March 17, 1834, in Maine and his service was credited to Salem. He was killed in action May 1, 1863, at the Battle of Chancellorsville, Virginia. His parents' names were Kneeland and Christina (Morgan). His father was from Waterville and mother from Surrey, Maine. He was married and lived at House 28 Dearborn, Salem and was also a brakeman for the Salem, and Lynn Railroad. Sources: Sources: Adjutant General Vol. 1–7 & 1–2; Salem Street Directory; Osgood, Ira, *A Genealogy*.

Oviatt, Charles, was drafted for three years as a private at age 21 into the 2nd Company August 28, 1863, at Camp Wightman Long Island, Boston. He was a teamster. He was born in 1842 in either New York, New York, or Canada and his service was credited to Swanzey-Taunton. He was wounded June 22, 1864, at Petersburg, Virginia, and deserted from the hospital October 15, 1864. He must have been captured or returned to his unit as he was transferred to the 32nd Massachusetts Volunteer Infantry, Company M, as the Sharpshooters were mustered out and he had time yet to serve. He was discharged from the 32nd June 28, 1865. Sources: Adjutant General Vol. 1–7 & 1–2; Stokinger; Adjutant Second Company.

Palmer, George L., enlisted for three years as a private at age 50 into the 2nd Company September 2, 1861, at Camp Saunders in Lynnfield. He was a shoemaker. He was born in 1811 at Salem and his service was credited to Lynn. He was given a disability discharge July 7, 1862. He enlisted on August 24, 1863, in the Detached Unassigned Veterans Reserve Corps at Salem, and Worcester was credited; he was mustered into that service at Washington, D.C., and received a $325.00 bounty. He received a disability discharge May 1, 1864, from the 114th Company, 2nd Battalion, Veterans Reserve Corps on May 17, 1864. He married Sarah A. Martin of Marblehead on July 25, 1830, and they had four children. Sources: Adjutant General Vol. 1–7 & 1–2; Essex, *Lynn*.

Parlin, Herman F., enlisted for three years as a private at age 20 into the 2nd Company January 4, 1864, at Camp Wightman Long Island, Boston, and received a $325.00 bounty. He was a trader. He was born May 31, 1843, in Natick and his service was credited to Natick. He was killed in action May 8, 1864, at the Battle of Laurel Hill, Virginia. His parents' names were Asher and Rebecca (Washburn). Sources: Adjutant General Vol. 1–7 & 1–2; Stokinger; Baldwin, Thomas, *Natick*.

Perkins, Nelson, enlisted for three years as a private at age 32 into the 2nd Company August 22, 1861, at Camp Saunders in Lynnfield. He was a farmer. He was born in 1829 at Reading and his service was credited to Boston. He reenlisted January 2, 1864, and received a $325.00 bounty. He deserted May 15, 1864, and surrendered May 15, 1865, under the President's Amnesty Proclamation. He was mustered out of the service May 15, 1865. Sources: Adjutant General Vol. 1–7 & 1–2; Adjutant Second Company.

Perley, Joseph A., enlisted for three years as a private at age 37 into the 2nd Company September 9, 1861, at Camp Saunders in Lynnfield. He was a farmer. He was born October 21, 1829, in Danvers and his service was credited to Lynn. He was given disability discharge September 15, 1862, at Boston. His parents' names were Joseph Gould and Mary Jane (Dodge). His father was from Boxford and his mother from Ipswich. Sources: Adjutant General Vol. 1–7 & 1–2; Perley, M.V.B., *The Perley Family*.

Pinkam, Charles Freeman, enlisted for three years as a private at age 32 into the 2nd Company August 29, 1861, at Camp Saunders in Lynnfield. He was a carpenter. He was born January 11, 1829, at Madbury, New Hampshire, and his service was credited to South Danvers. He was given a disability discharge December 30, 1862, at Falmouth, Virginia. His parents' names were Hicks and Mary Buffington (Phelps). Hicks and Mary adopted him. One source indicates his name as Penkham. Sources: Adjutant General Vol. 1–7 & 1–2; Essex, *Danvers*.

Pond, George Otis, enlisted for three years as a private at age 33 into the 2nd Company August 27, 1862, at Camp Wightman Long Island, Boston, and received a $100.00 bounty. He was a sailor. He was born September 22, 1829, in Franklin and his service was credited to Medway. He died of disease at Strasburg, Virginia. He was being transported by ambulance from a field hospital to a general hospital at the time of his death. While at the field hospital, he was given some medication; he began to vomit and was in great distress. He was very sick for the last two months of his life and was waiting for discharge papers he expected on a daily basis. He left a family in Dedham. The town of Medway paid $50.00 to have his body returned to West Medway. The town of Medway also aided his family with the sum of $215.60. He was baptized November 7, 1830, at the 2nd Congregational Church in Medway. His parents' names were Paul D. and Hilda (Hill). Sources: Adjutant General Vol. 1–7 & 1–2; Stokinger; Jameson, E.O., *Medway*.

Reed, James Smith, enlisted for three years as a private at age 42 into the 2nd Company August 24, 1861, at Camp Saunders in Lynnfield. He was a wheelwright. He was born April 13, 1819, at Deerfield and his service was credited to Lynn. He died of fever June 9, 1862, at the Division Hospital near New Bridge, Virginia. His friends made a crude box and went together to follow his body to the gravesite. They were interrupted and ordered to fall into ranks to receive a "distinguished foreigner," who turned out to be a general from Spain. His parents' names were John and Sophronia (Smith). Sources: Adjutant General Vol. 1–7 & 1–2; Haynes, Nathan, *Journal*; Microfilm Collection.

Rhoades, Amos Jr., enlisted for three years as a private at age 40 into the 2nd Company October 2, 1861, at Camp Saunders in Lynnfield. He was a shoemaker. He was born in 1821 at Salem; his service was credited to Lynn. He was given a disability discharge November 1, 1862. His parents' names were Amos and Mary (Johnson). Sources: Adjutant General Vol. 1–7 & 1–2; Essex, *Salem*.

Richardson, Sewell D., enlisted for three years as a private at age 26 into the 2nd Company September 17, 1861, at Camp Saunders in Lynnfield. He was a machinist. He was born in 1835 and his service was credited to West Springfield. He was wounded July 1, 1862, at the Battle of Malvern Hill, Virginia, and also was taken prisoner of war. He was returned by the Confederates November 10, 1862. He was wounded two more times, once December 13, 1862, at the Battle of Fredericksburg, Virginia and again June 2, 1864, at the Battle of Bethesda Church, Virginia. He was discharged October 17, 1864. Sources: Adjutant General Vol. 1–7 & 1–2.

Roberts John K., enlisted for three years as a private at age 38 into the 2nd Company September 6, 1861, at Camp Saunders in Lynnfield. He was a teamster. He was born in 1823 at Goffstown, New Hampshire, and his service was credited to Stoneham. He was given a disability discharge December 10, 1862, at David's Island, New York Harbor. He reenlisted March 23, 1864, for three years and was discharged from that enlistment June 30, 1865. He married Sarah P. Mayhew April 15, 1849, at Stoneham.

His parents' names were Ephraim and Jane (Kennedy). Sources: Adjutant General Vol. 1–7 & 1–2; Stokinger. Essex, *Stoneham*; Stoneham, *Civil War Papers*; Hadley, George, *Goffstown, N.H.*

Roberts, Stephen H., enlisted for three years as a private at age 38 into the 2nd Company August 30, 1862, at Camp Wightman Long Island, Boston. He was a teamster. He was born in 1824 and his service was credited to Salem. He was discharged October 17, 1864. He lived at House 3 Elm. Sources: Adjutant General Vol. 1–7 & 1–2; Stokinger; Salem Street Directory.

Robinson, Nathaniel D., enlisted for three years as a private at age 29 into the 2nd Company September 16, 1861, at Camp Saunders in Lynnfield. He was a tinsmith. He was born in 1832 and his service was credited to Lawrence-Somerville. He was wounded July 1, 1862, at Malvern Hill, Virginia while serving with the Sharpshooters. He was given a disability discharge February 20, 1863. He reenlisted January 4, 1864, in the 3rd Massachusetts Volunteer Cavalry, Company B and received a $325.00 bounty. He was promoted to sergeant and was wounded at Winchester, Virginia. He was discharged from the cavalry September 28, 1865. Sources: Adjutant General Vol. 1–7 & 1–2.

Sibley, William H., enlisted for three years as a private at age 44 into the 2nd Company August 11, 1862, at Camp Wightman Long Island, Boston. He was a carpenter. He was born October 29, 1818, at Salem and his service was credited to Salem. He was discharged October 17, 1864. His parents' names were Joseph and Dorcas (Valpey). Sources: Adjutant General Vol. 1–7 & 1–2; Stokinger; Essex, *Salem*.

Simonds, John, was drafted for three years as a private at age 21 and assigned to the 2nd Company September 1, 1863, at Camp Wightman Long Island, Boston. He was a shoemaker. He was born in 1842 and his service was credited to Albany, New York. He was transferred to the United States Navy May 2, 1864. His service and discharge dates with the navy are unknown as there was no further information found regarding his service. Sources: Adjutant General Vol. 1–7 & 1–2; Stokinger.

Smith, John, was drafted for three years as a private at age 23 and assigned to the 2nd Company September 1, 1863, at Camp Wightman Long Island, Boston. He was an engineer. He was born in 1840 in England and his service was credited to Philadelphia, Pennsylvania. He was transferred to the United States Navy May 2, 1864. His service and discharge dates with the Navy are unknown as there was no further information found regarding his service. Sources: Adjutant General Vol. 1–7 & 1–2; Stokinger.

Smith, Robert, enlisted for three years as a sergeant at age 21 into the 2nd Company September 16, 1861, at Camp Saunders, Lynnfield. He was a hairdresser. He was born in 1840 and his service was credited to Salem. He first enlisted in 5th Massachusetts Volunteer Infantry, Company A (known as the "Mechanic Light Infantry"), April 16, 1861 (3 months), and was discharged from that unit July 31, 1861. He then enlisted in the Sharpshooters and was commissioned 2nd lieutenant July 7, 1862, 1st lieutenant January 3, 1863 and captain May 19, 1863, He was wounded December 13, 1862, at the Battle of Fredericksburg, Virginia. He was discharged October 17, 1864 (Ref. #4 O.R.'s I, 25, 40) and cited for organization and bravery. He lived at House 16 Elm. Sources: Adjutant General Vol. 1–7 & 1–2; Salem Street Directory.

Sprague, Frederick E., enlisted for three years as a private at age 19 into the 2nd Company August 11, 1862, at Camp Wightman Long Island, Boston. He was a painter. He was born in 1843 and his service was credited to Lynn. He was given a disability discharge October 17, 1864. Sources: Adjutant General Vol. 1–7 & 1–2; Stokinger.

Steele, Walter, enlisted for three years as a private at age 25 into the 2nd Company August 25, 1862, at Camp Wightman Long Island, Boston. He was a bookkeeper. He was born in 1837 and his service was credited to Boston. He first enlisted in the Salem Cadets Massachusetts Volunteer Militia May 26, 1862, and was discharged from that unit June 19, 1862. He then enlisted in the Sharpshooters and was wounded December 13, 1862, at the Battle of Fredericksburg, Virginia. He was given a disability discharge March 31, 1863, as a result of that wound. Sources: Adjutant General Vol. 1–7 & 1–2; Stokinger.

Stiles, Charles D., was commissioned as an officer (1st lieutenant) at age 24, into the 2nd Company September 10, 1861, at Camp Saunders in Lynnfield. He was a carpenter. He was born April 10, 1836, in Salem and his service was credited to Salem. He first enlisted in 5th Massachusetts Volunteer Infantry Company A (known as the Mechanic Light Infantry), April 16, 1861 (3 months), as a 1st sergeant and was commissioned 2nd lieutenant July 6, 1861; he was mustered out of that unit July 31, 1861. He resigned his commission from the Sharpshooters August 4, 1862, and was discharged (Ref. #4 O.R.'s I.11 cites his bravery at the Seven Days' Battle in three separate entries). His parents' names were Dean and Rebeckah (Denet). His father, also a carpenter, was born in Middleton. Sources: Adjutant General Vol. 1–7 & 1–2; Root, Elihu; Essex, *Salem*.

Stiles, Henry, enlisted for three years as a private at age 21 into the 2nd Company September 9, 1861, at Camp Saunders in Lynnfield. He was a shoemaker. He was born May 23, 1841, at Andover and his service was credited to North Andover. He was given a disability discharge October 1, 1862. His parents' names were William and Elizabeth (Larrabee). His father was from Ossipee, New Hampshire. Sources: Adjutant General Vol. 1–7 & 1–2; Topsfield Historical Society, *Andover*; Essex, *Danvers*.

Stillman, Samuel, enlisted for three years as a private at age 23 into the 2nd Company August 11, 1862, at Camp Wightman Long Island, Boston. He was a clerk. He was born in 1839 and his service was credited to Salem. He died of disease March 27, 1863, at Potomac Creek, Virginia. He was a clerk at 210 Essex and boarded at 40 St. Peter. Sources: Adjutant General Vol. 1–7 & 1–2; Stokinger; Salem Street Directory.

Sturtevant, John Q.A., enlisted for three years as a sergeant at age 35 into the 2nd Company August 17, 1861, at Camp Saunders in Lynnfield. He was a farmer. He was born October 31, 1824, in Stoneham and his service was credited to Stoneham. While serving with the Sharpshooters he was wounded July 1, 1862, at the Battle of Malvern Hill, Virginia. He was given a disability discharge March 10, 1863, as a result of that wound. He reenlisted July 29, 1864, in the 13th Veterans Reserve Corps, Company C, and received a $325.00 bounty. He was discharged from that unit November 17, 1865. He married Elizabeth A. Stevens and his parents' names were Heman and Sarah (Green). His brother, Daniel also served in the 1st Company of Sharpshooters and Veteran Reserve Corps. Sources: Adjutant General Vol. 1–7 & 1–2; Essex, *Stoneham*; Stoneham, *Civil War Papers*.

Sweetser, Madison C., enlisted for three years as a private at age 21 into the 2nd Company October 2, 1861, at Camp Saunders in Lynnfield. He was a farmer. He was born June 18, 1840, in Wakefield and his service was credited to South Reading. He was discharged October 4, 1864. He enlisted December 29, 1864 in the Hancock's Corps, U. S. Veterans Volunteers 1st Regiment, Company B, and received a $240.00 bounty. He was discharged from that unit December 28, 1865, at Baltimore, Maryland. His parents' names were Madison and Phebe (Bayard). His father was from Lowell. Sources: Adjutant General Vol. 1–7 & 1–2; Baldwin, Thomas, *Wakefield*; Eaton, Lilley, *Reading*.

Sweet, Charles G., enlisted for three years as a private at age 39 into the 2nd Company August 27, 1861, at Camp Saunders in Lynnfield. He was a teamster. He was born in 1822 at Falmouth, Maine and his service was credited to Stoneham. He was wounded May 10, 1864, in the right arm and left hand at the Battle of Laurel Hill, Virginia. He was discharged October 17, 1864. He married Ellen E. Ireland from Lynn and his parents' names were Adam and Sarah. Sources: Adjutant General Vol. 1–7 & 1–2; Essex, *Stoneham*; Stoneham, *Civil War Papers*.

Sweet, Newell S., enlisted for three years as a private at age 25 into the 2nd Company August 29,

1861, at Camp Saunders in Lynnfield. He was a teamster. He was born in 1836 and his service was credited to Lowell. He was wounded May 10, 1864, at the Battle of Laurel Hill, Virginia. He was promoted to sergeant, no date indicated, but prior to May 10, 1864, as records indicate he was wounded as a sergeant. He was discharged October 17, 1864. Sources: Adjutant General Vol. 1–7 & 1–2.

Thomas, Charles S., enlisted for three years as a corporal at age 27 into the 2nd Company September 30, 1861, at Camp Saunders in Lynnfield. He was a carpenter. He was born in 1834 and his service was credited to Salem. He was given a disability discharge April 15, 1862. He lived at House 72 Summer. Sources: Adjutant General Vol. 1–7 & 1–2; Salem Street Directory.

Towne, John, enlisted for three years as a private at age 40 into the 2nd Company September 9, 1862, at Camp Wightman Long Island, Boston. He was a shoemaker. He was born August 11, 1821, in Andover and his service was credited to North Andover. He was transferred to the 12th Veterans Reserve Corps, Company A, in June of 1863 and was given a disability discharge December 15, 1863. His parents' names were John and Patty (Gray). Source *Andover*, indicates his parents' last name was spelled without an e at the end. Sources: Adjutant General Vol. 1–7 & 1–2; Topsfield Historical Society, *Andover*.

Trask, Moses A., enlisted for three years as a private at age 39 into the 2nd Company August 25, 1862, at Camp Wightman Long Island, Boston. He was a currier. He was born December 2, 1823, in Danvers and his service was credited to Salem. He was discharged October 17, 1864. His parents' names were Moses and Mary (Cole). Sources: Adjutant General Vol. 1–7 & 1–2; Stokinger; Essex, *Danvers*.

Truell, Zenas B., enlisted for three years as a private at age 35 into the 2nd Company August 22, 1861, at Camp Saunders in Lynnfield. He was a spinner. He was born in 1826 and his service was credited to Salem. He was wounded July 1, 1862, at the Battle of Malvern Hill, Virginia. He was killed in action May 8, 1864, at the Battle of Laurel Hill, Virginia. He was interred at the Battlefield Cemetery of Wilderness or Spotsylvania. There are two cemeteries there: one at Orange Court Turnpike about two miles from the Wilderness Tavern and the other at Orange Court House Plank Road, about 2 miles from Orange Court House Turnpike. Sources: Adjutant General Vol. 1–7 & 1–2; U.S. Quartermaster's Department.

Upton, Edward, enlisted for three years as a 1st sergeant at age 24 into the 2nd Company September 20, 1861, at Camp Saunders in Lynnfield. He was a currier. He was born April 23, 1837, in Salem and his service was credited to Salem. While serving with the Sharpshooters he was commissioned 1st lieutenant August 6, 1862. He was given a disability discharge January 29, 1863, by Special Order No. 48. He enlisted January 5, 1864, in the 59th Massachusetts Volunteer Infantry, Company B, as a private and received a $325.00 bounty. He soon was promoted to sergeant. He was wounded May 6, 1864, at the Battle of the Wilderness, Virginia, and again June 17, 1864, at the Battle of Petersburg, Virginia. He was discharged June 19, 1865, from the 59th Massachusetts. His parents' names were Benjamin and Elizabeth (Willis). Sources: Adjutant General Vol. 1–7 & 1–2; Essex, *Salem*.

Varrell, John B., enlisted for three years as a private at age 39 into the 2nd Company August 19, 1861, at Camp Saunders in Lynnfield. He was a polisher. He was born in 1822 at Chelsea and his service was credited to Boston. He was given a disability discharge October 6, 1862, at Washington, D.C. He was married. Sources: Adjutant General Vol. 1–7 & 1–2.

Walcott, George Henry, enlisted for three years as a private at age 19 into the 2nd Company December 28, 1863, at Camp Wightman Long Island, Boston, and received a $325.00 bounty. He was a student. He was born October 28, 1844, at Natick and his service was credited to Natick. He was discharged from the Sharpshooters February 24, 1864, to receive a promotion. He was commissioned 1st lieutenant in the 30th United States Colored Troops. He died of disease July 10, 1864, at Philadelphia, Pennsylvania. His parents' names were George and Sophronia C. (Davis). Sources: Adjutant General Vol. 1–7 & 1–2; Stokinger.

Ward, Winsor M., enlisted for three years as a corporal at age 19 into the 2nd Company September 18, 1861, at Camp Saunders in Lynnfield. He was a student. He was born December 30, 1833, at Danvers and his service was credited to South Danvers. He was promoted to sergeant September 20, 1863, promoted to 1st sergeant February 1, 1863, and commissioned 1st lieutenant May 18, 1863. He was wounded July 2, 1863 at the Battle of Gettysburg and by Special Order No. 313 was discharged as a result of that wound September 21, 1864 (Ref. #4 O.R.'s I, 36 cited for bravery and removing the wounded from the field). His parents' names were Alfred A. and Hannah S. (Osborn). Sources: Adjutant General Vol. 1–7 & 1–2; Root, Elihu; Essex, *Danvers*.

Wares, Daniel, enlisted for three years as a private at age 30 into the 2nd Company August 20, 1862, at Camp Wightman Long Island, Boston. He was a mechanic. He was born in 1832 and his service was credited to Ashby. He was promoted to corporal July 22, 1863. He was wounded May 5, 1864, at the Battle of the Wilderness, Virginia. He was discharged October 17, 1864. Sources: Adjutant General Vol. 1–7 & 1–2; Stokinger.

Welch, John F., enlisted for three years as a private at age 44 into the 2nd Company August 30, 1861, at Camp Saunders in Lynnfield. He was a cordwainer.

He was born September 29, 1815, in Reading and his service was credited to Reading. He was given a disability discharge March 17, 1863. He reenlisted October 28, 1864, in the 13th Veterans Reserve Corps, Company E, and received a $325.00 bounty. He was discharged from that unit November 15, 1865. Sources: Adjutant General Vol. 1–7 & 1–2; Baldwin, Thomas, *Reading*.

Wellman, William F., enlisted for three years as a private at age 18 into the 2nd Company August 11, 1862, at Camp Wightman Long Island, Boston. He was a carpenter. He was born June 4, 1844, in Lynn and his service was credited to Lynn. He was discharged October 17, 1864. His parents' names were Ebenezer W. and Martha A. (Williams). Sources: Adjutant General Vol. 1–7 & 1–2; Stokinger; Essex, Lynn; Microfilm Collection.

Wentworth, Lewis E., was commissioned as an officer (captain) at age 39 into the 2nd Company September 3, 1861, at Camp Saunders in Lynnfield. He was a tinsmith. He was born April 29, 1823, and his service was credited to Malden. He was commissioned 2nd lieutenant in the 5th Massachusetts Volunteer Infantry, Company A (known as the Mechanic Light Infantry), March 19, 1861 (3 months), made 1st lieutenant July 16, 1861, and was discharged from that unit July 31, 1861. He was discharged from the Sharpshooters July 16, 1862, when he resigned his commission. He was re-commissioned August 20, 1862, (credit Salem) and was discharged May 18, 1863. He married Mirinda Paine of Patrickstown, Lincoln County, Maine and they had two children. He then married Sara A. Ham of Dover, New Hampshire and they had one child. His parents' names were Lewis and Hannah (Everson). Sources: Adjutant General Vol. 1–7 & 1–2; Root, Elihu. Wentworth, John, *Wentworth Genealogy*.

Westover, Charles C., was drafted for three years as a private at age 32 into the 2nd Company July 9, 1863, at Camp Wightman Long Island, Boston. He was a machinist. He was born in 1830 at New Britain, Connecticut, and his service was credited to Boston. By Special Order of October 21, 1864, to complete his service requirement as the Sharpshooters were mustered out, he was transferred to the 32nd Massachusetts Volunteer Infantry, Company L. He was discharged June 25, 1865. Sources: Adjutant General Vol. 1–7 & 1–2; Stokinger; Adjutant Second Company.

William, James S., was drafted for three years as a private at age 23 into the 2nd Company August 29, 1863, at Camp Wightman Long Island, Boston. He was a joiner. He was born in 1840 in England and his service was credited to Philadelphia, Pennsylvania. He was discharged from the Sharpshooters May 3, 1864, so he could enlist in the U.S. Navy. He enlisted in the Navy May 9, 1864. He served on the receiving ship *Ohio*, *North Carolina*, USS *New Hampshire* and *South Carolina*. He was appointed acting master's mate November 13, 1864. As an officer he served on the *Racer*, *Harvest Moon* and receiving ship *Ohio*. He was discharged November 25, 1865. Sources: Adjutant General Vol. 1–7 & 1–2; Stokinger.

Williams, Henry, enlisted for three years as a private at age 32 into the 2nd Company October 2, 1861, at Camp Saunders in Lynnfield. He was a shoemaker. He was born November 27, 1827, at Lynn and his service was credited to Lynn. He died of typhoid fever December 20, 1861, while at Hall's Hill, Virginia. He was married and had three children; his parents' names were Henry and Mary (Galleucia). His brother John also served in the same company. Sources: Adjutant General Vol. 1–7 & 1–2; Essex, *Lynn*.

Williams, John Lindsey Galleucia, enlisted for three years as a private at age 28 into the 2nd Company September 2, 1861, at Camp Saunders in Lynnfield. He was a glue maker. He was born October 11, 1832, in Lynn and his service was credited to Lynn. He was discharged October 17, 1864. His parents' names were Henry and Mary (Galleucia). His brother Henry also served in the same company. Sources: Adjutant General Vol. 1–7 & 1–2; Essex, *Lynn*.

Wood, James O., enlisted for three years as a private at age 24 into the 2nd Company September 2, 1861, at Camp Saunders in Lynnfield. He was a farmer. He was born April 13, 1836, at Upton and his service was credited to Upton. He was discharged October 17, 1864. His parents' names were Orra and Fanny (Wood). Sources: Adjutant General Vol. 1–7 & 1–2; Rice, Franklin, *Upton*.

Wood William H., enlisted for three years as a private at age 25 into the 2nd Company August 6, 1862, at Camp Wightman Long Island, Boston. He was a shoemaker. He was born in 1837 and his service was credited to Webster. He reenlisted February 1, 1864, and received $325.00 and $60.00 bounties. He was transferred to the 19th Massachusetts Volunteer Infantry, Company M October 21, 1864, by Special Order as the Sharpshooters were being mustered out and he had time yet to serve. He was discharged June 29, 1865, from the 19th. It is possible he was born in Brookfield and his father was named Willard, but this could not be confirmed. Sources: Adjutant General Vol. 1–7 & 1–2; Stokinger; Microfilm Collection.

Woodbury, Benjamin F., enlisted for three years as a private at age 30 into the 2nd Company September 20, 1861, at Camp Saunders in Lynnfield. He was a painter. He was born July 6, 1833, in Danvers and his service was credited to South Danvers. He was promoted to sergeant. He was discharged October 17, 1864 (Ref. O.R.'s I, 40 cited for personal bravery on the 5th and 8th of May 1864). His parents' names were Benjamin and Emily Jane (Flower). Sources: Adjutant General Vol. 1–7 & 1–2; Root, Elihu; Essex, *Danvers*.

Wright, Abraham, enlisted for three years as a private at age 24 into the 2nd Company July 10, 1863, at Camp Wightman Long Island, Boston. He was a carriage maker. He was born in 1839 at Ballston, New York, and his service was credited to Lynn-Salisbury. He was transferred to the 19th Massachusetts Volunteer Infantry, Company M, October 26, 1864, as the Sharpshooters were being mustered out and he had time yet to serve. He was discharged June 29, 1865, from the 19th. He was in the battles of Rappahannock Station, Mine Run, the Wilderness, Laurel Hill, North Anna, Totopotomy Creek, and Petersburg, Virginia. Sources: Adjutant General Vol. 1–7 & 1–2; Stokinger; Adjutant Second Company.

Wyman, George W., enlisted for three years as a private at age 32 into the 2nd Company August 19, 1861, at Camp Saunders in Lynnfield. He was a blacksmith. He was born in 1827 and his service was credited to Lowell. He was given a disability discharge April 3, 1862, at New Market, Virginia. He was married and had three children. Sources: Adjutant General Vol. 1–7 & 1–2.

Young, George W., enlisted for three years as a private at age 42 into the 2nd Company August 27, 1861, at Camp Saunders in Lynnfield. He was a shoemaker. He was born in 1819 and his service was credited to Stoneham. He died of disease October 8, 1862, while at York, Pennsylvania. He was interred at Prospect Hill Cemetery in York. He married Rebecca Rowe at Stoneham June 2, 1837, and had a son, George William Parker Young on October 3, 1841. Sources: Adjutant General Vol. 1–7 & 1–2; U.S. Quartermaster's Department.

Glossary

Abatis: An obstruction made by felled trees or bent saplings pointed in the direction of the expected enemy attack.

Battery: Field artillery which consisted of six guns of the same caliber, each attached to a limber (two wheeled ammunition chest) pulled by three pairs of horses and supplied by six or more caissons (two or three ammunition chests mounted on four wheeled carts) each also pulled by six horses. The usual strength was 155 men, which consisted of one captain, four lieutenants, two staff sergeants, six sergeants, twelve corporals, six artificers, two buglers, fifty-two drivers and seventy cannoneers.

Breastworks: A low, temporary defense work built breast high and made of felled trees or rocks.

Conscripts: Drafted men. There was no draft in America until the Civil War. The Confederates started one in April of 1862 and the Union followed a year later.

Contrabands: Runaway slaves from Southern plantations who followed the Union Army and sought its protection. The term contraband of war was first used by General Benjamin Butler at Fort Monroe after he learned such slaves had built fortifications for the Confederates.

Copperheads: After the Battle of Manassas, the Democratic Party split into two factions: one supported the war efforts of the Union; the other wanted peace and would allow the South to secede. The latter faction was dubbed the Copperheads because they chose as badges the head of Liberty, which they cut from copper pennies; their contemporaries thought the name more appropriate in the sense of poisonous, treacherous snakes. The Copperheads worked against the Lincoln administration and supported the draft riots. They were unpopular with the Union soldiers.

Corduroy Road: A road in which logs were laid transversely to allow wagons to pass and not create deep ruts or sink in the mud.

Dirge: A tune which expresses grief or mourning, e.g., a hymn or choral service at a funeral.

Earthworks: Fortifications constructed with rocks, dirt, and other materials available. Often referred to as breastworks.

Haversack: A waterproof canvas bag about a foot square which carried soldiers' rations. It was slung over the right shoulder by a strap and rested on the left hip.

Knapsack: A backpack heavily painted and made of canvas, with the soldier's unit painted or stenciled on it, usually riding on a light wooden frame. In the summer it was heavy to carry on long marches and the soldiers preferred to wrap their belongings in a wool blanket slung over their left shoulder and tied at their right hip.

Mosby's Raiders: A band of partisan rangers which operated out of Middleburg in Loudoun County, Virginia, led by John Singleton Mosby. They were made up of men on leave from the Confederate Army, convalescents, and civilians who did not want to enlist in the Confederate Army. They used guerrilla tactics, and swift night operations. They attacked wagon trains and murdered picket guards and stragglers. They lived off the land and in residences in the area; they did not have a campsite. They were the greatest menace to Union troops in Northern Virginia. Orders were issued that if caught, they were to be hanged without a trial.

Pickets: An outpost of guards scattered far in advance of the main army's encampment. A picket guard was usually made up of one lieutenant, two sergeants, four corporals and forty privates. It was dangerous duty, as pickets would be the first to encounter any movement of the enemy. They were also shot at by snipers and partisan rangers.

Pioneers: Skilled soldiers taken from their units and assigned to pioneer duty, which consisted of labor to built fortifications, dig trenches, repair roads, construct bridges, fell trees, and any other manual labor needed by the army.

Reconnaissance: A small party of calvary or infantry which moved toward enemy lines to determine enemy positions, strength and movement. Regulations required daily reconnaissance when near an enemy force. Cavalry usually reconnoitered open space while infantry operated in mountainous terrain and wooded areas. They were not to engage the enemy — only observe.

Redan: A fortification with two parapets meeting at an angle which pointed outwards, very similar to a bastion.

Rifle pit: A shallow body length trench dug in the ground with the dirt dug from the hole piled up facing the enemy. The soldier lay prone on the ground and fired from that position.

Salt beef: A ration of one pound, four ounces of pickled beef, called salt beef or salt horse, preserved in brine and issued daily.

Sharps rifle: A breech-loading rifle designed by Christian Sharps. It was a thirty-inch-long single-shot percussion weapon with an open barrel sight. It was capable of being fired eight to ten times per minute versus three shots a minute by the muzzle loaders and was advantageous for skirmishes. The cavalry used the Sharps twenty-two inches long with a ring mounted on the side of it to clip to their saddles.

Skirmish: A clash of combatants on a small scale, without the engagement of the main army. A skirmish line was usually a loose formation ahead of, on each side of, and at the rear of the main body of marching troops. The skirmish line drew fire from the enemy, scouted the enemy position, and passed along that information to commanders.

Stack arms: A group of rifles in a pyramid shape, shoulder stock on the ground with their bayonets interlocked at the muzzle.

Sutler: A civilian business establishment officially appointed to a regiment to sell them approved goods at a set price. They operated out of wagons and set up tents which bulged with goods. They would extend credit to the soldiers for such items as razors, tin plates, cups, foods, tobacco, newspapers, books and many other items to comfort the soldier in the field. They charged exorbitant prices and were sometimes attacked and cleaned out by soldiers who felt they were being taken advantage of.

Vedette: A mounted sentry or picket guard on duty. The word is also spelled vidette and is derived from the Latin word *video* which meant to watch or see.

Notes

Chapter 1

1. William H. Hastings, *Letters From a Sharpshooter* (Belleville, WI: Historical Publications, 1993), iv–vi.
2. Commonwealth of Massachusetts, Executive Department, *War Record*. Maintained at the Office of the Adjutant General, Massachusetts National Guard Museum and Archives, Worcester, MA.
3. Alan Foulds, and Arthur Foulds, *Lynnfield: Two Centuries* (Lynnfield, MA: Bancroft Press, 1982), 28–29.
4. Adams, Sampson, and Co., *The Massachusetts Register, 1862, Containing A Record of the Government and Institutions of the State, Together With a Very Complete Account of the Massachusetts Volunteers* (Boston: Rand and Avery, 1862), 406–407.
5. James L. Bowen, *Massachusetts in the War, 1861–1865* (Springfield, MA: Bryan, 1889), 862.
6. Adams, Sampson, 406–407.
7. Commonwealth of Massachusetts, Executive Department, *War Record*.
8. Luke Emerson Bicknell, "The Sharpshooters" (Boston: Massachusetts Historical Society, 1883), 1–8.
9. Ibid., 2–3.
10. Ibid., 3.
11. Ibid., 4.
12. Ibid., 5.
13. Commonwealth of Massachusetts, Executive Department, *War Record*.
14. Bicknell, 5.
15. Ibid., 6.
16. General Order Book, [First Company Andrew Sharpshooters] September 1861 to June 1863, Massachusetts National Guard Museum and Archives. Worcester, MA.
17. Bicknell, 6–7.
18. General Order Book.
19. Ibid.
20. Bicknell, 6–7.

Chapter 2

1. General Order Book, [First Company Andrew Sharpshooters] September 1861 to June 1863, Massachusetts National Guard Museum and Archives. Worcester, MA.
2. Luke Emerson Bicknell, "The Sharpshooters" (Boston: Massachusetts Historical Society, 1883), 7.
3. Andrew E. Ford, *The Story of the Fifteenth Regiment Massachusetts Volunteer Infantry in the Civil War, 1861–1864* (Clinton, MA: Cutler. 1898), 66.
4. Ford, 75–79; Patricia L. Faust, ed., *Historical Times Illustrated Encyclopedia of the Civil War* (New York: Harper and Row, 1991), 720.
5. Ernest L. Waitt, *History of the Nineteenth Regiment Massachusetts Volunteer Infantry, 1861–1865* (Salem, MA: Salem Press, 1906), 21.
6. Adams, Sampson, and Co., *The Massachusetts Register, 1862, Containing A Record of the Government and Institutions of the State, Together with a Very Complete Account of the Massachusetts Volunteers* (Boston: Rand and Avery, 1862), 407.
7. Bicknell, 8.
8. Ibid., 9.
9. Waitt, 30–34.
10. Bicknell, 11.
11. Ibid., 12
12. Ibid., 13
13. General Order Book.
14. Bicknell, 13.
15. Ibid., 13–15.
16. Ibid., 15–17.
17. Ibid., 18.
18. Ibid., 18–19.
19. Ibid., 21.
20. Ibid., 22.
21. Ibid., 24.
22. Ibid., 25.
23. Ibid., 27.
24. Ford, 145.

Chapter 3

1. Luke Emerson Bicknell, "The Sharpshooters" (Boston: Massachusetts Historical Society, 1883), 27–28.
2. Ibid., 29.

3. Ibid., 30.
4. Ibid., 32–33.
5. Ibid., 34.
6. Ibid., 35.
7. Ibid., 36.
8. Ibid., 37–38.
9. Ibid., 39.

Chapter 4

1. Luke Emerson Bicknell, "The Sharpshooters" (Boston: Massachusetts Historical Society, 1883), 39–40.
2. Ibid., 42.
3. Ibid., 41.
4. Patricia L. Faust, ed., *Historical Times Illustrated Encyclopedia of the Civil War* (New York: Harper and Row, 1991), 471.
5. Bicknell, 43–44.
6. Ibid., 46–47.
7. Ibid., 48.
8. Faust, 129.
9. Antietam Battlefield Board, *Atlas of the Battlefield of Antietam* (Washington, D.C.: Government Printing Office, 1904), 48–50.
10. Bicknell, 50–51; Andrew E. Ford, *The Story of the Fifteenth Regiment Massachusetts Volunteer Infantry in the Civil War, 1861–1864* (Clinton, MA: Cutler. 1898), 194–195.
11. Bicknell, 5.
12. Ibid., 51; Ford, 164–169.
13. Bicknell, 51–52.
14. Ford, 210; Bicknell, 59.
15. Bicknell, 52–55.

Chapter 5

1. Tom A.C. Ellis, *Biographical Roster of Andrew Sharpshooters*. Information derived from that roster.
2. Luke Emerson Bicknell, "The Sharpshooters" (Boston: Massachusetts Historical Society, 1883), 56.
3. Andrew E. Ford, *The Story of the Fifteenth Regiment Massachusetts Volunteer Infantry in the Civil War, 1861–1864* (Clinton, MA: Cutler. 1898), 198.
4. Ford, 212.
5. Ibid., 213–214.
6. Ibid., 214.
7. Ibid., 220–221.
8. Bicknell, 57.
9. General Order Book, [First Company Andrew Sharpshooters] September 1861 to June 1863, Massachusetts National Guard Museum and Archives. Worcester, MA.
10. Bicknell, 58.
11. General Order Book.
12. Bicknell, 58–59.
13. Adjutant General, Commonwealth of Massachusetts, *Massachusetts Soldiers, Sailors, and Marines in the Civil War.* Vols. 1–7 (Boston: Wright & Potter, 1937).
14. General Order Book
15. Bicknell, 59–60; General Order Book.
16. Bicknell, 61–62.
17. General Order Book; Capt. William Plummer, O.R., Ser. 1, Vol. 21 [S# 31], December 11–15, 1862, Battle of Fredericksburg, Va., No. 83.
18. General Order Book.

Chapter 6

1. Luke Emerson Bicknell, "The Sharpshooters" (Boston: Massachusetts Historical Society, 1883), 62–63.
2. Ibid., 63–65.
3. Ibid., 65–68.
4. Gregory A. Coco, *From Ball's Bluff to Gettysburg, and Beyond.* (Gettysburg, PA: Thomas, 1994), 158.
5. Bicknell, 69–71.
6. Ibid., 71–75.
7. Ibid., 74–76.
8. Gettysburg National Park, *Battle Field Maps.* Three in total. One for each day.
9. Bicknell, 76–78.
10. Tom A. C. Ellis, *Biographical Roster of Andrew Sharpshooters.* Information derived from that roster.
11. Bicknell, 79–80; Robert U. Johnson, and Clarence C. Buel, *Battles and Leaders of the Civil War,* Vol. 3 (New York: Devine, 1884), 391–392.
12. Bicknell, 84.
13. Bicknell, 85–86.
14. Bicknell, 87–91; Adams, Sampson, and Co., *The Massachusetts Register, 1862, Containing A Record of the Government and Institutions of the State, Together with a Very Complete Account of the Massachusetts Volunteers* (Boston: Rand and Avery, 1862), 406–408.
15. Ellis; John B. Bachelder, Bachelder Papers, vols. 1–3, New Hampshire Historical Society.
16. Bicknell, 92.

Chapter 7

1. Luke Emerson Bicknell, "The Sharpshooters" (Boston: Massachusetts Historical Society, 1883), 93.
2. Company Records [First Company Andrew Sharpshooters] December 9, 1862, to August 9, 1864, Massachusetts National Guard Museum and Archives, Worcester, MA.
3. Ibid.
4. Bicknell, 93; Company Records.
5. Company Records.
6. Bicknell, 93.
7. Ibid., 94; Company Records.
8. Company Records
9. Bicknell, 98–99.
10. Company Records
11. General Order Book [*First Company Andrew Sharpshooters*], September 1861 to June 1863 Massachusetts National Guard Museum and Archives. Worcester, MA; Tom A. C. Ellis, *Biographical Roster of Andrew Sharpshooters.* Information derived from that roster.
12. General Order Book.
13. Company Records.
14. *Boston Journal,* morning edition, September 1,

1863, page two, column two, in the Boston Public Library's Micro-Text Division.
15. Company Records.
16. General Order Book
17. Richard F. Miller, *Harvard's Civil War, A History of the History of the Twentieth Massachusetts Volunteer Infantry* (Lebanon, NH: University Press of New England, 2005), 288–289.
18. Company Records.
19. Miller.
20. Major Abbott, October 9–22 1863 ,O.R., Seri. 1, vol. 29/1 [S#48].
21. Company Records.
22. Ibid.; Ellis.
23. Company Records.
24. John L. Parker, *History Of The Twenty-Second Massachusetts Infantry, The Second Company Sharpshooters, And The Third Light Battery, In The War Of The Rebellion* (Boston: Regimental Association, Press Of Rand Avery, 1887), 390–391.
25. Ellis.
26. Company Records; Ellis.

Chapter 8

1. Company Records [First Company Andrew Sharpshooters] December 9, 1862, to August 9, 1864, Massachusetts National Guard Museum and Archives. Worcester, MA; Tom A. C. Ellis, *Biographical Roster of Andrew Sharpshooters*. Information derived from that roster.
2. Company Records.
3. Ibid., Ellis.
4. Patricia L. Faust, ed., *Historical Times Illustrated Encyclopedia of the Civil War* (New York: Harper and Row, 1991), 68.
5. Company Records; Ellis.
6. Company Records; Ellis.
7. Company Records
8. Richard F. Miller, *Harvard's Civil War, A History Of The History Of The Twentieth Massachusetts Volunteer Infantry* (Lebanon, NH: University Press of New England, 2005), 389–390; Company Records.
9. Company Records
10. George A. Bruce, *The Twentieth Regiment Of Massachusetts Volunteer Infantry 1861–1865* (Cambridge, MA: Riverside Press, 1906), 416; Miller, 405.
11. Miller, 406.
12. Ibid., 407–409.
13. Ibid., 411–417.
14. Ellis; Miller, 417–419.

Chapter 9

1. John L. Parker, *History Of The Twenty-Second Massachusetts Infantry, The Second Company Sharpshooters, And The Third Light Battery, In The War Of The Rebellion* (Boston: Regimental Association, Press Of Rand Avery, 1887), 27; Lewis E. Wentworth, *Journal Of The Second Company*. Massachusetts Historical Society. Journal written and maintained by Sergeant Nathan W. Haynes. October 1861– April 1863, np.
2. Parker, 34; Wentworth.
3. Parker, 41; Wentworth.
4. Wentworth, Lewis E.
5. Wentworth; Parker, 41–44.
6. Parker, 44–48; Wentworth.
7. Parker, 48–53; Wentworth.
8. Parker, 53; Wentworth.
9. Parker, 57; Wentworth.
10. Wentworth.
11. Ibid.
12. General Orders, Headquarters 22nd Massachusetts Regiment, Halls Hill, Va., December 11, 1861, Adjutant Generals Office, Commonwealth of Massachusetts, Massachusetts National Guard Museum & Archives, Worcester, MA.
13. Wentworth.
14. Ibid.

Chapter 10

1. Lewis E. Wentworth, *Journal of the Second Company*. Massachusetts Historical Society. Journal written and maintained by Sergeant Nathan W. Haynes. October 1861–April 1863, np.
2. Ibid.
3. John L. Parker, *History of the Twenty-Second Massachusetts Infantry, The Second Company Sharpshooters, And the Third Light Battery, In the War of the Rebellion* (Boston: Regimental Association, Press of Rand Avery, 1887), 65; Wentworth.
4. Parker, 74; Wentworth.
5. Parker, 73; Wentworth.
6. Wentworth, Lewis E.
7. Parker, 76; Wentworth.
8. Parker, 76–80; Wentworth.
9. Parker, 83; Wentworth.
10. Wentworth.

Chapter 11

1. Lewis E. Wentworth, *Journal of the Second Company*. Massachusetts Historical Society. Journal written and maintained by Sergeant Nathan W. Haynes. October 1861— April 1863, np.
2. John L. Parker, *History of the Twenty-Second Massachusetts Infantry, The Second Company Sharpshooters, And the Third Light Battery, In the War of the Rebellion* (Boston: Regimental Association, Press of Rand Avery, 1887), 88–90; Wentworth.
3. Parker, 91; Wentworth.
4. Wentworth.
5. Parker, 93–94; Wentworth.
6. Wentworth.
7. Parker, 96.
8. Ibid., 99; Wentworth.
9. Parker, 101.
10. Wentworth.
11. Parker, 104; Wentworth.
12. Parker, 109; Wentworth.
13. Wentworth.

Chapter 12

1. John L. Parker, *History of the Twenty-Second Massachusetts Infantry, The Second Company Sharpshooters, And the Third Light Battery, In the War of the Rebellion* (Boston: Regimental Association, Press of Rand Avery, 1887), 112–113; Lewis E. Wentworth, *Journal Of The Second Company.* Massachusetts Historical Society. Journal written and maintained by Sergeant Nathan W. Haynes. October 1861–April 1863, np.
2. Parker, 114; Wentworth.
3. Parker, 116; Wentworth.
4. Wentworth, Lewis E.
5. Parker, 120; Wentworth.
6. Wentworth.
7. Parker, 127; Wentworth.
8. Wentworth.
9. Parker, 129–130; Wentworth.
10. Wentworth.
11. Parker, 153; Wentworth.
12. Wentworth.
13. Parker, 154–155; Wentworth.
14. Wentworth.
15. Parker, 156; Wentworth.
16. Parker, 157; Wentworth.
17. Wentworth, Lewis E.
18. Parker, 158–159; Wentworth.
19. Parker, 159–160; Wentworth.
20. Parker, 161–163; Wentworth.
21. Wentworth.
22. Parker, 186; Wentworth.
23. Parker, 187–194; Wentworth.
24. Wentworth.

Chapter 13

1. John L. Parker, *History of the Twenty-Second Massachusetts Infantry, The Second Company Sharpshooters, And the Third Light Battery, In the War of the Rebellion* (Boston: Regimental Association, Press of Rand Avery, 1887), 197; Lewis E. Wentworth, *Journal of the Second Company.* Massachusetts Historical Society. Journal written and maintained by Sergeant Nathan W. Haynes. October 1861— April 1863, np.
2. Parker, 204; Wentworth.
3. Wentworth, Lewis E.
4. Parker, 206; Wentworth.
5. Parker, 210; Wentworth.
6. Parker, 215; Wentworth.
7. Parker, 219; Wentworth.
8. Wentworth, Lewis E.
9. Parker, 224–225; Wentworth.
10. Parker, 226–229; Wentworth.
11. Parker, 236–237; Wentworth.
12. Parker, 237–238; Wentworth.
13. Parker, 243–244; Wentworth.
14. Wentworth, Lewis E.
15. Parker, 245–247; Wentworth.
16. Wentworth, Lewis E.
17. Parker, 250; Wentworth.
18. Tom A. C. Ellis, *Biographical Roster of Andrew Sharpshooters.* Information derived from that roster.
19. Wentworth.

Chapter 14

1. John L. Parker, *History of the Twenty-Second Massachusetts Infantry, The Second Company Sharpshooters, and the Third Light Battery, In the War of the Rebellion* (Boston: Regimental Association, Press of Rand Avery, 1887), 251; Lewis E. Wentworth, *Journal of the Second Company.* Massachusetts Historical Society. Journal written and maintained by Sergeant Nathan W. Haynes. October 1861— April 1863, np.
2. Parker, 284–285.
3. Ibid., 286–288.
4. Ibid., 289–292.
5. Ibid., 293–297.
6. Ibid., 320–324.
7. Ibid., 325–328.
8. Ibid., 325–334; General Orders, Headquarters 22nd Massachusetts Regiment, Halls Hill, Va., December 11, 1861, Adjutant Generals Office, Commonwealth of Massachusetts, Massachusetts National Guard Museum & Archives, Worcester, MA.
9. General Orders, Headquarters 22nd Massachusetts.
10. Parker, 335–338; General Orders, Headquarters 22nd Massachusetts.
11. Parker, 339–343; General Orders, Headquarters 22nd Massachusetts.

Chapter 15

1. Tom A. C. Ellis, *Biographical Roster of Andrew Sharpshooters.* Information derived from that roster; Elihu Root and Robert N. Scott. *War of the Rebellion: Official Records, Union and Confederate Armies,* vol. 1. (Washington, D.C.: Government Printing Office, 1880), 36.
2. John L. Parker, *History of the Twenty-Second Massachusetts Infantry, The Second Company Sharpshooters, and the Third Light Battery, In the War of the Rebellion* (Boston: Regimental Association, Press of Rand Avery, 1887), 345.
3. Ibid., 346–352.
4. Ibid., 354–372.
5. Ibid., 373–376.
6. Ibid., 382–386.
7. Ibid., 389.

Chapter 16

1. John L. Parker, *History of the Twenty-Second Massachusetts Infantry, The Second Company Sharpshooters, And the Third Light Battery, In the War of the Rebellion* (Boston: Regimental Association, Press of Rand Avery, 1887), 391–394.
2. Ibid., 395–398.
3. Ibid., 399–429.
4. Ibid., 432.
5. Tom A. C. Ellis, *Biographical Roster of Andrew Sharpshooters.* Information derived from that roster.
6. Parker, 432–445.
7. Ibid., 446–450.
8. Ellis.

9. Parker, 452–462; Ellis.
10. Parker, 464–473.
12. George A. Bruce, *The Twentieth Regiment of Massachusetts Volunteer Infantry, 1861–1865* (Cambridge, MA: Riverside Press, 1906).
13. Letter from Major Mason Burt to Adjutant General of the United States Army, August 11, 1864, Massachusetts National Guard Museum and Archives, Worcester, MA. Burt states enlistments expire September 16, 1864.
14. Parker, 474–486.
15. Ibid., 487–491.

Bibliography

Abbott, Lemuel Abijah. *Descendants of George Abbott of Rowley, Massachusetts.* Boston: T. R. Marvin, 1906.

Adjutant, Andrews Sharpshooters, 1st Company. *Descriptive Rolls,* Worcester, MA, 1861.

———. *Muster in Rolls,* Worcester, MA, 1861.

Adjutant, Andrews Sharpshooters, 2nd Company. *Descriptive Rolls,* Worcester, MA, 1861.

Adjutant General, Commonwealth of Massachusetts. *Massachusetts Soldiers, Sailors, and Marines in the Civil War.* Vols. 1–7. Boston: Wright & Potter, 1937.

———. *Record of the Massachusetts Volunteers.* Vols. 1–2. Boston: Wright & Potter, 1870.

Antietam Battlefield Board. *Atlas of the Battlefield of Antietam.* Washington, D.C.: Government Printing Office, 1904.

Baldwin, Thomas W. *Vital Records of Cambridge, Massachusetts, to the Year 1850.* Boston: Wright & Potter, 1914.

———. *Vital Records of Harvard, Massachusetts, to the Year 1850.* Boston: Wright & Potter, 1917.

———. *Vital Records of Natick, Massachusetts, to the Year 1850.* Boston: Stanhope, 1910.

———. *Vital Records of Northbridge, Massachusetts, to the Year 1850.* Boston: Wright & Potter, 1916.

———. *Vital Records of Reading, Massachusetts, to the Year 1850.* Boston: Wright & Potter, 1917.

———. *Vital Records of Wakefield, Massachusetts, to the Year 1850.* Boston: Wright & Potter, 1914.

Ballou, Adin. *History of the Town of Milford.* Boston: Franklin, 1882.

Bicknell, Luke Emerson. "The Sharpshooters." Boston: Massachusetts Historical Society, 1883.

Boston Public Library's Micro-Text Division published September 1, 1863, in the Morning Edition of the Boston Journal, page two, column two.

Bowen, James L. *Massachusetts in the War, 1861–1865.* Springfield, MA: Bryan, 1889.

Bowman, George Ernest. *Vital Records of the Town of Brewster, Massachusetts, to the End of the Year 1849.* Boston: Massachusetts Society of Mayflower Descendants, 1904.

Bruce, George A. *The Twentieth Regiment of Massachusetts Volunteer Infantry, 1861–1865.* Cambridge, MA: Riverside Press, 1906.

Burt, Mason. Letter from Major to Adjutant General of the United States Army, August 11, 1864. Massachusetts National Guard Museum and Archives. Worcester, MA.

Cambridge Historical Society. *History of Cambridge, Massachusetts, 1630–1877. Supplement and Index.* Cambridge, MA: Cambridge Historical Society, 1930.

Chapman, Henry Smith. *History of Winchester, Massachusetts.* Winchester, MA: Town of Winchester, 1936.

Civil War Papers. Stoneham Public Library, Stoneham, MA.

Clerk, Town of Hopkinton, Massachusetts. "Town Soldiers' Record." Historical Papers Collection. Hopkinton Public Library, Hopkinton, MA.

Coco, Gregory A. *From Ball's Bluff to Gettysburg, and Beyond.* Gettysburg, PA: Thomas, 1994.

Creasey, George W. *The City of Newburyport in the Civil War, 1861–1865.* Boston: Griffith-Sillings, 1903.

Dole, Samuel Thomas. *Windham in the Past.* Auburn, ME: Merrill & Webber, 1916.

Dwelley, Jedediah, and John Simmons. *History of the Town of Hanover, Massachusetts.* Hanover, MA: Town of Hanover, 1910.

Eaton, Lilley. *Genealogical History of the Town of Reading, Massachusetts.* Boston: Mudge, 1874.

Ellis, Harry H. *The Family of Lt. John and Elizabeth (Freeman) Ellis of Sandwich, Massachusetts.* Boston: New England Historic Genealogical Society, 1983.

Essex Institute. *Vital Records of Carlisle, Massachusetts, to the Year 1850.* Salem, MA: Newcomb & Gaus, 1918.

———. *Vital Records of Danvers, Massachusetts, to the Year 1850.* Salem, MA: Newcomb & Gaus, 1928.

———. *Vital Records of Georgetown, Massachusetts, to the Year 1850.* Salem, MA: Newcomb & Gaus, 1906.

———. *Vital Records of Ipswich, Massachusetts, to the Year 1850.* Salem, MA: Newcomb & Gaus, 1910.

———. *Vital Records of Lowell, Massachusetts, to the Year 1850.* Salem, MA: Newcomb & Gaus, 1930.

_____. *Vital Records of Lynn, Massachusetts, to the Year 1850.* Salem, MA: Newcomb & Gaus, 1905.

_____. *Vital Records of Lynnfield, Massachusetts, to the End of the Year 1849.* Salem, MA: Newcomb & Gaus, 1907.

_____. *Vital Records of Mansfield, Massachusetts, to the Year 1850.* Salem, MA: Newcomb & Gaus, 1933.

_____. *Vital Records of Marblehead, Massachusetts, to the End of the Year 1849.* Salem, MA: Newcomb & Gaus, 1903.

_____. *Vital Records of Newburyport, Massachusetts, to the Year 1850.* Salem, MA: Newcomb & Gaus, 1911.

_____. *Vital Records of Rowley, Massachusetts, to the Year 1850.* Salem, MA: Newcomb & Gaus, 1928.

_____. *Vital Records of Roxbury, Massachusetts, to the Year 1850.* Salem, MA: Newcomb & Gaus, 1926.

_____. *Vital Records of Salem, Massachusetts, to the Year 1850.* Salem, MA: Newcomb & Gaus, 1916.

_____. *Vital Records of Saugus, Massachusetts, to the Year 1850.* Salem, MA: Newcomb & Gaus, 1916.

_____. *Vital Records of Stoneham, Massachusetts, to the Year 1850.* Salem, MA: Newcomb & Gaus, 1918.

Everest, David Clark. *Descendants of Andrew Everest.* Concord, NH: Rumford, 1955.

Faust, Patricia L. *Historical Times Illustrated Encyclopedia of the Civil War.* New York: Harper & Row, 1986.

Ford, Andrew E. *The Story of the Fifteenth Regiment Massachusetts Volunteer Infantry in the Civil War, 1861–1864.* Clinton, MA: Cutler, 1898.

___. *History of the Origin of the Town of Clinton, Massachusetts, 1653–1865.* Clinton, MA: Coulter, 1896.

Foulds, Alan, and Arthur Foulds. *Lynnfield: Two Centuries.* Lynnfield, MA: Bancroft, 1982.

Furber, George C., and James R. Jackson. *History of Littleton, New Hampshire.* Cambridge, MA: University Press, 1905.

General Order Book, First Company Andrew Sharpshooters. Worcester, MA: Adjutant General, Commonwealth of Massachusetts, September 1861 to June 1863.

Hadley, George P. *History of the Town of Goffstown.* Concord, NH: Rumford, 1924.

Harnwell, Susan. Roster and Genealogies of the 15th Massachusetts Volunteer Infantry. http://www.nextech.de/ma15mvi/ma15mvi-p/index.htm?ssmain=p12.htm.

Hastings, William H. *Letters From A Sharpshooter.* Belleville, WI: Historic, 1993.

Haynes, Francis. *Walter Haynes and His Descendants.* Haverhill, MA: Record, 1929.

Haynes, Nathan W. "Journal of Second Company, Massachusetts Volunteer Sharpshooters." In *Historical Society Papers.* Boston: Massachusetts Historical Society, October 1861 to April 1863. Also referred to as Wentworth, Lewis.

Hill, Don Gleason. *The Record of Baptisms, Marriages, and Deaths, and Admissions to the Church and Dismissals Therefrom, Transcribed from the Church Records in the Town of Dedham, Massachusetts, 1638–1845.* Dedham, MA: Town of Dedham, 1888.

Hudson, Charles. *History of the Town of Lexington.* Boston: Wiggins & Lunt, 1868.

Jameson, E.O. *Medway, Massachusetts, 1713–1865.* Medway, MA: Town of Medway, 1886.

Johnson, Robert Underwood, and Clarence Clough Buel. *Battles and Leaders of the Civil War.* Vol. 3. New York: De Vinne, 1884.

Joslyn, Roger D. *Vital Records of Charlestown, Massachusetts, to the Year 1850.* Boston: New England Historic Genealogical Society, 1984.

Lainhart, Ann S. *1855 and 1865 Massachusetts State Census for Marlborough.* Boston: Privately printed, 1986.

_____. *1855 and 1865 Massachusetts State Census for Natick.* Boston: Privately printed, 1986.

Lewis, George Harlan. *Edmund Lewis, of Lynn, Massachusetts, and Some of His Descendants.* Salem, MA: Essex Institute, 1908.

"Lewis E. Wentworth, journal, 10 October 1861, *Civil War Correspondence, Diaries, and Journals at the Massachusetts Historical Society, 1754–1926,* microfilm edition, 1 reel. Boston: Massachusetts Historical Society, 1985.

Lynnfield Heritage Associates. *History of Lynnfield, 1635–1895.* New Canaan, NH: Phoenix, 1977.

Lynnfield Public Library Genealogy Microfilm Collection, Lynnfield Center, MA.

Massachusetts Register. *A Very Complete Account of the Massachusetts Volunteers.* Boston: Adams, Sampson, 1862.

Meserve, Charles A. *Record of Births and Deaths in the Town of Buxton.* Portland, ME: Maine Historical Society, 1891.

Miller, Richard F. *Harvard's Civil War: A History of the Twentieth Massachusetts Volunteer Infantry.* Hanover, NH: University Press of New England, 2006.

Mudgett, Mildred D., and Bruce D. Mudgett. *Thomas Mudgett of Salisbury, Massachusetts, and Some of His Descendants.* Bennington, VT: Privately printed, 1961.

New England Historic Genealogy Society, and Eddy Town Record Fund. *Vital Records of Bedford, Massachusetts, to the Year 1850.* Boston: Stanhope, 1903.

_____. *Vital Records of Medway, Massachusetts, to the Year 1850.* Boston: Stanhope, 1905.

_____. *Vital Records of Stow, Massachusetts, to the Year 1850.* Boston: Stanhope, 1911.

Orders, General Headquarters, 22nd Mass. Regt., Halls Hill, Va., December 11, 1861. Adjutant Generals Office, Commonwealth of Massachusetts. Massachusetts National Guard Museum and Archives, Worcester, MA.

Osgood, Ira A. *A Genealogy of the Descendants of John, Christopher, and William Osgood.* Salem, MA: Salem, 1984.

Parker, John L. *History of the Twenty-Second Massachusetts Infantry, The Second Company Sharpshooters, and the Third Light Battery, in the War of the Rebellion.* Boston: Regimental Association, Press of Rand Avery, 1887.

Peck, Theodore S. *Revised Roster of Vermont Volunteers.* Montpelier, VT: Watchman, 1892.

Perley, M.V.B. *The Perley Family.* Salem, MA: Privately printed, 1906.

Putnam, Eben. *Report of the Committee Appointed to Revise the Soldiers' Record.* Danvers, MA: Town of Danvers, 1895.

Rice, Franklin P. *Vital Records of Brookfield, Massachu-*

setts, to the End of the Year 1849. Worcester, MA: Systematic History Fund, 1909.

———. *Vital Records of Grafton, Massachusetts, to the Year 1850.* Boston: Stanhope, 1906.

———. *Vital Records of Shrewsbury, Massachusetts, to the Year 1850.* Boston: Stanhope, 1904.

———. *Vital Records of Sutton, Massachusetts, to the Year 1850.* Boston: Stanhope, 1907.

———. *Vital Records of Upton, Massachusetts, to the Year 1850.* Boston: Stanhope, 1904.

Root, Elihu, and Robert N. Scott. *War of the Rebellion: Official Records, Union and Confederate Armies.* Washington, D.C.: Government Printing Office, 1880.

Salem Street Directory, 1861. Salem, MA: Salem Public Library, 1861.

Sheldon, George. *History of Deerfield, Massachusetts.* Greenfield, MA: Hall, 1896.

Smith, Charles J. *History of Mount Vernon, New Hampshire.* Boston: Blanchard, 1907.

Stevens, William B. *History of Stoneham, Massachusetts.* Stoneham, MA: Whittier, 1891.

Stokinger, W. A., A. K. Schroeder, and Captain A. A. Swanson. *Civil War Camps at Readville.* Boston: Reservations and Historic Sites M.D.C., 1990.

Streeter, William, and Daphne Morris. *Vital Records of Cummington, 1782–1900.* Cummington, MA: Privately printed, 1979.

Sturtevant, Robert Hunter. *Descendants of Samuel Sturtevant.* Waco, TX: Texian, 1986.

Systematic History Fund, and Franklin Price. *Vital Records of Millbury, Massachusetts, to the Year 1850.* Boston: Stanhope, 1903.

"The Sharpshooters, 1883," in *Civil War Correspondence, Diaries, and Journals at the Massachusetts Historical Society,* 1754–1926, microfilm edition, 1 reel. Massachusetts Historical Society.

Topsfield Historical Society. *Vital Records of Andover, Massachusetts, to the End of the Year 1849.* Salem, MA: Newcomb & Gauss, 1912.

———. *Vital Records of Beverly, Massachusetts, to the End of the Year 1849.* Salem, MA: Newcomb & Gauss, 1907.

———. *Vital Records of Haverhill, Massachusetts, to the Year 1849.* Salem, MA: Newcomb & Gauss, 1910.

———. *Vital Records of Middleton, Massachusetts, to the Year 1849.* Salem, MA: Newcomb & Gauss, 1904.

Town of Lexington. *Vital Records of Lexington to 1898.* Boston: Wright & Potter, 1898.

U.S. Quartermaster Department. *Roll of Honor.* Vols.1–12. Washington, D.C.: Government Printing Office, 1868.

Waitt, Ernest L. *History of the Nineteenth Regiment Massachusetts Volunteer Infantry, 1861–1865.* Salem, MA: Salem Press, 1906.

Wentworth, John. *The Wentworth Genealogy.* Boston: Little, Brown, 1878.

Wentworth, Lewis E. Massachusetts Historical Society. Journal written and maintained by Sergeant Nathan W. Haynes. October 1861– April 1863.

Williamson, Joseph. *History of Belfast in the State of Maine.* Portland, ME: Loring, Short, & Harmon, 1877.

Index

Numbers in ***bold italics*** indicate pages with photographs and illustrations.

Abbott, Maj. Henry L. 76, 78, 82
Adams, Pvt. Henry H. 195
Adams, Pvt. John Quincy 43
Alexandria, VA 39, 96, 107, 109–110, 141; Roundhouse Station **29**
Allen, Pvt. George 84
Allen, Pvt. William H. 113
Allsop's Farm 194, 196, ***196***
Ambrose, Pvt. John B. 10
Ambulance Train ***69***
Andrew, Gov. John Albion 7, 10, ***12***, 14–15, 39, 52, 69–70, 99, 111, 154, 181
Andrew Sharpshooters ***6***
Andrews, Pvt. Edward A. 23
Antietam Battle 46, 144, ***144***
Antietam Creek 41
Antietam East Woods 41
Appomattox River 208
Aquia Creek, VA 138, ***138***
Armistead, Gen. Lewis Addison 1, 66
Arnold, Pvt. Marcus Palmer 51
Arnott, Pvt. John 51
Artillery at Fair Oaks, VA ***33***
Ashby, Gen. Turner 25–26, ***26***
Averill, Pvt. Trask Woodbury 51

Ball's Bluff 18, 96–97
Bancroft, Sgt. Robert B. 80
Banks, Gen. Nathaniel Prentiss 19–20, 27, 182
Barker, Pvt. Samuel S. (aka Samuel Sprague) 46
Barlow, Gen. Francis Channing 88
Barnes, Col. James 113, 132–134, 143, 155, 163, 168, 172
Barnes, U.S. Surgeon Joseph ***49***
Bartlett, Pvt. Alonzo W. 81, 83
Bartlett, Gen. Joseph Jackson 186
Bartlett, Pvt. Sylvanus 100
Batchelder, Pvt. Alfred A. 51, 65
Beauregard, CSA Gen. Pierre Gustave Toutant 204
Bellows, Rev. Henry 94

Bently, Pvt. Noah 51
Berdan, Col. Hiram 7–8, ***8***, 10
Berdan's Sharpshooters 7, 178
Berry, Gen. Hiram Gregory 169
Berry, 2nd Lt. William Burges 14, 30, 39, 41, 43
Bestwick, Pvt. Frederick Litchfield 51
Bicknell, Emerson Luke 10, 14, 17–25, 28, 30–32, 34, 37–39, 43–45, 49, 52–54, 57–60, 62–65, 67–70
Big Bethel, VA 111
Blenker, Gen. Louis 100, 103
Bloody Angle 83
Botts, John Minor 102–103, ***102***
Bowen, Pvt. Roland E. 58
Brandy Station 76, 78, 81, 183, 185, 188, 190, 192
Bristoe Station 78–79, 140, 172
Brown, Pvt. John H. 23
Bryan House, Gettysburg 64, ***64***
Bull Run 102
Burdett, Cpl. George 100
Burns, Gen. William Wallace 103
Burnside, Gen. Ambrose Everett 48, 52, 106, 145, 153, 159, 161–163, 201
Burrill, Pvt. Alden 94
Burrows, Pvt. John A. 10
Burt, Maj. Mason W. 207
Butterfield, Gen. Daniel Adams 103, 160
Butters, Pvt. Daniel H. 51

Cameron, Secretary of War Simon 15, 99, 103
Camp Benton, Poolesville, MD 15, 20
Camp Gove 166
Camp Saunders 9, 92
Camp Schouler 8
Camp Smokey 154
Catlett Station 78, 172, 183, ***184***, 197

Cemetery Ridge, Gettysburg 60
Centreville, VA 109, 141, 183
Chamberlain, Col. Joshua Lawrence 177
Champney, Pvt. John H. 51
Chancellor House 168–170
Chancellorsville, VA, battle 54, 56, 168–169, 171
Chapman, Pvt. Ezra 199
Charles City Courthouse 86, 136, 202–203
Chartres, Duc de 103
Chase, Pvt. Samuel E. 51, 83
Chickahominy River 37, 124–125, 136, 202
Christian Commission 109
City Point VA 87, ***207***, 208, ***209***
Clement, Oscar H. 29, 50, 68–69, 71–72, 76; court-martial 77
Coburn, Pvt. Horace G. 51
Colburn, Pvt. Henry F. 161
Cold Harbor 85, 121, 201–202, 204
Congress 137
Cookhouse ***106***
Corps of Engineers 50, ***51***, 53
Cowdrey, Pvt. Isaac B. 113–114
Crane, Pvt. Robert T. 51
Cromack, Rev. Joseph C. 100
Crossman, Pvt. Ferdinand J.F. 51, 57, 83
Culpepper Court House 76, 183, 186, 192
Cumberland 137
Cumberland, MD 22
Curtis, George 51, 78, 80–81, 83–84

Darbytown Road 88
Davidson, Pvt. Edward F. 94
Davis, CSA Pres. Jefferson 31, 34
Dearborn, Pvt. William H. 121
Deep Bottom 87, ***88***, 89
Deep Run at Rappahannock River 57, 62, 172
Deland, Pvt. Moses 201

263

Index

Devil's Den, Gettysburg 178
Dike, Pvt. William M. 28
Donelson, Fort 107
Dunkard Church, Antietam *42*

Early, CSA Gen. Jubal Anderson 192
Eaton, Pvt. Daniel W. 87, 90
Edward's Ferry 10, 40, 60, 175
Eighteenth Mass. Volunteer Infantry 103, 107, 113, 164, 188
Eighth Ohio Regiment 64, 80
Eleventh Mass. Volunteer Infantry 116
Ellis, Nathan B. 51, 81, 82
Ely Ford 80–81
Emmitsburg Road, Gettysburg 60–61, 65–67, 175, 179
Evans, 2nd Lt. Alvan Augustus 94, *95*
Ewell, CSA Gen. Richard Stoddert 193, 197

Fair Oaks, VA 33, 123
Fairfax, VA 40, 106, 108–109, 174–175, 183
Fairfax Seminary 142
Falmouth, VA 48, 50, 53, 139
Faneuil Hall *12*, 40
Faulkner, Pvt. John W. 125
Federal Gunboats 38
Fifteenth Mass. Volunteer Infantry 18, 40–41, 43, 47–48, 50, 54, 66, 80, 96
Fifth Mass. Battery 111
Fifth U.S. Battery 122
Fiftieth NY Eng. 171, ***171***
Fifty Ninth NY Infantry 43–44, 80
First Calif. Volunteer Infantry, 18
First Mass. Cavalry 174
First Mass. Volunteer Infantry 116
Fisher's Hill, VA 26
Floyd, CSA Gen. John Buchanan 107
Foinville, Prince de 103
Forbes, Pvt. William C. 10
Fortress Monroe, VA 29, 39, 110, 113
Forty-Fifth Pennsylvania Regiment 145
Forty-Fourth NY Regiment 122
Fourth Michigan Volunteer Infantry 164, 195, 201
Franklin, Gen. William Buel 119
Frederick, MD 46, 60, 68, 143, 175, 179
Fredericksburg, VA 49–50, 138, 153–154, 157, ***158***
French, Gen. William Henry 181, 186
Fuller Pvt. Sanford K. 62
Funkstown MD 180
Furness, Pvt. George 94
Fussell's Farm 89

Gaines's Mill 122, 125, 128, 202
Gainesville, VA 140, 183–184
Gainesville Battle 36, 131
Gardener, Pvt. Charles A. 51
Gardener, Pvt. James W. 201

Garibaldi Regiment 103
General Order No. 191 81, 189
Germanna Ford 187, 192
Gettysburg, PA 58, 60
Gibbon, Gen. John 50, 53–54, 60, 62, 83
Gilbreth, Samuel Gordon 10, 12, 19, 40, 50, 59, 62, 65, 78–79, 81, 86
Gleason, 1st Lt. William 14, 30
Goodwin, Pvt. Stephen H. 10
Goose Creek 19
Gorman, Gen. Willis A. 30, 34, 39, 47
Gove, Col. Jesse A. 97, 99, 102, 117, 122, 126, 128–129, 132
Graham, Pvt. James 131
Grant, Gen. Ulysses Simpson 87, 89, 190, 194–195, 199, 202, 205; headquarters at City Point ***208***
Gray, 2nd Lt. George C. 14
Gregg, Gen. David McMurtrie 183
Griffin Gen. Charles 141, 166, 167, 191, 201–202
Griswold, Col. Charles E. 132–133, 210
Grover, Cpl. Benjamin P. 121
Guerrillas, Rebel 172
Gum Spring VA ***173***, 173–174
Gunboats: Confederate ***130***; 130–131

Hagerstown, MD 180
Hall's Hill 95, 97, 103, 105, 109–110, 127, 142, 159
Hammond, Anselm C. 51, 78–79, 83
Hampton Roads 39
Hancock, Gen. Winfield Scott 1, 66, 89
Hancock, MD 22
Hanover Courthouse VA 122–123, 199–200
Harpers Ferry, West VA 27–28, 47, 70, ***150***, 151, 175
Harrington, Pvt. Charles F. 51, 83, 90
Harrison's Landing 38–39, 131, 140, 203
Hatch, Pvt. Cyrus K. 10, 25, 79, 83
Hatch, Pvt. Edwin B. 51
Haven, Surgeon Samuel F., Jr. 49
Havre de Grace, MD 94
Haynes, Cpl. Nathan Wheeler 98, 125–126, 134–135, 137, 141, 146–147, 149, 154–156, 158–159, 161–162, 166
Hays, Gen. Alexander 62–63, 65, 67, 82
Heath, Pvt. William 101
Heintzelman, Gen. Samuel Peter 99, 103
Herrick, Pvt. Charles Greely 195
Heth, CSA Gen. Henry 183
Hill, CSA Gen. Ambrose Powell 198
Hill, Pvt. William 73–75
Hixon, Pvt. Egbert Oswell (aka Egbert Hicks) 46

Hood, CSA Gen. John Bell 178, 202
Hooker, Gen. Joseph 42, 56, 127, 145, 153, 163, 167–168, 172, 175, 196
Hooper, Pvt. John 201
Hospital barn, Antietam *47*
Hospital, 2nd Corps ***191***
Houghton, Pvt. Chilon 51
Howe, Col. Frank 94
Howell, Gen. Joshua Blackwood 133
Hudson, Pvt. James L. 10
Humphreys, Gen. Andrew Atkinson 163, 180, 195
Hunt, Pvt. Josiah Harrison 51
Hutchins, Pvt. Edward 51, 67

"Infernal machines," land mines 117
Ingalls, 3rd Lt. Charles N. 14, 39
Ingalls, Pvt. Joseph S. 43
Ingalls, Nathan B.M. 123
Intrepid (observation balloon) 20, ***20***, 124

Jackson, CSA Gen. Thomas "Stonewall" 40, ***40***, 43–45, 169, 202
James, Morgan target rifle *9*
James River 126, 129
Jeffery, Sgt. David N. 194
Jericho Ford 197, ***198***, 199
Jones CSA Gen. David Rump 192

Keedysville MD 144, 180
Kelly's Ford VA 79, 139, 167, 185
Kennebec 210
Kilpatrick, Gen. Hugh Hudson 69
King, Gen. Rufus 103

Lacy House, Falmouth, VA 54, ***55***, 56
Ladd, Pvt. Otis K. 45
Lander, Gen. Frederick West 5, 13–15, 17–***18***, 19–24, 40
Lawler, Pvt. Patrick 201
Leach, Ivory Lowe 148, 166
Lee, CSA Gen. Fitzhugh 166, 194
Lee, CSA Gen. Robert Edward 1, 24, 46, 80, 84, 87, 89–90, 168, 170, 180, 183, 186, 197, 202
Leesburg, VA 17
Lewis, Pvt. Charles 123
Lewis, Pvt. Isaac H. 195
Lincoln, Pres. Abraham 47, ***48***, 52, 95, 99, 149, 167
Little Round Top, Gettysburg 61
Littlefield, Pvt. David M. 10, 31, 45
Long Bridge 95, ***96***
Longstreet, CSA Gen. James 195–196
Lowe, Prof. Thaddeus Sobieski Constantine 20

Macy, Col. George N. 88–89
Madden, Cpl. William H. 162, 179
Magruder, Gen. John Bankhead 31
Mallory, Pvt. William Henry Harrison 162

Index

Malvern Hill 37–38, *128*, 129, 131, 135, 202
Manassas, VA 109, 140, 141, 152
Manassas Gap, VA 71, 181
Manassas Station 79
Martin, Col. Augustus P. 210
Martin, Henry L. 10, 14, 17, 19, 26, 30–31, 38–39, 45, 50, 52
Martin, Pvt. Lysander 51, 57
Martindale, Gen. John Henry 96, 103, 107, 122, 125
Martinsburg, VA 24
Marye's Heights, VA 49, 54–55, 156–157
Matt, Pvt. Frank 51, 81
Mattoon, Pvt. Eleazer 34
Mayers, Pvt. Henry 51
McCall, Gen. George A. 99
McClellan, Gen. George Brinton 17, 20, 24, 31, 36–37, 39, 47, 98–99, 103, 108, 125, 128–129, 133, 153
McCook, Gen. Robert 136
McCown, CSA Gen. John Porter 123
McDowell, Gen. Irvin 40, 99, 103, 140
McKay, 1st Lt. Thomas 77
McKenzie, Pvt. John W. 195
McLaughlin, Pvt. Benjamin L. 84
Meade, Gen. George G. *61*, 65–66, 73, 79, 161, 167, 181, 183, 186–187, 189, 208–209
Meagher, Gen. Thomas Francis 145
Mechanicsville, VA 125–127, 200
Mechanicsville Battle 36
Merrell, Gen. Lewis 103
Merrimack 137
Mine Run 187
Morrell, Gen. George Webb 108, 121, 133
Morris, Pvt. George E. 121
Morrison, Pvt. John 195
Morse, Pvt. Henry 51, 81–83
Mosby, CSA Ranger John Singleton 136, 173
Mozart, NY Regiment 164
Mud March 162, 186
Mudgett, Sgt. Isaac Newton 50, 90
Mule Shoe 84
Munn, Sgt. George 166, 179
Munson Hill *99*, 106

Neal, Pvt. Thomas J. 201
New York riots 180
Newhall, Pvt. Edward E. 194
Nichols, Pvt. George Whitefield 160
Nineteenth Ma Volunteer Infantry 18
Ninth Mass. Volunteer Infantry 97, 166
North America 137
North Anna River *85*, 197, 199–201
North Woods, Antietam 43, *44*
Ny River 195, 197

Old Wilderness Tavern 186, 192
Orange and Alexandria Railroad 140
Orange Courthouse 192
Orange Plank Road 80–81, 194

Osgood, Pvt. Cyrus M. 169, 195
Oviatt, Pvt. Charles 205

Packard, Cpl. William H. 50, 81, 81, 82–84, 90
Pamunkey River 119, 199
Parker Col. Francis J. 141
Parlin, Pvt. Herman F. 195
Parmenter, Pvt. Marcus Morton 43
Patterson Creek, VA 22
Penniman, Pvt. Nathaniel W. 51, 68, 83
Perley, Sgt. John L. 10, 17, 31
Petersburg, VA 86–87, 89, 204, 206–207; bomb enclosure *206*
Petersburg Express 205
Pickett's Charge at Gettysburg 63, *63*
Pierpont, Reverend John 96, 100
Pillow, CSA Gen. Gideon Johnson 107
Pinkam, Pvt. Charles Freeman 125
Pleasanton, Gen. Alfred 174, 183
Plimpton, Pvt. Amos G. 51, 83
Plummer, Capt. William 50–54, 57–59–60, 62, 70, 77
Pond, Pvt. George Otis 162
Pontoon bridge *36*
Pope, Gen. John 40, 153
Porter, Gen. John Fitz 96, 98, 103, 116, 125, 133, 140, 147, 153
Power's Hill Gettysburg 175
Prim, General of Spain 125

Quaker Gun *139*, 141
Quarle's Ford 199, *200*

Rains, CSA Gen. Gabriel James 118
Randall, Pvt. Lot J. 51
Rapidan River 80, 82, 168, *170*
Rappahannock River *76*, 139, 167, 181, 185, 192
Rappahannock Station 76, 184, *185*, 188, 192
Ream's Station 87, 89
Recruiting poster *11*
Reed, Pvt. James Smith 125
Richardson, Pvt. Sewell D. 131, 201
Richmond, VA 200
Rines, Pvt. Jason S. 10, 81–82
Roach, Pvt. William 51
Robertson's Tavern 80, 186
Robinson, Gen. John Cleveland 194
Rockville, MD 143
Round Top Gettysburg 175, *177*, 177–179
Roundy, Pvt. George Pickering 67–68

Sampson, Capt. Walter S. 129
Sanitary Commission 206, 208
Saunders, Capt. John 5, *13*, 13–23, 25–26, 28–32, 37, 39–41, 43
Savage Station 37, *37*, *127*, 129
Schouler, Mass. Adjutant General 210
Second Battle Bull Run 40
Second Division Surgeons *38*

Second Maine Regiment 101–102, 160
Sedgwick, Gen. John 29, 32, 53, 58–59
Seminary Ridge, Gettysburg 61
Seward, Secretary of State William 99
Sharp rifle *10*, 39, 45, 103, 132–134
Shattuck, Sgt. Oramel C. 10
Shepard, Pvt. James W. 80
Shepherdstown, W. VA *147*
Sheridan, Gen. Philip Henry 90, 194, 200
Sherwin, Gen. Adj. Thomas 129, 186, 208, 210
Shields, Gen. James 24–27
Sickles, Gen. Daniel Edgar 61, 165
Sigel, Gen. Franz 164
Simmons, Surgeon Marshall E. *100*, 114
Six Virginia Cavalry 186
Sixth Mass. Volunteer Infantry 94
Slocum, Gen. Henry Warner 49
Smart, Pvt. Joseph T. 90
Smith, Pvt. John 51, 71, 73–75
Smith, 2nd Lt. Robert 150, 166
Snow, Pvt. Warren 43
South Mountain, MD 40–41, *41*, 68, 143, 180
Spindler's Farm 194, 196
Spotsylvania 194–195
Stearns, Surgeon George F. 210
Stevens, Cpl. Lewis 101
Stiles, 1st Lt. Charles D. 105, 114, 117–119, 124, 129, 132, 135
Stone, Gen. Charles Pomeroy 16, 18, 21
Stone, Wagoner Charles 90
strange fruit 69
Strong Pvt. Martin V. 43–44
Stuart, CSA Gen. James Ewell Brown 166
Sturtevant, Sgt. John Quincy Adams 124, 131, 162, 195
Sullivan, Pvt. Eugene 73–75
Sumner, Gen. Edwin Vose 43, 53
swapping goods 35, 86, 206
Sweet, Pvt. Charles G. 195
Sweet, Sgt. Newell S. 166, 195
Sykes, Gen. George 163, 168, 191
Symons, Capt. J. Henry 210

Taneytown Road, Gettysburg, PA 60, 62, 65, 67
Taylor, Gen. Joseph Pannell 126
Temple, Pvt. David H. 58
Tenth Mass. Battery 85
Thirteenth Mass. Volunteer Infantry 96
Thirty Eighth NY Infantry 164
Thirty Fourth NY Infantry 42–43
Thirty Second Mass. Volunteer Infantry 210
Thomas, Cpl. Charles S. 103
Tilton, Maj. William S. *97*, 98, 101, 118, 129, 160–161, 174, 188, 191, 194, 199, 209–210
Todd's Tavern 194
Townsend, Pvt. Thaddeus J. 51

Index

Trostle's Farm, Gettysburg 175, *176*
Truel, Pvt. Zenas B. 195
Twelfth RI Regiment 157
Twentieth MA Volunteer Infantry 18, 21, 45, 71, 76, 78–82, 84, 86–87, 89, 90
Twentieth Maine Regiment 157
Twenty Fifth NY Regiment 97–98
Twenty Second MA Volunteer Infantry 92, 99, 103, 105, 128, 152, 156, 160, 163, 174, 184, 188–189, 192, 195–196–199, 201, 206
Twenty Third Maine Reg 105
Tyler, Chaplain 189–191, 205, 210

Upton, Cpl. Austin 50, 83

Van Moll, Pvt. Richard A. 10, 43
Varrell, Pvt. John P. 51

Wadsworth, Gen. James Samuel 193
Walcott, Pvt. Charles O. 51
Walker, Dr. Mary 56, *56*
Ward, 1st Lt. Winsor M. 179
Wardwell, Capt. David K. 129
Wares, Cpl. Daniel 194
Warner, Pvt. William H. 51

Warren, Gen. Gouverneur Kemble 80, 187, 191, 197, 201
Warrenton 79
Warrenton Junction, VA 48, 71, 79, 140, 152, 181
Washington, DC 28, 143
Webb, Gen. Alexander Stewart M. 72–73, 83
Weldon Station 89, 90
Wentworth, Capt. Lewis E. 92–93, 95–97–98, 101, 103, 105–106, 109, 114–115, 118–119, 134, 146–148, 152, 154–155, 159–160
West Point, VA 32
Wheelock, Pvt. Henry Lincoln 51
White Hall Church 80
White Oaks Swamp 37, 129, 202
Whitehouse Landing, VA *120*
Whittemore, Pvt. George 14, 31, 43
Wilcox Landing 203, *203*
Wilderness Battle 192–194, *193*
Wildes, Pvt. Solomon 51
Wilkes, Cdre. Charles D. 103
Williams, Pvt. Henry 103
Williams, Pvt. John Lindsey Galleucia 100, 103
Williams, Pvt. Theodore 51, 70

Williams, Gen. Thomas 103
Williamsburg, VA 136–137
Willis, Pvt. Henry (1st Co.) 51, 68
Willis, Pvt. Henry (2nd Co.) 103
Wilson, Col. Henry 92–94, 97, 103, 159, 167, 180, 207
Wilson, Pvt. Robert A. 51
Winchester, VA 23–27
Winn's Mill at Yorktown *30*
Winter Quarters *102*, 189–190, *190*
Winthrop, Hon. Robert C. 93
Wood, Cpl. Joseph L. 50, 80
Wright's Georgia Brigade 66

York and Richmond Railroad 121
York River 116, 119
Yorktown, VA 29, 32–33, 111, 113–114, 118–119, 137; Augustine Moore House *117*, 118
Yorktown siege gun *115*
Young, Pvt. J. Albert 51, 83–84

Ziegler's Grove, Gettysburg 60, 62–65, 67–68